Instructor Resource Guide

APPLYING
AutoCAD® 2002

Keyed to the *Fundamentals* and *Advanced* Editions

Glencoe McGraw-Hill

New York, New York   Columbus, Ohio   Chicago, Illinois   Peoria, Illinois   Woodland Hills, California

Writers:

Gary L. Aguilar
American River College
Sacramento, California

John M. Felser
Pompano Beach High School
Pompano Beach, Florida

John Horstketter
Professor Emeritus
Spokane Community College
Spokane, Washington

Dan Obenchain
University High School
Spokane, Washington

Stuart Soman
Educational Consultant
Long Island, NY

Terry T. Wohlers
Wohlers Associates
Fort Collins, Colorado

Internet listings throughout this guide provide a source for extended information related to the textbook. We have made every effort to recommend sites that are informative and accurate. However, these sites are not under the control of Glencoe/McGraw-Hill, and, therefore, Glencoe/McGraw-Hill makes no representation concerning the content of these sites. We strongly encourage instructors to preview Internet sites before students use them. Many sites may eventually contain "hot links" to other sites that could lead to exposure to inappropriate material. Internet sites are sometimes "under construction" and may not always be available. Sites may also move or have been discontinued completely by the time you or your students attempt to access them.

AutoCAD is a registered trademark of Autodesk, Inc. Word, Excel, Access, PowerPoint, and Internet Explorer are registered trademarks of Microsoft, Inc. **Exam**View is a registered trademark of FSCreations, Inc.

Glencoe/McGraw-Hill
A Division of The McGraw·Hill Companies

Copyright © 2003 by Glencoe/McGraw-Hill, a division of The McGraw-Hill Companies. All rights reserved. Permission is granted to reproduce the material contained herein on the condition that such material be reproduced only for classroom use; be provided to students, teachers, or families without charge; and be used solely in conjunction with *Applying AutoCAD 2002*. Any other reproduction, for use or sale, is prohibited without prior written permission of the publisher, Glencoe/McGraw-Hill.

Send all inquires to:
Glencoe/McGraw-Hill
3008 W. Willow Knolls Drive
Peoria, IL 61614-1083

ISBN 0-07-828541-0 (Instructor Resource Guide)

ISBN 0-07-828540-2 (*Fundamentals* Student Edition)
ISBN 0-07-828542-9 (*Advanced* Student Edition)
ISBN 0-07-829881-4 (*Fundamentals* Instructor Productivity CD-ROM)
ISBN 0-07-829882-2 (*Advanced* Instructor Productivity CD-ROM)

Printed in the United States of America.

1 2 3 4 5 6 7 8 9 10   009   06 05 04 03 02

Table of Contents

Program Description................................. 4
Managing CAD Courses............................. 11
    Setting Up a CAD Facility..................... 13
    Classroom Management....................... 29
    Assessment.. 45
    Professional Resources......................... 47
    Student and Professional Organizations.......... 48
    National Skill Standards for CADD............. 57
Career Handouts.................................... 63

APPLYING AutoCAD 2002 FUNDAMENTALS

Scope and Sequence................................ 96
Instructional Plans................................. 99
Transparency Masters............................. 143
Chapter Tests..................................... 171
Answer Keys...................................... 207

APPLYING AutoCAD 2002 ADVANCED

Scope and Sequence............................... 224
Instructional Plans................................ 227
Transparency Masters............................ 267
Chapter Tests..................................... 293
Answer Keys...................................... 325

Copyright © Glencoe/McGraw-Hill

APPLYING
AutoCAD® 2002

Choose the Program That Meets Your Needs

Since the first edition was published in 1986, the clear, step-by-step instructions in *Applying AutoCAD* have helped thousands learn to use the popular AutoCAD® computer-aided drafting and design software. Now that tradition continues in a new, more convenient format. *Applying AutoCAD* is now available in two versions for beginning and advanced students.

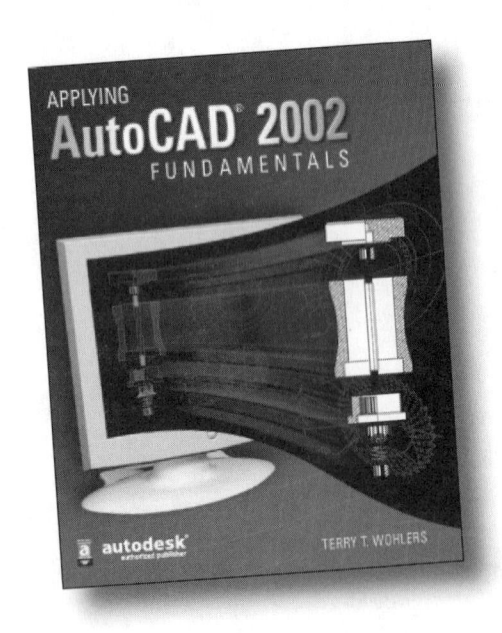

FUNDAMENTALS

This edition is targeted for those who are new to AutoCAD. It covers the AutoCAD commands and functions used to create, edit, store, and print engineering drawings.

ADVANCED

This edition assumes a basic knowledge of AutoCAD. It covers surface modeling, rendering, and solid modeling. It also provides instruction in customizing AutoCAD's menus, introduces AutoLISP, and explains how to use AutoCAD's commands and features to import, export, and share files.

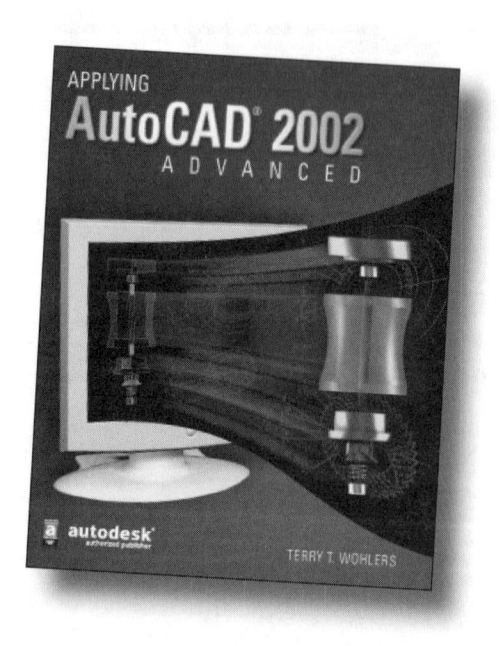

Copyright © Glencoe/McGraw-Hill

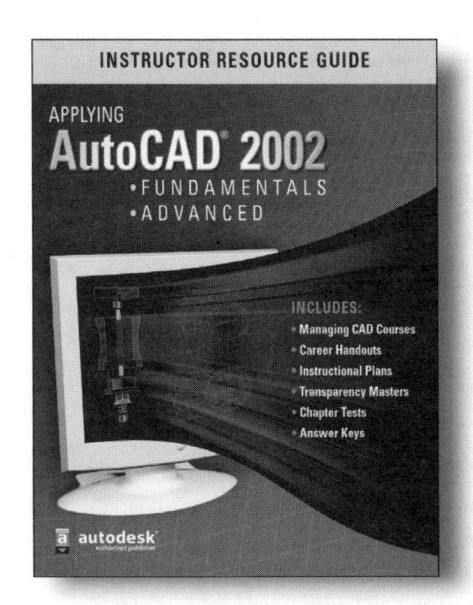

Instructor Resource Guide for Both Texts

The Instructor Resource Guide provides teaching aids and suggestions to help instructors plan, teach, manage, and assess.

- Managing CAD Courses
- Career Handouts
- Instructional Plans
- Transparency Masters
- Chapter Tests
- Answer Keys

Instructor Productivity CD-ROM for Fundamentals Text

- Instructional Plans
- PowerPoint® Presentations
- **Exam**View® Test Generator
- Student Practice Files

Instructor Productivity CD-ROM for Advanced Text

- Instructional Plans
- PowerPoint® Presentations
- **Exam**View® Test Generator
- Student Practice Files
- ACIS® Open Viewer

Copyright © Glencoe/McGraw-Hill

Student Texts

With its step-by-step approach, well-planned design, and clear, concise language, *Applying AutoCAD 2002* presents complex concepts in ways that are easy to grasp and retain. The student texts were developed with flexibility and adaptability in mind. Their structure lends itself to picking and choosing chapters and problems to suit individual needs.

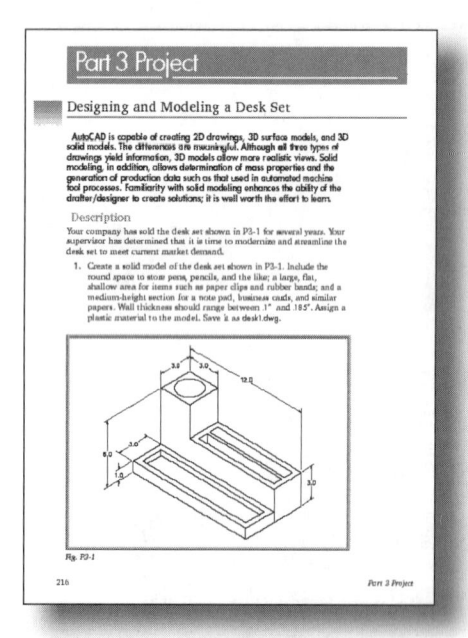

Parts

In each student text, the chapters are grouped into six parts. Each part comprises a broad area, such as drawing and editing or dimensioning and tolerancing. A culminating project ends each part. In this project, students apply the skills and techniques they have learned to a real-world situation.

Chapters

Each chapter includes features that guide student learning and help instructors evaluate progress.

- **Objectives** and **Key Terms** let students know what they can expect to learn from the chapter. The key terms are italicized and defined within the chapter as well as in the glossary.
- **Notes** and **Hints** help students effectively tap the full power of AutoCAD.
- **Review Questions** at the end of each chapter check students' comprehension of basic chapter content.
- **Challenge Your Thinking** questions at the end of each chapter encourage students to reason, research, and explore concepts in further detail.
- **Applying AutoCAD Skills** problems provide an opportunity to practice the skills learned in the chapter and apply them in a work-related context.
- **Using Problem-Solving Skills** activities challenge students to synthesize the AutoCAD skills they have learned and arrive at practical solutions.

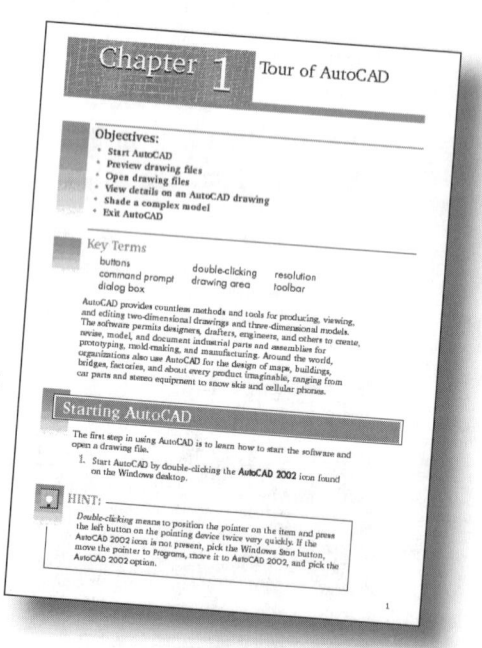

Copyright © Glencoe/McGraw-Hill

Careers

"Careers Using AutoCAD" articles help students explore the different types of careers open to people with AutoCAD knowledge and skills. Education and training requirements are described, and students are encouraged to explore each career in further detail.

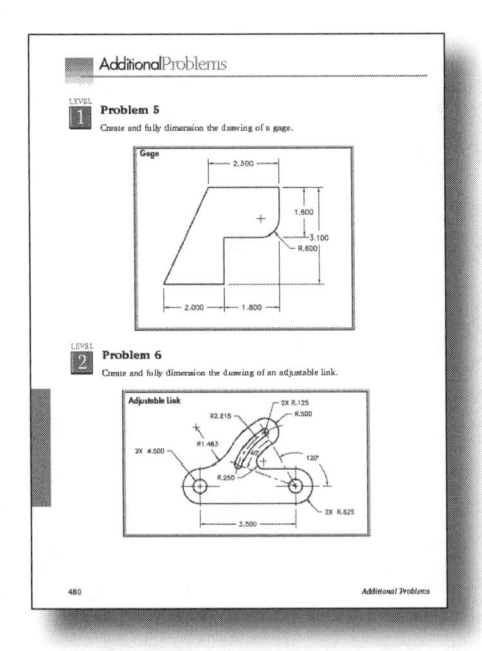

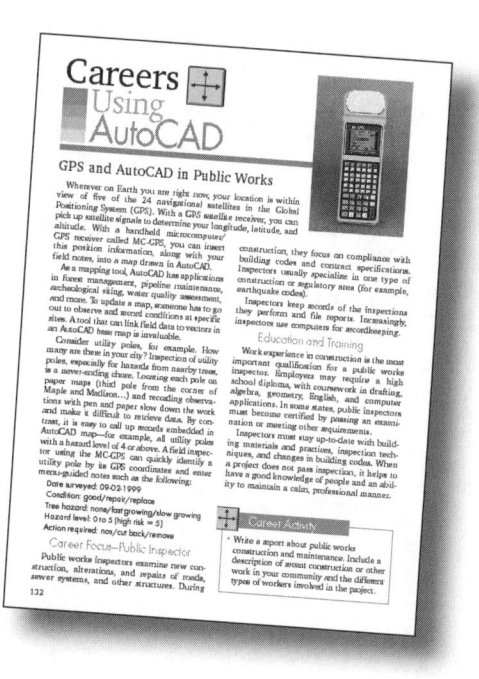

Additional Problems

An "Additional Problems" section at the back of each student text provides more opportunities for students to put their AutoCAD skills to work. Each problem is accompanied by specific instructions. Problems in the *Fundamentals* text are rated according to difficulty level.

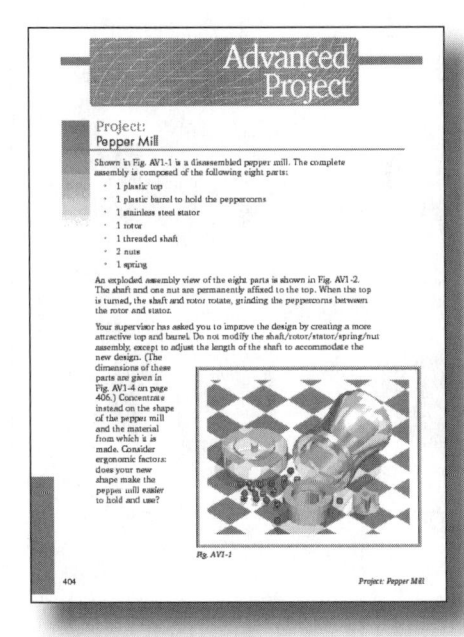

Advanced Projects

The "Advanced Projects" section in the *Advanced* text presents problems that might be encountered on the job. Minimal instruction is given. Students are asked to plan a solution and carry it out. These projects provide opportunities for students to show initiative and creativity on a long-term or group project.

Copyright © Glencoe/McGraw-Hill

Instructor Productivity CD-ROMs

An Instructor Productivity CD-ROM is available for both texts. Each CD-ROM contains files and software for use by both instructors and students. Included are Instructional Plans, PowerPoint® Presentations, an **ExamView®** Test Generator, and student practice files. The *Advanced* CD-ROM also includes the ACIS® Open Viewer software.

Instructional Plans

There is an instructional plan for each textbook chapter and part. The instructional plans are provided as Word® files so that instructors can easily customize them to their needs.

PowerPoint® Presentations

The PowerPoint Presentations help instructors explain topics visually and dynamically. The slide presentations are keyed to the textbook and are referenced in the Instructional Plans.

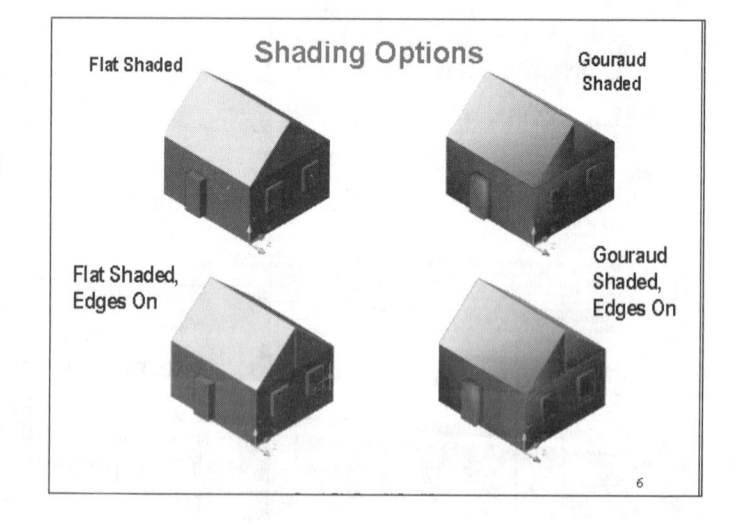

Copyright © Glencoe/McGraw-Hill

ExamView® Test Generator

The test generator includes software and question banks. There are questions for each textbook chapter plus a pre-/post-test for each textbook part. With this test generator, you can quickly and easily create tests from the available test banks and enter your own questions.

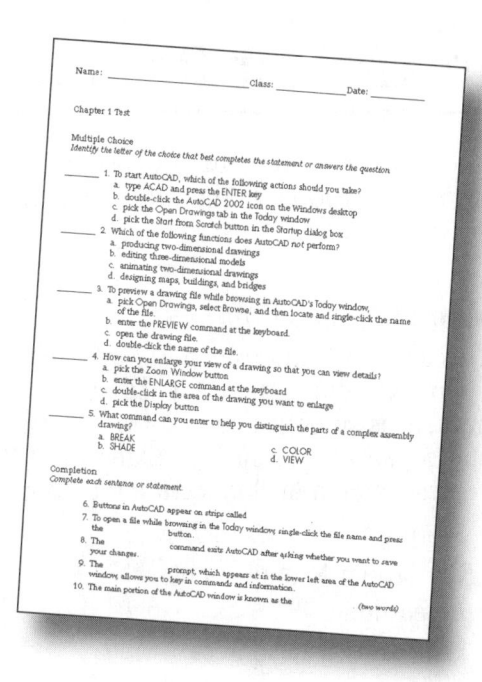

Student Practice Files

Student practice files are included on the CD-ROMs for use with exercises and problems in the textbook.

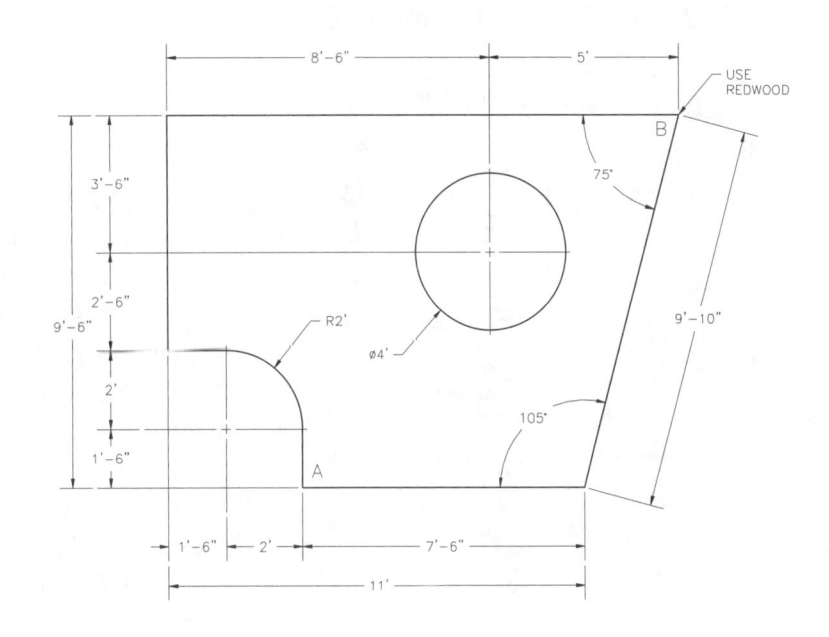

ACIS® Open Viewer

With this viewer, produced by Spatial Technology, users can access, view, and manipulate 3D models that were created in any ACIS-enabled application, such as AutoCAD. For example, AutoCAD drafters can embed their 3D models in software applications such a Word or PowerPoint. Others can then view the document, even if they don't have AutoCAD on their computers.

Copyright © Glencoe/McGraw-Hill

Instructor Resource Guide

The Instructor Resource Guide provides a variety of helpful teaching aids and suggestions. It includes material for both the *Fundamentals* and *Advanced* texts.

Managing CAD Courses

This section includes general information for setting up and conducting a CAD course. Also included are numerous student handouts on safety, computer use, and organizations such as SkillsUSA-VICA and ADDA. Topics covered in this section include:

- Setting Up a CAD Facility
- Classroom Management
- Assessment
- Professional Resources
- Student and Professional Organizations
- National Skill Standards for CADD

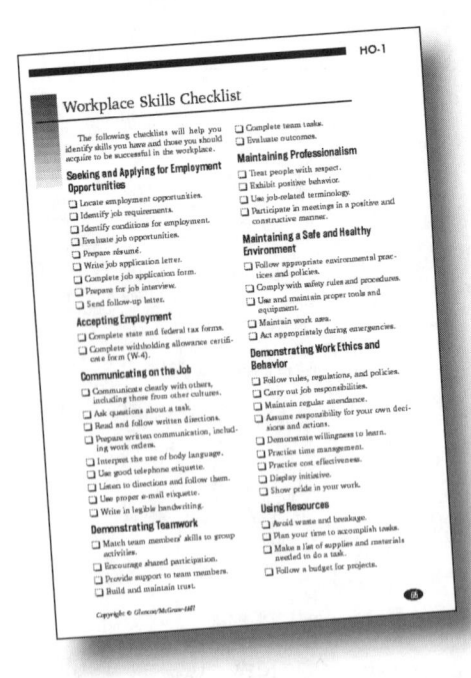

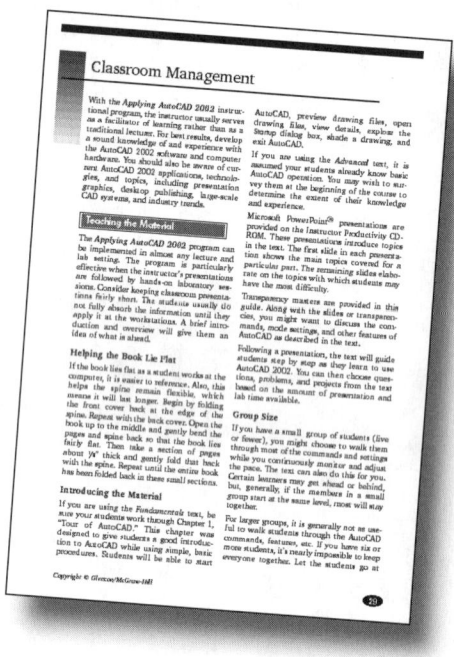

Career Handouts

These student handouts provide information for choosing a career, finding employment, succeeding on the job, and starting a business. Some examples are:

- Workplace Skills Checklist
- Setting Career Goals
- Sources of Career Information
- Creating a Portfolio
- Writing a Résumé
- Filling Out an Application Form
- The Job Interview
- Teamwork
- Entrepreneurship

Teaching Aids Keyed to the Student Texts

The Instructor Resource Guide includes sections related specifically to the *Fundamentals* and *Advanced* student texts. The following are included for each textbook:

- Scope and Sequence Chart
- Instructional Plans
- Transparency Masters
- Chapter Tests
- Answer Keys for tests and textbook review questions

Managing CAD Courses

This section provides information and suggestions to assist you with setting up and teaching an AutoCAD course.

Setting Up a CAD Facility 13
    Handouts:
    Computer Safety Checklist. 19
    Proper Care of Equipment 20
    Electrical Safety 21
    First Aid Can Save Lives 22
    Developing a Fire Emergency Plan. 23
    Fire Emergency Plan 24
    Extinguishing Fires 25
    Safety Color Codes 26
    Hazardous Waste. 27

Classroom Management 29
    Handouts:
    Basic Computer Skills 35
    E-Mail Etiquette 38
    Internet Permission Contract 39
    Internet Evaluation Sheet 40
    Using the Internet. 41
    Student Profile Form 43
    Course Evaluation Form 44

Assessment 45

Professional Resources 47

Student and Professional Organizations 48
    Handouts:
    Parliamentary Procedure 49
    Technology Student Association. 50
    SkillsUSA-VICA 51
    SkillsUSA Championships 53
    American Design Drafting Association 55
    Autodesk User Group International 55
    AutoCAD Testing and Certification. 56

National Skill Standards for CADD 57

Copyright © Glencoe/McGraw-Hill

Setting Up a CAD Facility

There is no one "best" way to lay out a CAD laboratory. The layout should meet your needs and the needs of your students. Asking yourself the following questions can help you determine what some of those needs are.

- How much space is available?
- How can you best take advantage of the available space?
- Will work areas be easily accessible, both by you and by students?
- What arrangements should you make for storage, both temporary and permanent?
- Will cables and electrical cords be easy to access, yet away from traffic?
- Will cords and cables be tucked up under desks and tabletops so they cannot be kicked or broken?
- Do you want to be able to see students' work as you stand in the center of the laboratory?
- Are student work areas accessible when you move about the room?
- While students are seated at the workstations, do you want them to be able to see a projection screen or marking board?

If you need to purchase hardware or the AutoCAD 2002 software, you may want to contact Autodesk, Inc. Their Web site provides product specifications and technical assistance, plus discussion groups and links to user's groups, such as AUGI, that can be a big help. (See page 47.) The authorized dealer from which the software was purchased might also be a resource.

When purchasing equipment and making plans, be aware that software and equipment should be upgraded every two or three years. Changes take place too rapidly for a system to remain current longer than that. Many colleges and universities are asking students to buy their own computers (usually laptops). When they bring them into the CAD lab, the computers are hooked up to the network server, which parcels out the programs they use.

Physical Layout

Figures 1, 2, and 3 on pages 14 and 15 show a few of the many layout options for CAD laboratories. You may wish to study these illustrations to discover new ideas for designing or improving your lab.

Figures 1 and 2 show enough workstations for fairly large classes—24 and 20, respectively. Both of these labs have a separate classroom area.

Figure 3 shows only 6 workstations in a combined laboratory/classroom. In this lab, students can remain at their workstations while you discuss new information. This setting is ideal for the small, two- to four-day workshops typically offered to practicing professionals and for small advanced classes.

Copyright © Glencoe/McGraw-Hill

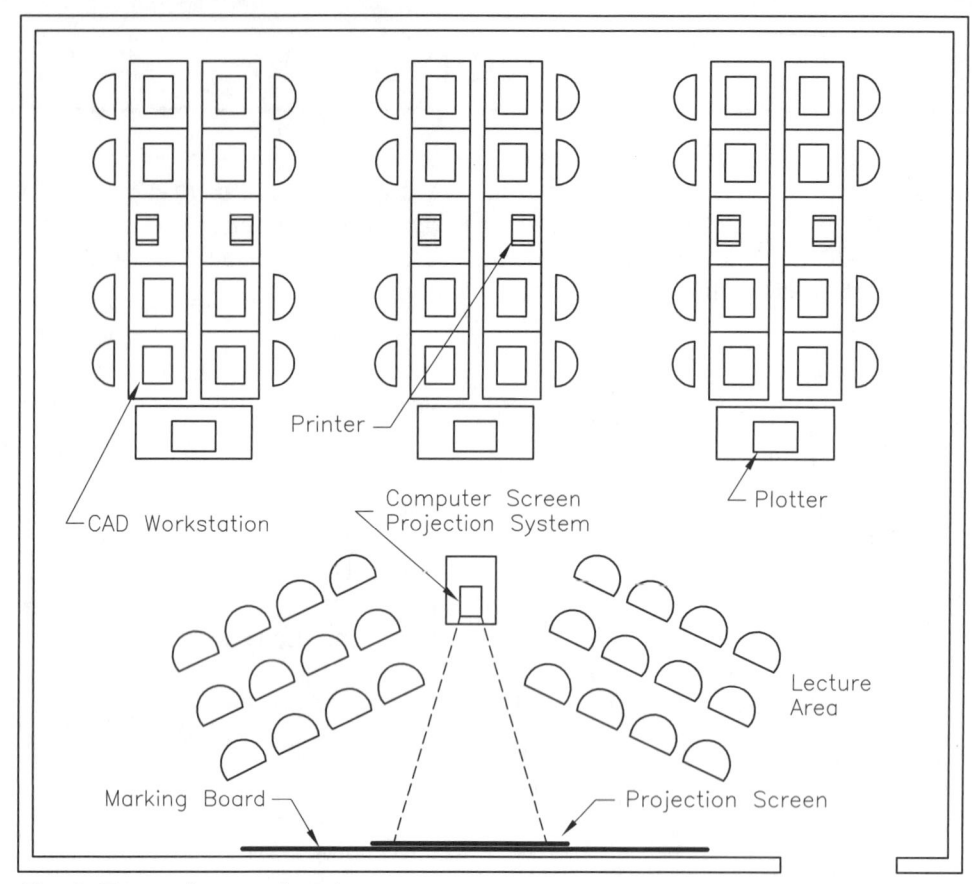

Fig. 1: Twenty-four workstations

Customizing Workstations

As you plan your laboratory, be sure to consider student (and instructor) comfort. Working at a computer can lead to eye strain; neck, wrist, and back discomfort; fatigue; and other problems that may interfere with student interest, performance, and productivity. Setting up CAD workstations with ergonomics in mind can help reduce these problems.

Ergonomic Adjustments

Correct placement of the computer monitor is critical. Ideally, the center of the screen should be a few degrees below eye level. Since student height will vary, this may be difficult to achieve. One solution is to set up most of the monitors at a level appropriate for a student of average height. Then one or two monitors can be placed a little higher than average and another one or two a little lower than average. Another solution is to provide chairs that are adjustable.

If the laboratory is brightly lit, dim the lights in the room if possible. Also, consider the position of the screens in relation to windows and other bright lights. This will help keep eye fatigue to a minimum.

Remember that CPUs and monitors generate heat. Be sure to provide for sufficient air flow through the work area.

Remind students to stretch frequently to relieve tension. For every hour at the computer, suggest a 10-minute break spent standing or walking around. Also suggest that they periodically focus their eyes on something other than the computer screen to reduce eye strain. Ideally, they should look out a window or at something in the distance.

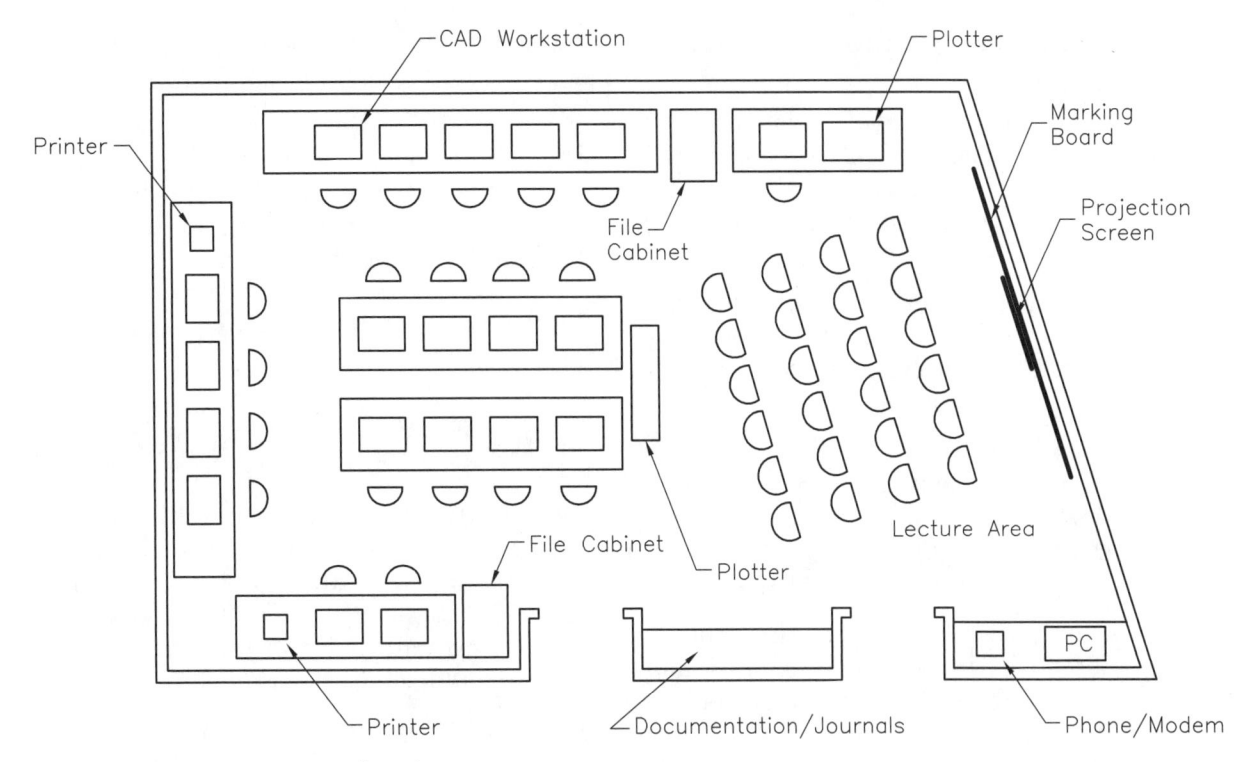

Fig. 2: Twenty workstations

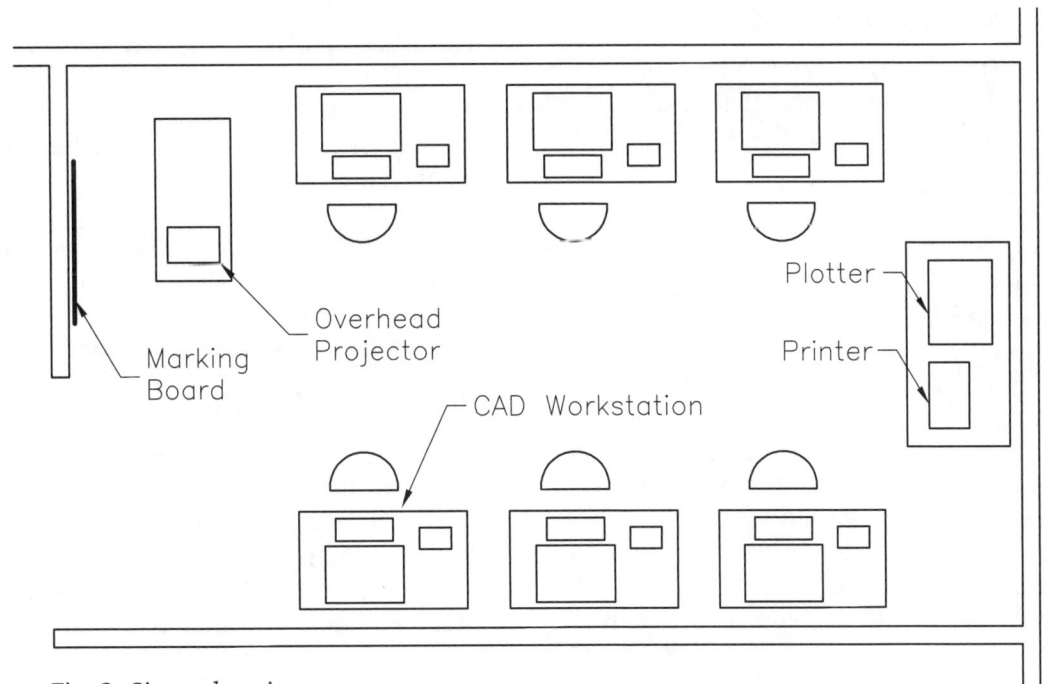

Fig. 3: Six workstations

Copyright © Glencoe/McGraw-Hill

Accommodating Students with Special Needs

Most students who have special needs have developed basic methods of coping with them. However, you can make their task easier by planning for their needs in the laboratory layout.

Consider possible problems students might have in accessing or using the CAD workstations. The following tips may help you meet these students' needs.

- For physically impaired students, make sure that at least some of the workstations are easily accessible by wheelchair. You might also need to add ramps for these students.

- People with back or hip problems should have elevated desks that allow them to stand; for some, high stools can then be used for sitting.

- Students with visual impairments may require larger monitors. If possible, have at least one larger monitor available. If this is not possible, try changing the screen colors, which often helps.

- Students with poor motor control often find it easier to use a roller ball or touch pad than a mouse.

Software and hardware adjustments may also help some students. Microsoft Windows operating system software provides several adjustment options to help special-needs students at no extra cost. For example, the MouseKeys feature allows physically impaired students to control the cursor using the numeric keypad rather than the mouse. For students with hearing impairments, a visual warning can be set to flash when a warning sound (such as a beep) occurs. High-contrast color schemes and large fonts allow visually impaired students to see the screen more easily. Also, alternative input devices can be integrated into the system using the SerialKeys feature. To activate any of these, pick the Windows Start button and select Settings and Control Panel. Then double-click the Accessibility Options icon. The Accessibility Properties dialog box appears from which you can set the appropriate features.

Windows 2000 provides several programs that enhance accessibility, including a screen magnifier, a narrator that reads the contents of the screen aloud, an on-screen keyboard, and a utility manager. To explore or activate these, pick the Windows Start button and select Programs, Accessories, and Accessibility.

Installing AutoCAD 2002

Most instructors prefer to install and configure the software prior to the school term. If you are not already familiar with AutoCAD 2002, read Appendix B, "Managing AutoCAD," in the student text before you begin installation.

In addition to hardware, you will need to manage the AutoCAD 2002 software. The electronic documentation that is provided as part of the software package contains useful information about the features, use, and management of the software.

The Microsoft Windows platform is noted for its ease of use. This is true of the AutoCAD 2002 software as well. AutoCAD 2002 allows you not only to reshape, reposition, and view or hide existing toolbars, but also to create new toolbars and customize the interface for your own needs. Students will enjoy creating an individual setup. However, this can create problems. One solution is to create profiles.

Customization Profiles

One of AutoCAD's best features is its flexibility, but this could cause major headaches in laboratory administration, particularly if you allow menu and toolbar customization. You will have to find a way to make sure that beginning students see what they expect to see when they open AutoCAD. (For example, in the standard setup, the Standard and Object Properties toolbars are docked at the top of the drawing area, and the Draw and Modify toolbars are docked on the left side.) This is also important

Copyright © Glencoe/McGraw-Hill

when using *Applying AutoCAD 2002* because the text assumes that the students are working with standard menus and toolbars. To avoid such problems, AutoCAD 2002 includes a profile feature that can help you manage the appearance of AutoCAD on student workstations.

A profile remembers all the parameters set by an individual, such as which toolbars are open on the screen, whether and where toolbars are docked, custom toolbars and pull-down menus, and the number of lines that appear in the Command prompt window.

Follow these steps to create a customized profile:

1. Open the Options dialog box by entering OPTIONS at the Command prompt or by selecting Options from the Tools pull-down menu. Select the last tab, labeled Profiles.

2. If no profiles have previously been defined, define the first one by selecting <<Unnamed Profile>> and picking the Rename button.

3. In the Change Profile window, type a name, such as Student 1, in the Profile name box. Select the Apply & Close button. The new profile appears in the Available profiles window.

4. To create additional profiles, select Add to List, enter a name, and select Apply & Close.

5. If you define more than one profile, pick the profile you want to use now and pick the Set Current button to make it the current profile.

Important: Any changes made by you or a student while a specific profile is current are recorded to that profile.

Creating Standard and Master Profiles

It is possible that students will change standard settings in AutoCAD 2002, even if they have been asked not to change them. Since any changes they make will be saved to the current profile, you should remind students at the end of each session to follow the directions in the text to close any toolbars they opened, and so on, returning everything to the way they found it before they exit the software. However, this method is not foolproof, and you may want to create an "out-of-the-box" standard profile on all student computers, as well as any custom profile with features you wish your classes to use. This will allow a user to return to either of these setups at any time.

For best results, keep a copy of your master profiles on a diskette. You can then restore them to any student's computer, as needed.

As students gain experience, you may want to allow them to create profiles of their own that they can use when they are in the lab. They also can store their profiles on a diskette.

Follow these steps to create a master profile:

1. Set up and make current the profile from which you want to create the master profile.

2. Pick the Export... button. The Export Profile dialog box appears.

3. Enter a name for the profile. (Notice that the file type is ARG. This is the standard file type for profiles in AutoCAD 2002.)

4. Specify the drive and folder in which you want to save the profile.

5. Pick the Save button to save the profile as an ARG file.

Importing a Profile

To reload a profile from a master copy you have made, follow these steps:

1. Display the Options dialog box and pick the Profiles tab.

2. Select and make current a profile other than the one you want to import, even if you have to create a new profile temporarily. (AutoCAD 2002 will not import a profile that is currently in use.)

3. Pick the Import... button. This displays the Import Profile dialog box.

Copyright © Glencoe/McGraw-Hill

4. Pick the drive and folder where the master profile is located, and double-click the file that contains the profile. Another dialog box, also named Import Profile, appears, allowing you to rename or change the description of the profile as you import it.

5. Make any necessary changes and pick Apply & Close.

6. If you are replacing a profile of the same name (because a student has changed the parameters, for example), AutoCAD warns you that the profile already exists and asks if you want to replace it. Pick Yes to reload the profile.

Using a Network

To avoid customization problems completely, consider serving AutoCAD 2002 over your lab's network. When a student logs onto the network and downloads AutoCAD, the original AutoCAD profile will appear, even if the previous student has made changes in the desktop preferences. *A cautionary note:* Give your students a login name such as AutoCAD01 or CAD02 and allow passwords that you assign. Have a secure copy of passwords and make new passwords for each change of class.

Computer Safety Checklist

Avoid Accidents

❏ Make sure cords and cables are tucked under desks and tabletops so they cannot be kicked or damaged.

Provide Proper Support

❏ Back of the chair should make full contact with your back. The backrest should provide support for the lower back. Most people are more comfortable if they recline slightly rather than sit upright.

❏ Make sure seat width and depth fit so that seat is not too large or too small.

❏ Make sure seat front does not press against back of knees and lower legs. Make sure seat has cushioning and does not have sharp edges.

❏ Armrests should support both forearms. If possible, use a chair with adjustable arms.

❏ Wrist rest should be padded and free of sharp and square edges. Wrist rest should not be used while keying. It should be used to rest the wrists between periods of keying.

Avoid Eye Strain

❏ To reduce glare, adjust room lighting and screen brightness. Consider position of screen in relation to windows and other bright lights.

❏ Look away from screen often and refocus on something in the distance.

Prevent Muscle Fatigue

❏ Take short breaks by walking around or standing after every hour spent at the computer.

❏ Make occasional changes in posture.

❏ Position mouse or trackball next to keyboard for use without reaching.

Optimize Working Conditions

❏ Arrange computer station so that head and neck are upright—not bent down or back. Center of monitor screen should be below eye level.

❏ Monitor distance should make screen readable without leaning head or trunk forward or backward.

❏ Head, neck, and trunk should face forward—they should not be twisted.

❏ Upper arms should be perpendicular to the floor (not stretched forward) and relaxed.

❏ Upper arms and elbows should be close to the body—not extended outward.

❏ Wrists and hands should be straight. They should not be bent up, down, or sideways.

❏ Thighs should be about parallel to floor, and lower legs should be perpendicular to floor.

❏ Feet should rest flat on floor or be supported by a stable footrest.

Make the Computer Accessible

❏ Check the computer's accessibility features. For example, you can adjust the appearance and behavior of Windows® to enhance accessibility for vision, hearing, or mobility.

❏ For impaired vision, use a large monitor. If you have Windows® 2000 or later, use the High Contrast accessibility tool to improve screen contrast with alternative colors and font sizes.

❏ Consider assistive technology, such as a voice input aid, if you have impairments in mobility. This type of device enables control of computers with the voice instead of a mouse or keyboard. For more information on assistive technology, go to Microsoft's site for accessibility at www.microsoft.com/enable.

Copyright © Glencoe/McGraw-Hill

Proper Care of Equipment

✓ The computer system should be on a sturdy, level surface.

✓ The computer and monitor should have at least 4 inches of space around the sides and back for heat to escape. Do not block any of the ventilation slots.

✓ The computer system should not be in direct sunlight or next to a heating device.

✓ Avoid dust, high humidity, and extreme heat or cold.

✓ Make sure there is surge protection.

✓ Keep liquids away from the computer and keyboard.

✓ Store diskettes, CDs, etc., in a clean, dry place. Avoid high humidity and extreme heat or cold.

✓ Keep disks away from magnets.

✓ Before moving any computer component, check the user's manual.

✓ Turn off and unplug the system before cleaning it. Check the user's manual for approved cleaning products and methods. Never spray cleaning products directly on the computer or other components. Spray a clean, lint-free cloth and then use the cloth to wipe the components.

Handout

Electrical Safety

Electrical equipment can be hazardous if not maintained and handled properly. Most injuries and deaths resulting from electrical shock occur because someone took needless chances.

Although many people think that the level of voltage is what determines danger from shock, this is not so. A shock of 10,000 volts may be no more deadly than a shock of 100 volts. The real danger lies in the amount of current, which is measured in milliamperes. Any amount of current over 10 milliamperes can produce severe shock, and currents over 100 milliamperes are usually fatal.

The Effects of Shock

At safe amounts of current, a shock may not even be felt. Any sensation is usually not painful and the person can easily let go of the appliance causing the shock.

Dangers increase with the number of amperes. Pain grows severe, accompanied by muscle contractions, and the victim may not be able to let go of the appliance. Breathing becomes difficult, and severe burns may occur. The heart begins to twitch and may go out of control. As a result, blood cannot be efficiently circulated to the brain. The longer the person is in contact with the current, the more harm is done. Eventually the muscle contractions reach the heart and stop it.

How to Help a Shock Victim

> **Don't** touch the person directly. You, too, could receive a shock.

- Turn off the power if possible.
- If you cannot turn off the power, use a nonconducting length of dry wood or a rope to push or pull the person away.
- Call for medical assistance.
- If the person is not breathing, start rescue breathing, *if you are trained to do so*.
- If the person is not breathing and is not showing signs of circulation, start CPR, *if you are trained to do so.*

General Safety Precautions

- Be sure all electrical equipment is grounded and maintained regularly. Do not use equipment if the cord is frayed or otherwise damaged.
- Never use equipment that has had the ground prong removed from the plug.
- Don't touch a broken electric wire. Touching it may cause a severe shock, burn, or even death.
- Do not overload a circuit. If possible, use a ground-fault circuit interrupter (GFCI). It provides extra protection because it is more sensitive than ordinary circuit breakers or fuses.

> **Contact Information**
> For information about CPR courses, contact your local American Heart Association.

Copyright © Glencoe/McGraw-Hill

Handout

First Aid Can Save Lives

It is important for everyone to learn basic first aid, especially if you are working near an area where equipment and materials may be hazardous if not used properly.

First Aid Actions

Do you know the sequence of first aid actions recommended by the Red Cross?

1. Rescue victim and yourself.
2. Restore or maintain breathing and heartbeat.
3. Control heavy bleeding.
4. Treat for poisoning.
5. Prevent traumatic shock.
6. Examine victim carefully to evaluate injury.
7. Seek medical help.
8. Keep checking and assisting victim until medical help is obtained.

Injured Person

When dealing with an injured person, remember that the first rule is to do no harm. Careless treatment can worsen the injury.

- Keep an injured person lying down.
- Do not try to give liquids to someone who is unconscious.
- If the person is not breathing, start rescue breathing.
- Keep pressure on the wound to control bleeding.
- Keep broken bones from moving.
- Cover burns lightly with a dry bandage to prevent contamination.
- Keep heart attack victims quiet.
- For eye injuries, pad and bandage both eyes.

First Aid Kit

Local Red Cross chapters often provide first aid kits. Suggestions for a first aid kit include

- Activated charcoal (use only if instructed by Poison Control Center)
- Adhesive tape
- Antiseptic ointment
- Adhesive bandages (assorted sizes)
- Blanket
- Cold pack
- Disposable gloves
- Gauze pads and roller gauze (assorted sizes)
- Hand cleaner
- Plastic bags
- Scissors and tweezers
- Small flashlight and extra batteries
- Syrup of ipecac (use only if instructed by Poison Control Center)
- Triangular bandage

Cardiopulmonary Resuscitation

Cardiopulmonary resuscitation (CPR) is a procedure designed to help a victim breathe and to restart the heart. It's a skill everyone should learn, especially those whose work may involve even moderately hazardous materials or duties.

CAUTION: To learn CPR, you need to be trained by qualified professionals. Injury can be caused if CPR is administered incorrectly. NEVER attempt CPR on a person who is breathing.

Contact Information

For information about CPR courses, contact your local American Heart Association.

Handout

Developing a Fire Emergency Plan

Your drafting lab should have a plan for use in a fire emergency. If your instructor has not explained it to you, ask about it. Be sure you know where all the exits are, where the fire extinguishers are kept, and what your responsibilities are in case a fire occurs. Then follow these steps to record the fire emergency plan.

1. On the next page, draw a floor plan of the lab. If there's not enough room, use a larger piece of paper.
2. Locate all the fire exits and label them on the floor plan. If the lab has no direct exit to the outside, use a separate piece of paper and draw a map of your section of the school. Show the location of the lab, and draw arrows from the doors in the lab to the nearest fire exits.
3. Locate and label any windows that could also be used for escape. (Check to be sure the opening will be large enough for an adult to pass through.)
4. Locate all the fire extinguishers and label them on the floor plan. Indicate on the plan the class of fire for which each extinguisher can be used.
5. Determine where you and your classmates should meet after you have left the building. This is important so that someone can check to be sure everyone has escaped safely.
6. Ask your instructor for procedures to follow if a fire occurs. If time allows, this may include such things as closing windows, turning off equipment, and grabbing the first aid kit. Someone should be responsible for reporting the fire. However, human safety is the most important consideration. Fires can spread quickly, and smoke can be just as deadly as flames. Your most important responsibility is to get out alive.
7. Be sure everyone has a chance to study the emergency plan. Then, with your instructor's approval, post it in a prominent place where it can be seen easily.

Copyright © Glencoe/McGraw-Hill

Fire Emergency Plan

Handout

Extinguishing Fires

Controlling a Fire

Most fires can be extinguished by

- **Reducing the heat.** The most common method of reducing the heat of a fire is to throw water on it. This method not only has a cooling action, but it also produces steam, which helps to exclude oxygen. However, water *should not* be used on Class B, C, or D fires. See the chart below.

- **Removing the source of fuel.** If a gas or liquid, such as gasoline, is feeding a fire, it can often be turned off in some way, which removes the fuel. In some cases, the fuel may be allowed to burn until it is used up and the fire goes out.

- **Preventing oxygen from reaching the fire.** Depriving a fire of oxygen can be accomplished by spraying it with an inert gas, such as carbon dioxide, which is contained in many fire extinguishers. This is also the method used when a person's clothing catches fire. The person is wrapped in a blanket, which smothers the fire.

Kinds of Fire Extinguishers

Fires are classified according to the type of fuel that is feeding them. Before using any fire extinguisher, look at its label to be sure you have the right one. Symbols with blue backgrounds indicate that the extinguisher can be used for the class of fire shown. If the symbol has a black background with a red line drawn through it, the extinguisher *cannot* be used for that class of fire.

Extinguishers must be tested periodically to be sure their contents are still active. Dry chemical extinguishers, for example, should be checked for moisture. Maintenance requirements appear on the label.

USING FIRE EXTINGUISHERS

Class of Fire	A — ORDINARY COMBUSTIBLES	B — FLAMMABLE LIQUIDS	C — ELECTRICAL EQUIPMENT	D — COMBUSTIBLE METALS
Material Burned	Ordinary combustibles, such as wood, paper, and cloth	Flammable liquids, such as oil, gasoline, paint, and solvents	Electrical equipment, such as power tools, electric motors, wiring, fuse boxes, and computers	Combustible metals, such as iron and magnesium
Types of Fire Extinguishers				
Pressurized Water	•			
Foam	•			
Ordinary Dry chemical		•	•	
Carbon Dioxide		•	•	
Multi-Purpose Dry chemical	•	•	•	
Halogenated	•	•	•	
Dry Powder				•

Copyright © Glencoe/McGraw-Hill

Handout

Safety Color Codes

Color	Common Uses	Meaning
Red	Used to identify • Fire equipment • Exit signs • Containers for flammable materials • Panic buttons on machinery • Signs for hazardous areas	**Danger**
Orange	Indicates machine hazards. Often used to outline and draw attention to • Machine guards • Electrical boxes that have start and stop buttons, levers, or toggles • Parts of machinery that can cut or crush • Pulleys, belts, and gears	**Warning**
Yellow	Used to indicate critical machine parts such as wheels, levers, and controls • Used along with black diagonal stripes to identify tripping or falling hazards, such as stairs • Used along with black for caution signs	**Caution**
Blue	Used on signs and bulletin boards	**Information**
Green	Used along with white to show location of • First aid stations • First aid kits • Safety equipment	**Safety**
White	Used alone or with black to direct traffic flow; stripes or arrows show direction, identify barricades, etc.	**Boundaries**
Magenta or purple on yellow	Used in areas where radiation is present	**Radiation caution**

Copyright © Glencoe/McGraw-Hill

Hazardous Waste

Hazardous waste is any waste material that either contributes to pollution or has the potential to create pollution. It may be a material that can cause personal injury or environmental damage. It also may be a material or product that becomes hazardous after use.

Hazardous wastes are generated and managed in a variety of settings. Those working in drafting professions may encounter varying types of wastes depending upon the type of business they are working in. For example, a manufacturing plant may produce hazardous waste as a result of normal production operations.

Environmental Protection Agency

The Environmental Protection Agency (EPA) regulates the management and disposal of hazardous wastes under the Resource Conservation and Recovery Act (RCRA). The RCRA has three goals:

- To protect both human health and the environment
- To reduce waste while conserving energy and natural resources
- To reduce or eliminate the generation of hazardous waste

The EPA requires businesses to follow rules for properly identifying and managing waste, without overly burdening their business practices. Businesses are classified by the amount of waste they produce. Those that produce larger volumes of waste must follow more stringent regulations. The EPA conducts inspections to make sure that individual facilities are in compliance with regulations. The EPA also offers incentives for those who report violations and promptly take care of the problem.

Types of Hazardous Waste

The EPA and the Code of Federal Regulations (CFR) list materials that can be considered hazardous wastes. State and local environmental agencies may list additional specific materials. Hazardous waste or material may be in the form of a liquid, a solid, or a gas.

According to the RCRA, waste is hazardous if it exhibits one of the following characteristics:

- **Ignitability.** Waste that is determined to be flammable under certain conditions
- **Corrosivity.** Waste that corrodes metals or has a very high or low pH
- **Reactivity.** Waste that readily explodes or undergoes violent reactions
- **Toxicity.** Waste that is known to be harmful or fatal when ingested and is known to leach into groundwater at certain levels; for example, waste with high levels of arsenic, lead, or mercury

If you work in an industry that produces wastes considered to be hazardous, always be aware of their presence. Wear protective clothing when working with these materials. Be careful not to mix or combine materials that may cause a chemical reaction. Always read and follow label directions before using any known hazardous material. If you are unsure of the use or application of any material, ask someone familiar with the material before proceeding. Remember, the only useless question is the one you don't ask. The proper use and containment of hazardous materials will provide a safer workplace.

Handout
Hazardous Waste (Continued)

Universal Waste Rule

The Universal Waste Rule is an amendment to the RCRA that encourages recycling and proper disposal of certain common hazardous wastes by reducing administrative requirements for businesses. It is designed to reduce the amount of hazardous waste in solid waste systems. Universal wastes that might be found in businesses employing drafting professionals include:

- Batteries, such as nickel-cadmium (Ni-Cd) and small sealed lead-acid batteries (SSLA), which are found in common items such as portable computers and computer backup devices
- Thermostats, which can contain as much as 3 grams of liquid mercury and are located in almost any building
- Lamps, which often contain mercury and lead. Common types of lamps include fluorescent, high-pressure sodium, and metal halide lamps.

Recycling Tips

State and local governments, businesses, and public agencies are involved in developing and promoting recycling programs. Businesses can develop collection programs and educate employees on the importance of recycling items that contain hazardous waste.

Here are ideas for recycling:

- The Rechargeable Battery Recycling Corporation (RBRC), a nonprofit organization representing many rechargeable battery manufacturers, has developed programs for recycling batteries. For more information, go the RBRC Web site at www.rbrc.com.
- Used cartridges for laser printers can be refilled or recycled. Empty toner cartridges can often be mailed to their manufacturers at little cost.
- Commercial mailing services will often accept plastic "peanuts" for reuse. For the nearest collection site that accepts them, contact the Peanut Pipeline. Look up Peanut Pipeline at www.epa.gov.
- For information on recycling expanded polystyrene (EPS) foam, check out the Alliance of Foam Packaging Recyclers at www.epspackaging.org.

Computer Hardware Components

A growing issue is how to dispose of computer hardware that has become obsolete. Environmental experts have identified toxic material in computers, such as lead, cadmium, and mercury. They are also studying the impact that computer peripherals could have on the environment.

Many states have laws that ban computer equipment from landfills. Many of the old computers can be recycled or refurbished, but other solutions are also needed.

Classroom Management

With the *Applying AutoCAD 2002* instructional program, the instructor usually serves as a facilitator of learning rather than as a traditional lecturer. For best results, develop a sound knowledge of and experience with the AutoCAD 2002 software and computer hardware. You should also be aware of current AutoCAD 2002 applications, technologies, and topics, including presentation graphics, desktop publishing, large-scale CAD systems, and industry trends.

Teaching the Material

The *Applying AutoCAD 2002* program can be implemented in almost any lecture and lab setting. The program is particularly effective when the instructor's presentations are followed by hands-on laboratory sessions. Consider keeping classroom presentations fairly short. The students usually do not fully absorb the information until they apply it at the workstations. A brief introduction and overview will give them an idea of what is ahead.

Helping the Book Lie Flat

If the book lies flat as a student works at the computer, it is easier to reference. Also, this helps the spine remain flexible, which means it will last longer. Begin by folding the front cover back at the edge of the spine. Repeat with the back cover. Open the book up to the middle and gently bend the pages and spine back so that the book lies fairly flat. Then take a section of pages about 1/8" thick and gently fold that back with the spine. Repeat until the entire book has been folded back in these small sections.

Introducing the Material

If you are using the *Fundamentals* text, be sure your students work through Chapter 1, "Tour of AutoCAD." This chapter was designed to give students a good introduction to AutoCAD while using simple, basic procedures. Students will be able to start AutoCAD, preview drawing files, open drawing files, view details, explore the **Startup** dialog box, shade a drawing, and exit AutoCAD.

If you are using the *Advanced* text, it is assumed your students already know basic AutoCAD operation. You may wish to survey them at the beginning of the course to determine the extent of their knowledge and experience.

Microsoft PowerPoint® presentations are provided on the Instructor Productivity CD-ROM. These presentations introduce topics in the text. The first slide in each presentation shows the main topics covered for a particular part. The remaining slides elaborate on the topics with which students may have the most difficulty.

Transparency masters are provided in this guide. Along with the slides or transparencies, you might want to discuss the commands, mode settings, and other features of AutoCAD as described in the text.

Following a presentation, the text will guide students step by step as they learn to use AutoCAD 2002. You can then choose questions, problems, and projects from the text based on the amount of presentation and lab time available.

Group Size

If you have a small group of students (five or fewer), you might choose to walk them through most of the commands and settings while you continuously monitor and adjust the pace. The text can also do this for you. Certain learners may get ahead or behind, but, generally, if the members in a small group start at the same level, most will stay together.

For larger groups, it is generally not as useful to walk students through the AutoCAD commands, features, etc. If you have six or more students, it's nearly impossible to keep everyone together. Let the students go at

Copyright © Glencoe/McGraw-Hill

their own pace in the lab, but do establish clear directions and goals. Emphasize to students the need for practice. This is one subject that can't be learned entirely out of a book. Some students will require more practice and others less.

Your course may consist of about one-half traditional drafting and design concepts that you've taught in the past and one-half new AutoCAD material. If so, consider introducing AutoCAD near the beginning of the course and allowing your students the opportunity to learn and apply traditional methods at the same time they are using *Applying AutoCAD 2002*. For example, if you are teaching isometric drawing, have your students draw isometric sketches not only by hand but also on the CAD system, using the appropriate chapter in the text as a guide.

Supervising the CAD Lab

Whether or not you are experienced with CAD, supervising a laboratory can be quite a challenge—especially if you have a relatively large class.

Student Assistants

Early in the course, select one or two of the better students and ask if they would be willing to serve as your lab assistants. Students are usually more than willing to help, and you'll be relieved from having to answer routine questions over and over again. Also, if you have open lab times, your assistants can help you supervise the lab.

It helps to make the boundaries and responsibilities of lab assistants clear and agreed to before they begin. You might want to consider having them sign a contract. If they do not live up to the agreement, they lose their supervisory privileges.

Preventing Problems in the Lab

If possible, have students use the same computer each time they are in the lab. This gives students a feeling of shared ownership. That, plus the opportunity to work on real-world projects that meet their interests, leads them to take responsibility for their computers and treat them with respect. Students don't want anything to happen to their computers, and they don't want others to damage them either.

Pride in ownership can also result from granting students the privilege of making their own AutoCAD profiles that they save on a diskette. This is a good option for students who have worked through some of the chapters in the text and know what options they will need to leave "as is" in order to follow the text. This kind of privilege can be granted with the understanding that any abuse of the computer results in loss of customized profile or other lab privileges. For information on creating profiles, see "Installing AutoCAD 2002," pp. 16-18.

A good source of ideas and support in any class that uses computer equipment is an e-mail discussion list called EDTECH. See the "Professional Resources" section (pp. 47-48) for more information.

Sharing Equipment

It is not uncommon for an instructor to have more students than workstations. If possible, make the best of it by staggering workstation schedules so that students can work at various times of the day or evening.

Make diskettes or CDs available to your students on which they can store backup copies of their drawing files. Students should take this diskette or CD with them when they leave the laboratory, but all other system and storage diskettes and files should remain in the lab.

You can also make more effective use of your equipment by assigning groups to work on the projects at the end of each part of *Applying AutoCAD 2002* or the Additional Problems at the end of the text.

One Workstation per Class

If you have access to only one CAD station, you are probably just starting to use CAD in your present drafting/design courses. Since you may have 20 or more students in your class, it may be difficult for you to provide even brief hands-on instruction to all of them. If so, the following ideas may be of help.

Introduce CAD near the beginning of your course by discussing its applications, capabilities, and limitations. Give your students a brief but dynamic demonstration of the system by plotting, zooming, dimensioning, and using other features such as array and dynamic drag. Show PowerPoint presentation slides from the Instructor Productivity CD-ROM.

Next, divide the class into teams of two students each. Develop a rotation schedule in which each team takes turns at the CAD workstation throughout the school term. The schedule should maximize use of the workstation so that it is seldom idle.

One Workstation per Small Group

If you have one workstation for each group of two to three students, you will be able to provide your students with more hands-on CAD experience. You may even consider a course dedicated entirely to CAD. Whether you are starting a new course or teaching CAD in an existing course, students should have ample time on the computer. More than three students per workstation is not effective and is not recommended.

Learner Differences

Develop an understanding of the challenges associated with teaching and learning AutoCAD and be sensitive to the needs of new learners. Classes are rarely homogeneous. No matter how hard you work to bring in a new group of learners all at the same level, you'll usually have at least one who is either a computer whiz or, at the other extreme, fairly unskilled with a computer. Teaching under these conditions presents a challenge (and a bit of tension) for both instructor and students. Be prepared to accommodate each individual's needs regardless of his or her knowledge level. Of course, this does not mean that every student should progress at a different rate, because it's almost impossible to teach a large CAD class that way, but be flexible. Don't be afraid to restructure after you've learned more about the students' abilities.

Student Interaction

Students can often help one another learn. For this reason, allow the class to form small groups, not only at the CAD workstations but also in classroom activities. For example, student pairs can work together to understand lecture material. They may study together or quiz each other before a major exam.

Cooperative Learning

CAD courses provide many excellent opportunities for cooperative learning. In fact, when there aren't enough computers for each student to work individually, cooperative learning is essential. Assign teams in such a way that student strengths are complementary, and try to maintain a good gender and ethnic mix.

Some people believe that cooperative learning activities are the same as group activities. To some extent, this may be true. However, true cooperative learning makes sure that each member of the group plays a part in the learning process. Rather than just working together, students combine their skills and knowledge to help each other understand the content or activity. In true cooperative learning activities, each member is responsible for ensuring that every other member learns the material.

Some cooperative learning techniques may work very well in your instructional setting, and others may be completely inappropriate. Choose those that you think will work in your courses and modify them as necessary to meet your needs. For example, when appropriate, have the class form groups of four or five students, depending on class size. Allow time in class for students to discuss and compare homework assignments and their answers to the Review Questions at the end of each chapter in *Applying AutoCAD 2002*. When members of the group come up with different answers, they should discuss the topic and choose what they believe to be the most correct answer. For written assignments, you may wish to collect only one paper from each group, without disclosing ahead of time whose paper you will choose. This method encourages students to work together to make sure that all students understand the material.

Brainstorming

Many CAD problems have no one "right" answer. This is particularly true in design assignments and problem-solving activities. Encourage students to brainstorm to find as many alternatives as possible. This exercise generally has two favorable outcomes. First, it helps students discover many solutions from which they can then choose the one they believe will work best. Also, students learn to work together to solve problems—a real-world skill that many students have little chance to learn before they enter the job market.

Group Projects

The learning experiences in *Applying AutoCAD 2002* include projects that are intended to challenge students and sharpen their thinking skills. There are projects at the end of each of the parts, plus Advanced Projects at the end of the *Advanced* text. The projects can be carried out individually or by teams of two or more students who are matched according to similar interests. However, individual students should be held accountable for the results. Assign teams in such a way that student strengths are complementary, and try to maintain a good gender and ethnic mix.

Suggestions for using the part projects are included in the Part Instructional Plans provided in this guide. The Chapter Instructional Plans for the *Advanced* text show which of the Advanced Projects are appropriate to use at that point in students' coursework.

Motivating Students

Motivation is a major factor in any learning process, and even the best facilities cannot teach an individual who does not want to learn. Sometimes, particularly in secondary and post-secondary courses, the student comes to class already motivated. A high-school student, for example, may need to complete a CAD course as a prerequisite for college. A mechanical engineer may have been promised a raise or bonus for learning to use CAD. Often, however, the motivation must come from the instructor.

Learning CAD can be an interesting, even exciting, experience. However, although many students enjoy working at the computer, the predictability of classwork may become dull if it is unrelieved. You can break the monotony by adding a few new elements at intervals. What you choose depends on the type and purpose of the CAD course and the age and interests of the students. The following suggestions are general in nature, and they can be used to some extent by instructors at all levels.

Guest Speakers

One way to add variety is to invite guest speakers to the class. Choose both the speaker and the topic with care. The topics should be timely and appropriate. For example, you won't want to schedule a speaker who talks excitedly about uses of mass properties gleaned from solid models before students are aware of what a solid model is. Also, boring speakers defeat the purpose. If possible, listen to the speaker before you ask him or her to visit the class.

You can sometimes find good motivational speakers by contacting local companies. An employee may be willing to share knowledge about how CAD is used in the company or in a specific industry. Local speakers have the added advantage, from the instructor's point of view, of perhaps being available again in the future. Otherwise, you may find appropriate speakers listed in journals or participating in various meetings or conferences.

Copyright © Glencoe/McGraw-Hill

Field Trips

Another way of adding variety and value is to organize a field trip to a setting in which CAD is being used. Many engineering firms and manufacturing companies are willing to allow school groups of all ages to visit their worksites. Field trips may be difficult to orchestrate, but in many cases they are more than worth the effort. In fact, an ongoing relationship with one or more local companies has been known to result in jobs, internships, and other opportunities for interested students and instructors.

Contests

Major companies and organizations often sponsor student contests, which offer good opportunities for students to make use of the knowledge they have gained. Course content seems more relevant when students must apply a learned principle to a design project. These kinds of activities should involve every student who is interested.

For more information about contests in your area, contact local companies, look in any technology journals you receive, and check the Internet. See the information about SkillsUSA-VICA found under "Student and Professional Organizations" in this Instructor Resource Guide. If entering a large contest is not feasible, create one of your own. For example, students can work in groups to create a design, and different classes can compete.

Cultivating Useful Skills

In addition to gaining valuable drafting skills, your students will benefit from learning problem solving and critical thinking, leadership, and entrepreneurship.

Problem Solving and Critical Thinking

Problems to be solved are everywhere, and you won't have to look far for them. You can also ask students to suggest problems. You may be surprised at how many interesting projects students can suggest and how creative—and effective—some of their solutions can be.

If possible, build problems to be solved into the coursework. In the text, each chapter's Review & Activities section includes a section called Using Problem-Solving Skills. These activities present students with a situation that might occur in the workplace. For example, "Your architectural office needs a drawing template setup that will accommodate the floor plans. . . . Create the template." Students will need to apply their knowledge of AutoCAD 2002, common sense, and their problem-solving skills to develop solutions.

At the back of the *Advanced* text are Advanced Projects. These, too, are problem-solving activities. These longer projects are designed to stimulate and challenge advanced students. Students redesign or partially redesign a part or an entire product.

A good puzzle can catch student interest, and carefully implemented problem-solving activities are also great motivational devices, especially if the students' own ideas are involved. It is amazing how word of a special project trickles down to students from year to year, increasing both interest and enrollment in the course.

Critical-thinking activities are similar to problem-solving activities, and there is overlap between the two. The primary difference is that critical-thinking activities are generally done on paper, either as a design or as a plan for a project or a solution to a problem. *Applying AutoCAD 2002* provides plenty of opportunities for students to use and hone their thinking skills. For example, the Challenge Your Thinking questions at the end of each chapter can provide a springboard from which students may delve deeper into topics that interest them.

Leadership

Encourage the students enrolled in your courses to develop skills that will help them become leaders. In fact, you may want to hold a class discussion about the characteristics of leaders. Remind students that good leaders are not confined to presidents, generals, and governors. Ask students what they think qualifies a person as a leader, and list their responses.

Good leaders are generally people who have most or all of the following attributes:

- good communication skills
- strong sense of purpose
- integrity
- ability to get along with people

Explain to students that everyone has these characteristics to a certain extent. Those who make an effort to improve their skills are usually the most successful leaders. The sense of purpose and integrity come from within the individual, but communication and people skills can and should be improved at every opportunity.

People communicate in many ways—possibly in more ways than students realize. Verbal expression and body language are common forms of communication, but many people (including CAD students) may not realize that CAD, too, is a form of communication. The ability to describe a part or structure accurately and fully using CAD enables others to understand the object's appearance and workings. CAD communication can be extremely valuable to employees as well as students considering a career in drafting, architecture, engineering, or any of several other fields.

Finally, point out that leaders must be able to follow as well as lead. The cooperative learning activities discussed earlier in this guide can help students learn to balance leadership with cooperation.

Entrepreneurship

The world of work can be an exciting and challenging place. Now more than ever, students need to know how to take charge of their careers. Many new opportunities are emerging as a result of technology. On the other hand, many companies routinely use "downsizing" or reorganization to solve fiscal problems, and hundreds of employees may find themselves suddenly without work. Some people go into business for themselves—they become entrepreneurs—and entrepreneurship is an important concept for students to master.

An entrepreneur is someone who, in addition to having a marketable skill, has the ability to organize and manage a business based on that skill. Managing your own business can be a lot of work, but many people believe it is worth the effort. In fact, some people believe that they have more job security working for themselves than they would have if they worked for a large company. In the final analysis, those people who are willing to work hard and be flexible are most likely to succeed.

CAD skills lend themselves to entrepreneurship. You may want to have students set up a mock company in the CAD lab, possibly in connection with a CAD project. There are many projects in the text that you might want to allow them to choose from. Consider the projects at the end of each of the parts in the texts as well as the Additional Projects at the end of the *Advanced* text.

Feedback from Students

Even the best course can always benefit from student input. The forms on pages 43 and 44 are designed to help you gather this kind of information. The first is the Student Profile Form. Use this form at the beginning of the course to gain an understanding of the students' needs, their experience with computers and software, and their expectations for the course.

The second form is the Course Evaluation Form. Ask students to complete this form near the end of the course. Student remarks on this form can be very helpful in pointing out areas that might need improvement.

Handout

Basic Computer Skills

Computers can help you become a productive and efficient drafting professional. They make collaboration with other drafting professionals more effective, especially when they are networked. Computers can also be used for such things as writing, finding and organizing information, calculating numbers, and controlling other devices.

Three basic operations of a computer are input, processing, and output. Input is received through input devices such as keyboards, mice, or trackballs. Processing is handled by the central processing unit (CPU) and other internal electronic devices. Output is produced by the monitor, printer, and other devices.

The computer's operating system controls the overall activity of the computer. For example, the operating system starts and runs application software, such as CAD programs. The operating system also enables the different components of the computer system (such as the disk drives, printer, and monitor) to work together.

Most CAD software runs on computers that use the Microsoft Windows operating system. This article describes basic operations of Windows 95, 98, and 2000.

Starting and Shutting Down

In most computers, Windows starts automatically when you turn on the computer. When startup is complete, the screen will display the Windows desktop. The exact look of the desktop varies depending on how your computer is set up but will probably have the following items:

- **Start button.** Selecting this button displays a menu of items, such as programs and documents. Selecting an item with an arrow next to it displays another menu. At the bottom of the Start menu is the Shut Down option.

- **Shortcut icons.** There will be one or more icons on the desktop. These are shortcuts, and they provide an easy way to open programs or documents.

- **Taskbar.** The taskbar is usually in the bottom area of the desktop. It shows which Windows features are in use and displays the name of any open programs (also called *applications*). You can have more than one program open at a time.

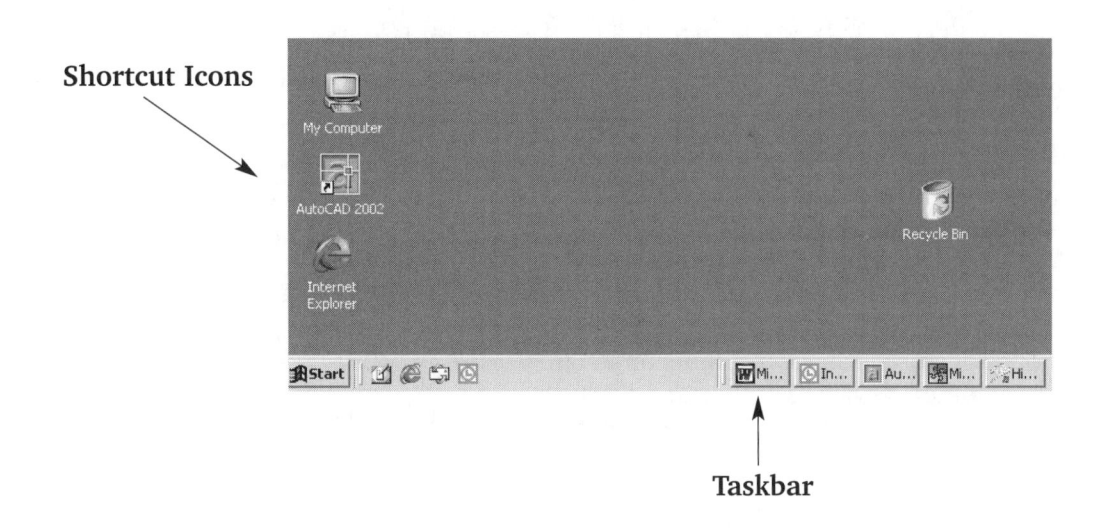

Copyright © Glencoe/McGraw-Hill

35

Handout
Basic Computer Skills (Continued)

Files and Folders

You will need to save each document or drawing you create as a file. The computer itself also has many different kinds of files it uses to operate. The files are organized into folders, much like paper documents are organized into folders in a filing cabinet. (Folders are sometimes referred to as *directories*.) Each folder is labeled for easy identification. Here are two ways to see the files and folders stored:

My Computer icon. If you select this icon on the desktop, a window displays the contents of your computer. You will see icons for the storage devices used by your computer. This may include a hard disk, compact disc, network drives, or removable storage devices. Selecting one of the icons will display the folders and files stored there. You can also search for and open files and folders.

Windows Explorer. This shows the hierarchical structure of files, folders, and storage systems or devices used by your computer. If you select a folder, Explorer will display its contents. You can copy, move, rename, delete, and search for files and folders. You can also create new folders.

Deleting Files

When you delete files or folders from your hard disk, Windows places them in the Recycle Bin, where you can retrieve them later if you need to. Files or folders deleted from a floppy disk or a network drive are permanently deleted and are not sent to the Recycle Bin.

Storing Data

To keep from losing the work you do on a computer, you must save it to some kind of storage medium. Storage devices may include a hard disk drive and various types of removable cartridges and disks. The amount of storage space available on a hard disk or other device is important because this is where you will store the files you have created.

Most hard disks are permanently connected to the drive (fixed disks), although there are also removable hard disks. Other removable devices include floppy disks, CDs, DVDs, and magnetic tape cartridges. Each type of removable storage medium works with a corresponding type of drive. Magnetic tape is often used for backup or archiving purposes.

The computer also has internal storage space called *memory* that it uses while it's operating. An adequate amount of memory makes it possible for the computer to handle large files, such as drawing files, while they are open and you are working on them. Two kinds of memory are RAM and ROM. RAM stands for *random-access memory* and is used for temporary storage. ROM stands for *read-only memory*. This is permanent storage for programs that the computer needs to run. It cannot be changed.

Staying Organized

You will be able to work much faster if your files and folders are organized. Follow these tips for managing files.

- Give your files and folders names that describe their contents. For example, suppose you created a drawing of a slide collar and another of a pipe collar. File names such as "collar1" and "collar2" would not be as descriptive as the names "slide collar" and "pipe collar."

- Avoid storing large numbers of files in a single folder. Organize them into several folders within that folder.

- Do not store your drawing files in the same folder as the CAD program.

- Save your work as you go. It is recommended that you save every fifteen minutes. Remember, though, that each time you save a file without renaming it, the previous version of your file is overwritten with the newer one.

- Regularly back up your files onto removable storage media, such as floppy disks, tapes, or writable compact discs. (If not preformatted, floppy disks must be formatted before use.) Keep the disks or

Copyright © Glencoe/McGraw-Hill

Handout
Basic Computer Skills (Continued)

tapes in a safe place, protected from extremes of temperature and humidity.

- To free up space on the hard disk, delete files that you are sure you no longer need. If you don't need the file now, but may need it later, copy the file to a backup disk or tape. It also helps to delete files that have been stored in the Recycle Bin.

Computer Care and Maintenance

- The computer system should be on a sturdy, level surface.

- The computer and monitor should have at least four inches of space around the sides and back for heat to escape. Do not block any of the ventilation slots.

- The computer system should not be in direct sunlight or next to a heating device. Avoid dust, high humidity, and extreme heat or cold.

- Make sure there is surge protection.

- Keep liquids away from the computer and keyboard. Keep disks away from magnets.

- Restart the computer every morning, even if you left it on overnight. This clears out all of the memory. Also, if some applications fail to quit completely, this closes them out.

- About once a month, run the utilities for defragmenting and diagnosing problems on the hard disk. For Windows 2000, the tools to use are Disk Defragmenter and Disk Cleanup. You can start these utility programs from the Start, Programs, Accessories, and System Tools menus.

- Protect the computer against viruses with an antivirus utility program. Two popular programs are Norton Antivirus by Symantec and McAfee VirusScan.

Copyright © Glencoe/McGraw-Hill

E-Mail Etiquette

Observing e-mail manners can mean the difference between success and failure in getting your messages read and understood.

Send the Right Message

When sending e-mail messages, you can't share facial expressions, gestures, or voice inflections the way you do when you're face-to-face with someone. Therefore it is easier to take a person's intentions the wrong way. Here are some things to keep in mind to prevent misunderstandings.

- The person you e-mail may not share your values, cultural background, or opinions. Before you send the message, consider how it will be received.

- Don't write anything in e-mail that you wouldn't write on a post card. E-mail is not entirely secure and can be intercepted by others. A message can also be saved or forwarded to anyone.

- Don't use e-mail to "let off steam." Cool off before sending it.

- Would you say the same thing if the person were in front of you? If not, rewrite the message.

- DON'T SHOUT! It's all right to emphasize a word or line in capitals, but use the CAPS lock button sparingly.

- Keep harassment and discrimination policies in mind. Don't write, send, or forward e-mail that is offensive, obscene, discriminatory, or sexist.

- E-mail is less formal than letter writing, so it's tempting to relax on the formalities of grammar and spelling. However, you will be judged by the quality of your writing. Like it or not, spelling and grammar do count.

- Make sure your notes are clear, logical, and concise. It is possible to write a paragraph that contains no errors in grammar or spelling but still makes no sense.

- Bad information spreads easily on the Internet. Once e-mail is sent, you lose control of where it might be forwarded. Before you send information, check the facts.

- Having good manners yourself doesn't give you the right to correct everyone else. If you decide to inform someone of an e-mail mistake, point it out politely and privately.

Respect Your Reader's Time

- Send messages only to those who really need the information. Mail to a group list only if it's appropriate for everyone on the list to receive the message.

- If you want your e-mail read, use a specific subject line.

- Recipients of your e-mail may not appreciate an inbox filled with recipes, jokes, inspiring stories, or requests for charitable donations.

- Don't use the school or organization's computers to send or forward electronic junk mail advertisements (spam).

- For urgent messages, try another medium. E-mail is quick and efficient, but your reader is not obligated to check or reply to it on a regular basis. If you have a pressing issue, try the phone or arrange a face-to-face meeting.

- When you return e-mail, don't reply to everyone the e-mail has been sent to, unless it's necessary. Delete the e-mail addresses of people who don't need to receive a reply.

- When replying, use the automatic quote feature and edit the quote. Quote just enough of the previous message so that the receiver can see at a glance what has gone on before in the conversation.

- Don't forward e-mail virus warnings; almost all are hoaxes. Antivirus software is the best defense against viruses.

Handout

Internet Permission Contract

This school is fortunate to have been equipped with access to the Internet. Our system has been established to help students learn and to help them develop their computer skills. It is our school's intention to use the computer(s) and the Internet responsibly and ethically.

Below is a list of rules and principles we intend to abide by and maintain:

1. Students will have access to the Internet, including e-mail.
2. No personal contact information (such as the student's home and school addresses, telephone numbers, etc.) will be posted or shared on the Internet.
3. Students will report any inappropriate messages to the instructor.
4. Students will not engage in any illegal act, including downloading illegal music, movies, or software and plagiarizing content from the Internet.
5. Students will not attempt to gain unauthorized access or disrupt any computer system by willfully destroying data or spreading viruses.
6. On the Internet, students will not use obscene language, engage in personal or discriminatory attacks, or post false or misleading information about individuals or organizations.
7. Students will not access lewd or obscene material.
8. Students will abide by any additional rules posted by the school.

These rules and principles must be adhered to and any violation of them will be met with zero tolerance.

- **Students must abide by their signed contracts.**
- **The use of the computer is a privilege, not a right.**
- **If this contract is broken, the student's privilege will be revoked.**

I have read the "Internet Permission Contract" above. By signing below, I fully understand and agree with the contents of this contract. If I breach any rules, I understand my Internet and computer privileges will be revoked.

Signed by:

Parent or Guardian: _____ Date: _____

Student: _____ Date: _____

Instructor: _____ Date: _____

Copyright © Glencoe/McGraw-Hill

Handout

Internet Evaluation Sheet

URL of website you are evaluating: http:// _____

Appropriateness: Is the site suitable for viewing? Does it provide the information you need? Is the information at your level and clearly written?

_____
_____
_____

Design and Technical Aspects: Is it attractive and easy to use? Are pages set up in a useful order? Does it download quickly? Do its links work? Are they clearly explained and relevant?

_____
_____
_____

Source: Is the information from a source you can trust? Who wrote the information? Does the site provide biographical information, such as the author's position, the organization the person is associated with, and the address, e-mail address, and telephone number?

_____
_____
_____

Accuracy: If facts or statistics are provided, does the author cite the sources so you can refer to them? How recent is the information? Do the links reveal any bias that the author might have?

_____
_____
_____

Point of View: Is the site's intention to teach something or to persuade you to adopt its point of view? What do you think the writer's point of view, or bias, is? Is the purpose of the site to sell a product?

_____
_____
_____

Copyright © Glencoe/McGraw-Hill

Using the Internet

The Internet is a worldwide network of computers linked together. Small groups of computers, such as those at a university, may be linked to form a local network. Then that network is linked to other small networks to form a large network. Many large networks make up what we know as the Internet.

E-Mail

Electronic mail (e-mail) is one part of the Internet. It has become an extremely popular method of communication. Using your computer, you can send and receive messages, letters, and documents 24 hours a day.

As with regular mail, e-mail must include an address. An e-mail address looks something like this: john_smith@company.com.

The World Wide Web

The World Wide Web is another part of the Internet that was created to make accessing information easier. It does this by means of hypertext markup language (HTML), a formatting system that allows you to receive information in the form of pictures, text, sound, and even video. Because of its ease of use, the Web is very popular.

Any individual or organization can set up a document on the Web, called a Web site, that other people can visit using their computers. A Web site may have several "pages," like the pages in a book, filled with information, pictures, and links to other Web sites. The primary page is called the *home page*. Each page has its own address, called a *uniform resource locator* or *universal resource locator* (URL). By typing that address in your computer, you can go to that Web page.

Many software programs, including AutoCAD design software, include links to online help. In addition, AutoCAD provides Web sites on which you can post drawings so that people in other locations can view and edit them online.

Search Tools

Newspaper and magazine articles, automobile ratings, travel information, and much, much more can be found on the Internet. Search tools, such as directories and search engines, organize lists of information to make it easier for you to find what you're looking for. For example, Yahoo is a directory created by people who visit and evaluate Web sites and then organize them into subject-based categories and subcategories. Yahoo also provides a search tool that can be used to find information in the categories. A search engine, such as Google, uses special software to organize and help you find the information you need.

To use Yahoo, for example, you first type in its URL: www.yahoo.com.

When Yahoo's home page appears, you can select a category or type in key words that describe the information you want. For example, if you are looking for information about pipe drafting, you might type in: pipe drafting.

After a moment, a list of links in which the words "pipe" and "drafting" occur will appear on your screen.

If the list you get has links that are not really related to what you're looking for, you can refine your search. Most search tools provide instructions that will save you time and effort. In the example above, typing "pipe drafting" (within quotation marks as shown here) would have narrowed your search to only those sites that have that exact term. Also, you may get clues for better search terms from words that appear in the links.

Viruses

A virus is a computer program designed to change the way your computer works. Some viruses are relatively harmless. Others may affect system operation, damage other programs, erase files, erase your hard disk, or cause the system to crash.

Most viruses enter your computer through e-mail attachments. If e-mail with

Handout
Using the Internet (Continued)

an attachment comes from an unknown sender, or unexpectedly from a known sender, it should not be opened. If you receive an unexpected attachment from someone you know, call to make sure of the mail's source before opening it.

The best protection is an antivirus utility program designed to track down viruses and eliminate them. Two popular antivirus programs are Norton Antivirus by Symantec and McAfee VirusScan. Antivirus software should be updated at least once a week. There is no need to forward e-mail virus warnings, as almost all are hoaxes.

Internet Communities

You can participate in several types of communities on the Internet, such as chat rooms, bulletin boards, news groups, and e-mail lists.

- Chat rooms are formed by groups of people who want to communicate instantly and directly about a topic of common interest.

- Bulletin boards are like chat rooms, except that they are used to post messages rather than to "talk" back and forth. You might post a question such as "What are government housing standards for drawing floor plans?" Another user might know the answer and respond.

- Newsgroups are similar to bulletin boards, except that you subscribe in order to participate. Newsgroups exist for a huge variety of topics, to which anyone can post thoughts, opinions, or advice.

- Mailing lists are another type of group that you can subscribe to. Messages sent to the group arrive in each person's e-mail box.

Job Searches

The Internet has become very popular with employers and job-seekers. Most large companies now have Web sites and provide a page listing their job opportunities. Most large newspapers and some trade magazines reproduce their "Help Wanted" section at their Web sites.

Commercial Web sites have also been created that allow job seekers to post their résumés. Prospective employers review the résumés and contact those people in whom they're interested. Usually, either the job seeker or the employer is charged a fee. You can also send a résumé with an e-mail message, which many companies prefer.

Protecting Yourself

- Don't give personal information, such as your full name, address, etc., to people or companies you don't know.

- Never give your password to anyone. If someone claiming to represent your Internet service provider asks for your password, don't comply. Contact the service provider yourself and find out whether the request came from them.

- Don't give your credit card number unless you are sure that you are dealing with a reputable company.

- Do not download or open files that are attached to e-mail unless you know the source. The attached file could contain a virus.

- Do not assume that all the information you find on the Internet is true.

- Things change quickly on the Internet. Sites may be redesigned, updated, or disappear. Be aware that what's here today may be gone tomorrow.

- Be aware that some schools may reserve the right to monitor your use of e-mail and Web sites you visit. This is also very common on the job.

Copyright © Glencoe/McGraw-Hill

Handout

Student Profile Form
(To be completed at the beginning of the course)

Name _____

Education Level _____

What do you hope to learn in this course?

_____
_____
_____

What experience have you had with manual methods of drafting and design? (e.g., two years, a course)

_____

What experience have you had with computers?

_____

What experience have you had with the Microsoft Windows operating environment?

_____

What experience have you had with computer-aided drafting/design (CAD)?

_____

Does your work or study currently involve graphics, computer graphics, or CAD? If so, explain.

_____
_____

Comments: _____

_____
_____
_____

Copyright © Glencoe/McGraw-Hill

Handout

Course Evaluation Form

(To be completed near the end of the course)

Please state at least one thing you liked and one thing you disliked about the course.

Liked _____

_____

Disliked _____

_____

Use the scale below to indicate how you would rate the course and the instructor on the following criteria.

5	4	3	2	1
Excellent	Good	Average (No Opinion)	Weak	Very Poor (No)

_____ Instructor was open to questions, problems, and discussions.

_____ Instructor demonstrated strong technical skills and understanding of techniques.

_____ Objectives were clearly presented and explained.

_____ Objectives of the course were met.

_____ Instructor presented information in a way that was easy to understand.

_____ Instructor's presentations and audiovisual aids were well organized.

_____ Instructional materials, including the textbook, were beneficial to my learning.

_____ Lab was effective for learning.

_____ Enough time was allowed to complete assignments.

_____ This course met my expectations.

_____ I would recommend this course to others.

Other Comments _____

_____

_____

_____

_____

_____

Assessment

Students who enroll in CAD courses are generally interested in a job or career that involves CAD. Thus, one of the objectives of the **Applying AutoCAD 2002** text is to help prepare students adequately for their chosen vocations. Evaluation of student work should also reflect this objective. Evaluation of CAD skills and the student's ability to apply them to solve problems and create new drawings is, in many cases, the most appropriate method of assessment. This can be achieved by assigning various drawing tasks, at the appropriate learning levels, throughout the course. Written tests provide excellent supplements to this type of evaluation.

Applying AutoCAD 2002 provides many types of materials that can be used to assist with the assessment process, including chapter review materials, chapter tests, problems, and projects. These are described here, along with ideas for using design problems and portfolios and ideas for grading student work.

Review & Activities

Each chapter of the text concludes with Review & Activities materials, including Review Questions, Challenge Your Thinking questions, Applying AutoCAD Skills activities, and Using Problem-Solving Skills activities. These materials can be used in a variety of ways for teaching the material and also for student assessment. For example, Review Questions can be used to give students a chance to assess themselves after they have worked through the chapter. Challenge Your Thinking questions provide opportunities to think critically. Applying AutoCAD Skills activities provide drawing practice. Using Problem-Solving Skills activities help students develop drawing skills as they solve a problem. Both types of questions and activities can also be scored and assigned points for conversion to a letter grade.

Chapter Tests

This Instructor Resource Guide includes chapter tests that you can photocopy and distribute to students. Question types include multiple choice, completion, and true-false. The answers for the chapter tests are included in this guide.

The Instructor Productivity CD-ROM also includes these chapter tests. They are in an editable, test generator format so that you can customize them to your needs. In addition, the test generator includes pre- and post-tests for each of the textbook's parts.

Projects and Problems

Each part of the text concludes with a project that can also be used for assessment. Additional Problems in both texts and Advanced Projects in the *Advanced* text provide additional opportunities for assessment.

To avoid confusion and frustration, inform students in advance of how you plan to evaluate CAD projects. For example, you may choose to provide a sheet that lists the following items to guide student efforts:

- Format and style of drawings (placement of lines, details, notes, etc.)
- Neatness and accuracy of drawings
- Correct usage of commands, command options, and mode settings (layers, linetypes, dimensions, text styles, units, limits, etc.)
- Overall initiative and effort

Design Problems

Another way to approach evaluation, particularly as a final or comprehensive exam, is to give students a design problem. The exam can consist of solving the problem, creating a drawing that contains all the nec-

Copyright © Glencoe/McGraw-Hill

essay views, and writing a summary of 1) the problem as the student sees it, 2) the way the student believes the problem should be solved, and 3) any limitations to the solution that the student recognizes. Be aware, however, that lab time should be available to give students sufficient access to the computers to complete the exam.

Portfolios

Portfolios, notebooks, or folders can be an important type of assessment tool. They show a representative sample of student work that is collected over a period of time. Portfolios can be assigned a grade based on the instructor's judgment. They can also be used to show the student's best work to a future instructor or employer.

Students can keep all of their work in one portfolio and then organize samples of their best work throughout the course into a final assessment portfolio. You might also want students to write an essay describing their progress during the course.

Grading

Grading should be based on all student work, including computer assignments as well as written assignments. A suggested scenario is to derive sixty percent of the grade from weekly assignments and computer-generated work. The remaining 40 percent can be based on quizzes and examinations. Class participation, attendance, promptness, attitude, and initiative can also be considered during the evaluation process.

Copyright © Glencoe/McGraw-Hill

Professional Resources

Autodesk, Inc.

Contact Autodesk, Inc. for information on AutoCAD 2002, including how to purchase the software, product specifications, products from independent developers, and technical assistance. Autodesk also provides a free knowledge base and links to user's groups.

Autodesk, Inc., 111 McInnis Parkway, San Rafael, CA 94903; Web site:

http://www.autodesk.com/autocad

CADALYST

CADALYST is published 12 times yearly. It provides AutoCAD users with articles, user tips and experiences, suggestions for program improvement, industry happenings, and product information.

Advanstar Communications, 201 Sand Pointe 600, Santa Ana, CA 92707; Web site:

http://www.cadonline.com

CADENCE

CADENCE is a journal developed for the professional AutoCAD user community. It contains a variety of articles, AutoCAD-supported product information, applications for AutoCAD, and information about user problems and potential solutions to those problems.

CMP Media, 600 Harrison Street, San Francisco, CA 94107; Web site:

http://www.cadenceweb.com

Computer-Aided Engineering

Computer-Aided Engineering, a monthly publication, concentrates on the application of CAD/CAM/CAE products, including AutoCAD. Some subscribers qualify for a free subscription.

Penton Media, Inc., 1300 E. 9th St., Cleveland, OH 44114; Web site:

http://www.penton.com

The contact information and Internet listings in this article and in the handouts that follow are a source for extended information related to our text. We have made every effort to recommend sources that are informative and accurate. However, the Internet sites are not under the control of Glencoe/McGraw-Hill, and, therefore, Glencoe/McGraw-Hill makes no representation concerning the content of these sites. We strongly encourage teachers to preview Internet sites before students use them. Many sites may eventually contain "hot links" to other sites that could lead to exposure to inappropriate material. Internet sites are sometimes "under construction" and may not always be available. Sites may also move or have been discontinued completely by the time you or your students attempt to access them.

Computer Graphics World

CGW focuses on various computer graphics applications, including computer-aided design and drafting and AutoCAD. This quality magazine is published monthly.

Computer Graphics World, Pennwell Publishing, 98 Spit Brook Rd., Nashua, NH 03062-2801. Web site:

http://www.cgw.com/

EDTECH

EDTECH is an e-mail discussion list for educational technology users. You can subscribe from the Web archive site, which also gives you access to archives and references offered by the many subscribers and participants in the EDTECH discussion list.

EDTECH Web site:

http://www.h-net.msu.edu/~edweb

InfoWorld

InfoWorld is published weekly and offers news on personal computer and network products.

InfoWorld, 155 Bovet Rd., Suite 800, San Mateo, CA 94402; Web site:

http://www.infoworld.com

PC Magazine

PC Magazine is a weekly publication that provides news and information on personal computer developments and products.

Ziff-Davis Media, Inc., 28 E. 28th St., New York, NY 10016; Web site:

http://www.pcmag.com/pcweek

Student and Professional Organizations

Student and professional organizations help keep members aware of mandates and trends in their fields. On the following pages you will find handouts about the Technology Student Association, SkillsUSA-VICA, the American Design Drafting Association, and Autodesk User Group International. Also included is a handout about parliamentary procedure.

Parliamentary Procedure

Parliamentary procedures are the generally accepted rules used for business meetings. The purpose of the rules is to help a group make decisions in an orderly manner and to promote cooperation and harmony. *Robert's Rules of Order* is a commonly used guide to parliamentary procedures.

To make sure that issues are decided fairly, a quorum must be present. A *quorum* is usually defined as a majority of the members, unless otherwise defined by the organization's by-laws or other rules.

To keep order, only one issue can be considered at one time. No member may speak until recognized by the chair (group leader), and the chair should, of course, be strictly impartial.

Addressing Issues with a Motion

When a member has an issue to deal with, it must be presented in the form of a motion before it can be discussed. There are three steps for making a motion:

1. The member stands up, is recognized, and makes a motion. For example, "I move that we buy new uniforms, including hats."
2. Another member seconds the motion.
3. Without rewording, the chair states the issue being considered in the motion.

The members then debate the motion. After debate is complete, the chair puts the motion to a vote, and later the chair announces the results of the vote.

Voting on the Motion

Three basic methods are often used for voting:

- **Voice vote.** The chair says, "All in favor of the motion, say 'aye' and "those opposed, say 'no'."
- **Show of hands.** Members vote by raising their hand. For example, the chair might say, "All in favor, raise your right hand," and so on.
- **Rising vote.** Members stand to vote yes or no.

A roll call vote can also be used. This places each member's vote on record. If a secret vote is necessary, a ballot can be used.

A majority vote usually decides if a motion is approved. *Majority* usually means more than one-half of the voting members. Some organizations require a two-thirds vote to pass a motion.

Amending the Motion

There are three ways to amend a motion. You can also amend the amendment.

1. You can move to amend by inserting words or paragraphs. For example, "I move to amend by inserting the phrase 'with the total cost no more than $500.'"
2. You can move to amend by striking (not deleting) words or paragraphs. For example, "I move to amend by striking out the words 'including hats.'"
3. You can move to amend by striking out and inserting words or paragraphs. You can even replace the entire motion. For example, "I move to amend by striking out 'buy new uniforms, including hats' and inserting the words 'rent a van for the national competition.'"

Four Types of Motions

- **Main.** A proposed action presented for consideration and decision.
- **Subsidiary.** These help resolve the main motion. Examples are an amendment and a referral.
- **Privileged.** Motions concerned with the rights of members. They take precedence over all other motions. Examples are to adjourn or to recess.
- **Incidental motions.** A type needed due to business being conducted at a meeting. One example is a point of order, which draws attention to a rule that is not being followed properly.

Copyright © Glencoe/McGraw-Hill

Handout

The Technology Student Association (TSA) is an organization for technology education students. It provides a national program of activities and competition that helps students become leaders and problem solvers. Members are supported by teachers, parents, and business leaders. TSA encourages the participation of local chapters in the national organization.

National Competitive Event

This annual event includes over fifty competitions for various skills and interests, ranging from structural engineering and computer-aided drafting to extemporaneous presentation and graphic design. Competitions of interest to drafting students include

- **Technical Sketching and Application.** Participants demonstrate their ability to analyze and interpret engineering graphic specifications, to use drafting terminology accurately, and to complete a Technical Sketching and Application test correctly. Finalists then demonstrate their ability to solve an on-site engineering graphic problem, using standard drafting techniques.

- **Computer-Aided Drafting and Design (CADD).** Participants develop technical drawings on site, using computer-aided drafting tools. There are three distinct categories to this event: engineering, architectural, and 3D modeling.

- **Architectural Model.** Participants develop a house design to be considered for use by an affiliate of Habitat for Humanity International.

Additional Programs

The following additional programs provide opportunities for the demonstration of leadership and service, as well as ideas for chapter activities.

- **Conferences.** These include the annual national conference and a leadership conference.

- **National Service Project.** Local chapters volunteer their efforts in support of a national cause, such as the American Red Cross (ARC). The ARC provides relief to disaster victims and helps people prevent, prepare for, and respond to emergencies.

- **National TSA Day.** To celebrate National Science and Technology Week, TSA provides suggestions for special chapter activities.

Contact Information
www.tsaweb.org

SkillsUSA
VICA

SkillsUSA-VICA serves high school and college students and professional members who are enrolled in training programs in technical, skilled, and service occupations, including health occupations.

Purpose

The purpose of SkillsUSA-VICA is to prepare high-performance workers. Its motto is "preparing leadership in the world of work." SkillsUSA-VICA

- Provides experiences for students in leadership, teamwork, citizenship, and character development
- Builds and reinforces self-confidence, work attitudes, and communication skills
- Emphasizes total quality at work, high ethical standards, superior work skills, life-long education, and pride in the dignity of work
- Promotes understanding of the free enterprise system and involvement in community service activities

History

SkillsUSA-VICA began in 1965 as the Vocational Industrial Clubs of America, Inc. (VICA). It was founded by students and teachers who were serious about their professions and saw the need for more training in the areas of leadership to complement their chosen vocation.

In 1967, VICA began holding competitive events (Skill Olympics). In 1981 VICA hosted the International Youth Skill Olympics, where VICA members joined 274 international contestants from 14 countries in 33 contests.

In 1994, the name Skill Olympics was changed to SkillsUSA Championships. In 1999 VICA officially changed its name to SkillsUSA-VICA.

Programs

SkillsUSA-VICA hosts local, state, and national competitions in which students demonstrate occupational and leadership skills. SkillsUSA-VICA programs also help to establish industry standards for job skill training in the classroom.

Two additional programs help prepare students for the world of work. The *Total Quality Curriculum* emphasizes basic employability skills. The *Professional Development Program* guides students through 84 employability skills lessons. These include goal setting, career planning, and community service.

SkillsUSA-VICA Chapters

Each chapter has an advisor, elects officers, and follows SkillsUSA-VICA regulations. Each chapter also develops an operating plan, which is called the program of work. This includes the activities in which members participate. SkillsUSA-VICA recommends an emphasis on activities such as leadership development, social development, community service, fund raising, career development, skills competition, and public relations.

The national organization makes publications available to guide chapters in how to set up the program of work, as well as other issues concerning how to operate. For example, each chapter needs to know the types of memberships available, what officers to elect and what each officer's duties are, requirements for a club to conduct business legally, and the procedures to complete a business meeting. This includes how to use *parliamentary procedures*, which are the generally accepted rules for conducting business meetings.

Contact Information
www.skillsusa.org

Handout
SkillsUSA-VICA (Continued)

SkillsUSA-VICA Pledge

Upon my honor, I pledge

- To prepare myself by diligent study and ardent practice to become a worker whose services will be recognized as honorable by my employer and fellow workers
- To base my expectations of reward upon the solid foundation of service
- To honor and respect my vocation in such a way as to bring repute to myself
- And further, to spare no effort in upholding the ideals of SkillsUSA-VICA

SkillsUSA-VICA Creed

- **I believe in the dignity of work.**
  I hold that society has advanced to its present culture through the use of the worker's hands and mind. I will maintain a feeling of humbleness for the knowledge and skills that I receive from professionals, and I will conduct myself with dignity in the work I do.

- **I believe in the American way of life.**
  I know our culture is the result of freedom of action and opportunities won by the founders of our American republic, and I will uphold their ideals.

- **I believe in education.**
  I will endeavor to make the best use of knowledge, skills, and experience that I will learn in order that I may be a better worker in my chosen occupation and a better citizen in my community. To this end, I will continue my learning now and in the future.

- **I believe in fair play.**
  I will, through honesty and fair play, respect the rights of others. I will always conduct myself in the manner of the best professionals in my occupation and treat those with whom I work as I would like to be treated.

- **I believe satisfaction is achieved by good work.**
  I feel that compensation and personal satisfaction received for my work and services will be in proportion to my creative and productive ability.

- **I believe in high moral and spiritual standards.**
  I will endeavor to conduct myself in such a manner as to set an example for others by living a wholesome life and by fulfilling my responsibilities as a citizen of my community.

SkillsUSA-VICA Colors

The colors red, white, blue, and gold represent the national SkillsUSA-VICA organization.

- Red and white represent the individual states and chapters.
- Blue represents the common union of the states and of the chapters.
- Gold represents the individual, the most important element of the organization.

Handout

SKILLS USA CHAMPIONSHIPS

SkillsUSA-VICA provides local, state, and national competitions in which students demonstrate their occupational and leadership skills. These contests recognize the achievements of career and technical education students and encourage them to strive for excellence and pride in their chosen fields.

The national SkillsUSA Championships event is held annually. Thousands of students compete in over 70 occupational and leadership skill areas. Working against the clock and each other, the participants prove their expertise in skills such as technical drafting, electronics, and precision machining. There are also competitions in leadership skills, such as extemporaneous speaking and conducting meetings by parliamentary procedure.

The contests are planned by technical committees made up of representatives of labor and management. The national technical committee is assisted by local representatives of education and industry. Safety practices and procedures are judged and graded.

Students benefit from the competition no matter how they place in the finals. They learn more about their skills and often make future job contacts.

Technical Drafting

This contest requires contestants to demonstrate their ability to work productively in today's modern drafting department. CAD skills, as well as traditional board drafting skills, are used to create drawings and data files that solve industry-developed engineering design problems. Contestants are evaluated on the basis of productivity, time, and quality.

Automated Manufacturing Technology

This contest evaluates teams of three in preparation for employment in the manufacturing technology fields of computer-aided drafting and design, computer-aided manufacturing, and computer numerical controlled machining. The competition runs much like industry. The CAD operator constructs the part geometry, the CAM operator generates the toolpaths, and the CNC operator does the setup and machines the part.

Architectural Drafting

Contestants are given a problem consisting of background information, building requirements, and a description of the drawings required. The contestants develop an appropriate plan (within four to five hours of time) from design notes and instructions. Judging criteria include the correct solution to the problem, line work, layout, and accuracy.

3-D Visualization and Animation

The 3D Visualization and Animation competition is designed to evaluate each contestant's preparation for employment and to recognize outstanding students for excellence and professionalism in the field of 3D visualization and animation. The competition is a team event (team of two). This contest evaluates students' proficiency in creating a 3D image and animation within specified time, hardware, and design constraints. The contest includes 3D visualization and animation skills, plus a written test.

Copyright © Glencoe/McGraw-Hill

Handout
SkillsUSA CHAMPIONSHIPS (Continued)

TQM Contest

The Total Quality Management (TQM) contest provides student teams an opportunity to demonstrate their skills in the continuous improvement process. Teams use and document a process that will effect positive change within their school.

Teams in this contest first present the Total Quality Management project from their school. Teams are then presented with a real problem by a sponsoring business. Real data is collected and analyzed, with possible solutions presented by the team.

Job Interview

The contest is divided into three phases: completion of employment application, preliminary interview with receptionist, and an in-depth interview. The contestant's understanding of employment procedures he or she will face in applying for positions in the occupational areas in which he or she is training is evaluated.

Job Skill Demonstration A

The ability of the contestant to demonstrate and explain an entry-level skill used in the occupational area for which he or she is training is evaluated. Contestants in Job Skill A must demonstrate a career objective in an area that is included in one of the contest areas of the SkillsUSA Championships.

Job Skill Demonstration B

The ability of the contestant to demonstrate and explain an entry-level skill used in the occupational area for which he or she is training is evaluated. Contestants in Job Skill B may demonstrate any career objective.

World Skills Competition

The World Skills Competition (WSC) is a biennial contest in skilled occupations. Through competition at the WSC, students learn what it means to be a competitor in the global market. The United States' top career and technical students test their skills against teams from other countries in an international showcase of occupational training. More than 600 young people from over 30 participating countries compete in over 40 skills and techniques competitions.

Contact Information
www.skillsusa.org

Handout

AMERICAN DESIGN DRAFTING ASSOCIATION

The American Design Drafting Association (ADDA) serves drafting professionals such as designers, drafters, architects, and technical illustrators in all disciplines, including manufacturing, construction, and engineering. It is open to designers, drafters, instructors, students, and managers in industry, government, and education. Institutional memberships are available to academic institutions offering design/drafting programs.

- **National Drafting Design Contest.** Each year the ADDA sponsors a national contest for students.

- **The Drafter Certification Program.** Drafting professionals can demonstrate their knowledge and skills in drafting concepts, standards, and practices by passing the certification exam. Many employers prefer hiring certified drafters.

- **School Certification.** The ADDA provides recognition to schools whose curriculum meets its established standards. Some states require ADDA certification, including Alabama, Georgia, New Jersey, and Tennessee.

- **Newsletter.** *Design Drafting News* keeps ADDA members informed about the rapidly transitioning work environment, computer-aided design and drafting technologies, and quality management.

- **Annual Conference.** The conference features technical sessions to educate and inform participants.

Autodesk User Group International (AUGI) is a nonprofit, professional association whose members use Autodesk products, including AutoCAD design and drafting software. AUGI provides training, technical support, networking opportunities, and other resources. Membership is free. Here are some of the resources offered at the AUGI Web site:

- **Guilds.** Information about guilds is provided. Guilds are groups of dedicated AUGI members who help each other solve day-to-day problems. Support is handled by e-mail. All questions and answers are sent to all members. Questions range from basic questions and tough technical questions to discussions about CAD management.

- **Articles.** Technical and industry-specific articles deal with various aspects of Autodesk software.

- **Dialog.** Discussions among users, Autodesk, and other industry experts provide practical information.

- **Publications.** Current and past issues of the *AUGI WorldView* and *PaperSpace* newsletters are provided.

- **Training.** A schedule of online training offered by AUGI is provided.

- **Demonstrations.** Demonstration software and links to other software downloads are available.

- **Gallery.** Animations and visual images are supplied by members.

Contact Information
www.adda.org

Contact Information
www.augi.com

Copyright © Glencoe/McGraw-Hill

AutoCAD Testing and Certification

You can become certified for AutoCAD software through the Autodesk Certification Program. The Autodesk Certification Program is a joint effort of Autodesk, Inc., the makers of AutoCAD software, and Brainbench.com, a company that specializes in online skills certifications. A certification test for AutoCAD 2000 was released in 2001, with additional tests under development.

The exams in this program are designed to test an individual's knowledge of AutoCAD and the ability to apply AutoCAD skills. You will need a comprehensive knowledge of AutoCAD to pass the tests.

Why Take the Certification Exam?

The certification exam helps different people in different ways. For students hoping to land a job or begin a career in which AutoCAD knowledge is required, certification provides proof that the individual has the skills required for the job. Even if a specific job does not currently require AutoCAD skills, certification often gives individuals an advantage over other job applicants.

For engineering and design employees in nearly every industrial field, certification provides the employer with a reliable measure of employee skill level. Certification also gives employers an objective method of evaluation for annual employee reviews. Some employers use the comprehensive report received at the end of the exam as a basis for both raises and promotions. Certification gives employees and job applicants an edge when an employer asks them why they deserve a promotion or why the company should hire them.

Taking the exam also helps you discover your own strengths and weaknesses. By finding your weaker areas, you can work on them to round out your skills, making yourself a more valuable asset to a company or organization.

Contact Information
www.brainbench.com/links/autodesk.html
www.autodesk.com/training

National Skill Standards for CADD

The Foundation for Industrial Modernization (FIM), in conjunction with business, education, and labor organizations, has developed national skill standards for computer-aided drafting and design (CADD). FIM serves as the research and education affiliate of the National Coalition for Advanced Manufacturing (NACFAM). The following table correlates the skill standards to *Applying AutoCAD 2002*.

1. Fundamental Drafting Skills	*Fundamentals* Text	*Advanced* Text
1.1 Drafting Skills Related Academic		
1.1.1 Use drawing media and related drafting materials (*e.g.*, papers, vellum, mylar; plotter pens, toner cartridges)	Chs. 21, 23, 24	
1.1.2 Use basic measurement systems (*e.g.*, fractions, decimals, and metric measurements)	Chs. 18, 21, 25, 27	
1.1.3 Add correct annotation to drawing	Chs. 18, 19, 34	
1.1.4 Identify line styles and weights	Ch. 22	
1.1.5 Prepare title blocks and other drafting formats	Chs. 21, 22, 23, 24	Ch. 16
1.1.6 Apply metric and/or dual dimensioning drawing standards	Chs. 26, 27	
1.1.7 Identify and use appropriate standard symbols	Chs. 20, 28, 32	
1.1.8 Reproduction of originals using different methods (*e.g.*, photocopy, plot, blueprint)	Ch. 23	Chs. 20, 24
1.1.9 Create freehand technical sketches	Part 1 Project	Advanced Projects
1.2 Orthographic Projections		
1.2.1 Identify, create, and place appropriate orthographic views	Ch. 11, Additional Problems	Chs. 14, 16, Additional Problems, Advanced Projects
1.2.2 Identify, create, and place appropriate auxiliary views	Additional Problems	Ch. 16, Additional Problems, Advanced Projects
1.2.3 Identify, create, and place appropriate section views	Additional Problems	Chs. 15, 16, Additional Problems, Advanced Projects

Copyright © Glencoe/McGraw-Hill

1.3	**Pictorial Drawings**		
1.3.1	Identify and create axonometric drawings (*e.g.*, isometric, dimetric, trimetric)		Ch. 1
1.3.2	Identify and create oblique drawings (*e.g.*, cabinet, cavalier)		Additional Problems
1.3.3	Identify perspective drawings (*e.g.*, 1-point, 2-point, 3-point)		Chs. 3, 4
1.4	**Dimensioning**		
1.4.1	Apply dimensioning rules correctly (*e.g.*, avoid redundant dimensioning, avoid dimensioning to hidden lines)	Chs. 25, 26, 27	Ch. 1
1.4.2	Use correct dimension line terminators (*e.g.*, arrowheads, ticks, slashes)	Chs. 25, 26	
1.4.3	Dimension objects (*e.g.*, lines, arcs, angles, circular)	Ch. 25, Additional Problems	Additional Problems, Advanced Projects
1.4.4	Dimension complex shapes (*e.g.*, spheres, cylinders, tapers, pyramids)	Chs. 25, 26, 27	Chs. 1, 15, 16
1.4.5	Dimension features from a center line	Ch. 26, Additional Problems	Additional Problems, Advanced Projects
1.4.6	Dimension a theoretical point of intersection		
1.4.7	Use appropriate dual dimensioning standards	Ch. 27	
1.4.8	Use size and location dimension practices	Chs. 25, 26, 27	
1.4.9	Use various dimensioning styles (*e.g.*, Cartesian, polar, ordinate, datum)	Chs. 25, 27, 28	
1.4.10	Place tolerance dimensioning and Geometric Dimensioning and Tolerancing (GD&T) on drawings when appropriate	Ch. 28, Part 5 Project	Advanced Projects
2. Fundamental Computer Skills			
2.1	**Hardware**		
2.1.1	Demonstrate proper care of equipment	Handout on p. 20 of this Instructor Resource Guide	Handout on p. 20 of this Instructor Resource Guide
2.1.2	Operate and adjust input devices (*e.g.*, mouse, keyboard, digitizer)	Chs. 1, 2, 3	

2.1.3	Operate and adjust output devices (*e.g.,* printers, plotters)	Ch. 23	
2.1.4	Correct handling and operation of storage media	Handout on p. 35 of this IRG	Handout on p. 35 of this IRG
2.1.5	Start and shut down workstation	Handout on p. 35 of this IRG	Handout on p. 35 of this IRG
2.1.6	Adjust monitor controls for maximum comfort and usability	Handout on p. 19 of this IRG	Chs. 26, 28, 29, 30, Handout on p. 19 of this IRG
2.1.7	Recognize availability of information services (*e.g.,* electronic mail, bulletin boards)	Handouts on pp. 38 and 41 of this IRG	Chs. 29, 30, Handouts on pp. 38 and 41 of this IRG
2.2	**Physical and Safety Needs**		
2.2.1	Demonstrate an understanding of ergonomic considerations (*e.g.,* keyboard position, screen position, lighting)	Part 5 Project, Handout on p. 19 of this IRG	Advanced Projects, Handout on p. 19 of this IRG
2.2.2	Demonstrate personal safety (*e.g.,* electrical and mechanical hazards)	Handouts on pp. 21-28 of this IRG	Handouts on pp. 21-28 of this IRG
2.3	**Operating Systems**		
2.3.1	Start and exit a software program as required	Ch. 1, Handout on p. 35 of this IRG	Ch. 1, Handout on p. 35 of this IRG
2.3.2	Demonstrate proper file management techniques (*e.g.,* copying, deleting)	Chs. 8, 19, Appendix B, Handout on p. 35 of this IRG	Chs. 29, 30, Appendix B, Handout on p. 35 of this IRG
2.3.3	Format floppy disk	Handout on p. 35 of this IRG	Handout on p. 35 of this IRG
2.3.4	Identify, create, and use directory structure and change directory paths	Chs. 2, 8, Handout on p. 35 of this IRG	Handout on p. 35 of this IRG
2.3.5	Demonstrate proper file maintenance and backup procedures	Ch. 8, Handout on p. 35 of this IRG	Handout on p. 35 of this IRG
2.3.6	Translate, import, and export data files between formats (*e.g.,* IGES< DXF)	Ch. 18	Chs. 17, 24, 29
2.3.7	Use on-line help	Ch. 7	
2.3.8	Save drawings to storage devices	Chs. 3, 4, Handout on p. 35 of this IRG	Handout on p. 35 of this IRG

Copyright © Glencoe/McGraw-Hill

3. Basic CAD Skills

The following skills must be performed in 2D and/or 3D as appropriate.

3.1	Create		
3.1.1	Create new drawing	Chs. 3, 4, 5, 6	
3.1.2	Perform drawing setup	Chs. 21, 22, 23, 24, 25	
3.1.3	Construct geometric figures (*e.g.,* lines, splines, circles, and arcs)	Chs. 3, 4, 5, 14, 15	
3.1.4	Create text using appropriate style and size to annotate drawings	Chs. 8, 19	
3.1.5	Use and control accuracy enhancement tools (*e.g.,* entity positioning methods such as snap and XYZ)	Chs. 6, 9, 10, 11, 12	Ch. 3
3.1.6	Identify, create, store, and use appropriate symbols/libraries	Chs. 31, 32, 33, 34, Additional Problems	Additional Problems
3.1.7	Create wireframe/solid models		Chs. 5, 17
3.1.8	Create objects using primitives		Chs. 7, 11
3.1.9	Create 2D geometry from 3D models		Chs. 15, 16
3.1.10	Revolve a profile to create a 3D object		Chs. 5, 12
3.1.11	Create 3D wireframe models from 2D geometry		Chs. 2, 10, 12
3.2	**Edit**		
3.2.1	Utilize geometry editing commands (*e.g.,* trimming, extending, scaling)	Chs. 15, 16, 17, 29	Ch. 14
3.2.2	Utilize non-geometric editing commands (*e.g.,* text, drawing format)	Chs. 18, 19, 21, 27, 29	
3.3	**Manipulate**		
3.3.1	Control coordinates and display scale	Chs. 6, 10, 17, 21	Ch. 4
3.3.2	Control entity properties (*e.g.,* color, linetype)	Chs. 21, 22, 32	
3.3.3	Use viewing commands (*e.g.,* dynamic rotation, zooming, panning)	Chs. 12, 13, 18	Ch. 2
3.3.4	Use display commands (*e.g.,* hidden line removal, shading)	Chs. 22, 24	Chs. 2, 3, 8, 9

3.3.5	Use standard parts and/or symbol libraries	Chs. 32, 33, 34	
3.3.6	Plot drawings on media using correct layout and scale	Chs. 21, 23	Advanced Projects
3.3.7	Use layering techniques	Chs. 22-27	Chs. 5, 6
3.3.8	Use grouping techniques	Ch. 30	
3.3.9	Minimize file size	Ch. 31	Chs. 24, 25, 26, 27, 29
3.4	**Analyze**		
	Use query commands to interrogate database (*e.g.,* entity characteristics, distance, area, status)		Ch. 28
3.5	**Dimensioning**		
	Use associative dimensioning correctly	Chs. 26, 27	
4. Advanced CAD Skills			
4.1	**Create**		
4.1.1	Create wireframe and/or solid models		Chs. 5, 17
4.1.2	Create non-analytic surfaces using appropriate modeling (*e.g.,* non-analytic: NURBS, B-spline, Gordon, Bezier, Coons)	Ch. 14	Ch. 6
4.1.3	Create analytic surfaces using appropriate modeling with planes and analytic curves (*e.g.,* conic, cylinder, revolution, ruled)	Ch. 4	Chs. 5-17
4.1.4	Create offset surfaces	Chs. 11, 15, Additional Problems	Additional Problems, Advanced Projects
4.1.5	Find intersection of two surfaces		Ch. 14
4.1.6	Create joined surfaces		Chs. 6, 10, 13
4.1.7	Create a fillet or blend between two surfaces		Ch. 14, Additional Problems, Advanced Projects
4.1.8	Create feature based geometry (*e.g.,* holes, slots, rounds)	Chs. 4, 15, 25, 26, 27, 28	Chs. 1, 10, 13
4.1.9	Create cut sections		Chs. 15, 16
4.1.10	Construct and label exploded assembly drawings	Ch. 27	Advanced Projects
4.1.11	Perform Boolean operations (*e.g.,* union, subtraction, intersection)		Additional Problems, Advanced Projects

Copyright © Glencoe/McGraw-Hill

4.2	**Edit**		
4.2.1	Trim surface	Ch. 17	
4.2.2	Manipulate surface normals		Chs. 3, 4, 5
4.2.3	Extend surface	Chs. 11, 17	
4.2.4	Edit control points (*e.g.,* surfaces, Bezier)		Ch. 6
4.2.5	Modify geometry via Boolean operations		Chs. 13, 14
4.2.6	Edit primitives (*e.g.,* moving, copying, resizing)		Ch. 7
4.3	**Manipulate**		
4.3.1	Perform axis view clipping		Chs. 2, 26
4.3.2	Extract wireframe data from surface/solid geometry		Chs. 8, 9, 10, 12
4.3.3	Shade/render object (*e.g.,* reflectivity, opacity)		Chs. 8, 9, 10, 11
4.4	**Analyze**		
4.4.1	Extract geometric data		Chs. 10, 17
4.4.2	Extract attribute data	Ch. 34	
4.4.3	Identify gaps in non-intersecting surfaces		Ch. 14
4.4.4	Obtain surface properties (*e.g.,* area, perimeter, bounded volume)	Ch. 29	
4.4.5	Obtain mass properties data (*e.g.,* moments of inertia, centroids)		Chs. 10, 17
4.5	**CADD Productivity and Work Habits**		
4.5.1	Perform customization to improve productivity (*e.g.,* customize menus, function keys, script files, macros)		Chs. 18, 19, 20, 29
4.5.2	Manipulate associated non-graphical data	Ch. 19	
4.5.3	Use template and library files to establish drawing standard presets	Chs. 21, 23, 32	Ch. 5
4.5.4	Develop geometry using parametric programs		Ch. 23

Copyright © Glencoe/McGraw-Hill

Career Handouts

These handouts are designed to be photocopied and distributed to students. They provide information for choosing a career, finding employment, succeeding on the job, and starting a business.

HO-1	Workplace Skills Checklist	65
HO-2	Setting Career Goals	67
HO-3	Sources of Career Information	68
HO-4	Occupational Outlook Handbook	69
HO-5	The O*NET	70
HO-6	Is This Career for Me?	71
HO-7	Selecting a School or Training Program	72
HO-8	Creating a Portfolio	73
HO-9	Finding a Job Opening	74
HO-10	Writing a Résumé	75
HO-11	A Sample Résumé	76
HO-12	Writing a Letter of Application	77
HO-13	Filling Out an Application Form	78
HO-14	Application for Employment	79
HO-15	The Job Interview	81
HO-16	Keeping the Job	83
HO-17	Teamwork	84
HO-18	Stress Management/Substance Abuse	87
HO-19	What You Can Expect from an Employer	88
HO-20	A Safe Workplace	89
HO-21	Labor Laws	91
HO-22	Making a Job Change	92
HO-23	Entrepreneurship	93

Copyright © Glencoe/McGraw-Hill

Workplace Skills Checklist

The following checklists will help you identify skills you have and those you should acquire to be successful in the workplace.

Seeking and Applying for Employment Opportunities

- ❏ Locate employment opportunities.
- ❏ Identify job requirements.
- ❏ Identify conditions for employment.
- ❏ Evaluate job opportunities.
- ❏ Prepare résumé.
- ❏ Write job application letter.
- ❏ Complete job application form.
- ❏ Prepare for job interview.
- ❏ Send follow-up letter.

Accepting Employment

- ❏ Complete state and federal tax forms.
- ❏ Complete withholding allowance certificate form (W-4).

Communicating on the Job

- ❏ Communicate clearly with others, including those from other cultures.
- ❏ Ask questions about a task.
- ❏ Read and follow written directions.
- ❏ Prepare written communication, including work orders.
- ❏ Interpret the use of body language.
- ❏ Use good telephone etiquette.
- ❏ Listen to directions and follow them.
- ❏ Use proper e-mail etiquette.
- ❏ Write in legible handwriting.

Demonstrating Teamwork

- ❏ Match team members' skills to group activities.
- ❏ Encourage shared participation.
- ❏ Provide support to team members.
- ❏ Build and maintain trust.
- ❏ Complete team tasks.
- ❏ Evaluate outcomes.

Maintaining Professionalism

- ❏ Treat people with respect.
- ❏ Exhibit positive behavior.
- ❏ Use job-related terminology.
- ❏ Participate in meetings in a positive and constructive manner.

Maintaining a Safe and Healthy Environment

- ❏ Follow appropriate environmental practices and policies.
- ❏ Comply with safety rules and procedures.
- ❏ Use and maintain proper tools and equipment.
- ❏ Maintain work area.
- ❏ Act appropriately during emergencies.

Demonstrating Work Ethics and Behavior

- ❏ Follow rules, regulations, and policies.
- ❏ Carry out job responsibilities.
- ❏ Maintain regular attendance.
- ❏ Assume responsibility for your own decisions and actions.
- ❏ Demonstrate willingness to learn.
- ❏ Practice time management.
- ❏ Practice cost effectiveness.
- ❏ Display initiative.
- ❏ Show pride in your work.

Using Resources

- ❏ Avoid waste and breakage.
- ❏ Plan your time to accomplish tasks.
- ❏ Make a list of supplies and materials needed to do a task.
- ❏ Follow a budget for projects.

Copyright © Glencoe/McGraw-Hill

Using Information

- ☐ Read instructions and understand how it affects your job.
- ☐ Check supplies or products received against an invoice or packing slip.
- ☐ Find and evaluate information.
- ☐ Use a telephone directory.

Using Systems

- ☐ Understand how your department fits within the whole operation.
- ☐ Find out what work is done in each department and how it fits into the operation.

Using Interpersonal Skills

- ☐ Teach others how to perform a task.
- ☐ Assist customers with problems.
- ☐ Work well with people from different ethnic or cultural backgrounds.
- ☐ Respond to praise or criticism.
- ☐ Provide constructive criticism.
- ☐ Properly channel and control emotional reactions.
- ☐ Help resolve conflicts.
- ☐ Report any sexual harassment.

Demonstrating Technology Literacy

- ☐ Operate and maintain tools and equipment safely and properly.
- ☐ Enter data into a computer system.
- ☐ Use word-processing software.
- ☐ Use the computer to locate information via the Internet.

Interpreting the Economics of Work

- ☐ Describe responsibilities of employees.
- ☐ Describe responsibilities of employers.

Solving Problems

- ☐ Identify the problem.
- ☐ Use reasoning skills.
- ☐ Assess employer and employee responsibility in solving a problem.
- ☐ Identify solutions to the problem.
- ☐ Select and implement solutions.
- ☐ Evaluate options.
- ☐ Estimate results of chosen options.

Adapting/Coping with Change

- ☐ Exhibit ability to handle stress.
- ☐ Recognize need to change or quit a job.
- ☐ Write a letter of resignation.

Personal Employability Traits

One way to make yourself more employable is to develop your personal employability traits. This table will help you become more aware of your strengths and weaknesses. Place a check in the column that best describes you. Be honest!

Employability Rating

Trait	Excellent	Good	Fair	Poor	Very Poor
Communication					
Honesty					
Dependability					
Constructive Criticism					
Teamwork					
Responsibility					
Initiative					
Positive Attitude					
Willingness to Learn					
Personal Care					

Setting Career Goals

Your goals are the targets you are aiming for. They give direction to your life, providing a focus for your energy, resources, and time. Setting goals is one of the most important things you can do when planning your career. Here are some guidelines for setting goals:

- ✓ **Make your goals specific.**
  Reaching a goal is easier if you understand exactly what you want to achieve.

- ✓ **Set both short-term and long-term goals.**
  Short-term goals can act as steppingstones toward reaching your long-term goals. Achieving each short-term goal takes you another step closer to achieving your long-term goals. The feeling of accomplishment makes you feel good about yourself. You build your self-esteem.

- ✓ **Be sure your goals are realistic.**
  Aim high, but be practical. Don't set goals that are unattainable (such as becoming a professional athlete without ever training for it). Neither should you underestimate what you are capable of achieving. Recognize that achieving a goal takes determination, work, and self-discipline.

- ✓ **Make sure your goals are in keeping with your values.**
  If one of the things you value is spending time with family, for example, then you will want to schedule time for it in your plans each week.

- ✓ **Make the goals your own.**
  Your goals should not be simply what someone else wants you to achieve. If you are working toward a goal you want for you, you will be more likely to put forth your best efforts. Achieving your goals will be more satisfying.

- ✓ **Set a due-date for achieving your goals.**
  Setting a deadline will help you plan time to do all the things necessary to reach the goal. Just make sure that the deadline is realistic.

- ✓ **Prioritize your goals.**
  Knowing which goals are most important to you will help you use your energy, resources, and time more efficiently and effectively.

Copyright © Glencoe/McGraw-Hill

Sources of Career Information

Gathering information about careers will help you make wise career decisions. Some things you will want to find out include:

- Types of careers available
- Tasks involved in particular jobs
- Education, special skills, and/or training required
- Salary and benefits

Career information is available from a number of sources. You can obtain it by:

- Visiting your school and local libraries. Reference materials they provide include:
    — Books, particularly the *Occupational Outlook Handbook* (OOH)
    — Computer software, particularly the Occupational Information Network (O*NET)
    — Magazines
    — Pamphlets
    — Filmstrips
    — Videotapes
    — Audiotapes
- Using the Internet. For example, the *Occupational Outlook Handbook* is on the Internet at: http://stats.bls.gov/ocohome.htm
- Speaking with people employed in your field of interest
- Speaking with teachers or counselors at your school
- Contacting professional associations
- Getting a part-time job in the field
- Doing volunteer work in the field

Occupational Outlook Handbook

When researching careers, an important source of information is the *Occupational Outlook Handbook* (OOH). This valuable resource is produced by the U.S. Department of Labor. The *Occupational Outlook Handbook* divides occupations into ten basic categories. There is also a section that describes the various types of training done in the armed forces that could prepare you for a career.

The OOH provides information about approximately 250 kinds of jobs. For each job, it provides the following types of information:

- **Significant points**
  Description of key occupational characteristics, such as training/skills needed or employment outlook.

- **Nature of the work**
  Detailed description of what the work involves, such as duties and responsibilities of workers.

- **Working conditions**
  Description of the work environment, including things such as safety considerations.

- **Training, other qualifications, and advancement**
  Description of the educational background and special skills that may be required and the potential for advancement.

- **Job outlook**
  Prediction of the relative number of job openings in the future.

- **Earnings**
  Information about the typical pay and benefits workers can expect.

- **Related occupations**
  Listing of occupations that require similar aptitudes and education or training.

- **Sources of additional information**
  Information about agencies and organizations that can provide you with useful occupational information.

The *Occupational Outlook Handbook* is available in book form, but it can also be found on the Internet. Its URL is:

http://stats.bls.gov/ocohome.htm

Keywords, indexes, and clusters (groups of similar types of jobs) can be used to find descriptions of particular jobs.

The O*NET

When researching careers, an important source of information is the Occupational Information Network (O*NET). This network is provided by the U.S. Department of Labor. You can find it on the Internet by keying O*NET into your search engine.

The O*NET offers up-to-date, comprehensive information about jobs and the skills and abilities needed. Over 1100 occupations are described, including the latest information about employment levels, outlook for the future, and wages. The most important facts about each occupation are provided in "Occupational Profiles."

Information is organized into six domains, or categories, as shown below. Keywords are used to locate specific occupations.

Category	Information Provided
Worker requirements	• Basic skills • Cross-functional skills • General knowledge • Education
Worker characteristics	• Abilities • Interests • Work styles
Experience requirements	• Training • Experience • Licensing
Occupation characteristics	• Labor market information • Occupational outlook • Wages
Occupation requirements	• Generalized work activities • Work context • Organizational context
Occupation specifics	• Occupational knowledge • Occupational skills • Tasks • Machines, tools, and equipment

Is This Career for Me?

Find information about a career that interests you. Think about how well it suits your interests, aptitudes, attitudes, and values. Then ask yourself the following questions and note your answers on the lines provided.

1. Will I find the duties and responsibilities of the career interesting? Why or why not?

   _____
   _____

2. Do I have the skills needed for this career? _____

   If not, can I develop the skills? _____
   _____

3. Does this career match well with my values? Why or why not?

   _____

4. Am I willing to continue my education as long as necessary to be qualified to work in this career? Can I afford to do so?

   _____
   _____

5. Will I feel comfortable in this work environment? Why or why not?

   _____

6. Will the working hours fit well with my desired lifestyle? _____
   If not, what changes will be needed?

   _____
   _____

7. Will this career pay well enough for me to live the way I want to live? _____
   Will there be opportunities for advancement?

   _____

8. What is the career outlook? _____ Will jobs be available when I am ready to enter the work world? _____ What is the long-term outlook?

   _____

9. Will this be a good career for me? _____ Why or why not?

   _____
   _____

Repeat for other careers in which you become interested.

Copyright © Glencoe/McGraw-Hill

Selecting a School or Training Program

The type of education you will need depends on the career you are interested in. To meet the various needs, many programs are available. Find out now which schools or training programs can best prepare you for the career of your choice.

On-the-Job Training

On-the-job training is training that a person receives after he or she has been hired. A company may hire a person without experience if that person has an appropriate educational background and is willing to work hard. The employer may offer special training sessions to provide the knowledge and skills required.

Apprenticeship

One way to begin a career in a skilled craft is through apprentice training. An apprentice learns from a skilled worker while on the job. The apprentice also receives classroom instruction. In exchange for this training, the apprentice may be asked to sign an agreement to work and learn for a period of two to five years. Carpentry and tool-and-die making are examples of careers in which apprenticeships are available.

Technical Institutes and Community Colleges

Some careers may require only two years of schooling beyond high school. In two-year programs, only career-related courses are offered, and they usually include hands-on training. A technical institute offers training for specific careers. For example, you could take courses at a technical institute that would prepare you to be a drafter.

A community college is a two-year school established to serve the needs of the local community. Many community colleges offer programs in technical fields, such as computer-aided drafting and design.

Four-Year Colleges

Many technical and professional careers, such as those in engineering and architecture, require at least a bachelor's degree. Obtaining a bachelor's degree involves four years of courses in both general education and a major area of study. A person's major area of study is related to the career for which he or she is preparing.

The Armed Forces

The armed forces (Army, Navy, Air Force, Marines, and Coast Guard) need highly trained persons to defend our country. The armed forces provide a wide range of technical training opportunities to new recruits. In fact, the armed forces probably have the largest technical training program in the country.

Creating a Portfolio

A portfolio is a collection of materials that you put together to tell employers about yourself and show them what you can do. A portfolio is useful in many careers but particularly in those that involve making drawings. Portfolios may consist of drawings on paper, in electronic computer files, or both. Paper materials are usually placed in a large, portable carrying case (much like a large, closable envelope) so they can be protected and yet taken to interviews.

Just as people are different, portfolios are different. Your portfolio should be a reflection of you. Most portfolios contain some or all of the following:

- A list or description of your career goals
- Your résumé
- Samples of your work
- Letters of recommendation
- Any certificates or diplomas you have earned
- A list of academic achievements
- Written recognition of achievements or personal contributions, such as for community service
- References

Your portfolio should be well organized. Include tabs so that the person reading it can go from section to section easily.

The samples of your work (school and/or employment) will be your largest section. This, too, should be organized and tabbed for easy access. If you have several divisions—drawings, written articles, special projects, and the like—write brief summaries of what each division contains to include with those materials. You may wish to tell why the items you chose for your portfolio have special significance to you or how they show special skills or strengths in your work.

Use your portfolio to present to potential employers the best you have to offer.

Copyright © Glencoe/McGraw-Hill

Finding a Job Opening

There are many different ways to locate jobs that you are interested in. Listed below are methods that are often used:

- **Personal contacts.** Network with friends, relatives, and acquaintances to find out about possible job opportunities.

- **Direct contact with employers.** Companies often have unadvertised openings available. By getting in direct contact with possible employers, you are telling them that you have initiative, a desirable quality in an employee.

- **The Internet.** Many Web sites are available to help employees find suitable employers, and vice versa.

- **Professional associations.** These groups often maintain areas on their Web sites where companies can post job openings and members can post résumés.

- **Job counseling.** Many schools offer job counseling as well as provide a list of job openings.

- **Help-wanted ads.** Watch the ads in newspapers, professional journals, and other sources. If you want to move out of the area, read newspapers from areas of interest. Many newspapers have Web sites that include job listings.

- **Employment agencies.** Both public and private employment agencies help people find jobs. These agencies have listings of available jobs, many of which may not be advertised in a newspaper. The agencies ask information about job seekers' skills, interests, and other qualifications. Then they try to match the job seekers with the jobs on their lists.

Abbreviations Used in Job Ads

Abbreviation	Meaning
appl.	applicants, applications
avail.	available
appt.	appointment
asst.	assistant
co.	company
comm.	commission
const.	construction
dept.	department
eves.	evenings
exp.	experience
ft	fulltime
hr.	hour
immed.	immediate
incl.	included
M-F	Monday through Friday
max.	maximum
mfg.	manufacturing
mgr.	manager
min.	minimum
mo.	month
nec.	necessary
pt	part-time
pos.	position
pref.	prefer, preferred
ref.	references
req.	require, required
sal.	salary
tel.	telephone
w/	with
wk.	week, work
yr., yrs.	year, years

Copyright © Glencoe/McGraw-Hill

HO-10

Writing a Résumé

Employers need information about you in order to determine whether you are qualified to work for them. You can provide this information by preparing a résumé. A résumé is basically a "sales-catalog" description of yourself. It tells who you are and what you have done. Your instructor will give you an example of a résumé. A résumé should include the following:

- Your full name
- Your address
- Your telephone number (including your area code)
- A brief description of your career objectives and the type of job you want
- Your qualifications

Include anything that indicates you would be good for the job, such as special training, aptitudes, and other relevant information.

- Your work experience. For each job you list, identify the position you held. Describe your job responsibilities and duties. Include the dates you started and left (if applicable) that position.
- Special interests or activities related to the job you want

There are many different types of résumés. Information is available in reference materials (including computer software) to help you write one.

Copyright © Glencoe/McGraw-Hill

A Sample Résumé

Lynn Matthews

SCHOOL ADDRESS	**HOME ADDRESS**
2431 W. Mitchell Avenue, Apt. 3	1219 O'Brien Street
Normal, IL 61761	Bloomington, IL 61702
(309) 555-5674	(309) 555-4277

CAREER OBJECTIVE To develop specialized drafting skills and gain practical experience in the field of manufacturing or electronics.

EDUCATION Heartland Community College, Bloomington, IL. Current student, majoring in computer-aided drafting and design. September, 2000, to present.

Bloomington High School, Bloomington, IL. Graduated June, 2000. Grade Point Average, 3.2 on 4.0 scale.

HONORS AND ACTIVITIES Student council 1998-1999.
Technology club; vice-president, 1998-1999.
Science fair, 1998, 1999, 2000.
Marching band, 1998, 1999, 2000.

WORK EXPERIENCE Schroeder Electronics, 311 Smith St., Bloomington, IL 61702; (309) 555-1000.
Sales associate and repair person, part-time, July 1999 to present.
Responsible for stocking shelves, waiting on customers, making some routine repairs on electronic equipment.

Farmland Food Stores, 1400 Oak Ave., Normal, IL 61703; (309) 555-2194.
Stock assistant and customer service clerk, part-time, May 1998 to July 1999.
Duties included stocking shelves, bagging groceries, and assisting with carry-outs.

HOBBIES Jazz band, remote-controlled airplanes, golf.

REFERENCES On request.

Writing a Letter of Application

When you apply for a job by mail or e-mail, the cover letter that accompanies your résumé (or application) is often as important as the résumé itself. The cover letter introduces you and sparks interest in reading your résumé. It's like an advertisement for *you*.

A cover letter should be no longer than one page. It should be friendly but businesslike. Also, it must be clearly written and contain no errors in spelling or grammar.

Following is a general outline of how a successful cover letter can be organized:

First Paragraph: Introduction

The introductory paragraph establishes the tone of the letter and captures the potential employer's attention. It should include the following:

- Your source of information about the position
- The position in which you are interested
- A statement expressing your desire to be considered for the position

These elements do not have to be in any particular order or covered in a single sentence. The more important—and more difficult—goal is to establish a tone of modest self-confidence.

Middle Paragraphs: Experience and Education

The next paragraphs describe your experience and/or educational background. Start with the area that is stronger. For example, if your work experience is more pertinent to the position you want, discuss it first.

Do not restate the contents of your résumé. Choose two or three points that will most interest the employer and develop those points. Then refer the employer to your résumé for more details.

Final Paragraph: Conclusion

The goal of the concluding paragraph is to get an interview. If you have not already referred to your résumé, do so here. Explain why you want to work for the company. Conclude with a polite, confident request for an interview at the employer's convenience.

Filling Out an Application Form

In order to choose the best person for the job, employers need information about the applicants. When you apply for a job, most employers ask you to fill out a job application form. On the form you are asked to provide information in a certain order.

Your instructor will give you an example of an application form. Here are a few tips for filling it out. Following these tips will increase your chances of getting the job you desire.

- **Read and follow the instructions.** For example, does the application form tell you to print, write, or type the information? Does it call for your last name to come first?

- **Answer all the questions asked on the application.** If a question or section does not apply to you, put NA, for "not applicable." This will show the employer that you did not overlook the question and that you have nothing to hide.

- **Fill out the form neatly.** You might want to photocopy the form and fill it in for a "trial run." Then you can follow it to fill in the final form more neatly.

- **Be as specific as you can possibly be in all areas.**

- **Reread your application before you hand it in.** Check for spelling errors. Be sure all phone numbers and addresses are correct.

HO-14

Application for Employment

Equal Opportunity Employer

Personal Information

Please print clearly.

Full Name: _____
                  First   Middle   Last

Present Address: _____
                  Number and Street   City   State   Zip

Social Security Number: _____ Phone Number: _____

Are you 18 years or older? ❏ Yes   ❏ No   If not, what is your date of birth? _____

Have you ever been convicted of a felony or misdemeanor? ❏ Yes   ❏ No
If yes, please explain in the space below. *(A conviction record will not necessarily preclude employment.)*

_____

_____

Are you aware of any reason that you cannot perform essential functions of the job with or without reasonable accommodations? ❏ Yes   ❏ No
If yes, please specify: _____

Availability

Total hours available per week: _____ Position or shift applied for: _____
Please indicate the time you are available for work each day.

DAY	Su	M	Tu	W	Th	F	Sa
FROM							
TO							

Education

SCHOOL TYPE	SCHOOL NAME/ADDRESS	CITY/STATE
Senior High School		
College/University		
Graduate School		
Trade/Business/Night Courses		
Other		

(Continued on back)

Copyright © Glencoe/McGraw-Hill

HO-14
(Continued)

Work History

List most recent jobs first.

Company: _____ From: _____ _____
Address: _____   Month   Year
                                                          To: _____ _____
City/State: _____ Phone: _____   Month   Year
Position: _____ Salary: _____ Supervisor: _____
List of duties: _____
Reason for leaving: _____

Company: _____ From: _____ _____
Address: _____   Month   Year
                                                          To: _____ _____
City/State: _____ Phone: _____   Month   Year
Position: _____ Salary: _____ Supervisor: _____
List of duties: _____
Reason for leaving: _____

Company: _____ From: _____ _____
Address: _____   Month   Year
                                                          To: _____ _____
City/State: _____ Phone: _____   Month   Year
Position: _____ Salary: _____ Supervisor: _____
List of duties: _____
Reason for leaving: _____

To comply with the Federal Employment Eligibility Verification Law, you must bring **EITHER** one document from List A **OR** one document from List B and one document from List C below:

List A
- United States Passport
- Certificate of United States Citizenship
- Certificate of Naturalization
- Unexpired Foreign Passport with Employment Authorization
- Alien Registration Card with Photograph

List B
- Unexpired State-issued Drivers License
- Unexpired State-issued Identification Card
- School Identification Card with Photograph
- Voter's Registration Card
- United States Military Card

List C
- Social Security Number Card (Original)
- An Original or Certified Copy of a Birth Certificate Issued by a State or County, Bearing an Official Seal

Fair Credit Reporting Act and Employment At Will Disclosure

I understand that I am applying for employment "at will." If I am hired, employment can be terminated at any time for any reason with or without prior notice or cause. Any oral statements or promises to the contrary are not binding upon the employer.

I confirm that all my answers to the questions in this employment application are accurate and complete. I also understand that the submission of any false information in connection with this employment application may be cause for immediate termination at any time thereafter should I be employed by this company. I understand that my employment will be contingent upon the accuracy, completeness, and acceptability of the information furnished by me. I acknowledge that this company has permission to verify all statements in this employment application.

I certify that the information on this application is accurate and complete.

Signature _____   Date _____

The Job Interview

For some people, an interview is the most difficult part of getting a job. There are many books that give tips on how to handle an interview. Following are some of the most useful tips.

Preparing for the Interview

You'll feel more confident and make a better impression if you prepare for the interview ahead of time.

- Do some research about the company. What business is it in? Is it local or national? Ask at the library for information or look for a Web site.

- Check to be sure your portfolio is well organized and up to date.

- Prepare a list of dates, names and addresses, and other relevant information that you may be asked for. Even if you've already sent in a résumé, take an extra copy with you. Do the same with references.

- Think about why you want the job and what you have to offer this particular employer that makes you a good choice.

- Plan what you will wear in advance so it will be clean, pressed, and ready for you on the big day. It's usually a good idea to wear the kind of clothing you would wear on the job. If you're not sure how employees are expected to dress, call the human resources office and ask. However, avoid anything too casual, like jeans, even if others wear them.

- Make transportation plans ahead of time. If the route is unfamiliar, make a practice trip. It will also help you know how much time to allow for the journey. Plan to arrive five to seven minutes early, so you're sure to be on time.

Putting Your Best Foot Forward

During the interview, you must be a salesperson for yourself. Give it your best!

- Greet the interviewer with a friendly smile and a firm handshake. Pronounce his or her name correctly. (If you're not sure, ask politely.)

- Dust off your very best manners and use them! Don't be rude or disrespectful.

- Don't put anything on the interviewer's desk unless it is asked for.

- Wait until you are asked to be seated.

- Maintain good posture; don't slouch in your chair. Lean slightly forward as you listen or speak.

- Sit quietly and keep your hands and feet still. Don't fidget. Don't chew gum or smoke.

- Speak clearly and use good grammar. Avoid profanity, slang, and mumbled replies.

- Be enthusiastic about the job and the company. If possible, work some of the information you've learned about the company into the conversation.

- Be prepared to answer questions about school or previous employment. Answer questions honestly and completely. Don't try to fake it.

- Don't say anything negative about a former employer. If you were treated badly or if working conditions seemed intolerable, just say something like, "I would rather work under different conditions."

- Don't complain or talk about your personal problems.

- When the interview is over, shake hands and express your appreciation for the chance to interview for the job. Leave as soon as it is polite to do so; don't keep the interviewer from other duties.

- Follow up the next day with a thank-you note.

Copyright © Glencoe/McGraw-Hill

HO-15
(Continued)

Practicing for an Interview

Following are some questions commonly asked during job interviews. It's not likely that you'll be asked all of these questions in a single interview. However, think about how you would answer them for a job you would like to have. Then set up a mock interview. Have a friend or classmate interview you, using the questions from this list. If possible, do this in front of others. Have them look for ways in which you can improve your performance.

- Tell me why you want to work for this company.
- How did you find out about this job opening?
- Why do you think you are suited for this job?
- Tell me about your education or training. What are your qualifications for this job.
- Which courses in school did you like best? Which did you do best in? Which did you like least?
- What are your strengths and weaknesses?
- What jobs have you had in the past? Why did you leave them?
- Are you looking for a permanent job?
- Would you rather work alone or with others?
- What kinds of work do you like to do?
- What type of work do you want to be doing five years from now?
- What do you like to do in your spare time?
- What salary do you expect to receive?
- How would you respond if you were asked to work overtime?
- What questions would you like to ask me?

Keeping the Job

After you are hired for a job, do your job as well as you can. Look for opportunities to learn. Even if this job is just a steppingstone along your career path, think of it as an opportunity to prove yourself and to grow.

Your Health

Good health, good grooming, and a good appearance are important to job success. If you don't feel your best, you can't do your best. Follow these tips to maintain good health:

- Eat a balanced diet including lots of fruits, vegetables, and whole grains. Avoid "junk" foods.
- Get plenty of exercise and fresh air.
- Bathe regularly and practice good dental hygiene.

Your Appearance

A survey of employers showed that poor appearance during the job interview was the main reason many young people were not hired. Having a good appearance means being neat and clean and dressed properly for the job. Jeans and a T-shirt may be acceptable for some jobs but not for others. It pays to find out in advance what type of dress is expected. Clothes need not be expensive as long as they are clean and neat.

Personal Skills and Qualities

The following personal skills and qualities are also major keys to job success. Start now to develop and improve these skills.

- **Cooperation.** Cooperation can mean many things. It can mean pitching in and helping out when others need it. It can mean respecting others' ideas or doing your fair share of the work.
- **Self-control.** Being able to control your emotions is valuable when working with others. You cannot be effective in a job situation if you lose your temper often or get easily frustrated. Try to remain calm and think the situation through.
- **Accepting criticism.** For some people criticism is hard to accept. They think every mistake they make is proof they are failures. This is not true. Everyone makes mistakes. Making mistakes is one way we learn. Criticism is the only way an employer has of letting you know how the job must be done. Some employers may not be as tactful or fair as they should be. Try to take the criticism good-naturedly. Then use it to help you become a better worker.
- **Initiative.** Initiative means seeing what needs to be done and doing it. If you have downtime, ask if you can help in ways not limited to your own assigned tasks.
- **Tact.** Tact is saying and doing things in a way that will not offend others. Successful people know how to point out mistakes and problems without making others angry or hurting their feelings. Consider how you would like to be treated and then treat others that way.
- **Being a good listener.** Listening is just as important as speaking. Here are a few guidelines for being a good listener:
  - Give the speaker your full attention. Don't be thinking about what you will be saying in response.
  - Don't interrupt.
  - Where appropriate, take notes of what is being said. Don't trust your memory.
  - Ask questions when appropriate. Part of listening is to get more information.

Teamwork

Teamwork is a skill you will use in all aspects of your personal life as well as your work life. Working in a team can be fun and challenging. Like any skill, it takes practice.

Companies today rely very heavily on teams of workers to get jobs done. For example, there are design teams, surgical teams, sales teams, and investment teams. In each case, the team members must work together to reach a common goal.

Each person on a team has something unique to contribute. For example, to design and build a house, there must be people who know kitchen design, electrical work, plumbing, landscaping, and so on. Each contributes to making a house functional and attractive. Besides providing a variety of skills, a team that really works well together can accomplish more than each of the members could on their own.

Your Own Experience

Working as a team member is probably already a part of your everyday life. Think of the ways you work with other people on a daily basis. For example, at home you are responsible for certain jobs. At school you might be a member of a committee that has to make decisions about a school activity. You might also be on a sports team. Those teamwork experiences have probably helped you prepare for the workplace.

Team Roles

Typically, a team has three or more members. Initially, the role you play on the team might fall into one of the categories shown in the table below. As the project continues, you may find that you play more than one role. For example, all team members are contributors and encouragers.

Team Roles

Role	Primary Functions
Leader	Keep members focused on the team's goal. Make sure everyone understands his or her job. Watch the time line. Set a good example.
Contributor	Help others stay on task. Support other team members. Ask questions. Complete tasks. Evaluate outcomes.
Encourager	Listen. Share ideas. Encourage everyone to participate.

Teambuilding

As part of a team, you need to focus on two things: completing the task and building and maintaining positive relationships with team members. Building a team that works well doesn't happen automatically.

Teams commonly go through four stages before they function at a high level. The first two stages are usually awkward and produce conflict that team members must resolve. They must get to know each other and see how they fit within the team. Some teams may exist for too short a time to reach the highest level of functioning. However, working through the stages will help your team reach the highest level possible.

Stages of Teambuilding

Stage	Tasks	Relationships
1	Set specific goals. Decide what to do and when. Decide who will do what. Decide who will lead or if leadership will be shared.	Get to know each other. See where members fit within the team. Share enthusiasm. Encourage shared participation.
2	Stay focused on goals. Make decisions. Develop processes for carrying out team plans.	Recognize and accept differences. Develop ways to behave that are acceptable to all. Resolve basic conflicts and build trust. Form a team image.
3	May use individual ways of getting own parts done. Follow planned process for making all the parts work together.	Make team goals as important as individual goals. Cooperate and get along well; learn to function better. Support, encourage, and guide each other.
4	Achieve high levels of productivity. Work independently. Take initiative. Focus primarily on getting the work done.	Know how to work together. Achieve a high level of trust. All members contribute equally. Resolve conflicts and make decisions quickly. Reach a level of win-win cooperation.

Leadership Styles

In a team, you will often play a leadership role. There are several leadership styles that you may use as you complete a task. Each one is useful for varying stages of completing a project.

Democratic Leaders

The democratic leader makes decisions by consulting team members and allowing them to decide how the task will be tackled and who will perform each part. He or she makes sure that team members know their jobs and stay focused on the goal. This type of leader values group discussion and input from the team. He or she draws from a pool of team members' strong points in order to obtain the best performance. He or she motivates the team by empowering the members to direct themselves and guides them with a loose rein.

Copyright © Glencoe/McGraw-Hill

Coaching Leaders

As a project progresses and teams function at a higher level, the team leader can become more like a coach. This type of leader helps team members stay focused on the goal, watches the schedule, and provides guidance as needed.

Autocratic Leaders

The autocratic leader dominates team members and delegates tasks. Generally, an authoritarian style is not a good approach to getting the best performance from a team at the beginning of a project. It may become necessary towards the end as time runs out. Also, some situations may call for urgent action, and in these cases an autocratic style of leadership may be best. In some situations, team members may actually prefer an autocratic style.

Laissez-Faire Leaders

The laissez-faire leader uses little control, leaving team members to sort out their roles and tackle their work. This approach can leave the team floundering with little direction or motivation. However, it can be very effective when a team of highly skilled, highly motivated people have reached a high level of functioning. Once a leader has established that a team is confident, capable, and motivated, it is often best to step back and let the team get on with the task. Interfering can generate resentment and detract from effectiveness. By handing over ownership, a leader can empower a team to achieve its goals.

Team Problem Solving

In the workplace you may be assigned to a team. The team is given a problem to solve. Here are some basic steps for solving problems.

1. **State the problem clearly.** Stating the problem clearly in a sentence or two often helps clarify the problem. Figuring out what the problem really is may bring you halfway to a solution.
2. **Collect information.** Gather as much information as possible that could be used to solve the problem.
3. **Develop possible solutions.** There is usually more than one possible solution to a problem. Brainstorm. The more solutions the team can think of, the more options available to you.
4. **Select the best solution.** Weigh the advantages and disadvantages of each possible solution. Consider all the factors, and base the decision on the team's goals and the particular situation the problem presents.
5. **Implement the solution.** Try out the best choice. Now you will see if the solution is workable.
6. **Evaluate the solution.** This is not the end of the problem-solving process. A good solution should be evaluated carefully to make sure it is appropriate to the problem at hand. If it doesn't work, try another.

Real-World Problems

Think of a recent problem you had to solve.

- How do you think the concepts of teamwork could have helped you?
- Would a team have made your job easier or harder? Why?
- Would it have changed your work habits or your approach to the job?

Stress Management

In school, on the job, and in your personal life certain situations can cause stress. A little stress can actually be good. It helps us be more alert and stay focused. Too much stress, though, is harmful to physical, mental, and emotional health. You cannot avoid stress, but you can control your response to it. You can take steps to protect your health. Here are some tips for dealing positively with stress.

- **Talk to someone.** Talk with a trusted relative or friend about your problems. Often, someone who is not directly involved can see solutions that you cannot.
- **Keep a journal.** Writing about events, thoughts, and feelings can help you identify the real causes of stress and provide an emotional outlet.
- **Set priorities.** What is the most important thing that must be done today? What can be done later? Recognize that time is limited.
- **Relax.** Learn and practice relaxation techniques, such as deep breathing or meditation. Give your mind and body a chance to recover.
- **Exercise regularly.** Exercise can relieve stress by releasing tension and making your muscles more flexible.
- **Eat healthy.** Your body needs good nutrition to deal with the effects of stress.
- **Limit your intake of caffeine.** Too much caffeine will make you nervous and can interfere with sleep.
- **Avoid alcohol and other drugs.** Using drugs to cope with stress will only multiply your problems.
- **Help others.** It will make you feel good, and it will take your mind off your own troubles.
- **Set goals.** Set realistic goals that reflect your values. Identify what is truly important to you. Understand and accept your limits.
- **Laugh.** Laughter can relieve tension and give you a new perspective.

Substance Abuse: Why Risk It?

Using drugs can harm you emotionally, physically, and socially. Effects of drug use include:

- **Lack of concentration.** Whether you are in school or at a job, you need to be focused on the tasks at hand. Lack of concentration can make you fall behind. If you work with machinery, chemicals, or other dangerous equipment or products, a lack of focus can cause accidents.
- **Alienation.** Those who are on drugs often alienate their friends and family. As your attitude and personality change from the effects of substance abuse, you may hurt those close to you. You may experience irritation, anxiety, depression, or other negative feelings.
- **Addiction.** Whether it's alcohol, tobacco, or another substance, addiction can lead people to take desperate measures to get what they want. Withdrawal symptoms can occur when you try to quit. Some of these symptoms include nausea, headaches, vomiting, chills, and cramps. In the most severe cases, death may occur.
- **Financial difficulty.** Taking drugs is an expensive habit, and drug abusers may spend money on them instead of paying the rent or other bills. Drug use on the job can lead to being fired. Lack of attention or difficulty in getting along with others can also cause a drug abuser to lose a job.
- **Increase in crime.** Users may steal to get the money for drugs, sell drugs to make money, or even kill someone to get what they need. Drug-related crimes destroy families, neighborhoods, and lives.

What You Can Expect from an Employer

Just as your employer expects certain things from you, you also have the right to expect certain things from your employer. Your employer should:

- **Explain to you how the company operates.**
  You should understand what your duties are and what your working relationships with others are. You should be informed of company policies and rules.

- **Provide safe working conditions.**
  Your employer should keep the workplace in good repair and be responsive to employee safety concerns. You should have all the safety equipment that you need to perform your job. If hazards exist that are not directly connected with your job (such as toxic or flammable materials on the premises), you should be made aware of it and know what to do in an emergency. The "Right to Know" law requires employers to inform their workers about hazardous materials in the workplace.

- **Provide all necessary training for you to perform the job for which you've been hired.**
  The type and amount of training will vary depending on the job. You should not be expected to work with or near toxic materials or work in dangerous situations or with dangerous equipment without full and proper training for doing so safely.

- **Pay you for your work.**
  You should receive the pay you were promised when you were hired. In addition, employers must provide services such as withholding taxes from your check and paying into Social Security and the Worker's Compensation Program (in case of injury on the job).

- **Provide feedback for how well you are doing your job.**
  Your employer will evaluate your work, usually in written form. You may also have the opportunity to discuss your strengths and weaknesses. Use this evaluation as the chance to identify how you need to improve your work and then do so. In addition, your employer will need to correct you when you make mistakes. Again, accept this as a learning experience and try to improve.

- **Be honest with you.**
  Your employer does not have to tell you all the company's secrets, but he or she should be honest about such things as your chances for promotion.

- **Treat you without discrimination.**
  Federal law prohibits employers from discriminating on the basis of race, color, religion, sex, national origin, disability, or age (over 40).

A Safe Workplace

Accidents and personal injuries in the workplace always have a negative effect. Accidents that result in material damage can mean the loss of business and personal income. The loss of an employee to injury can mean a loss in productivity while a new employee is trained.

Health and Safety Awareness

In any industry, employees must be aware of safety, health, and environmental hazards. They must be aware of the effect these hazards can have on property, as well as on themselves. Employees should be able to detect, identify, and access information and procedures related to safety and health issues.

Occupational Safety and Health Administration (OSHA)

The Occupational Safety and Health Act promotes safe and healthful working conditions. Employers are responsible for making sure that the workplace and the job are free from recognized hazards that could cause death or serious harm. Employees are responsible for complying with health and safety standards, rules, regulations, and orders issued under the Act that apply to their actions and conduct on the job.

The Act assigns to the Occupational Safety and Health Administration (OSHA) two principal functions: setting standards and conducting workplace inspections to ensure that employers are complying with the standards and providing a safe and healthful workplace. Citations must be posted. Employees or their representatives have the right to file a complaint with the nearest OSHA office requesting an inspection if they believe unsafe or unhealthful conditions exist in their workplace. OSHA will withhold, on request, the name of the person complaining.

OSHA also encourages efforts by labor and management to reduce workplace hazards voluntarily and to develop and improve safety and health programs in all workplaces and industries. Safety in the workplace is a benefit to all concerned.

American Red Cross (ARC)

The American Red Cross promotes health and safety in the workplace through safety training programs. Red Cross training ranges from first aid to making automated external defibrillators (AEDs) available to save victims of sudden cardiac arrest. An AED is a device that can restart a heart. Many businesses now include AEDs in their emergency equipment.

General Work Environment

Always review your worksite for safety and health problems and follow all posted rules and procedures. Equipment must be properly cared for in order to make sure the worksite is safe. Everyone must be encouraged to report what he or she perceives to be unsafe or unhealthy conditions. Once reported, appropriate action must be taken to resolve the situation.

The general work area must be kept clean and free of unnecessary materials and safety hazards. Exits must be sufficient to permit the prompt escape of occupants in case of fire or other emergency. Work area procedures may include, but may not be limited to

- Providing multiple exits from areas where material is stored or in elevated work and storage areas

- Keeping walk surfaces clean, free of debris, and coated with a non-skid material

- Properly marking all doors by purpose, such as Exit, Not an Exit, Storeroom, or Entry Only

Copyright © Glencoe/McGraw-Hill

HO-20
(Continued)

Fire Protection

Effective fire protection planning should include, but may not be limited to

- Availability of fire extinguishers that are correctly placed, properly charged and tagged, and regularly serviced
- Installation and certification of properly tested and approved fire alarm and sprinkler systems
- An employee alarm system and an emergency evacuation plan
- Employee training on the proper use of fire protection procedures and firefighting equipment

Ergonomics

Programs that focus on ergonomics can prevent musculoskeletal disorders (MSD) that can occur when there is a mismatch between the worker and the task. MSDs include such medical conditions as low back pain, tension neck syndrome, and carpal tunnel syndrome.

In mechanical drawing professions, the areas of body most at risk are the neck, shoulder, wrist, and hands. Risk factors include forced awkward postures and repetitive motion. Eye strain is also a concern. Changes can be made in the way an employee performs the work to prevent problems. Suggestions include, but are not limited to

- Stretching frequently and taking breaks to walk around or stand
- Using neutral postures to perform tasks, such as using straight wrists—not bent up or down
- Adjusting the seat position, chair height, and arm rest of the chair for support of the back, thighs, and arms
- Reducing eye strain with computer monitors by adjusting room lighting and screen brightness to reduce glare
- Looking away from the screen often and refocusing on distant objects

Hazard Prevention and Control

Chemical manufacturers and importers must evaluate the hazards of the chemicals they produce or import. Using that information, they must then prepare labels for containers and more detailed technical bulletins called material safety data sheets (MSDS). These requirements are part of OSHA's Hazard Communication Standard (HCS), which is intended to ensure that employees know the hazards and identities of the chemicals they are exposed to when working.

A plan for preventing and controlling hazards in the workplace should provide a list of actions to address any potential health and safety issues. The plan should include, but may not be limited to

- A list and description of all identified safety and health hazards
- The identification and labeling of harmful or toxic substances
- The availability of Material Safety Data Sheets (MSDS) that address those issues
- A description of protective equipment or devices that must be used or worn
- Rules and procedures that describe how to respond to each safety and health hazard or exposure
- Emergency response and notification telephone numbers
- Signage indicating exits

A safe workplace is also a matter of personal responsibility. Accidents occur when safety and health procedures are taken for granted. Personal injuries occur when processes and procedures are ignored. When in doubt, always ask a knowledgeable person for guidance and advice.

Copyright © Glencoe/McGraw-Hill

Labor Laws

Labor laws (listed below) affect everyone who works in business and industry. To learn more about them, divide into teams of three to five students and research one of the laws and the federal agency responsible for enforcing it. Create a presentation in which you

- Identify major provisions of the law
- Discuss how the provisions of the law protect workers
- Describe the implications for employers
- Describe how the law affects workers in your industry. For example, did passage of the Americans with Disabilities Act require design changes in CAD workstations? If so, what were the changes?

Each team should make its presentation to the entire class.

Fair Labor Standards Act	This act establishes standards for employment issues such as minimum wages, overtime pay, record-keeping, and child labor.
Civil Rights Act	Employers may not discriminate on the basis of race, color, national origin, sex, or religion. This act also protects U.S. citizens working for U.S. companies overseas.
Equal Employment Opportunities Act	This is an extension of the Civil Rights Act. It requires businesses to have affirmative action programs for locating, hiring, training, and promoting women and people of color.
The Age Discrimination in Employment Act	People 40 years of age and older are protected from being discriminated against in any aspect of employment.
Americans with Disabilities Act	The purpose of this act is to prevent employers from refusing to hire or promote disabled persons and to ensure that all employees are treated equally. It requires that public facilities make "reasonable accommodations" for the disabled.
Immigration Reform and Control Act	Only U.S. citizens and people who are authorized to work in the U.S. may be legally hired.
Immigration and Nationality Act	This act applies to people who want to immigrate to the U.S. The law gives preference to immigrants who are educated and have certain job skills.
Federal Employment Compensation Act	This act protects employees who are injured or disabled due to work-related accidents.
Occupational Safety and Health Act (OSHA)	This act promotes safe and healthful working conditions.

Copyright © Glencoe/McGraw-Hill

Making a Job Change

Most people will change jobs a number of times during their work life. Sometimes people change jobs voluntarily. They believe a new job will offer career advancement or an increase in pay. Perhaps they are looking for a completely new career or want to live in a different location. At other times the job change may be involuntary. A spouse may be transferred to a different town, or a company may close or downsize. Whatever the reason, making a job change must be done in a thoughtful way.

Changing Jobs by Necessity

If you lose a job, don't be discouraged. Try to learn positive things from the experience. Consider the following questions:

- Why am I losing my job?
- Do I need to improve my job and/or personal skills in order to get a new job? If so, how?
- Do I want the same type of job, or do I need/want to make a career change?

Occasionally, companies that close or downsize will help laid-off workers enter training programs or find new positions. Whatever the situation, try to stay on good terms with your present employer. A good recommendation from the company will help you secure a new position. Look on the bright side. You may like the next job better, and it may be better for you.

Choosing to Make a Job Change

When considering a job change, ask yourself several questions:

- Will changing jobs help me advance in my career?
- Is the pay better in the new job?
- Will I have more responsibility?
- What is the work environment like in the new company? How does it compare with that in my present company? Will I "fit in"?
- How do benefits offered by the new company compare with those of my present company?
- Will I need more training?

Leaving Your Present Position

Don't quit your present job before you have secured a new one. Then, when the right time comes to give up your position, observe certain courtesies and follow your company's resignation policy. Generally, it will include some or all of these steps:

- Tell your immediate supervisor that you intend to leave.
- Notify the personnel office.
- Write a letter of resignation.
- Give advance notice. Depending on your position (and company policy), the minimum time to allow is two weeks or one pay period. This gives the company time to find a replacement for you.

Entrepreneurship

Starting a Business

Entrepreneurs start, develop, and then run their own businesses. They may start their business venture in one of four ways.

1. **Starting a new business.** Some entrepreneurs start their businesses from scratch. They see a need and start a business to meet that need. There are many challenges to starting a new business. The entrepreneur must find a location, buy or build a facility, purchase equipment, hire employees, and find ways to attract and keep customers. He or she must obtain financing and develop a business plan. A business plan identifies the goods or services that will be offered, tells where the business will be located, outlines the owner's goals, and describes customers and the type of marketing that will be done. The advantage of starting a new business is that the owner can decide just how the business will be developed and run.

2. **Buying an existing business.** People who buy an existing business get the facility, equipment, and even employees. However, it's important to find answers to the following questions before buying. Why is the business being sold? Was it making a profit? Does it have a good reputation? Are the current employees skilled and motivated? What is the condition of the building, the equipment, and the inventory?

3. **Taking over a family business.** Entrepreneurs who take over a family business usually have the advantage of years of experience with the business. However, they must consider the same issues as those who are buying an existing business. In addition, they need to consider possible concerns and conflicts with other family members.

4. **Buying a franchise.** Many businesses are franchises. The entrepreneur who buys a franchise obtains the right to sell a company's products or services within a given area, or territory. The company provides the location, management training, and help with advertising and employee recruiting. In return, the franchise operator pays the company a share of the sales, in addition to the initial purchase price, and agrees to operate the business according to the company's policies.

Characteristics of an Entrepreneur

It takes a special kind of person to be a successful entrepreneur. An entrepreneur is

- **Persistent.** Entrepreneurs work until the job is done, no matter what. They know their livelihood depends on getting the job done and reaching the goals they have set for themselves.

- **Risk-taking.** A good entrepreneur does a lot of research and planning before starting a business. Still, in the final analysis, the entrepreneur must put his or her money and reputation on the line.

- **Responsible.** Successful entrepreneurs take responsibility for their actions. They know they are accountable to their customers, employees, and investors. They keep their promises and treat people honestly and fairly.

- **Creative.** Entrepreneurs recognize opportunities and are always looking for ways to improve their business. They may develop new products or find new markets for their products.

- **Self-confident.** If you don't believe in yourself, how can you expect your investors, customers, and employees to believe in you? Entrepreneurs must be confident in their business actions.

- **Independent.** Entrepreneurs make their own decisions. They run their businesses the way they believe is best. They will ask for advice, but they make the final decisions themselves.

Copyright © Glencoe/McGraw-Hill

HO-23
(Continued)

- **Goal-oriented.** Entrepreneurs set goals and then "go for it." They know what they want and work hard to achieve it. They are driven to reach their goals.

- **Competitive.** Entrepreneurs are always looking for ways to make their product or service better than the competition's. They learn as much as possible about things that might affect their business.

- **Demanding.** Entrepreneurs expect a lot from their employees, but they expect even more from themselves. Entrepreneurs need to focus on all areas of their business. In order to do that, they expect a great deal from everyone involved in the business, including themselves.

Could You Be an Entrepreneur?

Read each statement in the table below. If a statement strongly describes you, rate it a #5. If it doesn't describe you at all, rate it a #1. If the statement partly describes you, rate it as a #2, #3, or #4. Total your answers and divide by 10. The closer your total score is to 5, the more likely it is that you would enjoy being an entrepreneur.

Rate Your Entrepreneurship Qualities

Qualities	1	2	3	4	5
I am creative.					
I take responsibility for my actions.					
I am independent and like to make my own decisions.					
I am persistent and finish a task, despite difficulties.					
I set goals and try to reach them.					
I like to work at my own pace.					
I believe in myself and what I'm doing.					
I like challenges and am willing to take risks.					
I set high standards for myself.					
I am willing to learn in order to make wise decisions.					

Total Score _____ ÷ **10** = _____

APPLYING AutoCAD® 2002 FUNDAMENTALS

This section contains materials related specifically to the *Fundamentals* student textbook. Included are

- A scope and sequence chart, starting on page 96.
- Instructional plans for each of the textbook's 6 parts and 34 chapters. These begin on page 99.
- Transparency masters keyed to the textbook's 6 parts. The transparency masters begin on page 143.
- Chapter tests, starting on page 171.
- Answer keys for the chapter review questions and for the chapter tests, starting on page 207.

Scope and Sequence for *Fundamentals* Text

Themes and Concepts	Part 1	Part 2
Careers, Productivity, and Employability	Careers Using AutoCAD: Pages 20, 49, 86, and 96 Ch. 3: Introduction Ch. 4: Polygons (Hint)	Careers Using AutoCAD: Pages 132 and 174 Ch. 10: Introduction; Tracking Time
Communication	Ch. 2: Challenge Your Thinking #1 Ch. 4: Challenge Your Thinking #1	Ch. 11: Challenge Your Thinking #1
Mathematics	Ch. 4: Entire chapter Ch. 6: Entire chapter Part 1 Project	Ch. 9: Entire chapter Ch. 10: Coordinate Display; Ortho Mode Ch. 11: Alignment Grid; Snap Grid; Orthographic Projection
Design and Problem Solving	All chapters: Using Problem-Solving Skills Part 1 Project	All chapters: Using Problem-Solving Skills Part 2 Project
Standards, Symbols, and Conventions		
Creating, Editing, Manipulating, and Analyzing Drawings	Ch. 1: Shading the Model Ch. 2: Scrollbars Ch. 3: All end-of-chapter problems Ch. 4: Creating Circles; Polygons; all end-of-chapter problems Ch. 5: Entire chapter Ch. 6: Applying Methods of Coordinate Entry; all end-of-chapter problems Ch. 8: Using Problem-Solving Skills Part 1 Project	Ch. 9: Using Preset Object Snaps; Object Snap Tracking; all end-of-chapter problems Ch. 10: Copying and Pasting; Undoing Your Work; all end-of-chapter problems Ch. 11: Entire chapter Ch. 12: Zooming; all end-of-chapter problems Ch. 13: Applying AutoCAD Skills #2 and #5 Part 2 Project
Dimensioning and Tolerancing		
2D, 3D, and Solid Objects	Ch. 3: Reentering Last Command; Applying AutoCAD Skills Ch. 4: Entire chapter Part 1 Project	Ch. 11: Orthographic Projection; all end-of-chapter problems Ch. 13: Applying AutoCAD Skills Part 2 Project
Viewing, Printing, and Plotting	Ch. 1: Previewing Drawing Files; Viewing Details Ch. 7: Browsing and Searching	Chs. 12 and 13: Entire chapter Part 2 Project
Computer Equipment and Software	Ch. 1: Starting AutoCAD; Viewing Details; Exiting AutoCAD Chs. 2, 3, 4, 7, 8: Entire chapter Ch. 5: Using Grips; Using Grips with Commands Part 1 Project	Ch. 9: Entire chapter Ch. 10: AutoCAD Text Window; Command Line Window Ch. 11: Alignment Grid; Snap Grid Ch. 12: Zooming; Controlling View Resolution

Copyright © Glencoe/McGraw-Hill

Scope and Sequence, *Fundamentals* (Continued)

Themes and Concepts	Part 3	Part 4
Careers, Productivity, and Employability	Careers Using AutoCAD: Pages 209, 255, and 280	Careers Using AutoCAD: Pages 312 and 340 Ch. 21: Pages 281 and 287 Ch. 23: Previewing a Plot
Communication	Ch. 15: Challenge Your Thinking #3 Chs. 18 and 19: Entire chapter Ch. 20: Challenge Your Thinking #2	Ch. 22: Challenge Your Thinking #2; Using Problem-Solving Skills Ch. 23: Challenge Your Thinking #2
Mathematics	Ch. 15: Applying AutoCAD Skills Ch. 16: Changing Object Properties; Producing Arrays; all end-of-chapter problems	Ch. 21: Initial Template Setup; Establishing Other Settings; all end-of-chapter problems Ch. 22: All end-of-chapter problems
Design and Problem Solving	All chapters: Using Problem-Solving Skills Ch. 16: Applying AutoCAD Skills #5 Part 3 Project	All chapters: Using Problem-Solving Skills Ch. 22: Applying AutoCAD Skills Part 4 Project
Standards, Symbols, and Conventions	Ch. 14: Drawing a Thick Polyline; Applying AutoCAD Skills	Ch. 22: Assigning Linetypes; Scaling Linetypes
Creating, Editing, Manipulating, and Analyzing Drawings	Chs. 14 through 17, 20: Entire chapter Ch. 18: Applying Text in Drawings Part 3 Project	Ch. 21: All end-of-chapter problems Chs. 22 and 24: Entire chapter Ch. 23: Setting the Drawing Scale Part 4 Project
Dimensioning and Tolerancing		
2D, 3D, and Solid Objects	Ch. 14: Drawing Solid Shapes; Applying AutoCAD Skills Ch. 17: Stretching Objects; Scaling Objects; Rotating Objects; Applying AutoCAD Skills Part 3 Projects	Ch. 24: Objects in Viewports Part 4 Project
Viewing, Printing, and Plotting		Chs. 23 and 24: Entire chapter Part 4 Project
Computer Equipment and Software	Chs. 14, 16, 18, 19: Entire chapter Ch. 15: Creating Chamfers; Breaking Objects; Creating Fillets and Rounds; Offsetting Objects; Setting Multiline Styles; Applying a New Style Ch. 20: Hatching; Editing a Hatch	Chs. 21, 22, 23: Entire chapter Ch. 24: Viewports in Model Space; Viewports in Paper Space

Copyright © Glencoe/McGraw-Hill

Scope and Sequence, *Fundamentals* (Continued)

Themes and Concepts	Part 5	Part 6
Careers, Productivity, and Employability	Careers Using AutoCAD: Pages 376 and 422	Careers Using AutoCAD: Pages 440 and 476 Part 6 Project
Communication	Ch. 25: Challenge Your Thinking #2 Ch. 29: Challenge Your Thinking #2; Using Problem-Solving Skills #2	Chs. 33 and 34: Entire chapter Part 6 Project
Mathematics	Ch. 25: Dimensioning Overall Size; Dimensioning Angles; Ordinate Dimensioning Ch. 28: GD&T Practices Ch. 29: Entire chapter Part 5 Project	Ch. 33: Using Problem-Solving Skills #2
Design and Problem Solving	All chapters: Using Problem-Solving Skills Part 5 Project	All chapters: Using Problem-Solving Skills Ch. 32: Using AutoCAD DesignCenter; Applying AutoCAD Skills #1, #2 Ch. 33: Applying AutoCAD Skills #1-#3
Standards, Symbols, and Conventions	Ch. 28: GD&T Practices	Ch. 32: Entire chapter Part 6 Project
Creating, Editing, Manipulating, and Analyzing Drawings	Ch. 25: Using Other Types of Dimensioning; all end-of-chapter problems Ch. 26: Introduction; Applying a Dimension Style; Editing a Dimension; Working with Associative Dimensions; Applying AutoCAD Skills Ch. 27: Entire chapter Ch. 28: Applying AutoCAD Skills Ch. 29: Editing Objects Mathematically; all end-of-chapter problems Part 5 Project	Chs. 30, 31, 32: Entire chapter Ch. 33: Variable Attributes Part 6 Project
Dimensioning and Tolerancing	Chs. 25 through 28: Entire chapter Part 5 Project	
2D, 3D, and Solid Objects	Ch. 25: Applying AutoCAD Skills Part 5 Project	
Viewing, Printing, and Plotting		Ch. 34: Creating a Report
Computer Equipment and Software	Chs. 25, 27, 29: Entire chapter Ch. 26: Creating a Dimension Style; Changing a Dimension Style; Adding Dimension Styles to Templates Ch. 28: Methods of Tolerancing Part 5 Project	Ch. 30: Creating a Group Chs. 31 through 34: Entire chapter Part 6 Project

Copyright © Glencoe/McGraw-Hill

Instructional Plans for Fundamentals Text

In the instructional plans, you will find teaching suggestions for each of the *Fundamentals* text's 34 chapters and 6 parts.

Part 1 Groundwork **101**
Chapter 1   Tour of AutoCAD 102
Chapter 2   User Interface 103
Chapter 3   Entering Commands 104
Chapter 4   Basic Objects 105
Chapter 5   Object Selection 106
Chapter 6   Entering Coordinates 107
Chapter 7   Securing Help 108
Chapter 8   File Maintenance 109

Part 2 Drawing Aids and Controls **111**
Chapter 9   Object Snap 112
Chapter 10   Helpful Drawing Features 113
Chapter 11   Construction Aids 114
Chapter 12   AutoCAD's Magnifying Glass 115
Chapter 13   Panning and Viewing 116

Part 3 Drawing and Editing **117**
Chapter 14   Solid and Curved Objects 118
Chapter 15   Adding and Altering Objects 119
Chapter 16   Moving and Duplicating Objects 120
Chapter 17   Modifying and Maneuvering 121
Chapter 18   Notes and Specifications 122
Chapter 19   Text Editing and Spell Checking 123
Chapter 20   Hatching and Sketching 124

Part 4 Preparing and Printing a Drawing **125**
Chapter 21   Drawing Setup 126
Chapter 22   Layers and Linetypes 127
Chapter 23   Plotting and Printing 128
Chapter 24   Multiple Viewports 129

Copyright © Glencoe/McGraw-Hill

Part 5 Dimensioning and Tolerancing............ 131
Chapter 25　Basic Dimensioning 132
Chapter 26　Advanced Dimensioning 133
Chapter 27　Fine-Tuning Dimensions 134
Chapter 28　Tolerancing 135
Chapter 29　A Calculating Strategy 136

Part 6 Groups and Details 137
Chapter 30　Groups 138
Chapter 31　Building Blocks 139
Chapter 32　Symbol Libraries 140
Chapter 33　Attributes 141
Chapter 34　Bills of Materials 142

Name		Class Period		Time	
Date	M	Tu	W	Th	F

Instructional Plan - Fundamentals Text — *Part 1* Groundwork

CHAPTERS AND MAIN TOPICS

Chapter 1: Tour of AutoCAD—an exploration of AutoCAD to introduce users to this versatile software. Topics include starting AutoCAD, the Today window, previewing drawing files, opening drawing files, viewing details, shading a model, and exiting AutoCAD.

Chapter 2: User Interface—navigating through AutoCAD by using the pull-down menus, docked and floating toolbars, Command window, status bar, and scrollbars

Chapter 3: Entering Commands—entering commands using the keyboard and toolbars; shortcuts for entering commands; creating, saving, and opening a drawing file

Chapter 4: Basic Objects—holes, cylinders, rounded and polygonal features; circles, arcs, ellipses, and donuts; rectangles and regular polygons

Chapter 5: Object Selection—types of objects in AutoCAD; creating a selection set; adding and removing objects from the selection set; erasing and restoring objects

Chapter 6: Entering Coordinates—the absolute, relative, polar, polar tracking, and direct distance methods of entering coordinates

Chapter 7: Securing Help—browsing and searching for files, using the HELP command

Chapter 8: File Maintenance—copying, renaming, moving, and deleting drawing files; creating and deleting folders; auditing and recovering damaged drawing files

CD-ROM

Use the following from the *Fundamentals Instructor Productivity CD-ROM* to help you present the textbook's topics and assess student progress.

- Pre-/Post-Test for Part 1, found in the **Exam**View test generator.
- PowerPoint presentation for Part 1. The first slide shows the main topics covered in Part 1 of the textbook. The remaining slides elaborate on the more complex topics. You may want to use the PowerPoint presentations to introduce all the topics in this part before students begin working through the chapters. Later, as they begin each chapter, you could show the related slides for that chapter.

TRANSPARENCY MASTERS

Transparency masters for Part 1 begin on page 145 of this guide.

Title	Use with
TM-1A: Groundwork	Introduction to Part 1
TM-1B: Opening Drawings from AutoCAD's Today Window	Chapter 1
TM-1C: Creating Drawings Using AutoCAD's Today Window	Chapter 1
TM-1D: Drawing Ellipses	Chapter 4
TM-1E: Selecting Objects	Chapter 5
TM-1F: Entering Coordinates	Chapter 6

HANDOUTS

Safety (see pages 19-28)

Computer skills (see pages 35-42)

PART 1 PROJECT: Rocker Arm

This project, found at the end of Part 1 in the textbook, provides students the opportunity to apply the AutoCAD commands and procedures they have learned in this part.

- Remind students to read the Hints and Suggestions before they begin drawing.
- Summary Questions/Self-Evaluation may be answered in writing or used as a springboard to class discussion. Students could compare their procedures and exchange ideas about improving efficiency and accuracy.
- Point out the importance of drawing as a means of communication. What information will the drawing of the rocker arm provide to potential customers who see the product brochure?

Copyright © Glencoe/McGraw-Hill

Name		Class Period		Time	
Date	M	Tu	W	Th	F

Instructional Plan - Fundamentals Text — *Chapter 1* Tour of AutoCAD

FOCUS

- **Gaining Attention.** Like many things—jobs, sports, other software programs—AutoCAD has a unique vocabulary. Explain to students that AutoCAD has terminology they need to learn, use, and apply to gain competence.
- **Objectives.** Discuss the objectives listed at the beginning of the textbook chapter.
- **Orientation.** Make sure students understand the Windows directory and subdirectory structure and know how to locate files and maneuver through the file structure.

TEACH

- **Key Terms.** Ask students to write out the meaning of each term in their own words. Discuss the terms with the class until you arrive at a consensus about the meaning of each term.
- **Drawing Skills.** Assign the step-by-step instructions in the chapter. Use projection equipment to display the drawings being created as students complete the steps. Students will be able to start AutoCAD, preview drawing files, open drawing files, view details, explore the Startup graphics screen, shade, and exit AutoCAD.
- **Today Window Options.** Have students explore the options of the Today window. Have students sketch the window and label the various icons and buttons.

ASSESS

- **Review Questions.** Ask students to complete the Review Questions. Discuss their answers in class. Answers are found in the Answer Keys section of this guide.
- **Applying AutoCAD Skills.** Assign the activities at the end of the chapter.
- **Reteaching.** Students often get lost in the folders, subfolders, and levels. Think of the hard drive (usually drive C) as being a filing cabinet. Each folder is a drawer and each drawer has subfolders. Opening the file folders shows more subdirectories or files.
- **Enrichment.** Assign the Challenge Your Thinking questions at the end of the chapter. Assign the Using Problem-Solving Skills activities at the end of the chapter.
- **Communication.** Assign Challenge Your Thinking questions 1 and 2.
- **Test.** Use the Chapter Test printed in this guide, or create a test using the **Exam**View test generator software on the CD-ROM.

CLOSE

- Have students open and preview watch.dwg from the Sample directory. Have them write down the size and date modified information.

Name		Class Period		Time	
Date	M	Tu	W	Th	F

Instructional Plan - Fundamentals Text — *Chapter 2* User Interface

FOCUS

- **Gaining Attention.** Windows-based software has many common graphic interfaces, menu bars, and icons. AutoCAD 2002 shares these traits but also has unique shortcuts and commands to make the software user friendly.
- **Objectives.** Discuss the objectives listed at the beginning of the textbook chapter.
- **Orientation.** If necessary, review the concepts of directories, subdirectories, and file extensions to organize and find files.

TEACH

- **Key Terms.** Ask students to write out the meaning of each term in their own words. Discuss the terms with the class until you arrive at a consensus about the meaning of each term.
- **PowerPoint.** Review the PowerPoint presentation for Part 1, provided on the CD-ROM. Slides 2, 3, and 4 apply to this chapter.
- **Drawing Skills.** Assign the step-by-step instructions in the chapter. Use projection equipment to display the drawings being created as students complete the steps. Students will be able to identify the parts of the graphics screen and the cascading menu bars, create new drawings, open existing drawings, and configure toolbars.
- **Toolbars.** Print out the AutoCAD graphics screen and have students identify and list the icons for a specific toolbar.

ASSESS

- **Review Questions.** Ask students to complete the Review Questions. Discuss their answers in class. Answers are found in the Answer Keys section of this guide.
- **Applying AutoCAD Skills.** Assign the activities at the end of the chapter.
- **Reteaching.** Students may need practice to become familiar with the names of the toolbars and what they contain. Ask students to write a brief description of each toolbar, stating its purpose. Have them list examples of what is found in each toolbar.
- **Enrichment.** Assign the Challenge Your Thinking questions at the end of the chapter. Assign the Using Problem-Solving Skills activities at the end of the chapter.
- **Communication.** Assign Challenge Your Thinking questions 1 and 2.
- **Test.** Use the Chapter Test printed in this guide, or create a test using the **Exam**View test generator on the CD-ROM. The answers can be found in the Answer Keys section of this guide.

CLOSE

- Have students create their own subdirectory inside AutoCAD to store and organize their drawings.

Copyright © Glencoe/McGraw-Hill

Name		Class Period			Time	
Date	M	Tu	W	Th	F	

Instructional Plan - Fundamentals Text
Chapter 3 Entering Commands

FOCUS

- **Gaining Attention.** Patterns are designed into software to make it more user-friendly. AutoCAD has patterns that can be repeated from the keyboard and mouse. These patterns will enable students to gain proficiency and competence using the software.

- **Objectives.** Discuss the objectives listed at the beginning of the textbook chapter.

- **Orientation.** Briefly review with students material they have previously learned that they will need in order to learn this chapter.

TEACH

- **Key Terms.** Ask students to write out the meaning of each term in their own words. Discuss the terms with the class until you arrive at a consensus about the meaning of each term.

- **PowerPoint.** Review the PowerPoint presentation for Part 1, provided on the CD-ROM. Slides 5 through 8 apply to this chapter.

- **Drawing Skills.** Assign the step-by-step instructions in the chapter. Use projection equipment to display the drawings being created as students complete the steps. Students will learn how to enter commands using toolbars, keyboards, cascading menus, and command aliases.

- **Command Aliases.** Have students create a list of the letter aliases for AutoCAD commands (*i.e.,* a = ARC, do = DONUT).

- **Command Line.** After entering a command, students need to develop the habit of reading the command line to find out the next step in completing the command.

- **CTRL key.** Have students experiment with the CTRL + ___ (any other alphabetic key to discover other AutoCAD shortcuts.)

ASSESS

- **Review Questions.** Ask students to complete the Review Questions. Discuss their answers in class. Answers are found in the Answer Keys section of this guide.

- **Applying AutoCAD Skills.** Assign the activities at the end of the chapter.

- **Reteaching.** Students need to develop a personal strategy for using AutoCAD that best fits their style. Encourage students to try various methods of entering commands. Those who keyboard well will probably prefer using the keyboard to enter commands. Those with less keyboarding skill will use cascading menus and icons.

- **Enrichment.** Assign the Challenge Your Thinking questions at the end of the chapter. Assign the Using Problem-Solving Skills activities at the end of the chapter.

- **Communication.** Assign Challenge Your Thinking questions 1 and 2.

- **Test.** Use the Chapter Test printed in this guide, or create a test using the **Exam**View test generator on the CD-ROM. The answers can be found in the Answer Keys section of this guide.

CLOSE

- Have students create a list of CTRL + ___ keys that are shortcuts for commands and object snaps. There are over 20 combinations for command shortcuts.

Name		Class Period		Time	
Date	M	Tu	W	Th	F

Instructional Plan - Fundamentals Text — *Chapter 4* Basic Objects

FOCUS

- **Gaining Attention.** Point out that individual parts and entire pieces of equipment, machinery, and other items that are in our everyday lives are combinations of basic objects. From simple to complex, our world is made up of lines, arcs, circles, rectangles, ellipses, and polygons.

- **Objectives.** Discuss the objectives listed at the beginning of the textbook chapter.

- **Orientation.** Students will need to continue applying skills from earlier chapters, such as using a variety of methods of entering. They will continue to see keyboard and mouse sequences that will assist them in gaining speed and efficiency using AutoCAD. Remind them to read and study the **command** line for directions on completing a command.

TEACH

- **Key Terms.** Ask students to write out the meaning of each term in their own words. Discuss the terms with the class until you arrive at a consensus about the meaning of each term.

- **PowerPoint.** Review the PowerPoint presentation for Part 1, provided on the CD-ROM. Slides 9 and 10 apply to this chapter.

- **Drawing Skills.** Assign the step-by-step instructions in the chapter. Use projection equipment to display the drawings being created as students complete the steps. Students will learn how to draw lines, arcs, rectangles, circles, ellipses, donuts, and polygons.

ASSESS

- **Review Questions.** Ask students to complete the Review Questions. Discuss their answers in class. Answers are found in the Answer Keys section of this guide.

- **Applying AutoCAD Skills.** Assign the activities at the end of the chapter.

- **Reteaching.** Technical math vocabulary will need to be taught and retaught as students begin to construct geometric shapes and figures. Terms such as *concentric*, *tangent*, *radius*, *diameter*, *circumference*, and *perpendicular* may be new to some students.

- **Enrichment.** Assign the Challenge Your Thinking questions at the end of the chapter. Assign the Using Problem-Solving Skills activities at the end of the chapter.

- **Mathematics.** Assign Challenge Your Thinking questions 1 and 2.

- **Test.** Use the Chapter Test printed in this guide, or create a test using the **Exam**View test generator on the CD-ROM. The answers can be found in the Answer Keys section of this guide.

CLOSE

- **Portfolio Cover Design Project.** Assign students to design a portfolio cover using the basic objects discussed in the chapter. Encourage creativity and fluency in design.

Copyright © Glencoe/McGraw-Hill

Name		Class Period		Time	
Date	M	Tu	W	Th	F

Instructional Plan - Fundamentals Text — *Chapter 5* Object Selection

FOCUS

- **Gaining Attention.** Alterations and modifications take place frequently while using AutoCAD. Mistakes have to be corrected and changes have to be made to drawings. Selecting specific objects is a key skill for using AutoCAD efficiently.
- **Objectives.** Discuss the objectives listed at the beginning of the textbook chapter.
- **Orientation.** Briefly review with students material they have previously learned that they will need in order to learn this chapter.

TEACH

- **Key Terms.** Ask students to write out the meaning of each term in their own words. Discuss the terms with the class until you arrive at a consensus about the meaning of each term.
- **PowerPoint.** Review the PowerPoint presentation for Part 1, provided on the CD-ROM. Slides 11 through 13 apply to this chapter.
- **Drawing Skills.** Assign the step-by-step instructions in the chapter. Use projection equipment to display the drawings being created as students complete the steps. Students will use the UNDO and ERASE commands while learning how to select specific objects.
- **Verb/Noun vs. Noun/Verb.** Traditionally AutoCAD users have used the verb/noun option of completing commands where they determine the action and then they select the entity (for example: enter ERASE, then pick the line). The GRIPS command reverses this process.

ASSESS

- **Review Questions.** Ask students to complete the Review Questions. Discuss their answers in class. Answers are found in the Answer Keys section of this guide.
- **Applying AutoCAD Skills.** Assign the activities at the end of the chapter.
- **Reteaching.** Learners will need continual review of the object selection options throughout the course session. These options assist the learner in gaining efficiency and skill in solving design/drafting problems using AutoCAD.
- **Enrichment.** Assign the Challenge Your Thinking questions at the end of the chapter. Assign the Using Problem-Solving Skills activities at the end of the chapter.
- **Communication.** Assign Challenge Your Thinking questions 1 and 2.
- **Test.** Use the Chapter Test printed in this guide, or create a test using the **Exam**View test generator on the CD-ROM. The answers can be found in the Answer Keys section of this guide.

CLOSE

- **Writing.** Give students a problem from Chapter 5 in the textbook related to Object Selection. Have them write and illustrate how they used the Object Selection options to solve the problem.

Name		Class Period		Time	
Date	M	Tu	W	Th	F

Instructional Plan - Fundamentals Text — *Chapter 6* Entering Coordinates

FOCUS

- **Gaining Attention.** AutoCAD provides a practical application of geometry and the Cartesian coordinate system. Knowing how to use the various techniques for line input is a critical AutoCAD skill.

- **Objectives.** Discuss the objectives listed at the beginning of the textbook chapter.

- **Orientation.** Briefly review with students material they have previously learned that they will need in order to learn this chapter.

TEACH

- **Key Terms.** Ask students to write out the meaning of each term in their own words. Discuss the terms with the class until you arrive at a consensus about the meaning of each term.

- **PowerPoint.** Review the PowerPoint presentation for Part 1, provided on the CD-ROM. Slides 14 and 15 apply to this chapter.

- **Drawing Skills.** Assign the step-by-step instructions in the chapter. Use projection equipment to display the drawings being created as students complete the steps. Learners will use the LINE command and the absolute, relative, polar, polar tracking, and direct distance techniques for creating lines.

- **Individuality at the Keyboard.** Encourage students to try all five basic line creation techniques. After they experiment, students will use the technique that best matches their learning style and math preference.

- **New Line Coordinate Techniques.** Students who have used older versions of AutoCAD will need to learn the polar tracking and direct distance techniques.

- **Cartesian Coordinate System.** Make sure students understand this critical concept. It will reinforce the graphing taught in math classes and will help the students develop a high level of competence.

ASSESS

- **Review Questions.** Ask students to complete the Review Questions. Discuss their answers in class. Answers are found in the Answer Keys section of this guide.

- **Applying AutoCAD Skills.** Assign the activities at the end of the chapter.

- **Reteaching.** Learners often have difficulty understanding the polar method for creating lines. Stress that AutoCAD measures counterclockwise from the three o'clock position.

- **Enrichment.** Assign the Challenge Your Thinking questions at the end of the chapter. Assign the Using Problem-Solving Skills activities at the end of the chapter.

- **Communication.** Assign Challenge Your Thinking questions 1 and 2.

- **Additional Problems.** Assign Problem 20, but replace the printed instructions with the following: Determine the coordinate pairs you could enter to create the block. Then use the coordinates to create the drawing.

- **Test.** Use the Chapter Test printed in this guide, or create a test using the **Exam**View test generator on the CD-ROM. The answers can be found in the Answer Keys section of this guide.

CLOSE

- Select a line drawing from the end of Chapter 6 and have the students write the coordinates for each line segment of the drawing using the absolute, relative and polar methods.

Copyright © Glencoe/McGraw-Hill

Name		Class Period		Time	
Date	M	Tu	W	Th	F

Instructional Plan - Fundamentals Text — *Chapter 7* Securing Help

FOCUS

- **Gaining Attention.** People need to become lifelong learners and problem solvers. Frequently you will encounter CAD situations that may not have an evident solution. At other times, you may need to use a command or technique that you have not used in a month or two. The HELP command will serve the learner well in these situations.

- **Objectives.** Discuss the objectives listed at the beginning of the textbook chapter.

- **Orientation.** Briefly review with students material they have previously learned that they will need in order to learn this chapter.

TEACH

- **Key Terms.** Ask students to write out the meaning of each term in their own words. Discuss the terms with the class until you arrive at a consensus about the meaning of each term.

- **PowerPoint.** Review the PowerPoint presentation for Part 1, provided on the CD-ROM. Slides 16 through 20 apply to this chapter.

- **Drawing Skills.** Assign the step-by-step instructions in the chapter. Use projection equipment to display the drawings being created as students complete the steps.

- **Context-Sensitive Help.** Be sure that students practice using context-sensitive help. Learners will often get started in a command and not know how to complete it. Being able to enter the HELP command in the middle of another command is a valuable AutoCAD feature.

ASSESS

- **Review Questions.** Ask students to complete the Review Questions. Discuss their answers in class. Answers are found in the Answer Keys section of this guide.

- **Applying AutoCAD Skills.** Assign the activities at the end of the chapter.

- **Reteaching.** Ask students to describe, in their own words, the difference between *browsing* and *searching*.

- **Enrichment.** Assign the Challenge Your Thinking questions at the end of the chapter. Assign the Using Problem-Solving Skills activities at the end of the chapter.

- **Communication.** Assign Challenge Your Thinking Questions 1 and 2.

- **Test.** Use the Chapter Test printed in this guide, or create a test using the **Exam**View test generator on the CD-ROM. The answers can be found in the Answer Keys section of this guide.

CLOSE

- Have students access help from the menu bar, then AutoCAD Help, Contents, Using AutoCAD Help, Overview, and Navigation tips to learn more about the HELP command. Students should print out results.

Name		Class Period		Time	
Date	M	Tu	W	Th	F

Instructional Plan - Fundamentals Text *Chapter 8* **File Maintenance**

FOCUS

- **Gaining Attention.** Ask students why it is important to keep drawings organized and to understand how to use the various file-related options in AutoCAD. What are the benefits of good organization?
- **Objectives.** Discuss the objectives listed at the beginning of the textbook chapter.
- **Orientation.** Briefly review with students material they have previously learned that they will need in order to learn this chapter.

TEACH

- **Key Terms.** Ask students to write out the meaning of each term in their own words. Discuss the terms with the class until you arrive at a consensus about the meaning of each term.
- **Drawing Skills.** Assign the step-by-step instructions in the chapter. Use projection equipment to display the drawings being created as students complete the steps. Students will learn how to navigate files and folders and how to use the **AUDIT** command.
- **Transfer of Skills.** The file maintenance skills learned in this chapter transfer to many other Windows-based software programs.
- **The Need for Organization.** Students often do not pay attention to the location where a drawing or file is saved. Stress that organizational skills in school and the workplace are very important. Organizing drawings by theme, project, or semester will save students time and free them of frustration associated with locating files.

ASSESS

- **Review Questions.** Ask students to complete the Review Questions. Discuss their answers in class. Answers are found in the Answer Keys section of this guide.
- **Applying AutoCAD Skills.** Assign the activities at the end of the chapter.
- **Reteaching.** Students need to have the concept of folders and subfolders reinforced and demonstrated periodically. Use an LCD projector and computer to demonstrate these concepts and, at the same time, have the students duplicate the process.
- **Enrichment.** Assign the Challenge Your Thinking questions at the end of the chapter. Assign the Using Problem-Solving Skills activities at the end of the chapter.
- **Communication.** Assign Challenge Your Thinking questions 1 and 2.
- **Test.** Use the Chapter Test printed in this guide, or create a test using the **ExamView** test generator on the CD-ROM. The answers can be found in the Answer Keys section of this guide.

CLOSE

- Have students develop a worksheet applying the file maintenance commands and techniques. They should then switch worksheets with fellow students, complete the assignment, and peer-grade the exercise.

Copyright © Glencoe/McGraw-Hill

Name		Class Period		Time	
Date	M	Tu	W	Th	F

Instructional Plan - Fundamentals Text — *Part 2* Drawing Aids and Controls

CHAPTERS AND MAIN TOPICS

Chapter 9: Object Snap—teaches how to use this timesaving, accuracy-enhancing feature. Describes object snap modes, presetting modes to run in the background, selecting modes on an as-needed basis, and tailoring object snaps to meet individual needs.

Chapter 10: Helpful Drawing Features—accessing and applying AutoCAD features that improve productivity. Topics include the coordinate display; the ORTHO, TIME, UNDO, and REDO commands; the AutoCAD Text window; and the command line window.

Chapter 11: Construction Aids—alignment grid, snap grid, construction lines (xlines), rays, orthographic projection

Chapter 12: AutoCAD's Magnifying Glass—applying the ZOOM command, transparent zooming, the relationship between screen regenerations and view resolution, controlling view resolution

Chapter 13: Panning and Viewing—more information on navigating within complex drawings. Topics include applying the PAN command, capturing views in order to return to them later, and using Aerial View.

CD-ROM

Use the following from the *Fundamentals Instructor Productivity CD-ROM* to help you present the textbook's topics and assess student progress.

- Pre-/Post-Test for Part 2, found in the **Exam**View test generator.
- PowerPoint presentation for Part 2. The first slide shows the main topics covered in Part 2 of the textbook. The remaining slides elaborate on the more complex topics. You may want to use the PowerPoint presentations to introduce all the topics in this part before students begin working through the chapters. Later, as they begin each chapter, you could show the related slides for that chapter.

TRANSPARENCY MASTERS

Transparency masters for Part 2 begin on page 151 of this guide.

Title	Use with
TM-2A: Drawing Aids and Controls	Introduction to Part 2
TM-2B: Quadrant Points	Chapter 9
TM-2C: Orthographic Projection	Chapter 11
TM-2D: Construction Lines	Chapter 11

HANDOUTS

Student and Professional Organizations (see pages 50-55)

PART 2 PROJECT: Patterns and Developments

This project, found at the end of Part 2 in the textbook, provides students the opportunity to apply the AutoCAD commands and procedures they have learned in this part.

- Bring to class a cereal box that has been opened into a flat pattern. Show students how the development is folded into a three-dimensional shape. Point out the need for overlapping parts to form a box that will close securely.

- Remind students to read the Hints and Suggestions before they begin drawing.

- Summary Questions/Self-Evaluation may be answered in writing or used as a springboard to class discussion. Students could compare their procedures and exchange ideas about improving efficiency and accuracy.

Copyright © Glencoe/McGraw-Hill

Name		Class Period		Time	
Date	M	Tu	W	Th	F

Instructional Plan - Fundamentals Text — *Chapter 9* **Object Snap**

FOCUS

- **Gaining Attention.** Drafting is a graphic language that requires precision and accuracy. Object snaps allow the designer/drafter to be mathematically precise when drawing houses, fixtures, or other technical features and parts.
- **Objectives.** Discuss the objectives listed at the beginning of the textbook chapter.
- **Orientation.** Briefly review with students material they have previously learned that they will need in order to learn this chapter.

TEACH

- **Key Terms.** Ask students to write out the meaning of each term in their own words. Discuss the terms with the class until you arrive at a consensus about the meaning of each term.
- **PowerPoint.** Review the PowerPoint presentation for Part 2, provided on the CD-ROM. Slides 2 through 6 apply to this chapter.
- **Drawing Skills.** Assign the step-by-step instructions in the chapter. Use projection equipment to display the drawings being created as students complete the steps. Students will learn how to use the OSNAP command and its many options.
- **Accuracy, Accuracy.** Students will initially try to "eyeball" a line that needs to start at the end of an existing line. They need to learn that they cannot do this accurately and that they must use object snaps to mathematically grab specific features of existing geometry.
- **Multiple Choices.** Often there are two or three different object snap options that students can use in a specific situation. Personal preference and experience will guide the decision making.

ASSESS

- **Review Questions.** Ask students to complete the Review Questions. Discuss their answers in class. Answers are found in the Answer Keys section of this guide.
- **Applying AutoCAD Skills.** Assign the activities at the end of the chapter.
- **Reteaching.** Students internalize CAD concepts at different rates. Periodic review of the various methods of accessing and using object snaps is critical to ensure that students will know how to apply these vital features while completing a drawing.
- **Enrichment.** Assign the Challenge Your Thinking questions at the end of the chapter. Assign the Using Problem-Solving Skills activities at the end of the chapter.
- **Mathematics.** Using object snaps reinforces the geometry concepts of quadrant, midpoint, perpendicular, intersection, and parallel.
- **Communication.** Assign Challenge Your Thinking questions 1 and 2.
- **Additional Problems.** Assign Problem 1, but replace the printed instructions with the following: Create the link according to the dimensions shown. Use the appropriate object snaps to make the lines meet accurately. Do not dimension.
- **Test.** Use the Chapter Test printed in this guide, or create a test using the **Exam**View test generator on the CD-ROM. The answers can be found in the Answer Keys section of this guide.

CLOSE

- After teaching the OSNAP command, have the students create a drawing that incorporates all the different object snaps. Have them label each type of object snap (END, INT, etc).

Name		Class Period		Time	
Date	M	Tu	W	Th	F

Instructional Plan - Fundamentals Text

Chapter 10 Helpful Drawing Features

FOCUS

- **Gaining Attention.** "Work smarter, not harder" is a popular adage. This also applies to using AutoCAD. There are built-in features designed to make your work easier and more efficient.

- **Objectives.** Discuss the objectives listed at the beginning of the textbook chapter.

- **Orientation.** Briefly review with students material they have previously learned that they will need in order to learn this chapter.

TEACH

- **Key Terms.** Ask students to write out the meaning of each term in their own words. Discuss the terms with the class until you arrive at a consensus about the meaning of each term.

- **PowerPoint.** Review the PowerPoint presentation for Part 2, provided on the CD-ROM. Slides 7 through 10 apply to this chapter.

- **Drawing Skills.** Assign the step-by-step instructions in the chapter. Use projection equipment to display the drawings being created as students complete the steps. Students will learn how to use the ORTHO, TIME, UNDO, and REDO commands and the function keys.

- **Where Am I?** Often in the middle of a drawing users want to know reference information such as the *x,y* coordinates or the length and angle of a line. The F6 function key allows the user to see this information.

- **Ortho.** Many drawings involve vertical and horizontal lines that are parallel or perpendicular to each other. *Ortho* is a root word that means "straight" or "true." The ORTHO command makes it easier to draw lines that are straight.

- **Copy/Paste.** The copy and paste options make it possible to use the Windows Clipboard from within AutoCAD. Text copied to the Clipboard can be pasted into other software applications, such as Microsoft Word documents.

ASSESS

- **Review Questions.** Ask students to complete the Review Questions. Discuss their answers in class. Answers are found in the Answer Keys section of this guide.

- **Applying AutoCAD Skills.** Assign the activities at the end of the chapter.

- **Reteaching.** Students will need extra practice and repetition in applying the copy/paste feature in the **AutoCAD Text** and **command** line windows.

- **Enrichment.** Assign the Challenge Your Thinking questions at the end of the chapter. Assign the Using Problem-Solving Skills activities at the end of the chapter.

- **Communication.** Assign Challenge Your Thinking questions 1 and 2.

- **Test.** Use the Chapter Test printed in this guide, or create a test using the **Exam**View test generator on the CD-ROM. The answers can be found in the Answer Keys section of this guide.

CLOSE

- Assign students an introductory CAD drawing. Have them copy and paste the history of their work to Windows Notepad or another word processor and print out the document. Ask students how information from this document could help them evaluate their work.

Copyright © Glencoe/McGraw-Hill

Name		Class Period			Time	
Date		M	Tu	W	Th	F

Instructional Plan - Fundamentals Text   *Chapter 11* **Construction Aids**

FOCUS

- **Gaining Attention.** Point out that taking a little time to prepare for a drawing can save a lot of time when actually creating the drawing. Before beginning a drawing, ask what units of measurement are being used and what is the smallest increment in the drawing. If the answers, for example, are "fractional" and "one-eighth inch," then setting the grid and snap values to 1/8″ will make the work easier.

- **Objectives.** Discuss the objectives listed at the beginning of the textbook chapter.

- **Orientation.** Students have probably used graph paper in their drafting classes. Point out that AutoCAD's grid system serves the same purpose as graph paper.

TEACH

- **Key Terms.** Ask students to write out the meaning of each term in their own words. Discuss the terms with the class until you arrive at a consensus about the meaning of each term.

- **PowerPoint.** Review the PowerPoint presentation for Part 2, provided on the CD-ROM. Slides 11 through 13 apply to this chapter.

- **Drawing Skills.** Assign the step-by-step instructions in the chapter. Use projection equipment to display the drawings being created as students complete the steps. Students will learn how to use the GRID and SNAP commands and how to create various types of construction lines. They will use these commands and capabilities in orthographic projection.

- **GRID vs. Snap Grid.** Discuss the difference between the GRID command and the snap grid feature. The GRID command sets up a visible alignment grid of dots. The grid serves as a visual guide for drawing lines, but the user has to position the lines. The snap grid is an invisible grid that forces the crosshairs to snap to points on the grid. The user cannot draw "between the lines" as long as snap grid is turned on.

- **Snap Grid vs. Object Snap.** Discuss the difference between snap grid and object snap. Object snap is used to position the crosshairs at specific parts of an object. The snap grid is unrelated to objects; it helps the user snap to specific coordinates within the drawing area.

ASSESS

- **Review Questions.** Ask students to complete the Review Questions. Discuss their answers in class. Answers are found in the Answer Keys section of this guide.

- **Applying AutoCAD Skills.** Assign the activities at the end of the chapter.

- **Reteaching.** Orthographic projection is a key concept in drafting, but it can be difficult for students to grasp. The "glass box," a cube that has different views of the same object drawn on its faces, is often used as a visual aid to explain this concept. The box is illustrated in many beginning drafting books.

- **Enrichment.** Assign the Using Problem-Solving Skills activities at the end of the chapter.

- **Communication.** Assign Challenge Your Thinking questions 1 and 2.

- **Additional Problems.** Assign Problem 61, but do not require students to dimension the drawing. Remind students to use snap and grid to create the cam accurately.

- **Test.** Use the Chapter Test printed in this guide, or create a test using the **Exam**View test generator on the CD-ROM. The answers can be found in the Answer Keys section of this guide.

CLOSE

- Now that students have practiced using AutoCAD's grid system, ask what advantages an electronic grid has over a paper grid.

Name		Class Period		Time	
Date	M	Tu	W	Th	F

Instructional Plan - Fundamentals Text

Chapter 12 AutoCAD's Magnifying Glass

FOCUS

- **Gaining Attention.** Bring to class a set of printed architectural plans. Point out that they include a vast amount of detail. Studying the plans requires one to focus on one area at a time. The same is true for viewing files on the computer screen. AutoCAD's ZOOM command makes it possible to select and enlarge portions of a drawing for a closer look.

- **Objectives.** Discuss the objectives listed at the beginning of the textbook chapter.

- **Orientation.** Most students will be familiar with camcorders. Relate the ZOOM command to the zoom capability of a camcorder.

TEACH

- **Key Terms.** Ask students to write out the meaning of each term in their own words. Discuss the terms with the class until you arrive at a consensus about the meaning of each term.

- **PowerPoint.** Review the PowerPoint presentation for Part 2, provided on the CD-ROM. Slides 14 and 15 apply to this chapter.

- **Drawing Skills.** Assign the step-by-step instructions in the chapter. Students will learn to use the ZOOM, REGEN, and VIEWRES commands.

- **Zooming.** Beginning students often make mistakes in geometric constructions and forget to use object snaps. Using the various ZOOM options allows students to zoom in and out of their drawings to see if lines intersect or overlap or to check for details of a large project.

- **Using the VIEWRES Command.** The VIEWRES command controls the apparent smoothness of curves on the screen. Setting VIEWRES to a higher value makes curved objects appear smoother.

ASSESS

- **Review Questions.** Ask students to complete the Review Questions. Discuss their answers in class. Answers are found in the Answer Keys section of this guide.

- **Applying AutoCAD Skills.** Assign the activities at the end of the chapter.

- **Reteaching.** Students often forget to use commands transparently by preceding them with an apostrophe. Remind them that most commands are transparent unless they select objects, create new objects, cause regenerations, or end a drawing session.

- **Enrichment.** Assign the Challenge Your Thinking questions at the end of the chapter. Assign the Using Problem-Solving Skills activities at the end of the chapter.

- **Communication.** Assign Challenge Your Thinking questions 1 and 2.

- **Mathematics.** AutoCAD objects are vector-based. Discuss the difference between vector-based and raster-based objects.

- **Additional Problems.** Assign Problem 7, but replace the printed instructions with the following: Use construction lines to create the orthographic views in their proper locations. Do not dimension.

- **Test.** Use the Chapter Test printed in this guide, or create a test using the **Exam**View test generator on the CD-ROM. The answers can be found in the Answer Keys section of this guide.

CLOSE

- Utilizing the instructor computer and an LCD projector, randomly call on students to demonstrate to the class a ZOOM option and have them explain the function of that option.

Copyright © Glencoe/McGraw-Hill

Name		Class Period		Time	
Date	M	Tu	W	Th	F

Instructional Plan - Fundamentals Text — *Chapter 13* Panning and Viewing

FOCUS

- **Gaining Attention.** Discuss why it is often necessary to move around while in a zoomed area. There may be questions to answer from a client or details that need to be analyzed. The PAN command lets users zoom to another part of a drawing while keeping the same magnification.

- **Objectives.** Discuss the objectives listed at the beginning of the textbook chapter.

- **Orientation.** If any student is still not familiar with the ZOOM command, review Chapter 12.

TEACH

- **Key Terms.** Ask students to write out the meaning of each term in their own words. Discuss the terms with the class until you arrive at a consensus about the meaning of each term.

- **PowerPoint.** Review the PowerPoint presentation for Part 2, provided on the CD-ROM. Slides 16 through 18 apply to this chapter.

- **Drawing Skills.** Assign the step-by-step instructions in the chapter. Students will learn to use the PAN and VIEW commands.

- **Entering the PAN Command.** The PAN command can be accessed at least five different ways: from the keyboard, as a transparent command ('PAN), with a mouse right-click, from the menu bar, and from the Standard toolbar. Some students may be more efficient using AutoCAD if they can keep their hand on the mouse as much as possible. Right-clicking with the mouse reveals the PAN command options and increases productivity.

ASSESS

- **Review Questions.** Ask students to complete the Review Questions. Discuss their answers in class. Answers are found in the Answer Keys section of this guide.

- **Applying AutoCAD Skills.** Assign the activities at the end of the chapter.

- **Reteaching.** The VIEW command is a powerful tool, but at this stage students may not understand its full capability. Review this command and its applications later during the course, after students have learned 3D modeling and orthographic projection applications.

- **Enrichment.** Assign the Challenge Your Thinking questions at the end of the chapter. Assign the Using Problem-Solving Skills activities at the end of the chapter.

- **Communication.** Assign Challenge Your Thinking questions 1 and 2.

- **Test.** Use the Chapter Test printed in this guide, or create a test using the **Exam**View test generator on the CD-ROM. The answers can be found in the Answer Keys section of this guide.

CLOSE

- Randomly choose a student to demonstrate to the class how to access the PAN command by one of the several techniques.

- Develop CAD competencies for each aspect of the VIEW command and have students demonstrate their skill in using the command.

Name		Class Period		Time	
Date	M	Tu	W	Th	F

Instructional Plan - Fundamentals Text — *Part 3* Drawing and Editing

CHAPTERS AND MAIN TOPICS

Chapter 14: Solid and Curved Objects—producing solid-filled objects; controlling the appearance of solid-filled objects; creating and editing polylines and splines

Chapter 15: Adding and Altering Objects—creating chamfered corners; breaking pieces out of lines, circles, and arcs; producing fillets and rounds; offsetting lines and circles; creating and editing multilines

Chapter 16: Moving and Duplicating Objects—changing an object's properties, such as color, layer, linetype, or geometry; moving objects to another part of the screen; copying objects; producing a mirror image of an object; creating rectangular and polar arrays

Chapter 17: Modifying and Maneuvering—stretching, scaling, and rotating objects; trimming and extending lines

Chapter 18: Notes and Specifications—creating and editing text dynamically; producing multiple-line text using AutoCAD's text editor; specifying the position and orientation of text; importing text from other software; creating new text styles; using TrueType fonts

Chapter 19: Text Editing and Spell Checking—editing text with AutoCAD's text editor; creating special text characters; finding and replacing text; spell-checking

Chapter 20: Hatching and Sketching—adding hatch patterns to objects; changing a hatch boundary; changing the characteristics of a hatch pattern; using sketching options

CD-ROM

Use the following from the *Fundamentals Instructor Productivity CD-ROM* to help you present the textbook's topics and assess student progress.

- Pre-/Post-Test for Part 3, found in the **Exam**View test generator.

- PowerPoint presentation for Part 3. The first slide shows the main topics covered in Part 3 of the textbook. The remaining slides elaborate on the more complex topics. You may want to use the PowerPoint presentations to introduce all the topics in this part before students begin working through the chapters. Later, as they begin each chapter, you could show the related slides for that chapter.

TRANSPARENCY MASTERS

Transparency masters for Part 3 begin on page 155 of this guide.

Title	Use with
TM-3A: Drawing and Editing	Introduction to Part 3
TM-3B: Arrays	Chapter 16
TM-3C: Stretching	Chapter 17
TM-3D: Hatching	Chapter 20

HANDOUTS

Career Handouts: HO-1 and HO-2

PART 3 PROJECT: Creating a Floor Plan

This project, found at the end of Part 3 in the textbook, provides students the opportunity to apply the AutoCAD commands and procedures they have learned in this part.

- Remind students to read the Hints and Suggestions before they begin drawing.

- Summary Questions/Self-Evaluation may be answered in writing or used as a springboard to class discussion. Students could compare their procedures and exchange ideas about improving efficiency and accuracy.

- A variation of this project is to create a floor plan of the school as a guide for visitors or new students. The rooms should be labeled with their room numbers.

Copyright © Glencoe/McGraw-Hill

Name		Class Period		Time	
Date	M	Tu	W	Th	F

Instructional Plan - Fundamentals Text — *Chapter 14* Solid and Curved Objects

FOCUS

- **Gaining Attention.** Use the analogy of a toolbox. Everyone likes to have a toolbox full of all the standard tools as well as the latest, greatest tools. In AutoCAD, knowing the basic commands is critical, but also knowing how to control the drawing environment to make the software work for you is a powerful additional skill.

- **Objectives.** Discuss the objectives listed at the beginning of the textbook chapter.

- **Orientation.** Students may need a quick review of basic objects, discussed in Chapter 4.

TEACH

- **Key Terms.** Ask students to write out the meaning of each term in their own words. Discuss the terms with the class until you arrive at a consensus about the meaning of each term.

- **PowerPoint.** Review the PowerPoint presentation for Part 3, provided on the CD-ROM. Slides 2 through 5 apply to this chapter.

- **Drawing Skills.** Assign the step-by-step instructions in the chapter. Students will learn to use the SOLID, FILL, REGEN, PLINE, PEDIT, EXPLODE, SPLINE, and SPLINEDIT commands.

- **Regeneration.** Circles that look like polygons when zoomed will return to their original circular shape with the REGEN command.

ASSESS

- **Review Questions.** Ask students to complete the Review Questions. Discuss their answers in class. Answers are found in the Answer Keys section of this guide.

- **Applying AutoCAD Skills.** Assign the activities at the end of the chapter.

- **Reteaching.** Make sure students practice both the PEDIT command, which can be used to combine polylines into a single entity, and its opposite, the EXPLODE command.

- **Enrichment.** Assign the Challenge Your Thinking questions at the end of the chapter. Assign the Using Problem-Solving Skills activities at the end of the chapter.

- **Communication.** Assign Challenge Your Thinking questions 1 and 2.

- **Mathematics.** When creating geometry, you may need to find the area and perimeter of a complex object made up of lines and arcs. Using the PEDIT command allows you to make the object a single entity; and with the LIST command, you can pick the object and find the answers. You can then explode the object back into its original geometry.

- **Additional Problems.** Assign Problem 50.

- **Test.** Use the Chapter Test printed in this guide, or create a test using the **Exam**View test generator on the CD-ROM. The answers can be found in the Answer Keys section of this guide.

CLOSE

- Have half of the class create a drawing from the chapter using standard drawing commands (line, arc, and circle). Have them calculate the area and perimeter. Have the other half of the class create the same object using PLINE and PEDIT. Have them calculate the area and perimeter. Use the TIME command to compare construction times. Check for accuracy.

Name		Class Period		Time	
Date		M	Tu	W	Th	F

Instructional Plan - Fundamentals Text — *Chapter 15* Adding and Altering Objects

FOCUS

- **Gaining Attention.** One of the goals of CAD software is to increase productivity. For students, one of the most powerful and simple commands to make drawing easier is the **OFFSET** command. Creating a twin object a certain distance from the original is a very practical and useful function of CAD software.

- **Objectives.** Discuss the objectives listed at the beginning of the textbook chapter.

- **Orientation.** Briefly review with students material they have previously learned that they will need in order to learn this chapter.

TEACH

- **Key Terms.** Ask students to write out the meaning of each term in their own words. Discuss the terms with the class until you arrive at a consensus about the meaning of each term.

- **PowerPoint.** Review the PowerPoint presentation for Part 3, provided on the CD-ROM. Slides 6 through 10 apply to this chapter.

- **Drawing Skills.** Assign the step-by-step instructions in the chapter. Students will learn to use the **CHAMFER**, **BREAK**, **FILLET**, **OFFSET**, **MLINE**, and **MLEDIT** command.

- **Clicking Patterns.** To increase productivity and to show students the patterns built into AutoCAD, demonstrate how a sequence of mouse clicks with the **OFFSET** command repeats the steps of the command (left, left, right, right, and left). This sequence enables students to use the command without taking their hands off the mouse.

- **Which Line Did I Pick First?** When you use the **CHAMFER** command, if the bevel distances are not equal, you must remember the sequence in which you entered the values and pick the line segments in the same sequence.

ASSESS

- **Review Questions.** Ask students to complete the Review Questions. Discuss their answers in class. Answers are found in the Answer Keys section of this guide.

- **Applying AutoCAD Skills.** Assign the activities at the end of the chapter.

- **Reteaching.** Have students practice the **OFFSET** command by drawing a dartboard or bull's-eye.

- **Enrichment.** Assign the Challenge Your Thinking questions at the end of the chapter. Assign the Using Problem-Solving Skills activities at the end of the chapter.

- **Mathematics.** Assign Challenge Your Thinking question 2.

- **Communication.** Assign Challenge Your Thinking questions 1 and 3.

- **Additional Problems.** Assign Problem 4, but do not require students to dimension the drawing. Remind students to use the commands presented in this chapter to make the drawing task easier.

- **Test.** Use the Chapter Test printed in this guide, or create a test using the **ExamView** test generator on the CD-ROM. The answers can be found in the Answer Keys section of this guide.

CLOSE

- Assign students to create a three-view drawing from the book. They are to use the **MLINE** and **OFFSET** commands as much as possible. Students should write a report describing the drawing sequence they used.

Copyright © Glencoe/McGraw-Hill

Name		Class Period			Time	
Date		M	Tu	W	Th	F

Instructional Plan - Fundamentals Text
Chapter 16 Moving and Duplicating Objects

FOCUS

- **Gaining Attention.** Producing complicated gears using traditional board drafting was a tedious task. Producing these same parts using the power of AutoCAD's duplicating commands is very easy. Drawings that would take one to two hours with a compass can be completed in minutes using the ARRAY command.

- **Objectives.** Discuss the objectives listed at the beginning of the textbook chapter.

- **Orientation.** Briefly review with students material they have previously learned that they will need in order to learn this chapter.

TEACH

- **Key Terms.** Ask students to write out the meaning of each term in their own words. Discuss the terms with the class until you arrive at a consensus about the meaning of each term.

- **Drawing Skills.** Assign the step-by-step instructions in the chapter. Students will learn to use the MOVE, COPY, MIRROR, and ARRAY commands.

- **Ortho with MIRROR.** When creating the mirror lines, pressing F8 to toggle ortho on will allow the drafter to quickly create the horizontal or vertical axis of symmetry.

- **Columns and Rows.** Students often confuse the terms *column* and *row*. Using the ARRAY (Rectangular) command to duplicate a classroom set of chairs will help them understand the difference. If the students set the values incorrectly, the results will be obvious.

- **The Hands of Time.** Drawing an analog clock face is a practical application of circular arrays.

ASSESS

- **Review Questions.** Ask students to complete the Review Questions. Discuss their answers in class. Answers are found in the Answer Keys section of this guide.

- **Applying AutoCAD Skills.** Assign the activities at the end of the chapter.

- **Reteaching.** Using the MOVE command with precision (object snaps) is a skill that students do not quickly understand. Moving from a specific intersection or end to another specific intersection or quadrant of another object is a great timesaver, and this procedure may need to be shown periodically.

- **Enrichment.** Assign the Challenge Your Thinking questions at the end of the chapter. Assign the Using Problem-Solving Skills activities at the end of the chapter.

- **Mathematics.** Assign Challenge Your Thinking question 2.

- **Communication.** Assign Challenge Your Thinking question 1.

- **Additional Problems.** Assign Problem 26, but do not require students to dimension the steel plate.

- **Test.** Use the Chapter Test printed in this guide, or create a test using the **Exam***View* test generator on the CD-ROM. The answers can be found in the Answer Keys section of this guide.

CLOSE

- Have students use the ARRAY (Rectangular) command to create a 6″ fractional ruler and/or an engineer's scale. This forces students to understand the units of division ($1/16''$ or $1/20''$). HINT: Draw the smallest division first.

Copyright © Glencoe/McGraw-Hill

Name		Class Period		Time	
Date		M	Tu	W	Th	F

Instructional Plan - Fundamentals Text

Chapter 17 Modifying and Maneuvering

FOCUS

- **Gaining Attention.** Point out that the TRIM and EXTEND commands are great timesavers when creating multiview and other two-dimensional drawings.

- **Objectives.** Discuss the objectives listed at the beginning of the textbook chapter.

- **Orientation.** Students may need a review of the XLINE and OFFSET commands.

TEACH

- **Key Terms.** Ask students to write out the meaning of each term in their own words. Discuss the terms with the class until you arrive at a consensus about the meaning of each term.

- **Drawing Skills.** Assign the step-by-step instructions in the chapter. Students will learn to use the STRETCH, SCALE, ROTATE, TRIM, and EXTEND commands.

- **Bring Out the Scissors.** When drawings are laid out using the XLINE or OFFSET commands, line segments are often too long. The TRIM command provides a quick and easy way to trim a line segment that is too long.

- **What? No Intersection!** Sometimes when students try to draw a line from an intersection, AutoCAD tells them that no intersection exists. Once they zoom in, students realize that the lines truly do not intersect. Using the EXTEND command solves that problem quickly. Pick the boundary line first, and then pick near the end of the short line. AutoCAD will extend the line, forming the intersection.

ASSESS

- **Review Questions.** Ask students to complete the Review Questions. Discuss their answers in class. Answers are found in the Answer Keys section of this guide.

- **Applying AutoCAD Skills.** Assign the activities at the end of the chapter.

- **Reteaching.** When using the ROTATE command, remember that the axis of rotation is the Z axis. This provides the opportunity to discuss the right-hand rule and the WCS (world coordinate system). *Right-hand rule:* Hold your right hand upright in front of you, palm facing toward you. Place your thumb and index finger so that they are in the same plane, with the thumb extended at a right angle to the index finger. These represent the X axis and Y axis. Point the middle finger toward yourself, at a right angle to the other two fingers. The middle finger represents the Z axis.

- **Enrichment.** Assign the Challenge Your Thinking questions at the end of the chapter. Assign the Using Problem-Solving Skills activities at the end of the chapter.

- **Mathematics.** Assign Challenge Your Thinking question 1.

- **Communication.** Assign Challenge Your Thinking question 2.

- **Additional Problems.** Assign Problem 59 using the instructions printed in the text.

- **Test.** Use the Chapter Test printed in this guide, or create a test using the **Exam**View test generator on the CD-ROM. The answers can be found in the Answer Keys section of this guide.

CLOSE

- Have students create a drawing from the chapter and use the SCALE command to practice enlarging and reducing the object.

Copyright © Glencoe/McGraw-Hill

Name		Class Period		Time	
Date	M	Tu	W	Th	F

Instructional Plan - Fundamentals Text *Chapter 18* Notes and Specifications

FOCUS

- **Gaining Attention.** The different disciplines of drafting (architecture, AEC, GIS, mechanical drawing, etc.) are all graphic languages. Many times, written explanations add to graphic images. AutoCAD provides a variety of text options for this purpose.

- **Objectives.** Discuss the objectives listed at the beginning of the textbook chapter.

- **Orientation.** Briefly review with students material they have previously learned that they will need in order to learn this chapter.

TEACH

- **Key Terms.** Ask students to write out the meaning of each term in their own words. Discuss the terms with the class until you arrive at a consensus about the meaning of each term.

- **PowerPoint.** Review the PowerPoint presentation for Part 3, provided on the CD-ROM. Slides 11 through 13 apply to this chapter.

- **Drawing Skills.** Assign the step-by-step instructions in the chapter. Students will learn to use the DTEXT, MTEXT, and STYLE commands; import text from a word processing program; and apply the TEXTQLTY system variable.

- **Enter Twice.** When using the DTEXT command, remember to enter twice when you are done inputting text. The first enter drops the cursor down one line and the second enter completes the command.

- **Where's the Height Option?** If you enter a height value in the STYLE command, you will not be given the option of selecting a text height. If you leave the height value at 0.00 in the STYLE command, you will have that option in the DTEXT command.

ASSESS

- **Review Questions.** Ask students to complete the Review Questions. Discuss their answers in class. Answers are found in the Answer Keys section of this guide.

- **Applying AutoCAD Skills.** Assign the activities at the end of the chapter.

- **Reteaching.** Creating text and drawings one time and then importing and exporting them to different software applications increases worker productivity. Teach the concept of importing text with the MTEXT command to add notes and specifications to drawings.

- **Enrichment.** Assign the Challenge Your Thinking questions at the end of the chapter. Assign the Using Problem-Solving Skills activities at the end of the chapter.

- **Communication.** Assign Challenge Your Thinking questions 1 and 2.

- **Test.** Use the Chapter Test printed in this guide, or create a test using the **Exam**View test generator on the CD-ROM. The answers can be found in the Answer Keys section of this guide.

CLOSE

- Have students draw a rectangle to represent their textbook and then have them add the book's title and the author's name. They can use existing fonts or create their own.

Copyright © Glencoe/McGraw-Hill

Name		Class Period		Time	
Date	M	Tu	W	Th	F

Instructional Plan - Fundamentals Text

Chapter 19 Text Editing and Spell Checking

FOCUS

- **Gaining Attention.** AutoCAD provides the ability to edit text, check spelling, and use special characters. Ask students how this ability might improve quality and productivity.
- **Objectives.** Discuss the objectives listed at the beginning of the textbook chapter.
- **Orientation.** Make sure students have completed Chapter 18 and have created a text.dwg file.

TEACH

- **Key Terms.** Ask students to write out the meaning of each term in their own words. Discuss the terms with the class until you arrive at a consensus about the meaning of each term.
- **Drawing Skills.** Assign the step-by-step instructions in the chapter. Students will learn to use the DDEDIT and SPELL commands and create special characters.
- **DINNING Room?** It's easy to misspell a word when adding notes or specifications to a drawing. Discuss the possible consequences of misspellings (miscommunication, clients or bosses getting a negative impression, etc.) Encourage students to develop the habit of spell checking their drawings before printing.

ASSESS

- **Review Questions.** Ask students to complete the Review Questions. Discuss their answers in class. Answers are found in the Answer Keys section of this guide.
- **Applying AutoCAD Skills.** Assign the activities at the end of the chapter.
- **Reteaching.** Create a drawing that includes text errors. Assign students to identify and correct the errors. They should use the MTEXT command to document their work.
- **Enrichment.** Assign the Challenge Your Thinking questions at the end of the chapter. Assign the Using Problem-Solving Skills activities at the end of the chapter.
- **Communication.** Assign Challenge Your Thinking questions 1 and 2.
- **Test.** Use the Chapter Test printed in this guide, or create a test using the **Exam**View test generator on the CD-ROM. The answers can be found in the Answer Keys section of this guide.

CLOSE

- Ask students to describe the limitations of a spell checker. (For example, it cannot identify words used incorrectly, such as "too" for "two.")

Name		Class Period		Time		
Date		M	Tu	W	Th	F

Instructional Plan - Fundamentals Text — *Chapter 20* Hatching and Sketching

FOCUS

- **Gaining Attention.** ANSI and ISO publish industry standards related to drawing and producing products. Discuss the importance of industry standards as they apply to drafting. Point out that AutoCAD provides ANSI- and ISO-compliant hatch patterns.

- **Objectives.** Discuss the objectives listed at the beginning of the textbook chapter.

- **Orientation.** Briefly review with students material they have previously learned that they will need in order to learn this chapter.

TEACH

- **Key Terms.** Ask students to write out the meaning of each term in their own words. Discuss the terms with the class until you arrive at a consensus about the meaning of each term.

- **PowerPoint.** Review the PowerPoint presentation for Part 3, provided on the CD-ROM. Slides 14 and 15 apply to this chapter.

- **Drawing Skills.** Assign the step-by-step instructions in the chapter. Students will learn to use the BHATCH and HATCHEDIT commands. They will also learn the SKETCH command and the SKPOLY system variable.

- **BHATCH vs. HATCH.** AutoCAD also has a HATCH command, which is text-driven. The BHATCH command is preferable it provides the user with a graphic dialog box loaded with a variety of options. BHATCH creates associative hatches; that is, it updates automatically when boundaries change.

- **Smoothing a Sketched Object.** Setting SKPOLY to 1 allows the user to smooth a sketched curve by applying the PEDIT command. Have students make sketches with SKPOLY set to 1 and to 0. Compare results.

ASSESS

- **Review Questions.** Ask students to complete the Review Questions. Discuss their answers in class. Answers are found in the Answer Keys section of this guide.

- **Applying AutoCAD Skills.** Assign the activities at the end of the chapter.

- **Reteaching.** Students may encounter some difficulty with the Island Detection Style option of the BHATCH command. A teacher demonstration is critical, but equally valuable is having the students experiment with the alternatives in different applications until they become competent with this concept.

- **Enrichment.** Assign the Challenge Your Thinking questions at the end of the chapter. Assign the Using Problem-Solving Skills activities at the end of the chapter.

- **Communication.** Assign Challenge Your Thinking questions 1 and 2.

- **Test.** Use the Chapter Test printed in this guide, or create a test using the **Exam**View test generator on the CD-ROM. The answers can be found in the Answer Keys section of this guide.

CLOSE

- Try something different and fun with the hatching and sketching commands. Have students create orthographic drawings and sketches and section views of a hamburger, hot dog, taco, and glass of iced tea or soda. Have students create a key that matches the various hatch symbols.

Name		Class Period		Time		
Date		M	Tu	W	Th	F

Instructional Plan - Fundamentals Text
Part 4 Preparing and Printing a Drawing

CHAPTERS AND MAIN TOPICS

Chapter 21: Drawing Setup—the purpose of a template file; common settings; choosing the appropriate unit of measurement for a drawing; determining appropriate sheet size and drawing scale; checking the status of a drawing file

Chapter 22: Layers and Linetypes—creating layers with appropriate characteristics; using layers to control the visibility and appearance of objects; changing an object's properties; filtering object selections; applying a custom template file

Chapter 23: Plotting and Printing—previewing a plot; adjusting plotter settings; plotting a drawing to scale

Chapter 24: Multiple Viewports—creating and using multiple viewports in model space and in paper space; positioning objects in paper space viewports; editing, positioning, and plotting paper space layouts

CD-ROM

Use the following from the *Fundamentals Instructor Productivity CD-ROM* to help you present the textbook's topics and assess student progress.

- Pre-/Post-Test for Part 4, found in the **Exam**View test generator.
- PowerPoint presentation for Part 4. The first slide shows the main topics covered in Part 4 of the textbook. The remaining slides elaborate on the more complex topics. You may want to use the PowerPoint presentations to introduce all the topics in this part before students begin working through the chapters. Later, as they begin each chapter, you could show the related slides for that chapter.

TRANSPARENCY MASTERS

Transparency masters for Part 4 begin on page 159 of this guide.

Title	Use with
TM-4A: Preparing and Printing a Drawing	Introduction to Part 4
TM-4B: Lineweights	Chapter 22
TM-4C: Layers	Chapter 22
TM-4D: Viewports in Model Space	Chapter 24

HANDOUTS

Career Handouts: HO-3 through HO-5

PART 4 PROJECT: Designing a Bookend

This project, found at the end of Part 4 in the textbook, provides students the opportunity to apply the AutoCAD commands and procedures they have learned in this part.

- Remind students to read the Hints and Suggestions before they begin drawing.

- Summary Questions/Self-Evaluation may be answered in writing or used as a springboard to class discussion. Students could compare their procedures and exchange ideas about improving efficiency and accuracy.

- As an additional challenge, have students create an actual model of the bookend using Styrofoam or a similar material of the appropriate thickness. For this model, students will need to determine exact dimensions of the bookend.

- Ask students what questions would need to be answered in order for the bookend to be manufactured. (Besides dimensions, the design would need to specify the type of material and the method of joining the parts.)

Copyright © Glencoe/McGraw-Hill

Name		Class Period		Time	
Date	M	Tu	W	Th	F

Instructional Plan - Fundamentals Text *Chapter 21* **Drawing Setup**

FOCUS

- **Gaining Attention.** In this chapter, students will learn how to create templates for their drawings. Point out that using templates is one way businesses streamline their procedures and thus save time and money.
- **Objectives.** Discuss the objectives listed at the beginning of the textbook chapter.
- **Orientation.** In manufacturing, a template is a pattern or mold used to form a piece. Electronic templates serve a similar purpose. Students may already be familiar with template files from other software applications.

TEACH

- **Key Terms.** Ask students to write out the meaning of each term in their own words. Discuss the terms with the class until you arrive at a consensus about the meaning of each term.
- **PowerPoint.** Review the PowerPoint presentation for Part 4, provided on the CD-ROM. Slides 2 through 6 apply to this chapter.
- **Drawing Skills.** Assign the step-by-step instructions in the chapter. Students will learn to use a predefined template and to create a custom template by specifying the units, angle measurements, limits, and other settings.
- **Units.** Students need to plan before they start to draw. It is easier to set the correct units, limits, etc., at the start than to change them later. Are the dimensions of a drawing to be in fractions? Then those units need to be chosen. How accurate does the denominator need to be—1/2″, 1/4″, 1/8″, or 1/16″? This can be specified in the **Precision** option.
- **What Are Limits?** Limits define the drawing area. Limits must be set correctly to ensure that a drawing will fit on a specific size of paper and plot to a desired scale.

ASSESS

- **Review Questions.** Ask students to complete the Review Questions. Discuss their answers in class. Answers are found in the Answer Keys section of this guide.
- **Applying AutoCAD Skills.** Assign the activities at the end of the chapter.
- **Reteaching.** The units settings are critical. For example, if the linear precision is set to 1/8″ and the size of an object is 3/16″, AutoCAD will round the value to 1/4″, the next multiple of 1/8″. Remind students to study the drawing for the smallest denominator and set the units accordingly.
- **Enrichment.** Assign the Challenge Your Thinking questions at the end of the chapter. Assign the Using Problem-Solving Skills activities at the end of the chapter.
- **Mathematics.** Assign Challenge Your Thinking question 2.
- **Communication.** Assign Challenge Your Thinking question 1.
- **Test.** Use the Chapter Test printed in this guide, or create a test using the **Exam**View test generator on the CD-ROM. The answers can be found in the Answer Keys section of this guide.

CLOSE

- Assign students two drawings from the earlier chapters. Have them develop template files for each and print out values.

Copyright © Glencoe/McGraw-Hill

Name		Class Period		Time	
Date	M	Tu	W	Th	F

Instructional Plan - Fundamentals Text *Chapter 22* Layers and Linetypes

FOCUS

- **Gaining Attention.** Students need to be aware of standards set up by specific companies and industries concerning layers (layer names, colors, linetypes, and lineweights). Taking a field trip to a local company or having a guest speaker talk to the class will strengthen this lesson and provide students with a workplace experience.

- **Objectives.** Discuss the objectives listed at the beginning of the textbook chapter.

- **Orientation.** Briefly review with students material they have previously learned that they will need in order to learn this chapter.

TEACH

- **Key Terms.** Ask students to write out the meaning of each term in their own words. Discuss the terms with the class until you arrive at a consensus about the meaning of each term.

- **PowerPoint.** Review the PowerPoint presentation for Part 4, provided on the CD-ROM. Slides 7 through 12 apply to this chapter.

- **Drawing Skills.** Assign the step-by-step instructions in the chapter. Students will learn to use layers, linetypes, and the LTSCALE command.

- **Why Don't Hidden Lines Show Correctly?** If the drawing area is set to any value other than the actual plotting area, noncontinuous lines may not show up properly. The LTSCALE command needs to be changed to one-half of the reciprocal of the plot scale. For example, $1/4" = 1'-0"$ is equal to $1/48$. Thus, LTSCALE needs to be 24.

- **Linetypes.** Drafting is the graphic language of industry. Various linetypes are used in the different sectors of industry. Students need to learn the basic linetype names and applications: continuous, hidden, center, phantom, and break lines.

ASSESS

- **Review Questions.** Ask students to complete the Review Questions. Discuss their answers in class. Answers are found in the Answer Keys section of this guide.

- **Applying AutoCAD Skills.** Assign the activities at the end of the chapter.

- **Reteaching.** Layers are like transparency film. Demonstrate with a drawing that has different classes of objects on different layers; for example, property lines, setbacks, roof outline, foundations, electrical, plumbing, and walls. Start by showing only the basic object (walls). Thaw layers one at a time until all features are visible.

- **Enrichment.** Assign the Challenge Your Thinking questions at the end of the chapter. Assign the Using Problem-Solving Skills activities at the end of the chapter.

- **Communication.** Assign Challenge Your Thinking questions 1 and 2.

- **Additional Problems.** Assign Problem 56, but replace the printed instructions with the following: Draw orthographic views of the stanchion, being sure to use the correct linetypes. Do not dimension.

- **Test.** Use the Chapter Test printed in this guide, or create a test using the **Exam**View test generator on the CD-ROM. The answers can be found in the Answer Keys section of this guide.

CLOSE

- Have students develop a set of class standards for creating layers.

Copyright © Glencoe/McGraw-Hill

Name		Class Period		Time	
Date	M	Tu	W	Th	F

Instructional Plan - Fundamentals Text — *Chapter 23* Plotting and Printing

FOCUS

- **Gaining Attention.** When architects present concept drawings to clients, the drawings are often on C size (24″ × 18″) or D size (36″ × 24″) sheets. They are usually plotted to a specific scale (1″ = 40″) for evaluation purposes. If questions arise, the architects can check sizes and distances. The clients need to understand the concept of scaling.
- **Objectives.** Discuss the objectives listed at the beginning of the textbook chapter.
- **Orientation.** Briefly review with students material they have previously learned that they will need in order to learn this chapter.

TEACH

- **Key Terms.** Ask students to write out the meaning of each term in their own words. Discuss the terms with the class until you arrive at a consensus about the meaning of each term.
- **PowerPoint.** Review the PowerPoint presentation for Part 4, provided on the CD-ROM. Slides 13 through 19 apply to this chapter.
- **Drawing Skills.** Assign the step-by-step instructions in the chapter. Students will learn to use the PLOT command and the LWSCALE system variable.
- **Equivalent Plot Values.** Scales on architectural drawings are listed with the fraction first, then one foot; for example, ¼″ = 1′-0″. There are forty-eight quarter-inches in one foot, so 1 = 48 or .5 = 24 or ¼ = 12 are values that will work when plotting.
- **Proper Planning Prevents Poor Performance!** Plan ahead to achieve good plots. If you are plotting to size A paper, and the printable area is 10.38 × 7.94, and if you are drawing an object that is 17″ × 10″, the drawing area should be 20″ × 16″ and plotted to 1 = 2. Use the Limits option when plotting.

ASSESS

- **Review Questions.** Ask students to complete the Review Questions. Discuss their answers in class. Answers are found in the Answer Keys section of this guide.
- **Applying AutoCAD Skills.** Assign the activities at the end of the chapter.
- **Reteaching.** After students have printed a drawing to a specific scale, have them use the appropriate (ruler) scale (metric, fractional, or engineering) and prove to you that they have properly printed the drawing to scale. Students will often make up their own scale or use the Scale to fit option.
- **Enrichment.** Assign the Challenge Your Thinking questions at the end of the chapter. Assign the Using Problem-Solving Skills activities at the end of the chapter.
- **Communication.** Assign Challenge Your Thinking questions 1 and 2.
- **Test.** Use the Chapter Test printed in this guide, or create a test using the **Exam**View test generator on the CD-ROM. The answers can be found in the Answer Keys section of this guide.

CLOSE

- Have students evaluate each other's drawings before instructor evaluation and have them check the drawings for proper scale value.

Name		Class Period		Time	
Date		M	Tu	W	Th	F

Instructional Plan - Fundamentals Text *Chapter 24* Multiple Viewports

FOCUS

- **Gaining Attention.** Presenting drawings that clearly communicate an idea or concept to clients, inspectors, builders, or contractors is critical. A picture is worth a thousand words and more. Viewports and their relation to model space and paper space are key concepts that students need to know when using AutoCAD.

- **Objectives.** Discuss the objectives listed at the beginning of the textbook chapter.

- **Orientation.** Briefly review with students material they have previously learned that they will need in order to learn this chapter.

TEACH

- **Key Terms.** Ask students to write out the meaning of each term in their own words. Discuss the terms with the class until you arrive at a consensus about the meaning of each term.

- **PowerPoint.** Review the PowerPoint presentation for Part 4, provided on the CD-ROM. Slides 20 through 26 apply to this chapter.

- **Drawing Skills.** Assign the step-by-step instructions in the chapter. Students will learn to apply the VPORTS command to model space and paper space.

- **Model Space vs. Paper Space.** Model space is the drawing environment in which most drawing work is done. Paper space allows you to lay out and plot one or more views of your model on one drawing sheet.

- **The THICKNESS System Variable.** Design experts stress the importance of presenting ideas using three-dimensional techniques. Orthographic drawings (with hidden and center lines) can be quite confusing. Three-dimensional drawings communicate ideas more readily to clients. The THICKNESS system variable adds depth to an object, making it three-dimensional.

ASSESS

- **Review Questions.** Ask students to complete the Review Questions. Discuss their answers in class. Answers are found in the Answer Keys section of this guide.

- **Applying AutoCAD Skills.** Assign the activities at the end of the chapter.

- **Reteaching.** Using viewports provides the instructor with another opportunity to explain orthographic projection and the relationships among views.

- **Enrichment.** Assign the Challenge Your Thinking questions at the end of the chapter. Assign the Using Problem-Solving Skills activities at the end of the chapter.

- **Communication.** Assign Challenge Your Thinking questions 1 and 2.

- **Test.** Use the Chapter Test printed in this guide, or create a test using the **Exam***View* test generator on the CD-ROM. The answers can be found in the Answer Keys section of this guide.

CLOSE

- Have students list the characteristics of paper space and model space. In which situations is it appropriate to use model space? Paper space?

Copyright © Glencoe/McGraw-Hill

Name		Class Period		Time	
Date	M	Tu	W	Th	F

Instructional Plan - Fundamentals Text

Part 5 Dimensioning and Tolerancing

CHAPTERS AND MAIN TOPICS

Chapter 25: Basic Dimensioning—setting up a text style for dimensions; producing linear dimensions; dimensioning round shapes, curves, holes, and angles; using baseline and ordinate dimensioning

Chapter 26: Advanced Dimensioning—creating a dimension style and applying it to a drawing and a template file; adjusting the text, arrowheads, center marks, and scale in a dimension style; editing individual dimensions; using associative dimensioning

Chapter 27: Fine-Tuning Dimensions—adjusting the appearance of dimension lines, arrowheads, and text; controlling the placement of dimension text; adjusting the format and precision of primary and alternate units; editing dimension properties; exploding dimensions

Chapter 28: Tolerancing—applying symmetrical, deviation, limits, and basic methods of tolerancing; inserting surface controls; creating geometric characteristic symbols and feature control frames; adding material condition symbols, datum references, data identifiers, and projected tolerance zones to drawings

Chapter 29: A Calculating Strategy—using AutoCAD's inquiry feature; calculating distance between points; calculating area and circumference; using the online geometry calculator; displaying database information; editing objects mathematically

CD-ROM

Use the following from the *Fundamentals Instructor Productivity CD-ROM* to help you present the textbook's topics and assess student progress.

- Pre-/Post-Test for Part 5, found in the **Exam***View* test generator.
- PowerPoint presentation for Part 5. The first slide shows the main topics covered in Part 5 of the textbook. The remaining slides elaborate on the more complex topics. You may want to use the PowerPoint presentations to introduce all the topics in this part before students begin working through the chapters.

Later, as they begin each chapter, you could show the related slides for that chapter.

TRANSPARENCY MASTERS

Transparency masters for Part 5 begin on page 163 of this guide.

Title	Use with
TM-5A: Dimensioning and Tolerancing	Introduction to Part 5
TM-5B: Linear and Baseline Dimensions	Chapter 25
TM-5C: Dimension Styles	Chapter 26
TM-5D: Tolerancing Methods	Chapter 28

HANDOUTS

Career Handouts: HO-6 through HO-8

PART 5 PROJECT: Designer Eyewear

This project, found at the end of Part 5 in the textbook, provides students the opportunity to apply the AutoCAD commands and procedures they have learned in this part.

- Remind students to read the Hints and Suggestions before they begin drawing.
- Summary Questions/Self-Evaluation may be answered in writing or used as a springboard to class discussion. Students could compare their procedures and exchange ideas about improving efficiency and accuracy.
- Designing eyewear that can be worn comfortably by many different people presents some interesting challenges. Unlike a part that is designed for a particular machine, eyewear must fit people of many different sizes. This project presents an opportunity to investigate the field of anthropometry—the study of the physical measurements and movements of the human body. Anthropometric data is used to produce ergonomic designs; that is, designs that are suited to the human body.

Copyright © Glencoe/McGraw-Hill

Name		Class Period		Time	
Date	M	Tu	W	Th	F

Instructional Plan - Fundamentals Text — *Chapter 25* Basic Dimensioning

FOCUS

- **Gaining Attention.** Divide the class into teams of four students. Assign each team an occupational title that relates to a career that uses dimensioning, *i.e.*, drafter, architect, or engineer. Have each team find out the type of dimensioning their occupation uses, including any professional standards. Have the team report their findings to the class. Encourage students to use the Internet to contact organizations such as the American Society of Mechanical Engineers (ASME) and the American National Standards Institute (ANSI) for additional information on standards.

- **Objectives.** Discuss the objectives listed at the beginning of the textbook chapter.

- **Orientation.** Due to the need for accuracy when using dimension commands, it would be beneficial to open and utilize the Object Snap toolbar. If necessary, review object snap modes with the students.

TEACH

- **Key Terms.** Ask students to write out the meaning of each term in their own words. Discuss the terms with the class until you arrive at a consensus about the meaning of each term.

- **PowerPoint.** Review the PowerPoint presentation for Part 5, provided on the CD-ROM. Slides 2 through 6 apply to this chapter.

- **Drawing Skills.** Assign the step-by-step instructions in the chapter. Skills covered include setting the dimension text style; creating linear, diameter, and angular dimensions; baseline and ordinate dimensioning techniques.

- **Dimensioning Methods.** The procedure for dimensioning drawings with AutoCAD 2002 is relatively easy. Allow students to determine which method works best for their application.

ASSESS

- **Review Questions.** Ask students to complete the Review Questions. Discuss their answers in class. Answers are found in the Answer Keys section of this guide.

- **Applying AutoCAD Skills.** Assign the activities at the end of the chapter.

- **Reteaching.** There are several correct methods for dimensioning the same line. Review the most common methods. This will allow your students to choose which method works best for them.

- **Enrichment.** Assign the Challenge Your Thinking questions at the end of the chapter. Assign the Using Problem-Solving Skills activities at the end of the chapter.

- **Communication.** Assign Challenge Your Thinking questions 1 and 2.

- **Additional Problems.** Assign one or more of the many dimensioning problems in the Additional Problems section. Have students follow the directions printed in the text.

- **Test.** Use the Chapter Test printed in this guide, or create a test using the **Exam**View test generator on the CD-ROM. The answers can be found in the Answer Keys section of this guide.

CLOSE

- Have students select a small object they use everyday, *i.e.*, pager, cell phone, watch, key chain, or TV remote control. Have them measure the dimensions of the object using a scale from the classroom and make a three-view drawing. Have them dimension each view as appropriate.

Name		Class Period		Time	
Date	M	Tu	W	Th	F

Instructional Plan - Fundamentals Text — *Chapter 26* Advanced Dimensioning

FOCUS

- **Gaining Attention.** Dimensioning is necessary to relay appropriate information, but the style in which it is done is often left to the discretion of the architect or designer. Have your students examine three different plans, including a floor plan, a working drawing, and a technical drawing, identifying differences and similarities.

- **Objectives.** Discuss the objectives listed at the beginning of the textbook chapter.

- **Orientation.** If students have not worked through Chapter 25, a quick review may be in order.

TEACH

- **Key Terms.** Ask students to write out the meaning of each term in their own words. Discuss the terms with the class until you arrive at a consensus about the meaning of each term.

- **PowerPoint.** Review the PowerPoint presentation for Part 5, provided on the CD-ROM. Slides 7 through 10 apply to this chapter.

- **Drawing Skills.** Assign the step-by-step instructions in the chapter. Skills covered include creating and changing dimension styles, changing the location of dimension lines and text, adding leaders, working with associative dimensions, and adding dimension styles to templates.

- **Dimension Style Manager.** It is said that "practice makes perfect," and dimensioning is definitely a skill for which that statement is true. The information in this chapter will be used repeatedly in a drafter's daily routine. Take the time to reinforce a good understanding of how to use the dimension style manager.

ASSESS

- **Review Questions.** Ask students to complete the Review Questions. Discuss their answers in class. Answers are found in the Answer Keys section of this guide.

- **Applying AutoCAD Skills.** Assign the activities at the end of the chapter.

- **Reteaching.** AutoCAD 2002's ability to modify dimension styles, or create a new one, is much improved over previous releases. Students need to practice using the Dimension Style Manager in a variety of settings. This is a good section to review periodically by providing students with modifications to the dimensioning style of their future drawings.

- **Enrichment.** Assign the Challenge Your Thinking questions at the end of the chapter. Assign the Using Problem-Solving Skills activities at the end of the chapter.

- **Communication.** Assign Challenge Your Thinking questions 1 and 2.

- **Additional Problems.** Assign one or more of the many dimensioning problems in the Additional Problems. Ask students to follow the instructions printed in the text.

- **Test.** Use the Chapter Test printed in this guide, or create a test using the **Exam**View test generator on the CD-ROM. The answers can be found in the Answer Keys section of this guide.

CLOSE

- Assign an existing CAD drawing from the Sample folder and have the students change the dimensioning style, drawing scale, arrowheads, and text style.

Copyright © Glencoe/McGraw-Hill

Name		Class Period			Time	
Date		M	Tu	W	Th	F

Instructional Plan - Fundamentals Text — *Chapter 27* Fine-Tuning Dimensions

FOCUS

- **Gaining Attention.** This chapter provides additional information for refining a drawing's dimension style, further helping to prepare your students for careers. Have them preview two sample drawings to determine similarities and differences between their respective dimensioning styles.

- **Objectives.** Discuss the objectives listed at the beginning of the textbook chapter.

- **Orientation.** Briefly review with students material they have previously learned that they will need in order to learn this chapter. Review the Dimension Style Manager with your students.

TEACH

- **Key Terms.** Ask students to write out the meaning of each term in their own words. Discuss the terms with the class until you arrive at a consensus about the meaning of each term.

- **PowerPoint.** Review the PowerPoint presentation for Part 5, provided on the CD-ROM. Slides 11 through 15 apply to this chapter.

- **Drawing Skills.** Assign the step-by-step instructions in the chapter. Skills covered include the use of primary and alternate units and exploding a dimension, as well as the application of additional dimension style options.

- **Zero Suppression.** The text discusses this topic briefly. It should be noted to the students in what instances manufacturing applies these standards.

- **Alternate Units.** Many companies have manufacturing facilities in several countries. Most countries use the metric system of measurement, and many drawings produced in the United States now show both English and metric measurements.

ASSESS

- **Review Questions.** Ask students to complete the Review Questions. Discuss their answers in class. Answers are found in the Answer Keys section of this guide.

- **Applying AutoCAD Skills.** Assign the activities at the end of the chapter.

- **Reteaching.** Being able to use the Dimension Style Manager effectively and efficiently is a valuable skill. You cannot over-emphasize the appropriate use of this feature.

- **Enrichment.** Assign the Challenge Your Thinking questions at the end of the chapter. Assign the Using Problem-Solving Skills activities at the end of the chapter.

- **Communication.** Assign Challenge Your Thinking questions 1 and 2.

- **Additional Problems.** Assign Problem 58 and ask students to follow the printed instructions, but have them add alternate dimensions to show the sizes in millimeters as well as inches. Also assign Problem 62.

- **Test.** Use the Chapter Test printed in this guide, or create a test using the **Exam**View test generator on the CD-ROM. The answers can be found in the Answer Keys section of this guide.

CLOSE

- Have students create a set of working drawings for an international business. Require the dimensions to be displayed in both English and metric measurements.

Name		Class Period		Time	
Date	M	Tu	W	Th	F

Instructional Plan - Fundamentals Text — *Chapter 28* Tolerancing

FOCUS

- **Gaining Attention.** Tolerancing a component is a common practice in the manufacturing industry. Have students find three different parts that would require a tolerance and discuss possible reasons why.
- **Objectives.** Discuss the objectives listed at the beginning of the textbook chapter.
- **Orientation.** Briefly review with students material they have previously learned that they will need in order to learn this chapter.

TEACH

- **Key Terms.** Ask students to write out the meaning of each term in their own words. Discuss the terms with the class until you arrive at a consensus about the meaning of each term.
- **PowerPoint.** Review the PowerPoint presentation for Part 5, provided on the CD-ROM. Slides 16 and 17 apply to this chapter.
- **Drawing Skills.** Assign the step-by-step instructions in the chapter. Topics covered include the various methods of tolerancing (symmetrical, deviation, limits, and basic) and the application of geometric dimensioning and tolerancing.
- **Precision Settings.** In most instances, the precision settings for both dimensioning and tolerancing should be set the same using the Symmetrical method, *i.e.*, .500±.005.
- **Tolerancing Method.** To have students better understand each method, describe their physical effects as follows:
  Symmetrical—Both values are the same.
  Deviation—The number values are different.
  Limits—The numbers state the range of acceptable sizes.
  Basic—A single number is given without allowances and tolerances.

ASSESS

- **Review Questions.** Ask students to complete the Review Questions. Discuss their answers in class. Answers are found in the Answer Keys section of this guide.
- **Applying AutoCAD Skills.** Assign the activities at the end of the chapter.
- **Reteaching.** This often-overlooked area should be stressed to your students as it is utilized across the board in most manufacturing processes. Take the necessary time to practice each method of tolerancing thoroughly.
- **Enrichment.** Assign the Challenge Your Thinking questions at the end of the chapter. Assign the Using Problem-Solving Skills activities at the end of the chapter.
- **Communication.** Assign Challenge Your Thinking questions 1, 2, and 3.
- **Additional Problems.** Assign problems 26 and 41. You may also wish to assign other Additional Problems and ask students to apply various tolerancing methods to the basic problems.
- **Test.** Use the Chapter Test printed in this guide, or create a test using the **Exam**View test generator on the CD-ROM. The answers can be found in the Answer Keys section of this guide.

CLOSE

- Have students draw and dimension a specific component requiring tolerancing, *i.e.*, camshaft, water pump impeller, intake valve, or other automotive engine part.

Copyright © Glencoe/McGraw-Hill

Name		Class Period			Time	
Date	M	Tu	W	Th	F	

Instructional Plan - Fundamentals Text — *Chapter 29* A Calculating Strategy

FOCUS

- **Gaining Attention.** Industry often requires drawings that display the distance between parts and their respective area measurements, as well as segmented parts. Review some of the possible uses of these functions with your students, including square footage measurements of floor plans, measuring the area of machined parts, and subdividing objects.

- **Objectives.** Discuss the objectives listed at the beginning of the textbook chapter.

- **Orientation.** Briefly review with students material they have previously learned that they will need in order to learn this chapter.

TEACH

- **Key Terms.** Ask students to write out the meaning of each term in their own words. Discuss the terms with the class until you arrive at a consensus about the meaning of each term.

- **PowerPoint.** Review the PowerPoint presentation for Part 5, provided on the CD-ROM. Slides 18 through 23 apply to this chapter.

- **Drawing Skills.** Assign the step-by-step instructions in the chapter. Topics covered include calculating distances and areas, using the online calculator, displaying and listing information, editing and dividing objects, and placing markers.

- **Calculating Feature.** The ability to calculate a specific distance or area, or to subdivide an object, is a standard feature in many CAD programs. Many occupations will require the use of this feature on a regular basis, while others will seldom use it. The best practice would be for students to experience the capabilities of this feature in a practical way by utilizing it as it relates to a possible career choice. For example, have a civil engineering student develop a plot plan calculating the land area, an architectural student determine the square footage of a home, and a mechanical engineering student subdivide a part that is to be milled into equal segments.

ASSESS

- **Review Questions.** Ask students to complete the Review Questions. Discuss their answers in class. Answers are found in the Answer Keys section of this guide.

- **Applying AutoCAD Skills.** Assign the activities at the end of the chapter.

- **Reteaching.** These functions are best taught in conjunction with drawings that are specifically geared to use these features. Review the steps of each and allow your students to practice them for reinforcement.

- **Enrichment.** Assign the Challenge Your Thinking questions at the end of the chapter. Assign the Using Problem-Solving Skills activities at the end of the chapter.

- **Communication.** Assign Challenge Your Thinking questions 1 and 2.

- **Test.** Use the Chapter Test printed in this guide, or create a test using the **Exam**View test generator on the CD-ROM. The answers can be found in the Answer Keys section of this guide.

CLOSE

- Give students an existing AutoCAD floor plan and have them determine the perimeter of the residential or commercial site, the area under roof, etc.

Name		Class Period			Time	
Date		M	Tu	W	Th	F

Instructional Plan - Fundamentals Text
Part 6 Groups and Details

CHAPTERS AND MAIN TOPICS

Chapter 30: Groups—creating a group; adding and deleting objects from a group; editing the group name and description; making a group selectable or unselectable; reordering the objects in a group

Chapter 31: Building Blocks—creating and inserting blocks; renaming, exploding, and purging blocks; inserting a drawing file into the current drawing; creating a drawing file from a block; copying and pasting objects from drawing to drawing

Chapter 32: Symbol Libraries—creating a symbol library; inserting blocks and other content into drawings using AutoCAD DesignCenter; inserting layers, dimension styles, and other content from other drawings using AutoCAD DesignCenter

Chapter 33: Attributes—creating fixed and variable attributes; storing attributes in blocks; editing individual attributes

Chapter 34: Bills of Materials—extracting attributes from blocks; creating a bill of materials with the extracted attributes

CD-ROM

Use the following from the *Fundamentals Instructor Productivity CD-ROM* to help you present the textbook's topics and assess student progress.

- Pre-/Post-Test for Part 6, found in the **Exam***View* test generator.
- PowerPoint presentation for Part 6. The first slide shows the main topics covered in Part 6 of the textbook. The remaining slides elaborate on the more complex topics. You may want to use the PowerPoint presentations to introduce all the topics in this part before students begin working through the chapters. Later, as they begin each chapter, you could show the related slides for that chapter.

TRANSPARENCY MASTERS

Transparency masters for Part 6 begin on page 167 of this guide.

Title	Use with
TM-6A: Groups and Details	Introduction to Part 6
TM-6B: Blocks	Chapter 31
TM-6C: Symbol Library	Chapter 32
TM-6D: AutoCAD DesignCenter	Chapter 32

HANDOUTS

Career Handouts: HO-9 through HO-11

PART 6 PROJECT: Computer Assembly Library

This project, found at the end of Part 6 of the textbook, provides students the opportunity to apply the AutoCAD commands and procedures they have learned in this part.

- Remind students to read the Hints and Suggestions before they begin drawing.
- Summary Questions/Self-Evaluation may be answered in writing or used as a springboard to class discussion. Students could compare their procedures and exchange ideas about improving efficiency and accuracy.
- Students may need to do some research to determine what components to draw, in addition to the CPU, hard drive, and CD-ROM drive. A good source of information is computer supply catalogs. These show pictures of many components and also include specifications and prices.

Copyright © Glencoe/McGraw-Hill

Name		Class Period		Time	
Date	M	Tu	W	Th	F

Instructional Plan - Fundamentals Text   *Chapter 30* Groups

FOCUS

- **Gaining Attention.** With the GROUP command, you can group several characteristics of a given object and copy or resize them easily using standard AutoCAD practices. Have students design a series of automotive wheels in various styles. They should have certain similarities, such as the same diameter, mounting bolt circle, and material. Encourage students to use the grouping feature as frequently as feasible.

- **Objectives.** Discuss the objectives listed at the beginning of the textbook chapter.

- **Orientation.** Briefly review with students material they have previously learned that they will need in order to learn this chapter.

TEACH

- **Key Terms.** Ask students to write out the meaning of each term in their own words. Discuss the terms with the class until you arrive at a consensus about the meaning of each term.

- **PowerPoint.** Review the PowerPoint presentation for Part 6, provided on the CD-ROM. Slides 2 through 11 apply to this chapter.

- **Drawing Skills.** Assign the step-by-step instructions in the chapter. Skills covered include creating a group, adding and editing objects in a group, modifying a group's name and description, using the selectable feature, and changing the order of objects.

- **Deleting or Changing Objects.** The purpose of grouping objects is to permit easy replication of an assembly of components that have common details. Often several objects possess many of the same details, with a few minor differences. In such a case, it may be easier to create the overall group, deleting or changing those details that need to be modified.

ASSESS

- **Review Questions.** Ask students to complete the Review Questions. Discuss their answers in class. Answers are found in the Answer Keys section of this guide.

- **Applying AutoCAD Skills.** Assign the activities at the end of the chapter.

- **Reteaching.** Review the steps for creating and modifying groups with your students. Continually encourage your students to incorporate these features into their everyday operation.

- **Enrichment.** Assign the Challenge Your Thinking questions at the end of the chapter. Assign the Using Problem-Solving Skills activities at the end of the chapter.

- **Communication.** Assign Challenge Your Thinking questions 1 and 2.

- **Test.** Use the Chapter Test printed in this guide, or create a test using the **Exam**View test generator on the CD-ROM. The answers can be found in the Answer Keys section of this guide.

CLOSE

- While this feature is "user friendly," students will benefit from any reinforcement activities assigned. Have students create a detailed object, such as an automotive cylinder head, guitar amplifier, or computer keyboard.

Name		Class Period		Time	
Date	M	Tu	W	Th	F

Instructional Plan - Fundamentals Text **Chapter 31** Building Blocks

FOCUS

- **Gaining Attention.** Blocks are most commonly used to establish a symbol library within a specific drawing. Some examples of these libraries are furniture or appliances to be used in a floor plan and symbols to be used in electrical schematics. Discuss the advantages of using blocks.

- **Objectives.** Discuss the objectives listed at the beginning of the textbook chapter.

- **Orientation.** Briefly review with students material they have previously learned that they will need in order to learn this chapter.

TEACH

- **Key Terms.** Ask students to write out the meaning of each term in their own words. Discuss the terms with the class until you arrive at a consensus about the meaning of each term.

- **PowerPoint.** Review the PowerPoint presentation for Part 6, provided on the CD-ROM. Slides 12 through 18 apply to this chapter.

- **Drawing Skills.** Assign the step-by-step instructions in the chapter. Skills covered include creating and inserting blocks; renaming, exploding, and purging blocks; inserting drawing files (DWG); creating a drawing file from a block; and using the copy and paste commands.

- **EXPLODE Command.** Use this command to dissolve a previously established block for further editing. Additionally, you can make a temporary modification to an existing block by checking the Explode box in the Insert Block dialog box.

- **WBLOCK Command.** One way to transfer blocks from drawing to drawing is to "write" the block to a new drawing file, as outlined in the chapter. While this procedure may not be the quickest method, it can adequately define each block for future use.

ASSESS

- **Review Questions.** Ask students to complete the Review Questions. Discuss their answers in class. Answers are found in the Answer Keys section of this guide.

- **Applying AutoCAD Skills.** Assign the activities at the end of the chapter.

- **Reteaching.** Students may have difficulty understanding the differences between blocks and groups. While these appear to be very similar, in reality they serve very different purposes. Review both blocks and groups, stressing particular applications for each.

- **Enrichment.** Assign the Challenge Your Thinking questions at the end of the chapter. Assign the Using Problem-Solving Skills activities at the end of the chapter.

- **Communication.** Assign Challenge Your Thinking questions 1 and 2.

- **Additional Problems.** Assign Problem 46. Have students use the instructions printed in the textbook.

- **Test.** Use the Chapter Test printed in this guide, or create a test using the **Exam**View test generator on the CD-ROM. The answers can be found in the Answer Keys section of this guide.

CLOSE

- Provide students with an existing AutoCAD floor plan and have them create a symbol library of all the furniture and appliances present. Have them use the WBLOCK command to create a drawing file of each block.

Copyright © Glencoe/McGraw-Hill

Name		Class Period		Time	
Date	M	Tu	W	Th	F

Instructional Plan - Fundamentals Text — *Chapter 32* Symbol Libraries

FOCUS

- **Gaining Attention.** Symbol libraries, as discussed in the previous chapter, are used to save time. Objects need to be created only once. While there are many aftermarket providers of AutoCAD symbol libraries, and AutoCAD 2002 supplies several more, this chapter will assist students in the quick creation of their own libraries for a variety of situations. Have your students "surf" the Internet to locate aftermarket providers of symbol libraries and report their findings. What types of symbol libraries are available? What are their prices?

- **Objectives.** Discuss the objectives listed at the beginning of the textbook chapter.

- **Orientation.** Briefly review with students material they have previously learned that they will need in order to learn this chapter.

TEACH

- **Key Terms.** Ask students to write out the meaning of each term in their own words. Discuss the terms with the class until you arrive at a consensus about the meaning of each term.

- **PowerPoint.** Review the PowerPoint presentation for Part 6, provided on the CD-ROM. Slides 19 through 23 apply to this chapter.

- **Drawing Skills.** Assign the step-by-step instructions in the chapter. Skills covered include creating a library of symbols and details and effectively using the AutoCAD DesignCenter.

- **AutoCAD DesignCenter.** The AutoCAD DesignCenter allows users to make use of blocks and other elements created in other drawings. Using this feature saves time when creating repetitive drawings, such as a series of townhouse floor plans or combustion chambers in an automotive cylinder head.

ASSESS

- **Review Questions.** Ask students to complete the Review Questions. Discuss their answers in class. Answers are found in the Answer Keys section of this guide.

- **Applying AutoCAD Skills.** Assign the activities at the end of the chapter.

- **Reteaching.** While the AutoCAD DesignCenter is very "user friendly," it is beneficial for students to practice using all the properties of this feature.

- **Enrichment.** Assign the Challenge Your Thinking questions at the end of the chapter. Assign the Using Problem-Solving Skills activities at the end of the chapter.

- **Communication.** Assign Challenge Your Thinking questions 1, 2, and 3.

- **Additional Problems.** Assign Problem 45. Have students use the instructions printed in the textbook.

- **Test.** Use the Chapter Test printed in this guide, or create a test using the **Exam**View test generator on the CD-ROM. The answers can be found in the Answer Keys section of this guide.

CLOSE

- Have students create a villa floor plan (a single-story, attached home) and mirror the finished plan to create five adjoined units. Have them add furniture and appliances for each home using AutoCAD DesignCenter.

Name		Class Period		Time	
Date	M	Tu	W	Th	F

Instructional Plan - Fundamentals Text *Chapter 33* **Attributes**

FOCUS

- **Gaining Attention.** Attributes are often used in preparation of bid proposals and cost analysis. Have students review plotted plans to determine three possible scenarios for using attributes with these drawings. Plotted plans may be available from local architects and manufacturing facilities.

- **Objectives.** Discuss the objectives listed at the beginning of the textbook chapter.

- **Orientation.** Briefly review with students material they have previously learned that they will need in order to learn this chapter.

TEACH

- **Key Terms.** Ask students to write out the meaning of each term in their own words. Discuss the terms with the class until you arrive at a consensus about the meaning of each term.

- **PowerPoint.** Review the PowerPoint presentation for Part 6, provided on the CD-ROM. Slides 24 through 27 apply to this chapter.

- **Drawing Skills.** Assign the step-by-step instructions in the chapter. Skills covered include creating, storing, and editing fixed and variable attributes within blocks.

- **Variable vs. Fixed.** Which attribute format to use in any given situation depends on the characteristics of the object. If the characteristics will always remain constant, use the fixed format. If it is possible that the object's shape, size, or cost will be altered, it is better to use the variable format.

- **Editing Attributes.** Because manufacturers make constant improvements and model changes, product lines are seldom static. It is necessary therefore to establish an easy method for modifying existing attributes when updating older drawings. The ATTEDIT command allows easy editing of existing variable attributes.

ASSESS

- **Review Questions.** Ask students to complete the Review Questions. Discuss their answers in class. Answers are found in the Answer Keys section of this guide.

- **Applying AutoCAD Skills.** Assign the activities at the end of the chapter.

- **Reteaching.** While creating attributes may appear to be easy, mastery of this skill requires hours of practice. Demonstrate the process of creating and displaying attributes. Use projection equipment so that students can easily see what you are doing and can follow along on their computers.

- **Enrichment.** Assign the Challenge Your Thinking questions at the end of the chapter. Assign the Using Problem-Solving Skills activities at the end of the chapter.

- **Communication.** Assign Challenge Your Thinking questions 1 and 2.

- **Test.** Use the Chapter Test printed in this guide, or create a test using the **Exam**View test generator on the CD-ROM. The answers can be found in the Answer Keys section of this guide.

CLOSE

- Refer to the closing activity in the Instructional Plan for Chapter 32. Have students add attributes to all of the furniture and appliances using the procedures outlined in Chapter 33.

Copyright © Glencoe/McGraw-Hill

Name		Class Period		Time	
Date	M	Tu	W	Th	F

Instructional Plan - Fundamentals Text *Chapter 34* **Bills of Materials**

FOCUS

- **Gaining Attention.** Creating a bill of materials is the culmination of skills learned throughout the last few chapters. Have students review existing sets of construction plans or working drawings to determine what common traits (or items) exist in the bill of materials.

- **Objectives.** Discuss the objectives listed at the beginning of the textbook chapter.

- **Orientation.** Briefly review with students material they have previously learned that they will need in order to learn this chapter.

TEACH

- **Key Terms.** Ask students to write out the meaning of each term in their own words. Discuss the terms with the class until you arrive at a consensus about the meaning of each term.

- **PowerPoint.** Review the PowerPoint presentation for Part 6, provided on the CD-ROM. Slides 28 through 33 apply to this chapter.

- **Drawing Skills.** Assign the step-by-step instructions in the chapter. This chapter teaches how to create a bill of materials by extracting attributes from existing blocks.

- **Extracting Attributes.** To complete the steps outlined in the textbook, students will need the *attext.txt*, *extract.dcl*, and *extract.lsp* files from the CD-ROM. These files must be copied to the same folder as the *extract.dwg* file. Otherwise, the exercise will not work.

ASSESS

- **Review Questions.** Ask students to complete the Review Questions. Discuss their answers in class. Answers are found in the Answer Keys section of this guide.

- **Applying AutoCAD Skills.** Assign the activities at the end of the chapter.

- **Reteaching.** Due to the culminating nature of this chapter, it is a good idea to periodically review the steps leading up to this point. This exercise will reinforce the learning process and benefit all students.

- **Enrichment.** Assign the Challenge Your Thinking questions at the end of the chapter. Assign the Using Problem-Solving Skills activities at the end of the chapter.

- **Communication.** Assign Challenge Your Thinking questions 1 and 2.

- **Test.** Use the Chapter Test printed in this guide, or create a test using the **Exam***View* test generator on the CD-ROM. The answers can be found in the Answer Keys section of this guide.

CLOSE

- Using the previously created villa floor plan, have your students generate a bill of materials. Use an architectural text to verify what items should be included in this list.

Transparency Masters for Fundamentals Text

The transparency masters correlate with the textbook's six parts. The first transparency master for each part lists the topics covered in that part of the textbook. The remaining transparencies illustrate specific topics covered in the part.

You may want to use the transparencies to introduce topics that will be covered in the part before students begin working through the chapters. Later, as students begin each chapter, you could show the related transparencies. See the Part Instructional Plans (such as page 101) for information on which transparencies to use with each chapter.

TM-1A	**Part 1 Groundwork**	**145**
TM-1B	Opening Drawings from AutoCAD's Today Window	146
TM-1C	Creating Drawings Using AutoCAD's Today Window	147
TM-1D	Drawing Ellipses	148
TM-1E	Selecting Objects	149
TM-1F	Entering Coordinates	150
TM-2A	**Part 2 Drawing Aids and Controls**	**151**
TM-2B	Quadrant Points	152
TM-2C	Orthographic Projection	153
TM-2D	Construction Lines	154
TM-3A	**Part 3 Drawing and Editing**	**155**
TM-3B	Arrays	156
TM-3C	Stretching	157
TM-3D	Hatching	158
TM-4A	**Part 4 Preparing and Printing a Drawing**	**159**
TM-4B	Lineweights	160
TM-4C	Layers	161
TM-4D	Viewports in Model Space	162

Copyright © Glencoe/McGraw-Hill

TM-5A	**Part 5 Dimensioning and Tolerancing**	**163**
TM-5B	Linear and Baseline Dimensions	164
TM-5C	Dimension Styles	165
TM-5D	Tolerancing Methods	166
TM-6A	**Part 6 Groups and Details**	**167**
TM-6B	Blocks	168
TM-6C	Symbol Library	169
TM-6D	AutoCAD DesignCenter	170

Part 1 Groundwork

- Ch. 1 Tour of AutoCAD
- Ch. 2 User Interface
- Ch. 3 Entering Commands
- Ch. 4 Basic Objects
- Ch. 5 Object Selection
- Ch. 6 Entering Coordinates
- Ch. 7 Securing Help
- Ch. 8 File Maintenance

TM-1B
Fundamentals

Opening Drawings from AutoCAD's Today Window

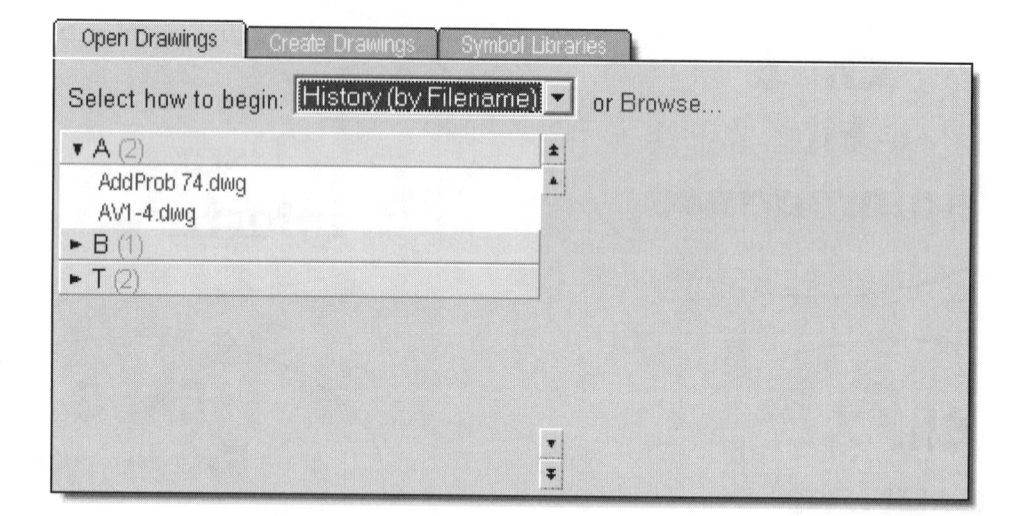

TM-1C
Fundamentals

Creating Drawings Using AutoCAD's Today Window

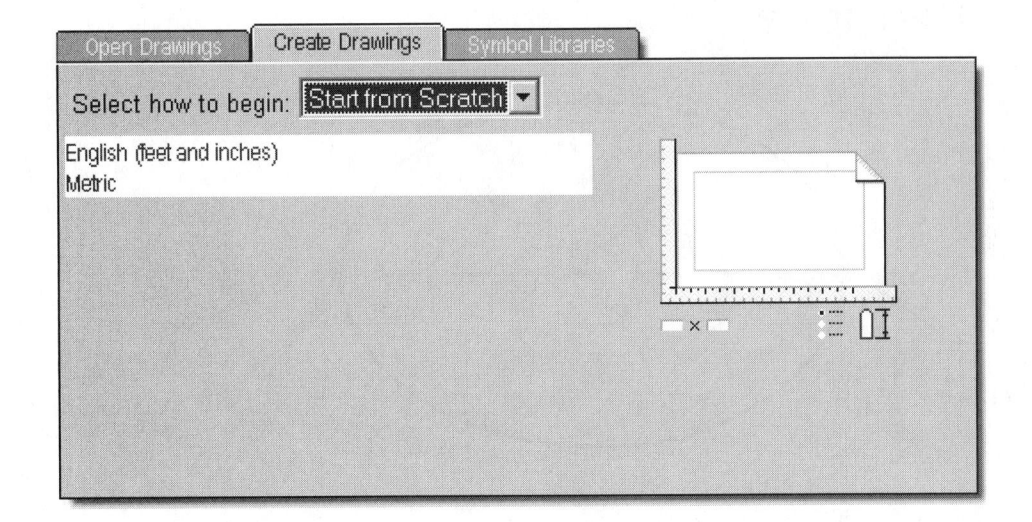

Drawing Ellipses

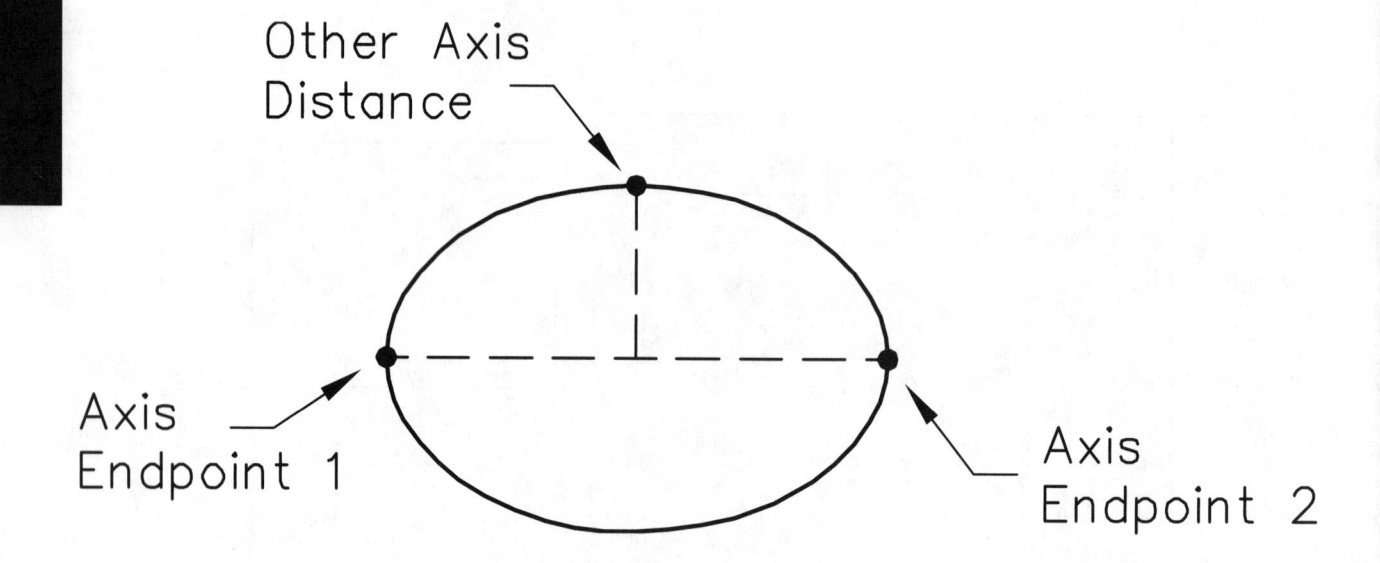

Other Axis Distance

Axis Endpoint 1

Axis Endpoint 2

TM-1D
Fundamentals

148

Copyright © Glencoe/McGraw-Hill

TM-1E
Fundamentals

Selecting Objects

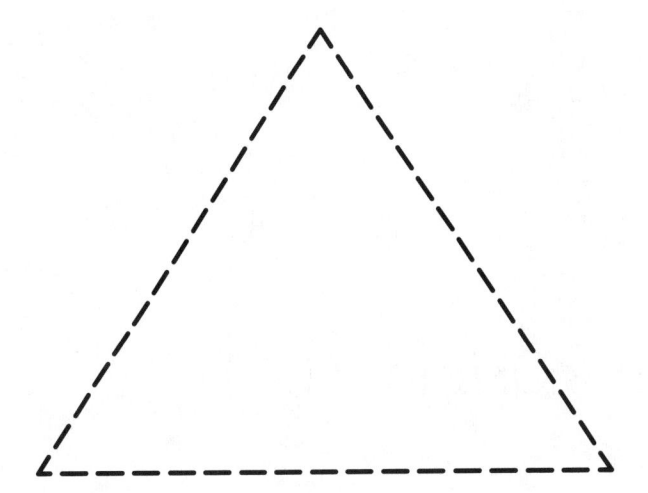

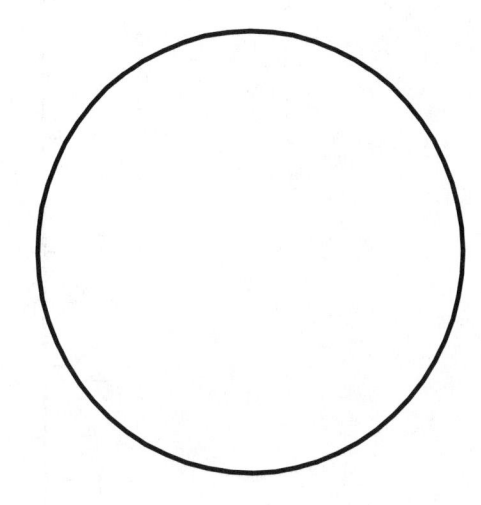

Entering Coordinates

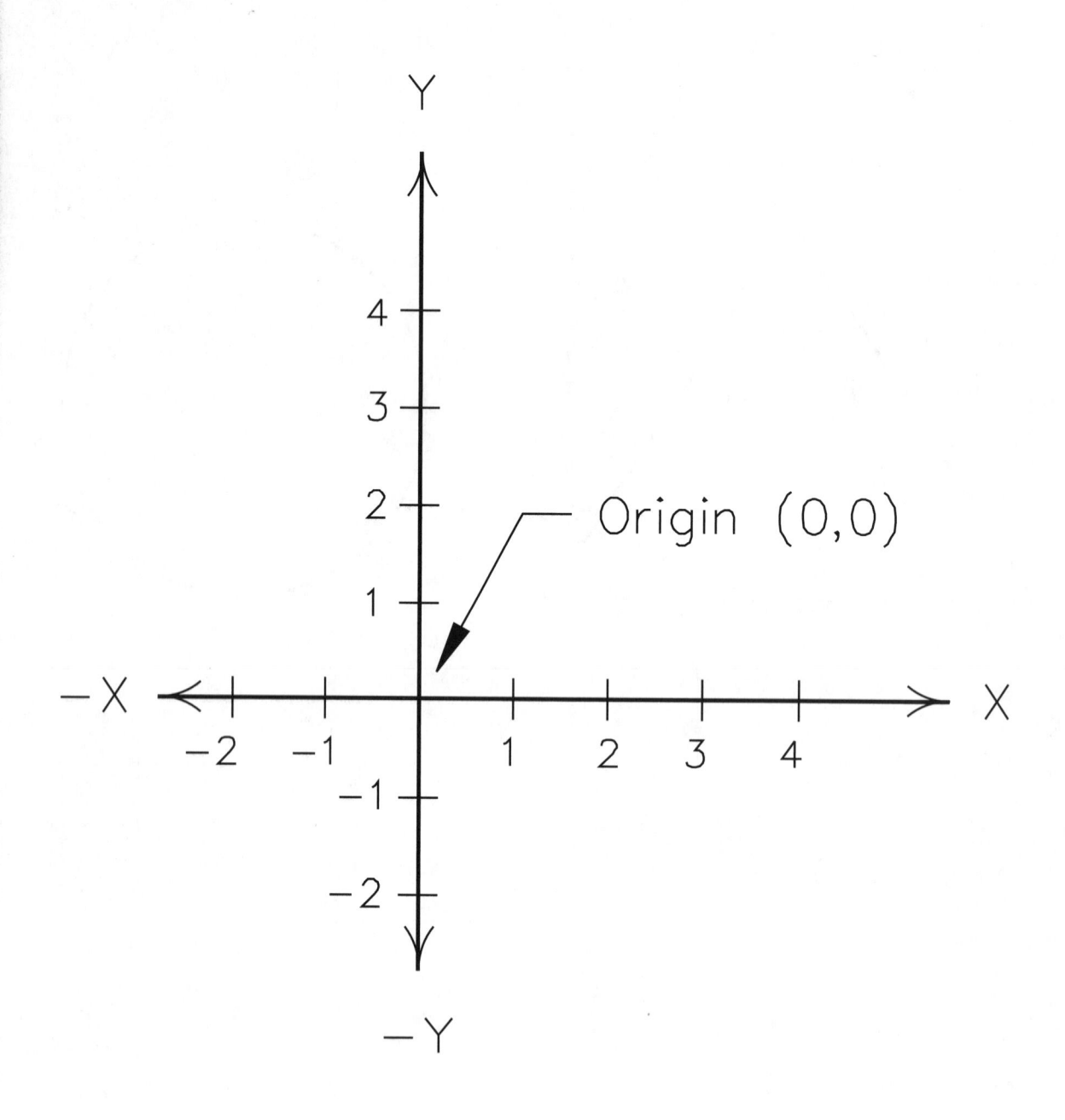

TM-1F
Fundamentals

Origin (0,0)

TM-2A
Fundamentals

Part 2 Drawing Aids and Controls

- Ch. 9 Object Snap
- Ch. 13 Panning and Viewing
- Ch. 10 Helpful Drawing Features
- Ch. 12 AutoCAD's Magnifying Glass
- Ch. 11 Construction Aids

Quadrant Points

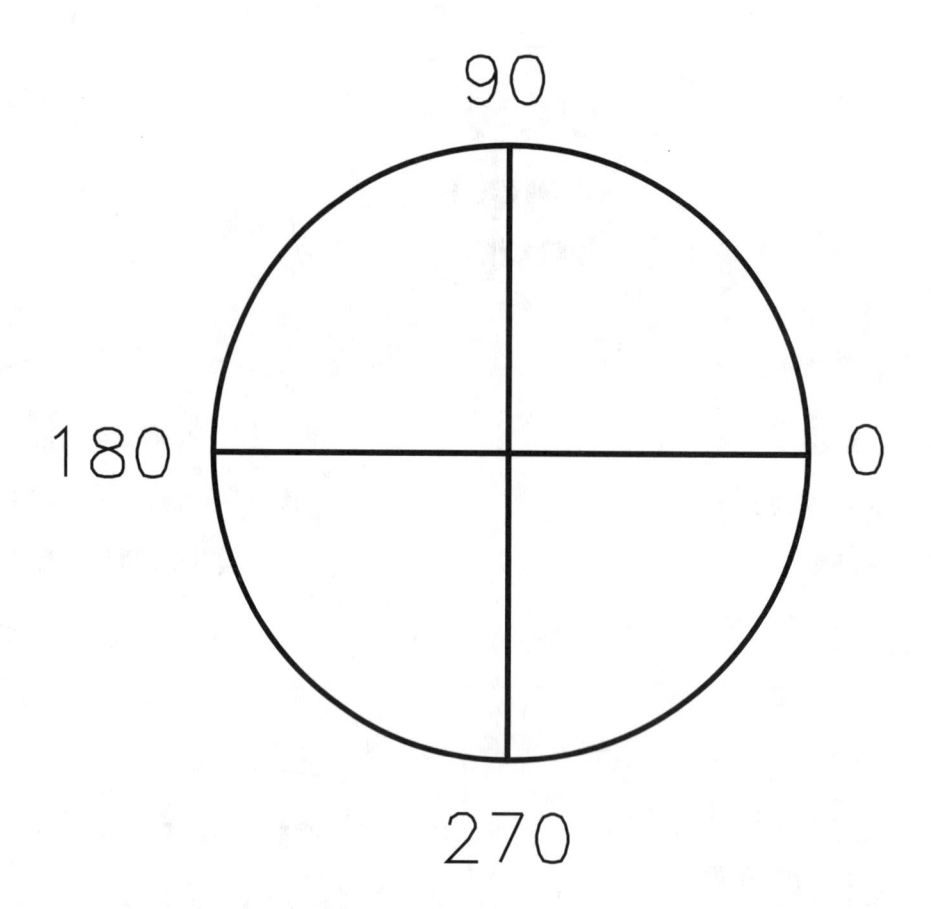

```
       90


180         0


      270
```

TM-2C
Fundamentals

Orthographic Projection

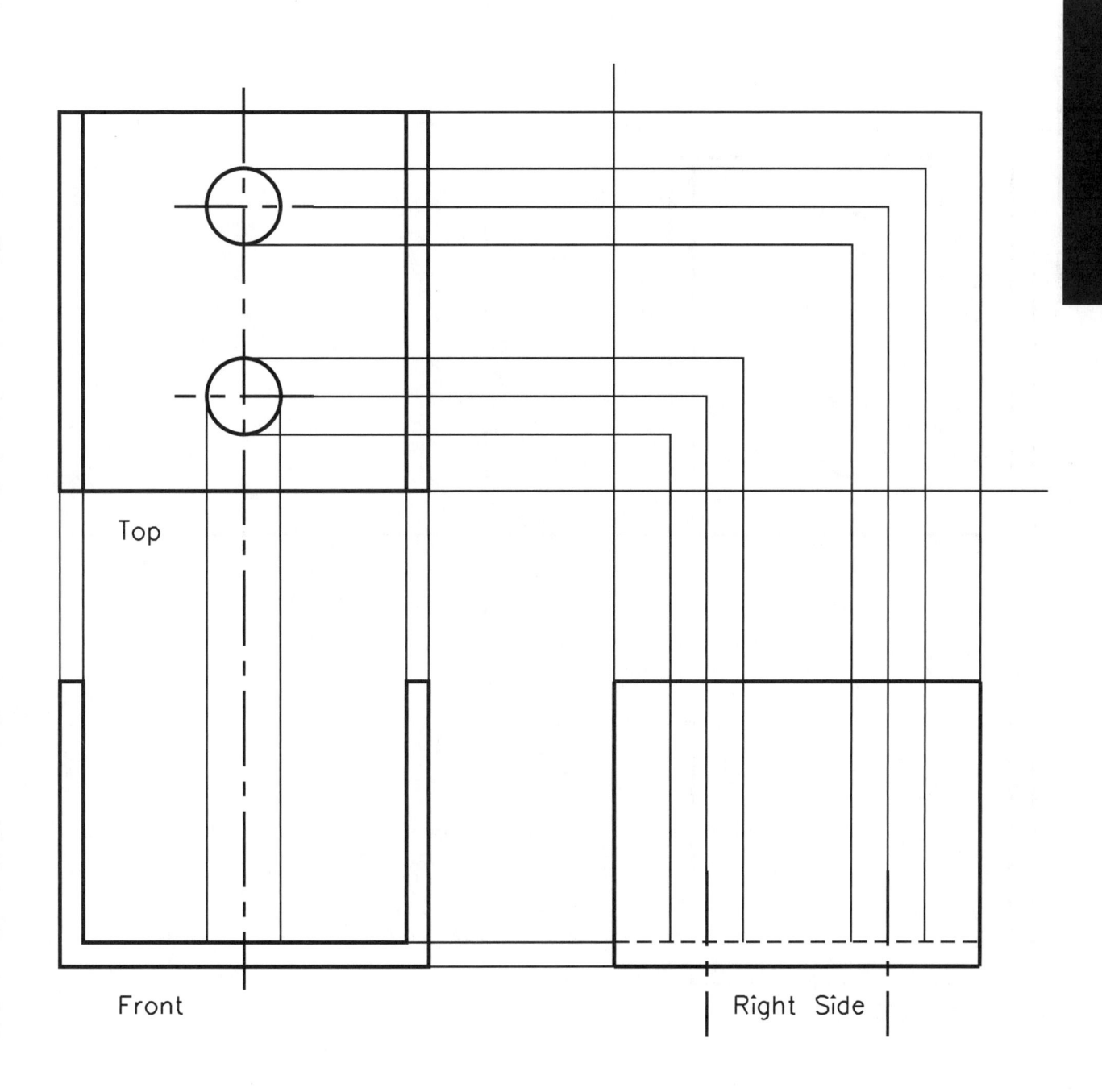

Top

Front

Right Side

Copyright © Glencoe/McGraw-Hill

Construction Lines

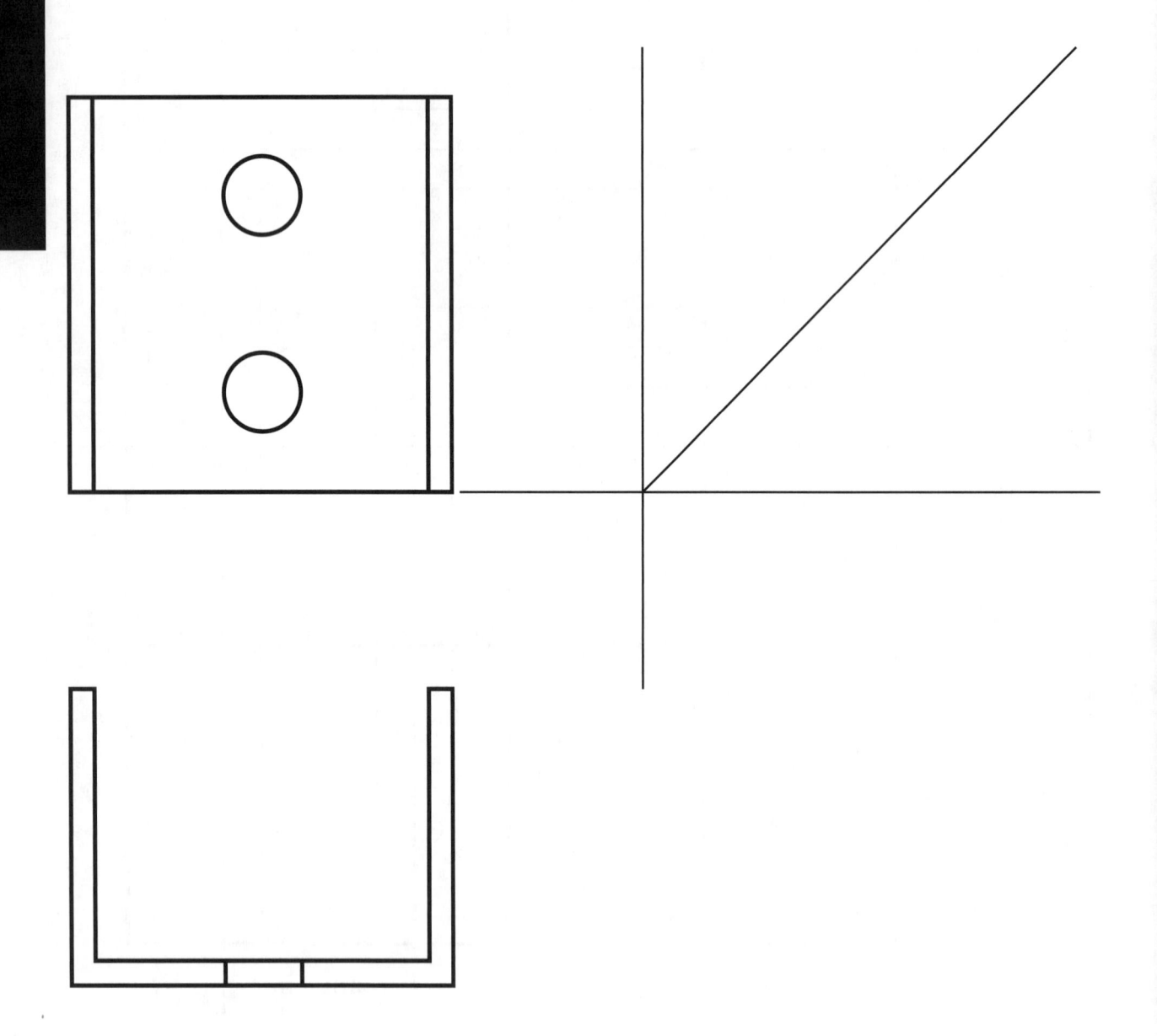

TM-2D
Fundamentals

Part 3 Drawing and Editing

TM-3A
Fundamentals

- Ch. 14 Solid and Curved Objects
- Ch. 20 Hatching and Sketching
- Ch. 15 Adding and Altering Objects
- Ch. 19 Text Editing and Spell Checking
- Ch. 16 Moving and Duplicating Objects
- Ch. 18 Notes and Specifications
- Ch. 17 Modifying and Maneuvering

Copyright © Glencoe/McGraw-Hill

Arrays

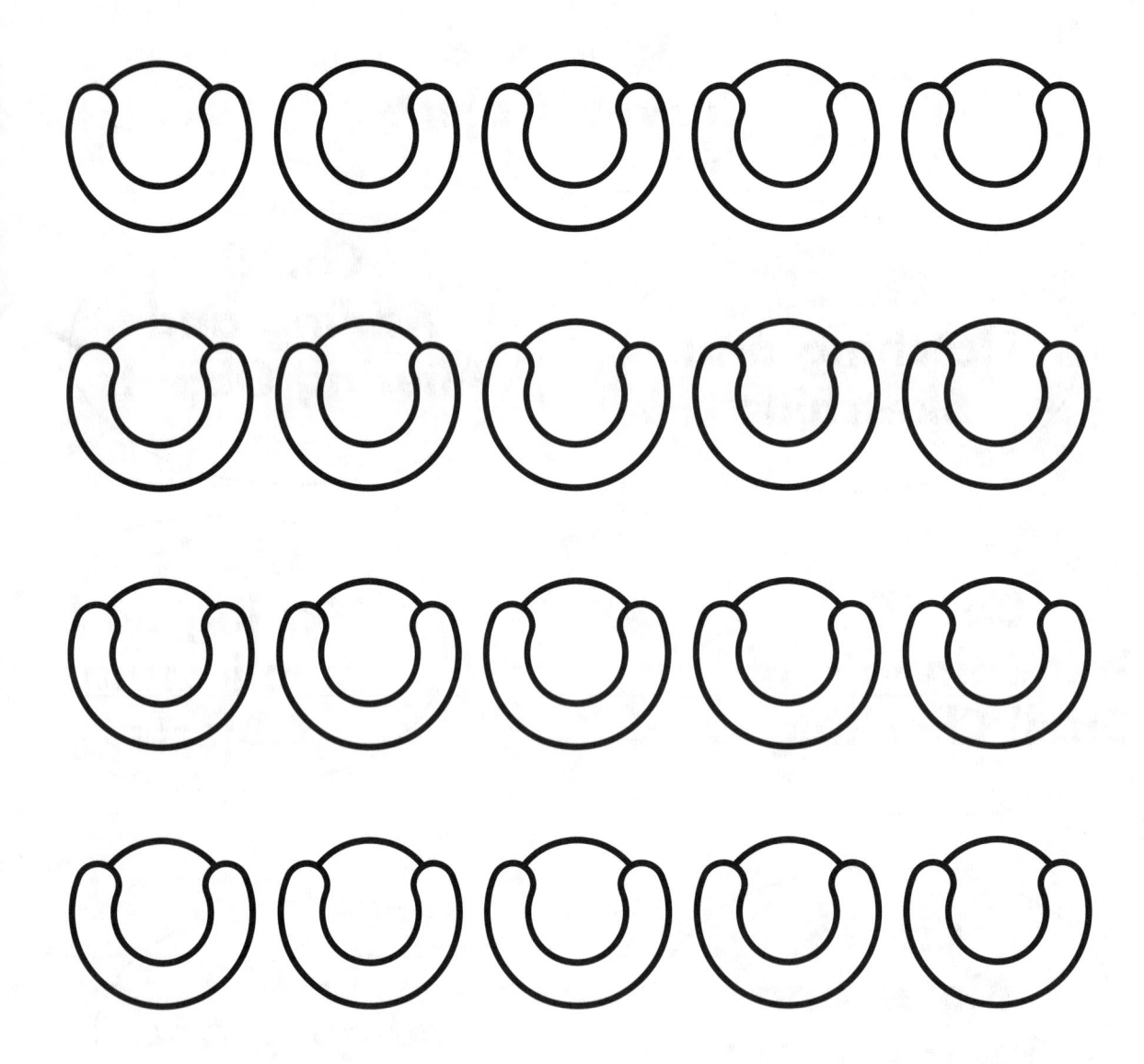

Stretching

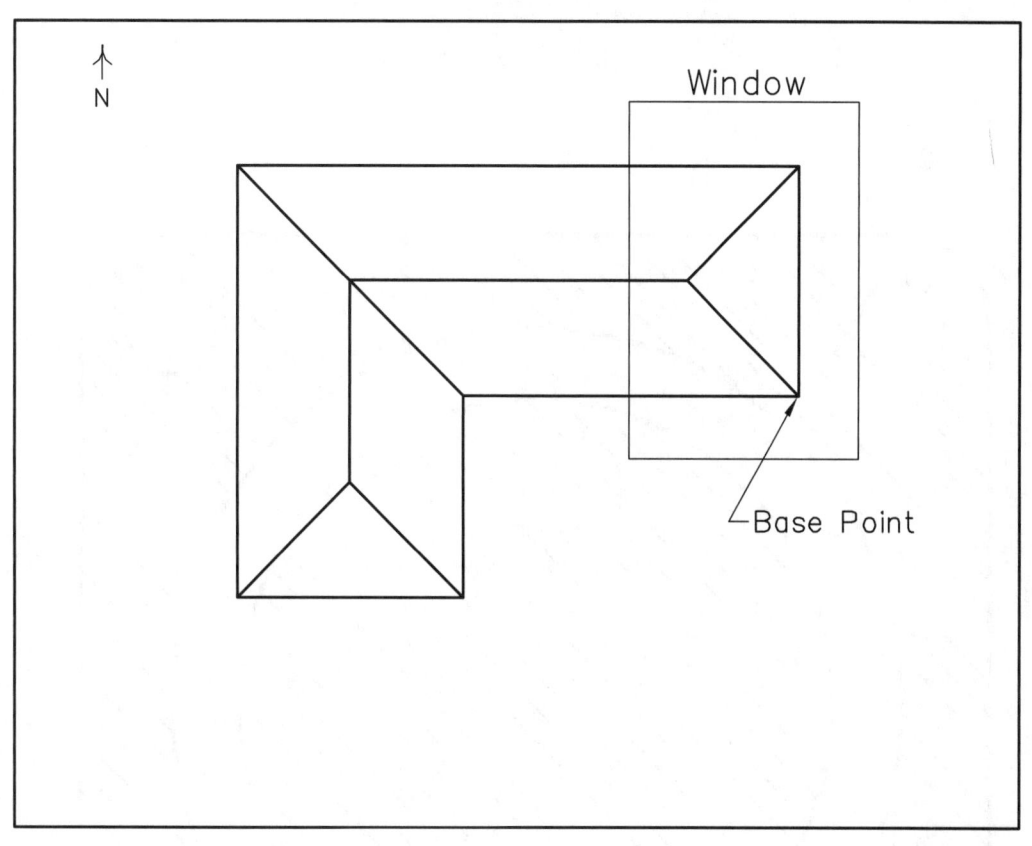

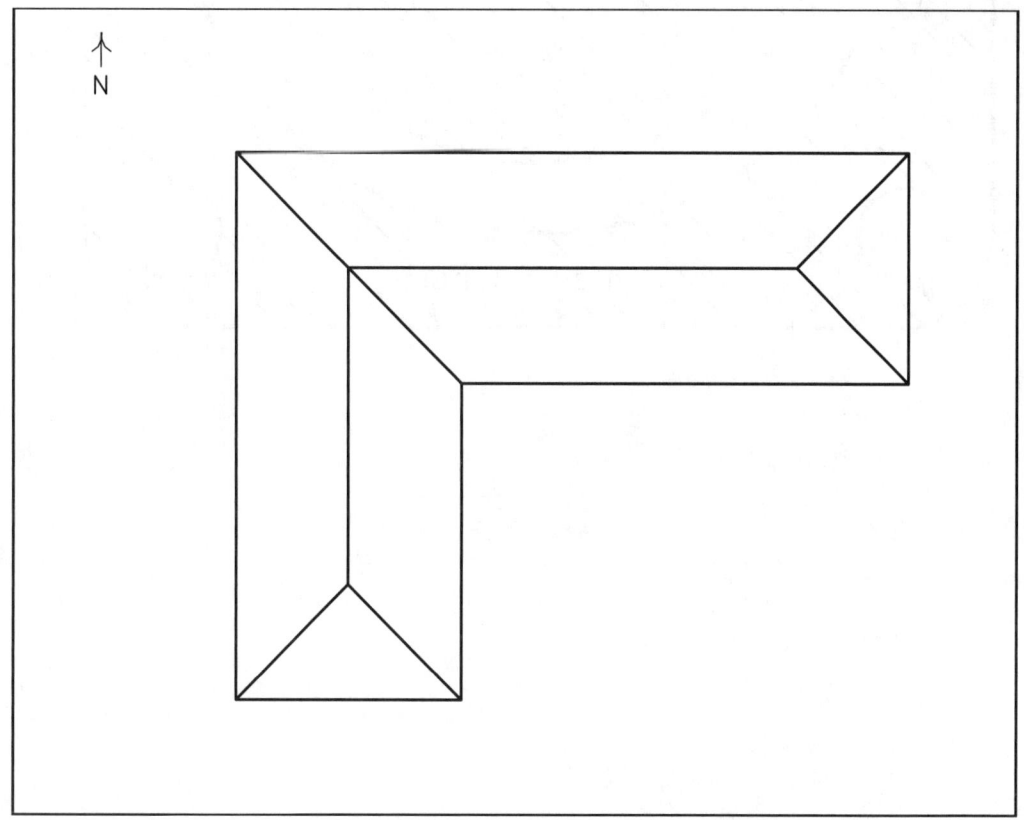

TM-3C
Fundamentals

Window

Base Point

N

Hatching

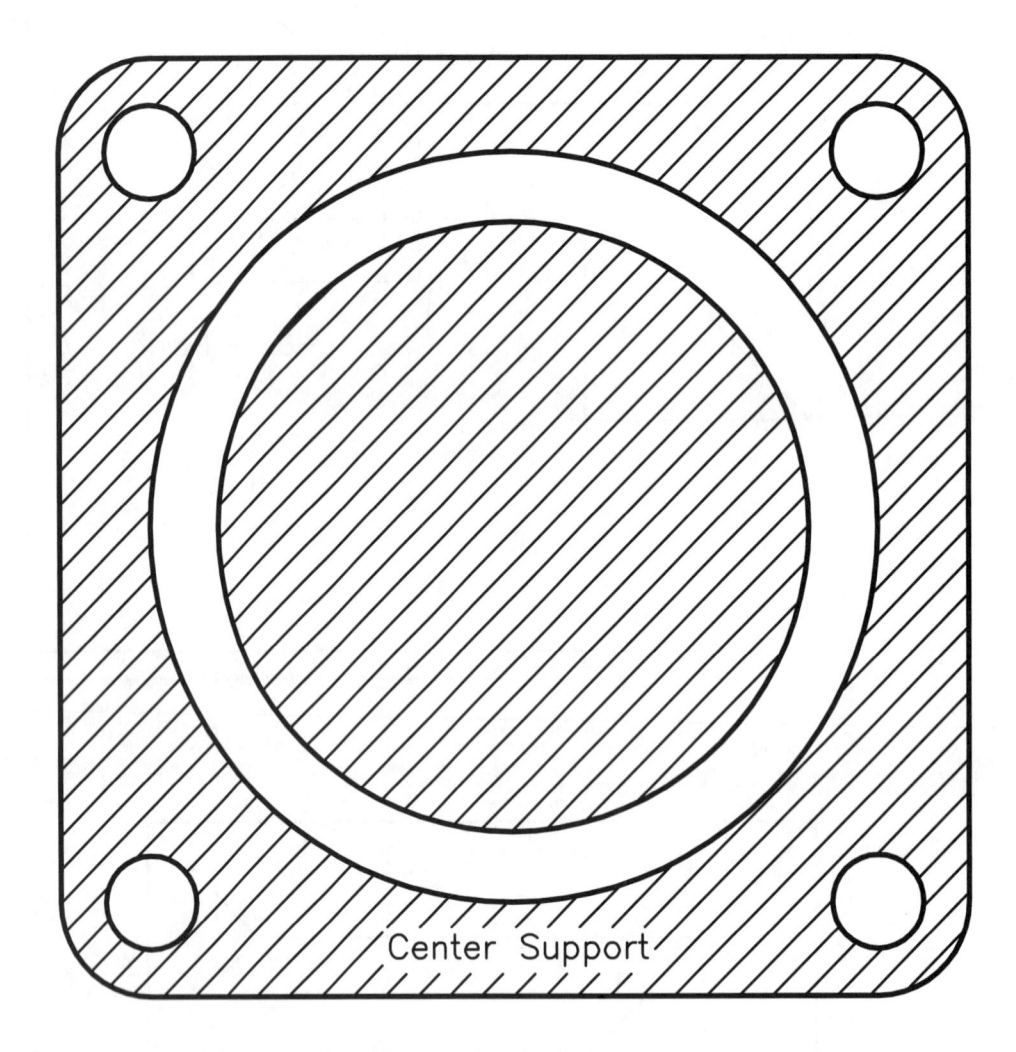

TM-3D
Fundamentals

Center Support

Part 4 Preparing and Printing a Drawing

TM-4A
Fundamentals

- Ch. 21 Drawing Setup
- Ch. 24 Multiple Viewports
- Ch. 22 Layers and Linetypes
- Ch. 23 Plotting and Printing

TM-4B
Fundamentals

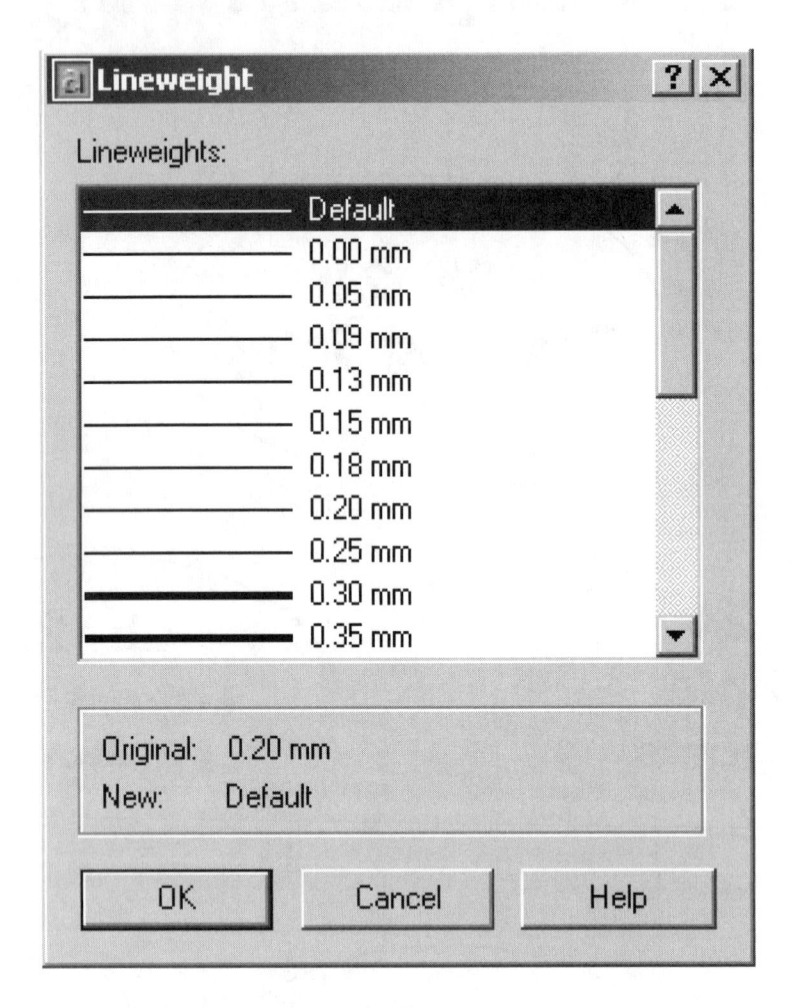

Lineweights

Lineweight	? ×

Lineweights:

———————	Default
———————	0.00 mm
———————	0.05 mm
———————	0.09 mm
———————	0.13 mm
———————	0.15 mm
———————	0.18 mm
———————	0.20 mm
———————	0.25 mm
———————	0.30 mm
———————	0.35 mm

Original: 0.20 mm
New: Default

[OK]   [Cancel]   [Help]

Layers

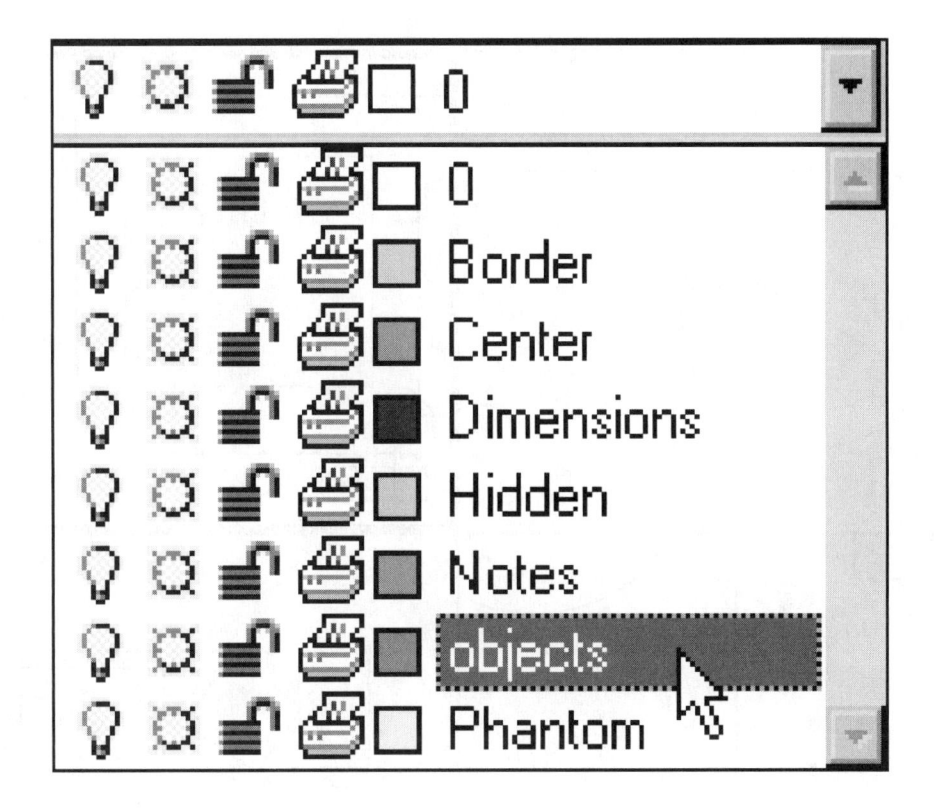

Viewports in Model Space

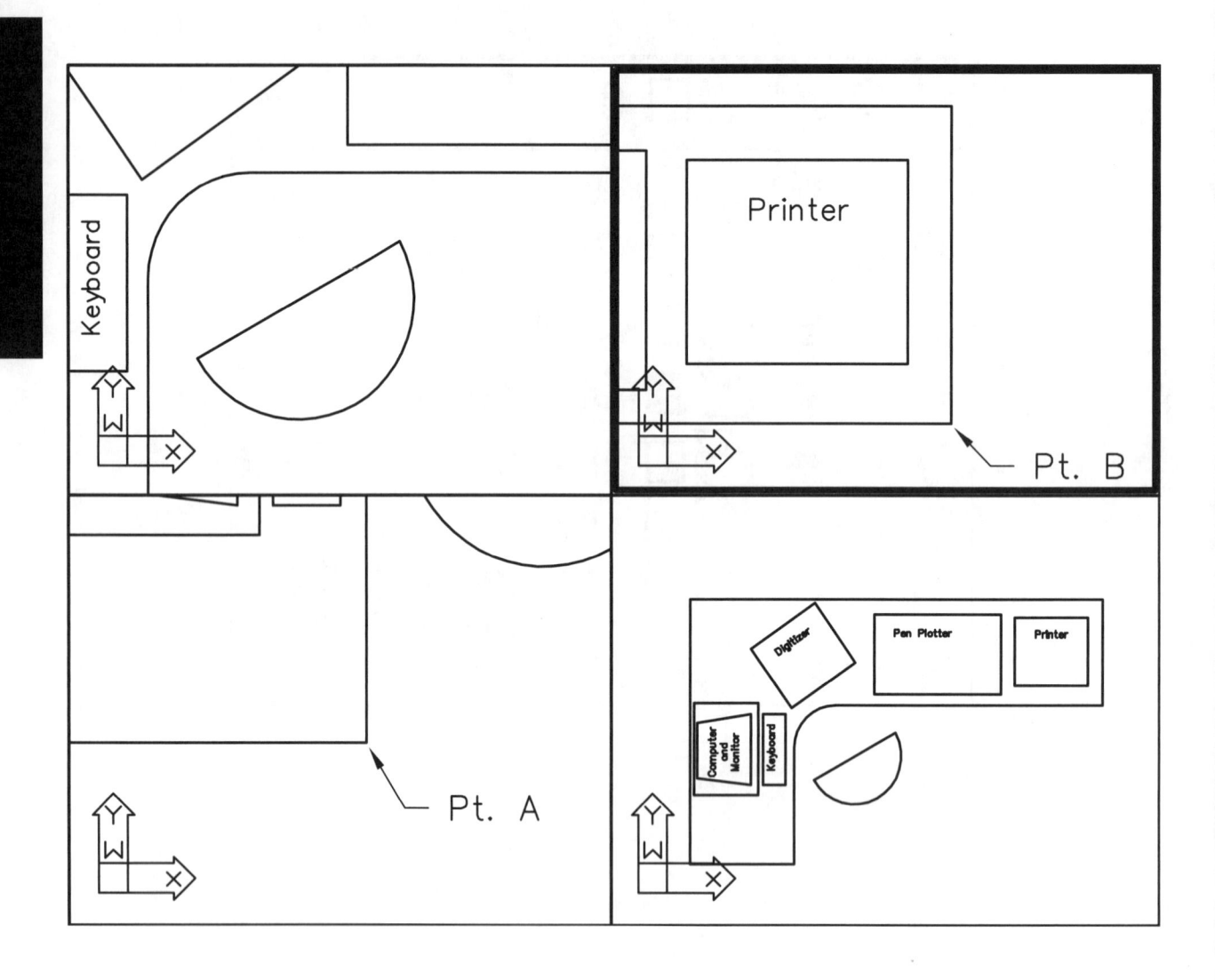

TM-4D
Fundamentals

Draw and edit in more than one view.

Part 5 Dimensioning and Tolerancing

Ch. 25 Basic Dimensioning

Ch. 29 A Calculating Strategy

Ch. 26 Advanced Dimensioning

Ch. 28 Tolerancing

Ch. 27 Fine-Tuning Dimensions

TM-5B
Fundamentals

Linear and Baseline Dimensions

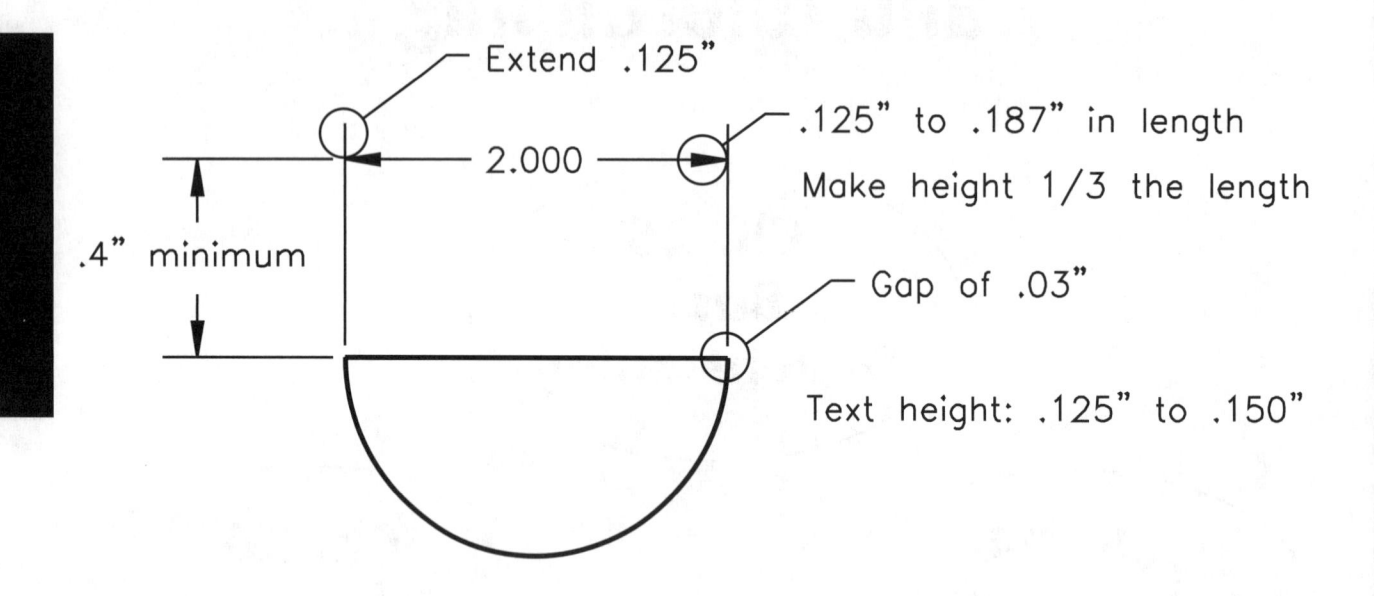

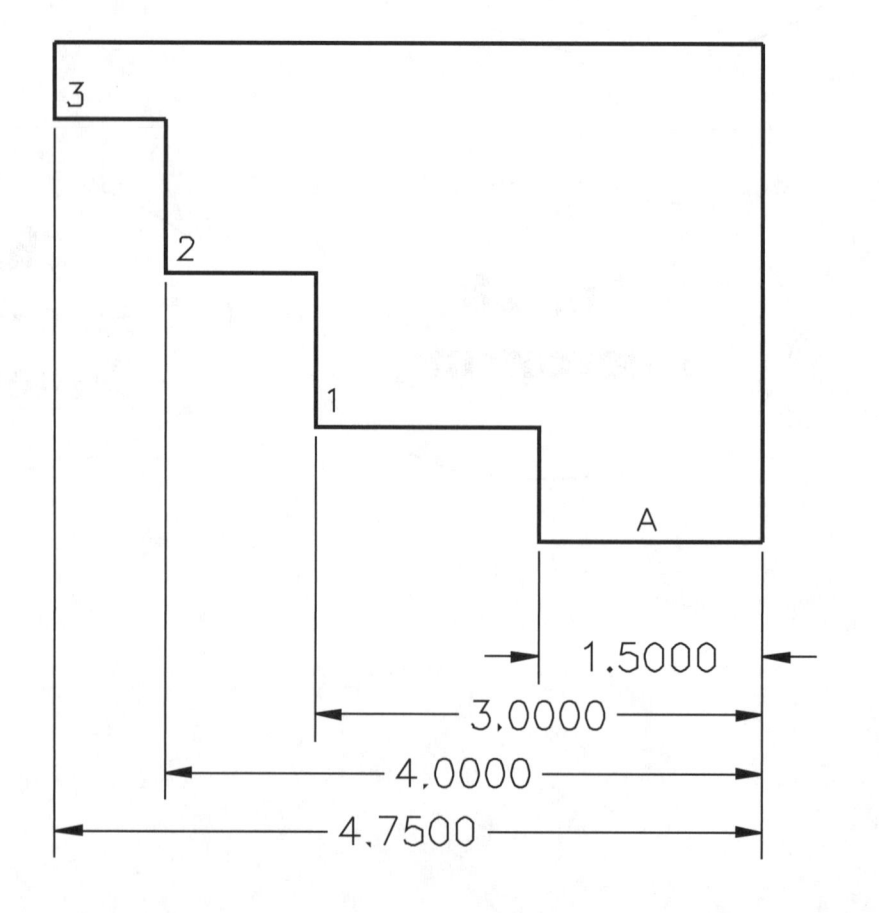

Extend .125"

2.000

.125" to .187" in length
Make height 1/3 the length

.4" minimum

Gap of .03"

Text height: .125" to .150"

3

2

1

A

1.5000

3.0000

4.0000

4.7500

Copyright © Glencoe/McGraw-Hill

TM-5C
Fundamentals

Dimension Styles

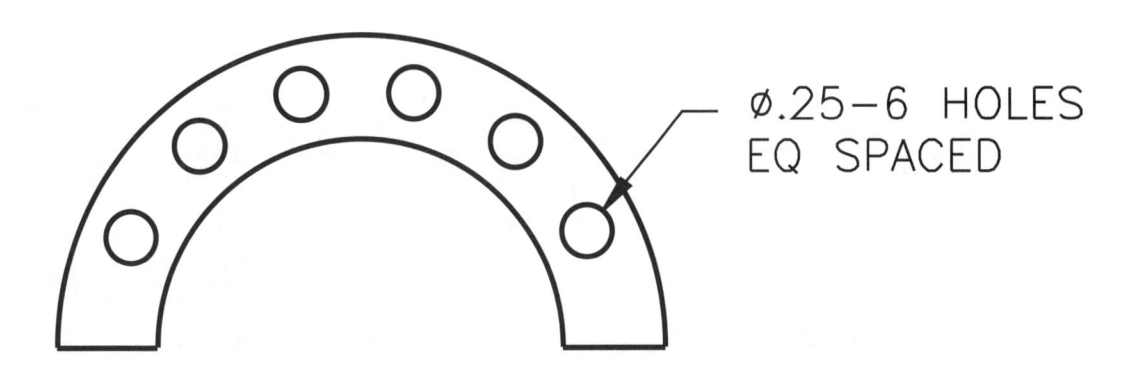

Ø.25−6 HOLES EQ SPACED

Leaders

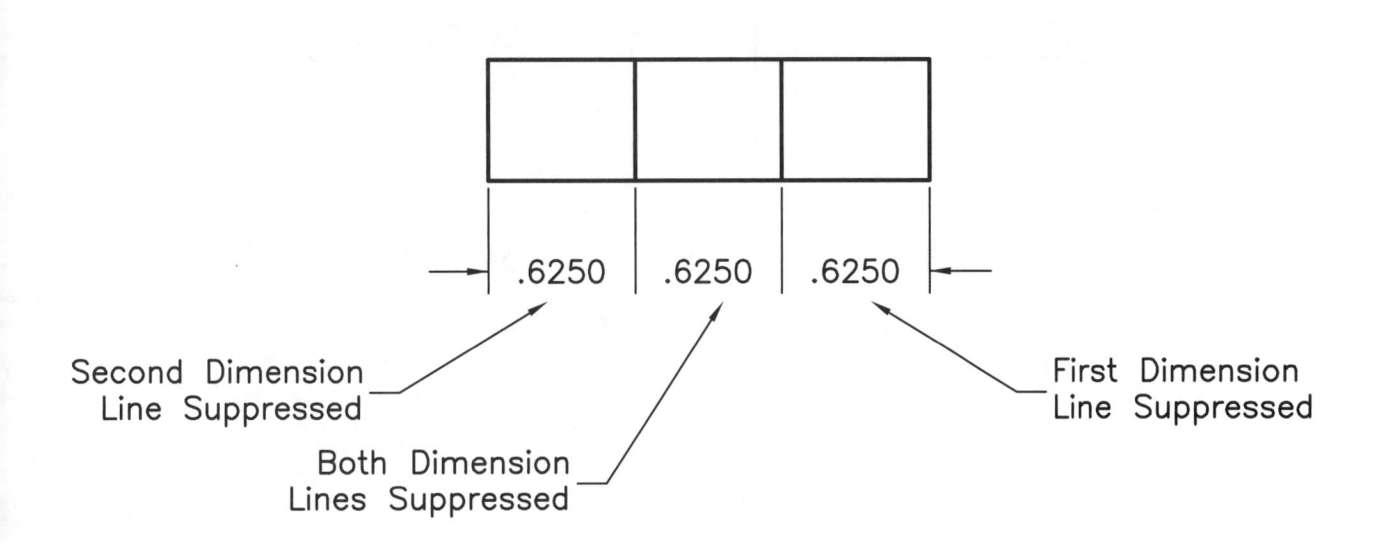

.6250 .6250 .6250

Second Dimension Line Suppressed

First Dimension Line Suppressed

Both Dimension Lines Suppressed

Dimension Style Options

TM-5D
Fundamentals

Tolerancing Methods

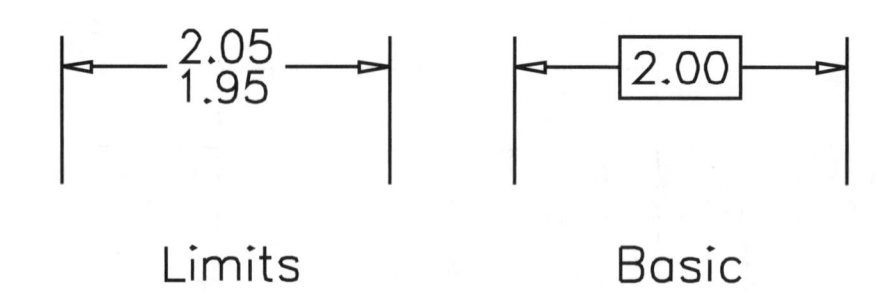

$\leftarrow 2.00 \pm .05 \rightarrow$ $\leftarrow 2.00^{+.10}_{-.05} \rightarrow$

Symmetrical   Deviation

$\leftarrow \begin{array}{c} 2.05 \\ 1.95 \end{array} \rightarrow$ $\leftarrow \boxed{2.00} \rightarrow$

Limits   Basic

TM-6A
Fundamentals

Part 6 Groups and Details

- Ch. 30 Groups
- Ch. 34 Bills of Materials
- Ch. 31 Building Blocks
- Ch. 33 Attributes
- Ch. 32 Symbol Libraries

TM-6B
Fundamentals

Blocks

Living Room

Coffee Table

End Table

Sofa

Chair

Easy Chair

Plant

Symbol Library

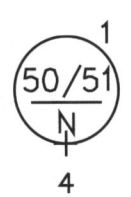

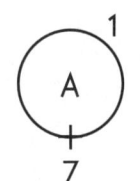

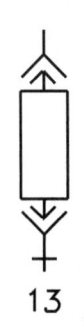

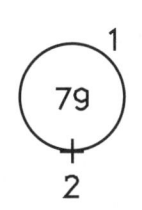

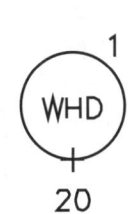

TM-6C
Fundamentals

TM-6D
Fundamentals

AutoCAD DesignCenter

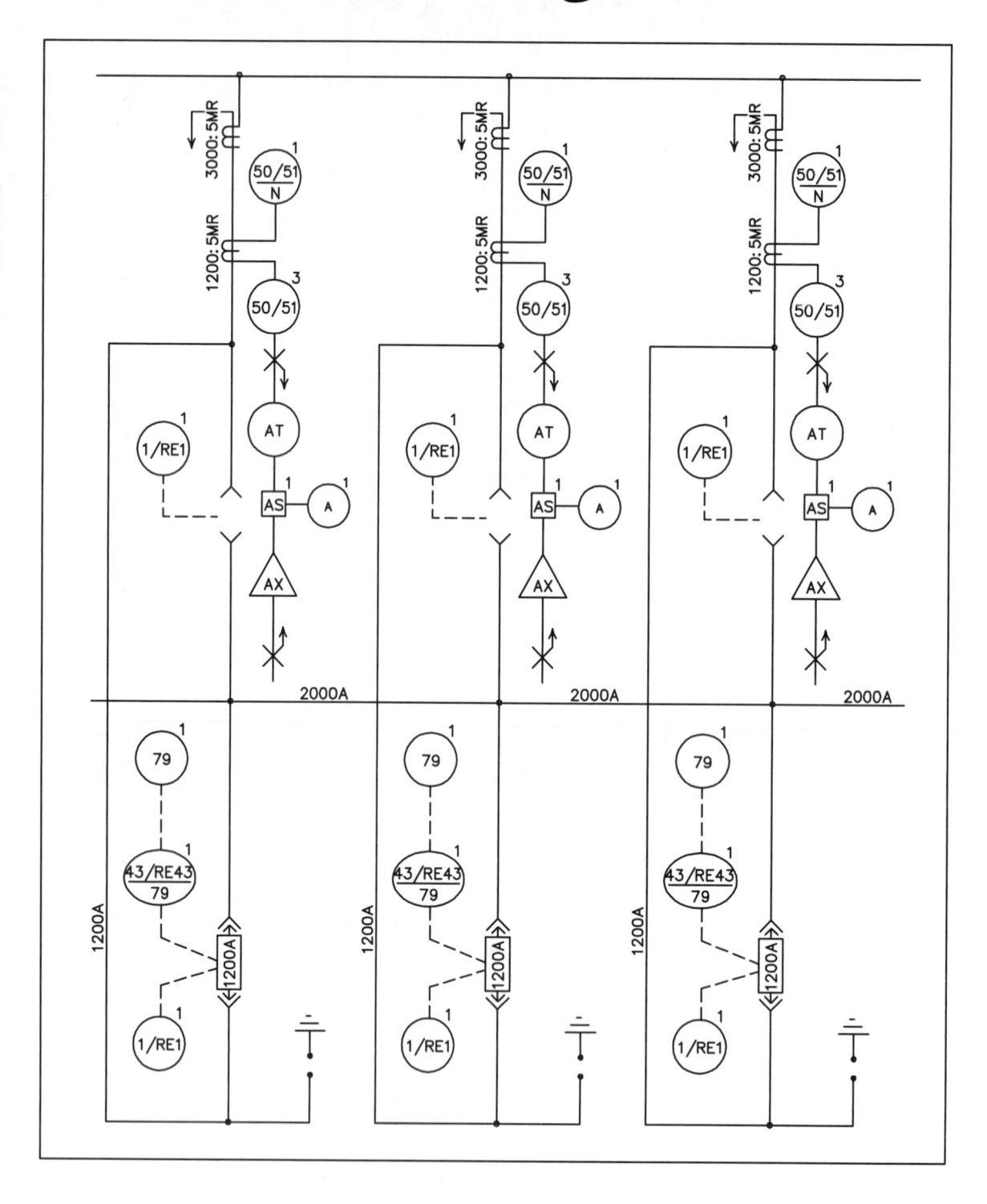

Use AutoCAD DesignCenter to insert symbols into a drawing.

Chapter Tests for Fundamentals Text

This section contains tests for each of the 34 chapters in the *Fundamentals* text. Answers can be found on pages 221-222.

Part 1 Groundwork
Chapter 1	Tour of AutoCAD	173
Chapter 2	User Interface	174
Chapter 3	Entering Commands	175
Chapter 4	Basic Objects	176
Chapter 5	Object Selection	177
Chapter 6	Entering Coordinates	178
Chapter 7	Securing Help	179
Chapter 8	File Maintenance	180

Part 2 Drawing Aids and Controls
Chapter 9	Object Snap	181
Chapter 10	Helpful Drawing Features	182
Chapter 11	Construction Aids	183
Chapter 12	AutoCAD's Magnifying Glass	184
Chapter 13	Panning and Viewing	185

Part 3 Drawing and Editing
Chapter 14	Solid and Curved Objects	186
Chapter 15	Adding and Altering Objects	187
Chapter 16	Moving and Duplicating Objects	188
Chapter 17	Modifying and Maneuvering	189
Chapter 18	Notes and Specifications	190
Chapter 19	Text Editing and Spell Checking	191
Chapter 20	Hatching and Sketching	192

Part 4 Preparing and Printing a Drawing
Chapter 21	Drawing Setup	193
Chapter 22	Layers and Linetypes	194
Chapter 23	Plotting and Printing	195
Chapter 24	Multiple Viewports	196

Copyright © Glencoe/McGraw-Hill

Part 5 Dimensioning and Tolerancing
Chapter 25   Basic Dimensioning 197
Chapter 26   Advanced Dimensioning 198
Chapter 27   Fine-Tuning Dimensions 199
Chapter 28   Tolerancing 200
Chapter 29   A Calculating Strategy 201

Part 6 Groups and Details
Chapter 30   Groups. 202
Chapter 31   Building Blocks 203
Chapter 32   Symbol Libraries 204
Chapter 33   Attributes. 205
Chapter 34   Bills of Materials 206

Name _____   Class Period _____   Time _____

TEST - Fundamentals Text   *Chapter 1* Tour of AutoCAD

Multiple Choice

Directions: Circle the letter of the choice that BEST completes the statement or answers the question.

1. To start AutoCAD, which of the following actions should you take?
   A. type ACAD and press the ENTER key
   B. double-click the AutoCAD 2002 icon on the Windows desktop
   C. pick the Open Drawings tab in the Today window
   D. pick the Start from Scratch button in the Startup dialog box

2. Which of the following functions does AutoCAD *not* perform?
   A. producing two-dimensional drawings
   B. editing three-dimensional models
   C. animating two-dimensional drawings
   D. designing maps, buildings, and bridges

3. To preview a drawing file while browsing in AutoCAD's Today window,
   A. pick Open Drawings, select Browse, and then locate and single-click the name of the file.
   B. enter the PREVIEW command at the keyboard.
   C. open the drawing file.
   D. double-click the name of the file.

4. How can you enlarge your view of a drawing so that you can view details?
   A. pick the Zoom Window button
   B. enter the ENLARGE command at the keyboard
   C. double-click in the area of the drawing you want to enlarge
   D. pick the Display button

5. What command can you enter to help you distinguish the parts of a complex assembly drawing?
   A. BREAK
   B. SHADE
   C. COLOR
   D. VIEW

Completion

Directions: In the space at the left, write the word or words that BEST complete the statement or answer the question.

_____   6. Buttons in AutoCAD appear on strips called _____.

_____   7. To open a file while browsing in the Today window, single-click the file name and press the _____ button.

_____   8. The _____ command exits AutoCAD after asking whether you want to save your changes.

_____   9. The _____ prompt, which appears at in the lower left area of the AutoCAD window, allows you to key in commands and information.

_____   10. The main portion of the AutoCAD window is known as the _____. (two words)

Copyright © Glencoe/McGraw-Hill

Name _____   Class Period _____   Time _____

TEST - Fundamentals Text   *Chapter 2* User Interface

Multiple Choice

Directions: Circle the letter of the choice that BEST completes the statement or answers the question.

1. The pull-down menus, docked and floating toolbars, command window, and status bar are all parts of the
   A. drawing area.
   B. Today window.
   C. toolbars.
   D. AutoCAD window.

2. In a pull-down menu, when you pick an item that contains a small arrow pointing to the right,
   A. a cascading menu appears.
   B. a dialog box appears.
   C. the command or function attached to that menu item executes.
   D. further options appear at the command line.

3. The status of various AutoCAD modes and settings is shown in the
   A. pull-down menus.
   B. command window.
   C. status bar.
   D. Toolbars dialog box.

4. When you right-click a button on a docked toolbar, it
   A. becomes a floating toolbar.
   B. closes.
   C. displays a list of toolbars from which you can open another toolbar.
   D. enters the command or function associated with the button.

5. To move a floating toolbar, you should
   A. click the x in the upper right corner of the toolbar.
   B. pick the top of the toolbar and drag it to a new location.
   C. move the pointer to the edge of the toolbar until a double arrow appears and then drag it to a new location.
   D. position the cursor over the toolbar, right-click, and select Move from the list of options.

Completion

Directions: In the space at the left, write the word or words that BEST complete the statement or answer the question.

_____   6. The special cursor AutoCAD displays in the drawing area is the _____.

_____   7. A _____ toolbar is one that is locked at the edge of the drawing area.

_____   8. To display a dialog box that allows you to manage which toolbars display on the screen, enter the _____ command.

_____   9. Vertical and horizontal _____ are used to move a drawing up and down and back and forth in the viewing window.

_____   10. Pull-down menu items that display ellipsis points (...) display a(n) _____ when you pick them. *(two words)*

Name _____ Class Period _____ Time _____

TEST - Fundamentals Text — *Chapter 3* Entering Commands

Multiple Choice

Directions: Circle the letter of the choice that BEST completes the statement or answers the question.

1. From which pull-down menu can you open a drawing file?
   A. File
   B. Edit
   C. Draw
   D. View

2. The original way to enter a command in AutoCAD was to
   A. pick a button from a toolbar.
   B. select an item from a pull-down menu.
   C. enter the command at the keyboard.
   D. right-click with the pointing device and choose from a list of commands.

3. The easiest way to find out what an unfamiliar button on a toolbar does is to
   A. rest the cursor on the button until a tooltip appears.
   B. position the cursor over the button and right-click.
   C. double-click the bar at the top of the toolbar.
   D. hold down the SHIFT key while picking the button.

4. To re-enter the most recently used command,
   A. type the letter R and press ENTER.
   B. press CTRL E.
   C. type EN and press ENTER.
   D. press the spacebar.

5. The default units in AutoCAD represent
   A. inches.
   B. feet.
   C. meters.
   D. any length; units are determined by the user.

Completion

Directions: In the space at the left, write the word or words that BEST complete the statement or answer the question.

_____ 6. A series of dialog boxes that steps you through a sequence or procedure is known as a(n) _____.

_____ 7. A _____ is an abbreviated version of a command that you can enter at the keyboard to enter the command quickly. *(two words)*

_____ 8. When you are using the LINE command, the stretching effect that occurs before you pick a second point is known as the _____ effect.

_____ 9. When you press the L key and then press ENTER, AutoCAD enters the _____ command.

_____ 10. Right-clicking in AutoCAD produces a context-sensitive _____. *(two words)*

Copyright © Glencoe/McGraw-Hill

175

Name _____   Class Period _____   Time _____

TEST - Fundamentals Text   *Chapter 4* Basic Objects

Multiple Choice

Directions: Circle the letter of the choice that BEST completes the statement or answers the question.

1. The POLYGON command
   A. is used to create any type of polygon.
   B. allows you to create regular polygons only.
   C. contains Octagon and Pentagon options.
   D. is limited to creating polygons of 12 or fewer sides.

2. The ARC Continue option allows you to
   A. continue an arc immediately after drawing a line.
   B. continue an arc tangent to the previous arc.
   C. increase the radius of an arc.
   D. create a new arc at another location in the drawing without reentering the ARC command.

3. To create an elliptical arc,
   A. enter the ELLIPSE command and select the Arc option.
   B. enter the ARC command and select the Elliptical option.
   C. enter the CIRCLE command and select the Elliptical arc option.
   D. enter the ARC command and specify beginning, center, and endpoints to define the elliptical arc.

4. The DONUT command
   A. lets you specify the inside and outside diameters as well as the center.
   B. lets you produce multiple donuts without re-entering the DONUT command.
   C. produces solid-filled donuts.
   D. all of the above.

Completion

Directions: In the space at the left, write the word or words that BEST complete the statement or answer the question.

_____   5. A _____ polygon is one in which all the sides have the same length.

_____   6. A(n) _____ feature is one on which every point is the same distance from an imaginary center point.

_____   7. Circles that share a common center are known as _____ circles.

_____   8. Circles are _____ when they meet at a single point.

_____   9. The distance across a circle measured through its center point is the circle's _____.

_____   10. _____ and arcs are commonly used in AutoCAD to create two-dimensional representations of holes, cylinders, and other round objects.

Name _____   Class Period _____   Time _____

TEST - Fundamentals Text   *Chapter 5* Object Selection

Multiple Choice

Directions: Circle the letter of the choice that BEST completes the statement or answers the question.

1. Which of the following are *not* examples of objects?
   A. lines, circles, and arcs
   B. text, lines, and dimensions
   C. grips and selection sets
   D. points, arcs, and text

2. The ERASE command
   A. erases selected parts of an object.
   B. clears the entire screen using the ERASE Clear option.
   C. erases selected objects.
   D. automatically erases all objects from the drawing file.

3. When you use a Crossing window to select objects, AutoCAD selects
   A. only those objects that are completely contained within the window.
   B. objects that are contained within the window and those that cross the window boundary.
   C. only those objects that touch or cross the window boundary.
   D. all objects except those enclosed in the window boundary.

4. To restore an object that you have accidentally erased,
   A. press the ESC key.
   B. press ENTER a second time.
   C. enter the RESTORE command at the keyboard.
   D. pick the Undo button on the docked Standard toolbar.

5. The Last object selection option selects
   A. the last object or objects you created in the current drawing.
   B. all the objects you created the previous drawing file.
   C. the last object or objects you selected in the current drawing.
   D. the last endpoint of a series of line segments.

Completion

Directions: In the space at the left, write the word or words that BEST complete the statement or answer the question.

_____ 6. In AutoCAD, another term for *object* is _____.

_____ 7. The selection mode in which you select objects and then specify the command to perform on those objects is known as _____ selection. *(two words)*

_____ 8. _____ are the small boxes or "handles" that you can select and use to change an object's position or properties.

_____ 9. When you use the _____ option to select objects, only those objects that touch the boundary are selected, and it is not necessary to close the selection polygon.

_____ 10. The _____ option allows you to deselect some or all of the objects in a selection set.

Copyright © Glencoe/McGraw-Hill

Name _____ Class Period _____ Time _____

TEST - Fundamentals Text — *Chapter 6* Entering Coordinates

Multiple Choice

Directions: Circle the letter of the choice that BEST completes the statement or answers the question.

1. Relative point specification using the keyboard refers to
   A. entering a length and angle relative to the last point entry.
   B. using the cursor control keys to move the crosshairs around the screen.
   C. entering an X distance and Y distance relative to the last point entry.
   D. entering absolute coordinates for a specific point.

2. In a series of line segments, if you specify a line endpoint at a 90-degree angle from the current point, the line will be
   A. horizontal; the new endpoint will be to the right of the current point.
   B. horizontal; the new endpoint will be to the left of the current point.
   C. vertical; the new endpoint will be in the upward direction from the current point.
   D. vertical; the new endpoint will be in the downward direction from the current point.

3. In polar point specification, @7.5<180
   A. specifies a point 7.5 units in the upward direction from the current position.
   B. specifies a point 7.5 units in the downward direction from the current position.
   C. displays an error message.
   D. specifies a point 7.5 units horizontally to the left of the current position.

4. A coordinate entry method in which you can specify precise positions and angles by entering a single distance value and using alignment paths is
   A. polar tracking.
   B. relative.
   C. absolute.
   D. direct distance.

5. In the two-dimensional version of AutoCAD's world coordinate system, how many axes are used?
   A. 1
   B. 2
   C. 3
   D. 4

Completion

Directions: In the space at the left, write the word or words that BEST complete the statement or answer the question.

_____ 6. Together, the *x* and *y* values that specify a point in AutoCAD are known as a(n) _____. *(two words)*

_____ 7. Point specification in AutoCAD is based on the _____ coordinate system.

_____ 8. The _____ is the point at which both the *x* and the *y* value equal 0.

_____ 9. In the world coordinate system, in which direction does the Y axis run?

_____ 10. What symbol should you use to specify relative coordinates in AutoCAD?

Copyright © Glencoe/McGraw-Hill

Name _____ Class Period _____ Time _____

TEST - Fundamentals Text — *Chapter 7* Securing Help

Multiple Choice

Directions: Circle the letter of the choice that BEST completes the statement or answers the question.

1. You can obtain help in AutoCAD by
   A. entering HELP.
   B. pressing the CTRL and ? keys.
   C. entering HP.
   D. pressing the ESC key.

2. In AutoCAD's Today window, you can select any viewing option *except*
   A. History (by Date).
   B. History (by Filename).
   C. History (by Location).
   D. History (by Author).

3. Picking the Help button while a command is entered at the command line
   A. displays the Help Topics: AutoCAD Help dialog box.
   B. displays context-sensitive help on the active command.
   C. presents an error message indicating that you must exit the command before accessing Help.
   D. terminates the active command.

4. The purpose of the drawing preview feature is to
   A. show how drawings created in previous AutoCAD releases will look in AutoCAD 2002.
   B. help you locate files by displaying the currently selected drawing in a preview box.
   C. help you visualize how your finished drawing will look.
   D. set drawing parameters for a new drawing.

5. The fastest way to review new commands and features in AutoCAD 2002 is to
   A. pick Learning Assistance from the Help pull-down menu.
   B. write to Autodesk.
   C. pick What's New from the Help pull-down menu.
   D. pick the Help icon from the docked Standard toolbar.

6. Which button on the help screens allows you to return to the previous help screen?
   A. Back   C. >>
   B. Glossary   D. <<

Completion

Directions: In the space at the left, write the word or words that BEST complete the statement or answer the question.

_____ 7. ____ are the small representations of drawings that appear when you are browsing files.

_____ 8. One way to obtain help in AutoCAD is to press the ____ function key.

_____ 9. The ____ tab of the Help Topics dialog box allows you to obtain help on a topic by entering only the first few letters of the topic at the keyboard.

_____ 10. The ____ tab of the Help Topics dialog box allows you to phrase a specific question that you want answered. *(two words)*

Copyright © Glencoe/McGraw-Hill

Name   Class Period   Time

TEST - Fundamentals Text   *Chapter 8* File Maintenance

Multiple Choice

Directions: Circle the letter of the choice that BEST completes the statement or answers the question.

1. To rename a drawing file within AutoCAD,
   A. double-click the file name and enter a new name for the file.
   B. right-click the file name, then select **Rename** from the shortcut menu and enter a new name for the file.
   C. enter the RENAME command at the keyboard and specify the new file name.
   D. right-click in the drawing area and select **Rename** from the list of options.

2. To create a new folder in AutoCAD,
   A. pick the **Create New Folder** button in the **Select File** dialog box.
   B. enter the NEW command and specify the new folder name.
   C. right-click on an existing folder and select **New...** from the shortcut menu.
   D. enter the FOLDER command and select the **New** option.

3. To move a file to another folder from within the **Select File** dialog box,
   A. enter the MOVE command, specify the file name, and then specify the new folder for the drawing file.
   B. right-click the file name, drag it to a new folder, and pick **Move Here**.
   C. double-click the file name to open the drawing and then save it with another name in the new location.
   D. none of the above.

4. How can you delete a file that is highlighted in the **Select File** dialog box?
   A. press the backspace key   C. select **Delete** from the shortcut menu
   B. press the spacebar   D. press the **END** key

5. Which of the following is *not* a probable cause of damaged files?
   A. an AutoCAD system crash
   B. a power surge while AutoCAD is writing the file to disk
   C. a disk error while AutoCAD is writing the file to disk
   D. saving the file too frequently while you are working

6. A damaged drawing file may cause
   A. an internal or fatal error in AutoCAD.
   B. errors in plotting the drawing.
   C. AutoCAD to refuse to open the drawing.
   D. all of the above.

Completion

Directions: In the space at the left, write the word or words that BEST complete the statement or answer the question.

_____ 7. A file's _____ include the name, size, and type of the file.

_____ 8. Which command examines the validity of a drawing file and can correct some of the errors it finds?

_____ 9. Which command automatically tries to repair and open a damaged drawing file?

_____ 10. When AutoCAD saves a drawing file, it automatically creates a backup file with a(n) _____ extension.

Name _____ Class Period _____ Time _____

TEST - Fundamentals Text
Chapter 9 Object Snap

Multiple Choice

Directions: Circle the letter of the choice that BEST completes the statement or answers the question.

1. AutoCAD's object snap feature allows you to
   A. snap to endpoints of lines.
   B. snap to the midpoints of lines.
   C. snap to the centers of circles.
   D. all of the above.

2. Object snap modes are useful because they
   A. can be entered easily using function keys F2 through F10.
   B. dimension the drawing as you specify the modes.
   C. allow you to snap to points that you otherwise could not reach easily and accurately.
   D. none of the above.

3. The Object Snap tab of the Drafting Settings dialog box allows you to
   A. turn running object snaps on and off.
   B. control the size and appearance of the aperture box.
   C. turn ortho, grid, and snap on and off.
   D. both A and B.

4. To use the Center object snap, you choose the center of the circle by picking
   A. a point as close to the center of the circle as possible.
   B. two points on the circle to establish the diameter, from which the center can be calculated using the Midpoint object snap.
   C. anywhere inside the boundary of the circle.
   D. a point on the circle itself.

5. AutoCAD's AutoSnap feature
   A. displays yellow symbols at available snap points when you move the cursor near an object.
   B. automatically snaps to the first snap point it finds.
   C. turns the selected object snaps on and off automatically, depending on the command you enter.
   D. all of the above.

Completion

Directions: In the space at the left, write the word or words that BEST complete the statement or answer the question.

_____ 6. Object snaps that have been set to work automatically in the background are called _____ object snaps.

_____ 7. AutoCAD's _____ are temporary lines that display at specific angles from an acquired object snap. *(two words)*

_____ 8. To specify an individual object snap, you can enter it at the keyboard or pick a button from the _____ toolbar. *(two words)*

_____ 9. The _____ is a box that defines an area around the center of the crosshairs within which an object or point will be selected when you press the pick button. *(two words)*

_____ 10. The POLAR and _____ buttons on the status bar toggle AutoTrack on and off.

Copyright © Glencoe/McGraw-Hill

Name _____ Class Period _____ Time _____

TEST - Fundamentals Text — *Chapter 10* Helpful Drawing Features

Multiple Choice

Directions: Circle the letter of the choice that BEST completes the statement or answers the question.

1. Coordinate information in AutoCAD is displayed
    A. by right-clicking in the drawing area.
    B. in the status bar whenever the coordinate display feature is turned on.
    C. in the top left corner of the drawing.
    D. by selecting Coordinates from the File pull-down menu.

2. The simplest and quickest way to back up one AutoCAD operation is to
    A. enter UNDO One.
    B. press CTRL C immediately.
    C. pick the Undo button.
    D. pick the Redo button twice.

3. UNDO Mark
    A. is used in conjunction with the U command.
    B. places a special mark in the Undo information to which you can later back up.
    C. places an x on any object. This object can be deleted later by entering UNDO Back.
    D. both A and B.

4. You have entered the TIME command, and the Last updated item displays a time of 19:20:00.000. At what time was this file last updated?
    A. 7:20 PM
    B. 2:20 PM
    C. 9:20 AM
    D. 6:20 AM

5. The AutoCAD text window
    A. displays a complete history of your activity in the current AutoCAD session.
    B. allows you to copy its entire contents to the Windows Clipboard for insertion into a word processing document.
    C. allows you to paste selected text to the command line.
    D. all of the above.

Completion

Directions: In the space at the left, write the word or words that BEST complete the statement or answer the question.

_____ 6. The _____ feature forces all lines to run exactly horizontal or vertical.

_____ 7. Which function key toggles among the coordinate display modes in AutoCAD?

_____ 8. The _____ function key allows you to display the AutoCAD text window.

_____ 9. To turn the ortho mode on and off, you can pick the ORTHO button in the status bar or press the _____ function key.

_____ 10. AutoCAD provides a(n) _____ timer that you can turn on and off to keep an accurate record of actual time you spend working on a project.

182

Copyright © Glencoe/McGraw-Hill

Name _____ Class Period _____ Time _____

TEST - Fundamentals Text — *Chapter 11* Construction Aids

Multiple Choice

Directions: Circle the letter of the choice that BEST completes the statement or answers the question.

1. The grid feature
   A. gives you a better sense of size and distance.
   B. displays an alignment grid of dots.
   C. can be toggled on and off using either CTRL G or the appropriate function key.
   D. all of the above.

2. The Aspect option of the SNAP command
   A. allows you to set the horizontal and vertical snap intervals differently.
   B. allows you to change the current view.
   C. performs exactly the same function as the Tangent object snap mode.
   D. all of the above.

3. The snap feature
   A. is useful in laying out a drawing.
   B. when on, snaps the crosshairs along an imaginary grid of dots.
   C. can be toggled off and on quickly.
   D. all of the above.

4. Xlines are construction lines that extend
   A. infinitely in both directions.
   B. from one edge of the screen to the opposite edge.
   C. infinitely in one direction.
   D. from a specified point to the edge of the screen.

5. The basic difference between an xline and a ray is that
   A. xlines extend infinitely in both directions, but rays extend infinitely in only one direction.
   B. rays are derived from the radius of a given circle or arc.
   C. rays extend only to the edges of the current drawing view.
   D. xlines extend only to the edges of the current drawing view.

Completion

Directions: In the space at the left, write the word or words that BEST complete the statement or answer the question.

_____ 6. The ratio of height to width of a region is its _____. *(two words)*

_____ 7. A(n) _____ drawing is one that describes a three-dimensional object completely using two or more two-dimensional views.

_____ 8. A technique in which views are projected at right angles to one another to create a drawing is known as _____. *(two words)*

_____ 9. You can create a second construction line at a specific distance from an existing construction line by _____ it.

_____ 10. To rotate the alignment grid, you would enter the Rotate option of the _____ command.

Copyright © Glencoe/McGraw-Hill

Name _____   Class Period _____   Time _____

TEST - Fundamentals Text   *Chapter 12* AutoCAD's Magnifying Glass

Multiple Choice

Directions: Circle the letter of the choice that BEST completes the statement or answers the question.

1. Picking the Zoom Realtime button allows you to zoom
   A. to a different part of the drawing at the same magnification.
   B. to a new magnification by dragging the cursor.
   C. to several magnifications consecutively without re-entering the ZOOM command.
   D. both B and C.

2. You can magnify a selected portion of a drawing by using the ZOOM
   A. Window option.
   B. In option.
   C. Extents option.
   D. all of the above.

3. ZOOM Previous
   A. restores the original view of the drawing.
   B. restores the previous zoom magnification of the drawing.
   C. displays the drawing boundaries defined by the LIMITS command.
   D. both B and C.

4. What sets the resolution of arcs and circles?
   A. the transparent zoom facility
   B. the VIEWRES command
   C. the REGEN command
   D. AutoCAD does not allow you to control the resolution of arcs and circles.

5. The difference between the All and Extents options of the ZOOM command is that
   A. All will not work if no objects exist in the drawing.
   B. All displays all the objects in the drawing, and Extents displays the entire drawing as determined by the drawing limits.
   C. All displays the entire drawing as determined by the drawing limits, and Extents zooms so that the objects in the drawing fill the entire drawing area.
   D. there is no difference between the All and Extents options.

Completion

Directions: In the space at the left, write the word or words that BEST complete the statement or answer the question.

_____ 6. A(n) _____ zoom is one that takes place while another command is in progress.

_____ 7. The recalculation of each vector in a drawing is called a screen _____ .

_____ 8. The accuracy with which curved lines appear on the screen is known as view _____ .

_____ 9. What is the command alias for the ZOOM command?

_____ 10. To zoom to a magnification at which objects appear at half their current size, what zoom factor should you enter?

184   Copyright © Glencoe/McGraw-Hill

Name   Class Period   Time

TEST - Fundamentals Text   *Chapter 13* Panning and Viewing

Multiple Choice

Directions: Circle the letter of the choice that BEST completes the statement or answers the question.

1. The PAN command
   A. always forces a regeneration of the drawing.
   B. is normally used in lieu of ZOOM All.
   C. is used to move around in the drawing.
   D. all of the above.

2. The VIEW command
   A. allows you to assign names to various views of a drawing.
   B. restores previously saved views of a drawing.
   C. is normally used on very small drawings.
   D. both A and B.

3. How do you activate the PAN command?
   A. by picking the Pan Realtime button on the Standard toolbar
   B. by entering the Pan option of the VIEW command
   C. by entering CTRL P at the keyboard
   D. both A and C

4. AutoCAD's Aerial View
   A. provides a quick and easy method of zooming and panning.
   B. shows the size and position of the current zoom window relative to the entire drawing area.
   C. allows you to zoom quickly to a portion of the drawing that you define using the view box in Aerial View.
   D. all of the above.

True-False

Directions: On the line beside each statement, write **True** if the statement is correct or **False** if the statement is incorrect.

_____ 5. The PAN command allows you to change the current zoom magnification.

_____ 6. The scrollbars provide a method of panning horizontally and vertically in a document.

_____ 7. The PAN command can be used transparently in much the same manner as the ZOOM command.

_____ 8. When PAN is active, the cursor changes to a hand.

_____ 9. Right-clicking while Zoom Realtime is active displays a shortcut menu from which you can alternate between pans and zooms.

_____ 10. After you have defined a view, you can use the View option of the ZOOM command to return to that view.

Copyright © Glencoe/McGraw-Hill

Name _____ Class Period _____ Time _____

TEST - Fundamentals Text — *Chapter 14* Solid and Curved Objects

Multiple Choice

Directions: Circle the letter of the choice that BEST completes the statement or answers the question.

1. With regard to using the SOLID command, which of the following statements is (are) true?
   A. The points must be picked in a particular order.
   B. The order of points is unimportant.
   C. FILL must be turned on in order to use SOLID.
   D. both B and C

2. You can change the appearance of solid objects to outlines by
   A. turning SOLID on.
   B. turning FILL off.
   C. using REGEN.
   D. turning on the OUTLINE command.

3. Which of the following objects is *not* affected by the FILL command?
   A. solid
   B. multiline
   C. text
   D. wide polyline

4. A polyline is
   A. made up of line and arc segments, each of which is treated as an individual object.
   B. a connected sequence of line and arc segments that is treated as a single object.
   C. a series of connected arcs created with the ARC Continue option.
   D. none of the above.

5. PEDIT allows you to change
   A. the width of a polyline.
   B. the X and Y scale of a polyline.
   C. both A and B.
   D. neither A nor B.

6. The EXPLODE command
   A. breaks a polyline into arc and line segments that you can edit individually.
   B. reverses the effect of the PEDIT command.
   C. erases all polylines from the screen in a single step.
   D. none of the above.

Completion

Directions: In the space at the left, write the word or words that BEST complete the statement or answer the question.

_____ 7. Another term for a spline curve is _____.

_____ 8. Which command should you use to transform a polyline into a spline curve?

_____ 9. _____ points are points that exert influence on the shape of a spline curve but do not necessarily lie on the curve.

_____ 10. Which command allows you to edit a spline curve?

Name _____ Class Period _____ Time _____

TEST - Fundamentals Text *Chapter 15* Adding and Altering Objects

Multiple Choice

Directions: Circle the letter of the choice that BEST completes the statement or answers the question.

1. The CHAMFER command
   A. allows you to draw concentric circles.
   B. alters the appearance of corners.
   C. is used to break portions of circles and arcs.
   D. both B and C.

2. You can erase or remove portions of objects by using the
   A. ERASE command.
   B. REMOVE command.
   C. BREAK command.
   D. EDIT command.

3. To create rounded inside and outside corners, use the
   A. CHAMFER command.
   B. appropriate function key.
   C. ERASE and ARC combination.
   D. FILLET command.

4. The OFFSET command
   A. produces a mirror image of all selected objects.
   B. contains a Solid-fill option.
   C. allows you to create a line that is parallel to another line.
   D. none of the above.

5. The Through option of the OFFSET command allows you to create a line
   A. perpendicular to the original line through a point you specify.
   B. from the current endpoint of the line through a point you specify.
   C. parallel to the original line through a point you specify.
   D. parallel to the original line through the origin (0,0).

6. To produce up to 16 parallel lines simultaneously, use the
   A. XLINE command.
   B. MLINE command.
   C. OFFSET command.
   D. FILLET command.

Completion

Directions: In the space at the left, write the word or words that BEST complete the statement or answer the question.

_____ 7. A(n) _____ is a rounded inside corner.

_____ 8. Two circles are _____ if they share the same center point.

_____ 9. Before you can use a new multiline style that you have created, you must _____ it.

_____ 10. Which command allows you to edit the intersections of multilines?

Copyright © Glencoe/McGraw-Hill

Name _____   Class Period _____   Time _____

TEST - Fundamentals Text   *Chapter 16* Moving and Duplicating Objects

Multiple Choice

Directions: Circle the letter of the choice that BEST completes the statement or answers the question.

1. The MOVE command allows you to
   A. move objects to new locations on the screen.
   B. move objects from one open drawing file to another.
   C. create mirror images of objects.
   D. both A and B.

2. The steps in using the COPY command
   A. are identical to the steps in using the ARRAY command.
   B. are similar to the steps in the MOVE command.
   C. provide the option of mirroring copies as you place them in the drawing.
   D. both B and C.

3. To mirror an object to form a symmetrical shape, use
   A. the MOVE command.
   B. the COPY command.
   C. the OFFSET command.
   D. none of the above.

4. The ARRAY command allows you to create
   A. circular arrays.
   B. rectangular arrays.
   C. a single row of multiple objects.
   D. all of the above.

5. To create circular arrays efficiently, use the
   A. ARRAY Circular option.
   B. ARRAY Polar option.
   C. COPY Multiple option.
   D. COPY and MOVE commands.

6. You can create rectangular arrays at any angle by
   A. changing the snap rotation angle before beginning the array.
   B. using the Rotation option of the ARRAY command.
   C. using the Polar option of the ARRAY command.
   D. none of the above.

True-False

Directions: On the line beside each statement, write **True** if the statement is correct or **False** if the statement is incorrect.

_____ 7. The Properties window allows you to change several of the characteristics of objects selected in the drawing area.

_____ 8. An array is any orderly grouping or arrangement of objects.

_____ 9. An array in which objects are arranged radially around a center point is called a symmetrical array.

_____ 10. You can create mirror images at any angle to the original object by entering an angular mirror line.

Copyright © Glencoe/McGraw-Hill

Name   Class Period   Time

TEST - Fundamentals Text   *Chapter 17* Modifying and Maneuvering

Multiple Choice

Directions: Circle the letter of the choice that BEST completes the statement or answers the question.

1. With the STRETCH command, you can
   A. lengthen objects both horizontally and vertically.
   B. stretch a circle to form an egg-shaped object.
   C. maintain the current proportions of an object while lengthening one end of it.
   D. both A and B.

2. To increase or decrease an object's overall size without changing its proportions, use
   A. the SCALE command.
   B. the SIZE command.
   C. a special technique in conjunction with the EXTEND command.
   D. both A and C.

3. The ROTATE command does not let you rotate
   A. single objects.
   B. numerous objects in a single operation.
   C. objects dynamically.
   D. and scale selected objects.

4. Which of the following commands would you most likely use to remove line segments drawn too far past an intersecting line?
   A. TRIM
   B. EXTEND
   C. STRETCH
   D. ERASE

True-False

Directions: On the line beside each statement, write **True** if the statement is correct or **False** if the statement is incorrect.

_____ 5. The ROTATE command allows you to change the size of an object as you turn it.

_____ 6. The SCALE command performs almost exactly the same function as the ZOOM command.

_____ 7. You can scale an object either by using a scale factor or by reference.

_____ 8. AutoCAD allows you to enter a specific angle of rotation when you use the ROTATE command.

_____ 9. The most efficient way to select objects to stretch is to use a crossing window.

_____ 10. Rotating an object 180° produces the same effect as mirroring the object.

Copyright © Glencoe/McGraw-Hill

Name _____   Class Period _____   Time _____

TEST - Fundamentals Text — *Chapter 18* Notes and Specifications

Multiple Choice

Directions: Circle the letter of the choice that BEST completes the statement or answers the question.

1. AutoCAD text can be
   A. left and right justified.
   B. centered and aligned between two points.
   C. created as large or as small as desired.
   D. all of the above.

2. The STYLE command
   A. is used to develop new text styles.
   B. is used in conjunction with the TEXTQLTY command.
   C. both A and B.
   D. neither A nor B.

3. DTEXT allows you to
   A. delete text.
   B. duplicate text.
   C. double-format text.
   D. none of the above.

4. To create a paragraph of text that can be edited as a single object, use the
   A. MTEXT command.
   B. TEXT command.
   C. DTEXT command.
   D. EDITTEXT command.

5. You can recognize TrueType fonts in AutoCAD's list of fonts by
   A. their TTX extension.
   B. the AutoCAD symbol to the left of the font name.
   C. the overlapping T's to the left of the font name.
   D. the asterisk (*) that follows the font name.

Completion

Directions: In the space at the left, write the word or words that BEST complete the statement or answer the question.

_____ 6. A(n) _____ is a set of characters, including letters, numbers, punctuation marks, and symbols, in a particular style.

_____ 7. An alternative to creating text in AutoCAD is to _____ it from a document created by a word processing program.

_____ 8. Which font in AutoCAD is recommended for most drafting applications?

_____ 9. What is the default text style in AutoCAD?

_____ 10. What font is used in AutoCAD's default text style?

Name _____ Class Period _____ Time _____

TEST - Fundamentals Text   *Chapter 19* Text Editing and Spell Checking

Multiple Choice

Directions: Circle the letter of the choice that BEST completes the statement or answers the question.

1. You can correct text using the
   A. DDEDIT command.
   B. MTPROP command.
   C. DTEXT command.
   D. both A and B.

2. In the Find and Replace dialog box,
   A. AutoCAD automatically highlights any word that is misspelled and suggests a replacement for it.
   B. you can specify files that you want to replace.
   C. you can specify text that you want to replace.
   D. AutoCAD automatically finds and replaces incorrect dimensions.

3. Which of the following codes inserts a diameter symbol in AutoCAD text?
   A. %%o
   B. %%p
   C. %%c
   D. none of the above

4. The easiest way to insert the degree symbol (°) into an mtext object is to
   A. minimize AutoCAD, pick the Windows Start button, select Accessories and Character Map, choose the degree symbol, and copy it to the clipboard.
   B. pick the Symbol drop-down list and choose Degrees %%d.
   C. pick the Layers button and create a layer that has a text style called Symbols; use that layer for all symbols, including the degree symbol.
   D. use the CTRL + SHIFT + D combination.

5. One of the fastest and easiest ways to edit text is to
   A. enter the DDEDIT command at the keyboard.
   B. highlight the text on the screen so that the cursor turns to a text editing symbol and edit the text as necessary.
   C. press CTRL E.
   D. select the text, right-click, and pick Text Edit... or Mtext Edit... from the shortcut menu.

True-False

Directions: On the line beside each statement, write **True** if the statement is correct or **False** if the statement is incorrect.

_____ 6. Text created with the DTEXT command can be edited using the Multiline Text Editor dialog box.

_____ 7. Special characters are those that are not normally available on the keyboard or in a basic text font.

_____ 8. AutoCAD allows you to do a search and replace on mtext objects, but not on text created with TEXT or DTEXT.

_____ 9. AutoCAD's spell checker checks the spelling, context, and grammar of text objects.

_____ 10. Text created with the MTEXT command can be edited using the DDEDIT command.

Copyright © Glencoe/McGraw-Hill

Name _____ Class Period _____ Time _____

TEST - Fundamentals Text   *Chapter 20* Hatching and Sketching

Multiple Choice

Directions: Circle the letter of the choice that BEST completes the statement or answers the question.

1. The AutoCAD hatch feature
   A. provides a selection of four hatch patterns.
   B. is issued with the PATTERN command.
   C. always hatches over the top of text when text is located inside the object to be hatched.
   D. none of the above.

2. The BHATCH command produces
   A. boundary hatches.
   B. associative hatches.
   C. hatches that update automatically.
   D. all of the above.

3. The SKETCH command
   A. is rarely used to make sketches.
   B. should not be used for making maps.
   C. enables you to produce drawings quickly and accurately.
   D. all of the above.

4. To make sure the hatch size corresponds to the drawing scale, you should set the pattern scale at
   A. 1.
   B. 0.
   C. a number that is equal to the plot scale.
   D. none of the above.

5. The Hatch Pattern Palette presents
   A. graphic examples of hatches that conform to ANSI and ISO standards.
   B. a master list of colors available for hatch patterns in AutoCAD.
   C. a workspace in which you can create new hatch patterns.
   D. all of the above.

Completion

Directions: In the space at the left, write the word or words that BEST complete the statement or answer the question.

_____ 6. A repetitive pattern of lines or symbols that indicate a related area of a drawing is called a hatch or _____.

_____ 7. _____ drawings are used to show the interior detail of a part.

_____ 8. A hatch pattern that updates automatically when you change the hatch boundaries is called a(n) _____ hatch.

_____ 9. Which command permits you to change the pattern and other characteristics of a hatch?

_____ 10. To what should the SKPOLY system variable be set if you want to edit a sketched object using PEDIT?

192   Copyright © Glencoe/McGraw-Hill

Name _____ Class Period _____ Time _____

TEST - Fundamentals Text — *Chapter 21* Drawing Setup

Multiple Choice

Directions: Circle the letter of the choice that BEST completes the statement or answers the question.

1. An AutoCAD drawing template file usually consists of
   A. a completed drawing, except for dimensions.
   B. numerous mode settings and drawing parameters stored in an audit report file.
   C. pre-established settings for units, grid, snap, and drawing area.
   D. both B and C.

2. When beginning a new drawing template,
   A. you should first identify the drawing, scale, and sheet size.
   B. you should identify the correct units and drawing area.
   C. it is good to plan ahead and foresee possible uses of the drawing for other new drawings.
   D. all of the above.

3. The **STATUS** command displays
   A. all layer names.
   B. the size of the drawing area.
   C. drawing files in the current directory.
   D. all of the above.

4. An advantage of using AutoCAD's predefined template files is that they
   A. save the time required to set up your own template files.
   B. allow you to choose from various ANSI- and ISO-standard drawing setups.
   C. provide a starting point for drawing setup but can be modified as needed to suit specific needs.
   D. all of the above.

5. You can set the units in a drawing file by
   A. entering the **UNITS** or **DDUNITS** command.
   B. using the **Quick Setup** or **Advanced Setup** wizard to create the drawing.
   C. picking the **Units** button on the docked **Standard** toolbar.
   D. A and B.

6. When does scaling actually occur in AutoCAD?
   A. when you plot the drawing
   B. when you set the drawing scale
   C. when you create the drawing
   D. none of the above

Completion

Directions: In the space at the left, write the word or words that BEST complete the statement or answer the question.

_____ 7. An AutoCAD template file has a file extension of _____.

_____ 8. To set the drawing area is to set the _____ of the drawing.

_____ 9. A(n) _____ is a means of reducing or enlarging a representation of an actual object or part that is too small or large to be shown on a drawing sheet. *(two words)*

_____ 10. What should the drawing area be in a drawing for a 17″ × 11″ sheet and a scale of $1/4″ = 1'$?

Copyright © Glencoe/McGraw-Hill

Name   Class Period   Time

TEST - Fundamentals Text   *Chapter 22* Layers and Linetypes

Multiple Choice

Directions: Circle the letter of the choice that BEST completes the statement or answers the question.

1. The **Layer Properties Manager** dialog box allows you to
   A. assign colors and linetypes to layers.
   B. delete layers.
   C. turn off one or more layers.
   D. all of the above.

2. Layers are used for the following reason(s):
   A. to organize drawing objects for color and linetype assignments and plotting.
   B. so layers can selectively be frozen and thawed.
   C. to filter object selection sets.
   D. all of the above.

3. The best way to assign colors to objects is to
   A. assign colors to layers.
   B. use the **DDCOLOR** command.
   C. choose the color from the **Color** control drop-down box in the **Object Properties** toolbar.
   D. select the object, display the **Properties** dialog box, and select the desired color.

4. The correct linetype scale for a drawing is
   A. the same as the plot scale.
   B. the reciprocal of the drawing scale.
   C. $\frac{1}{2}$ the reciprocal of the plot scale.
   D. $\frac{1}{2}$ the drawing scale.

5. Lineweights are used to
   A. distinguish among layers in a drawing.
   B. distinguish among the types of lines (object lines, dimension lines, etc.) in a drawing.
   C. improve the appearance of lines that have been scaled using the **LTSCALE** command.
   D. none of the above.

Completion

Directions: In the space at the left, write the word or words that BEST complete the statement or answer the question.

_____   6. The _____ linetype is used to show invisible edges on drawings.

_____   7. The _____ linetype is made up of alternating long and short dashes.

_____   8. To remove a layer from view without deleting it from the drawing, you can either turn it off or _____ it.

_____   9. To avoid editing an object accidentally, you can _____ the layer on which the object was drawn.

_____   10. _____ is the process of selectively including or excluding objects from a selection set using specific criteria.

Copyright © Glencoe/McGraw-Hill

TEST - Fundamentals Text
Chapter 23 Plotting and Printing

Multiple Choice

Directions: Circle the letter of the choice that BEST completes the statement or answers the question.

1. The Full Preview provided from the Plot dialog box
   A. shows how the drawing will look on the printed sheet.
   B. is useful for spotting errors.
   C. lets you zoom and pan.
   D. all of the above.

2. The Scaled to Fit option
   A. scales the drawing to fit within the defined drawing area.
   B. allows you to scale the drawing using grips to fit within a specified area of the drawing sheet.
   C. scales the drawing to fit on the drawing sheet.
   D. allows you to specify the scale at which the drawing is plotted.

3. Which option would you choose in the Plot area portion of the Plot dialog box to print only the part of the drawing that is currently shown on the screen?
   A. View
   B. Display
   C. Extents
   D. none of the above

4. The Paper size drop-down box allows you to select
   A. sheet sizes available for the selected printer.
   B. the correct printer for the paper size you want to use.
   C. any paper size that conforms to ANSI standards.
   D. all of the above.

True-False

Directions: On the line beside each statement, write **True** if the statement is correct or **False** if the statement is incorrect.

_____ 5. The plot scale is the scale at which the drawing is plotted to fit on the drawing sheet.

_____ 6. In landscape paper orientation, the drawing is positioned so that "north" or "up" falls on the narrower edge of the paper.

_____ 7. To plot a saved view of a drawing, you must first restore the view to the screen.

_____ 8. There is no longer a clear distinction between plotting and printing, and the two terms are often used synonymously.

_____ 9. It is possible to zoom and pan while you are previewing a plot.

_____ 10. Regardless of the current display, you can plot the entire drawing area by selecting the Limits radio button in the Plot dialog box.

Name _____ Class Period _____ Time _____

TEST - Fundamentals Text   *Chapter 24* Multiple Viewports

Multiple Choice

Directions: Circle the letter of the choice that BEST completes the statement or answers the question.

1. The model space viewport facility enables you to
    A. create a maximum of four viewports.
    B. open up to four individual drawing files, each in a separate viewport.
    C. begin an AutoCAD operation, such as a line, in one viewport and finish it in another.
    D. all of the above.

2. To make a viewport the current (active) viewport,
    A. enter the desired viewport number at the keyboard.
    B. enter the **Restore** option.
    C. pick the desired viewport with the pointing device.
    D. both A and C.

3. To regenerate all the viewports in a drawing that contains multiple viewports, enter the
    A. REGEN command.
    B. REGENALL command.
    C. REDRAW command.
    D. VPREGEN command.

4. Most AutoCAD drafting and design work is done in
    A. paper space.
    B. model space.
    C. layout space.
    D. none of the above.

True-False

Directions: On the line beside each statement, write **True** if the statement is correct or **False** if the statement is incorrect.

_____ 5. AutoCAD allows you to insert viewports of any polygonal shape.

_____ 6. Objects created in paper space cannot be edited in model space.

_____ 7. Objects created in model space cannot be edited in paper space.

_____ 8. You can plot only one viewport at a time in paper space; however, you can plot more than one viewport at a time in model space.

_____ 9. Viewports are objects; therefore you can edit their size and shape using standard AutoCAD commands.

_____ 10. A scale factor of $1/24$ xp specifies the plotting scale relative to the paper space scale.

Copyright © Glencoe/McGraw-Hill

Name _____ Class Period _____ Time _____

TEST - Fundamentals Text — *Chapter 25* Basic Dimensioning

Multiple Choice

Directions: Circle the letter of the choice that BEST completes the statement or answers the question.

1. The dimension text style is determined by the
   A. DIMSTYL command.
   B. types of dimensions you use.
   C. current text style.
   D. none of the above.

2. The most appropriate command for dimensioning inclined lines is the
   A. DIMANGULAR command.
   B. DIMALIGNED command.
   C. DIMLINEAR command.
   D. DIMBASELINE command.

3. Which of the following commands should you use to dimension the angle at which two lines meet?
   A. DIMANGULAR
   B. DIMRADIUS
   C. DIMDIAMETER
   D. none of the above

4. Ordinate dimensioning
   A. incorporates a datum that is assumed to be correct.
   B. helps prevent cumulative dimensioning errors.
   C. both A and B.
   D. neither A nor B.

5. AutoCAD's dimensioning capability allows for
   A. fractional or decimal dimensioning.
   B. linear, angular, and radial dimensioning.
   C. changing certain dimensioning aspects, such as text height and arrowhead size.
   D. all of the above.

6. To specify full center lines with 1/8" center marks, enter
   A. CENTER.
   B. DIMCEN and 1/8".
   C. CENTER and 1/8".
   D. none of the above.

Completion

Directions: In the space at the left, write the word or words that BEST complete the statement or answer the question.

_____ 7. _____ dimensions are progressive, each starting at the same place.

_____ 8. A(n) _____ is a surface or edge that is assumed to be correct.

_____ 9. _____ dimensioning helps prevent cumulative errors by allowing you to reference successive features in an object to a given feature that is assumed to be correct.

_____ 10. Which command is used to set the text style for dimensions?

Copyright © Glencoe/McGraw-Hill

Name _____ Class Period _____ Time _____

TEST - Fundamentals Text — *Chapter 26* Advanced Dimensioning

Multiple Choice

Directions: Circle the letter of the choice that BEST completes the statement or answers the question.

1. A dimension style
   A. is a collection of dimension settings.
   B. controls the format and appearance of dimensions.
   C. can help you apply appropriate drafting settings.
   D. all of the above.

2. To create a new dimension style,
   A. pick the **Dimension Style** button on the **Dimension** toolbar.
   B. select **Dimension** from the **Edit** pull-down menu.
   C. enter the STYLE command at the keyboard.
   D. enter the DST command alias at the keyboard.

3. The default dimension style in AutoCAD is
   A. DIM1.
   B. DIMSTYLE.
   C. Standard.
   D. none of the above.

4. Leaders are used to
   A. point out a particular feature in a drawing.
   B. identify radial dimensions.
   C. identify diameter dimensions.
   D. all of the above.

True-False

Directions: On the line beside each statement, write **True** if the statement is correct or **False** if the statement is incorrect.

_____ 5. The **Multiline Text Editor** can be used to produce notes for leaders.

_____ 6. Spline leaders are not permitted on formal drafted drawings.

_____ 7. A spline leader is similar to a regular leader, except the leader line points to a spline.

_____ 8. You can edit individual dimensions quickly by right-clicking on the dimension and using the resulting shortcut menu.

_____ 9. You should set the primary units for a dimension style in the **Alternate Units** tab of the **New Dimension Style** dialog box.

_____ 10. When dimensioning to the center of a circle, you should select the end of the center mark or line, rather than the center of the circle, as the endpoint for the extension line.

Name _____ Class Period _____ Time _____

TEST - Fundamentals Text — *Chapter 27* Fine-Tuning Dimensions

Multiple Choice

Directions: Circle the letter of the choice that BEST completes the statement or answers the question.

1. Baseline spacing sets
   A. the distance between the dimension lines of a baseline dimension.
   B. the space between the object and the extension lines of a dimension.
   C. the distance the extension lines extend beyond the dimension line.
   D. none of the above.

2. What type of units are typically used by manufacturers of consumer and industrial products?
   A. decimal
   B. architectural
   C. fractional
   D. none of the above

3. The Fit tab contains options that
   A. alter the dimension scale to fit the current drawing.
   B. control the placement of dimension text and arrows when there is not enough space to place them inside the extension lines.
   C. alter the size of the dimension text so that it fits between the extension lines.
   D. changes the size of the object to fit the specified dimension.

4. The units that appear by default when you add dimensions to a drawing are called
   A. basic units.
   B. primary units.
   C. alternate units.
   D. automatic units.

5. When you check Leading in the Zero Suppression area, a 2.500 dimension is shown as
   A. 2.500.
   B. 2.5.
   C. 0.500.
   D. .500.

True-False

Directions: On the line beside each statement, write **True** if the statement is correct or **False** if the statement is incorrect.

_____ 6. The Text Alignment area of the Text tab allows you to change the text orientation to meet ISO or ANSI standards.

_____ 7. In most cases, it is better to change dimension text to a color that is different from the dimensions so that it stands out and can be read more easily.

_____ 8. Because metric units are the most common form of alternate unit, AutoCAD shows millimeters by default when you activate alternate units.

_____ 9. You can change a dimension's properties easily by selecting the dimension, right-clicking, and selecting Properties from the shortcut menu.

_____ 10. The most efficient way to change the position of text in a dimension is to explode the dimension.

Copyright © Glencoe/McGraw-Hill

Name _____   Class Period _____   Time _____

TEST - Fundamentals Text   *Chapter 28* Tolerancing

Multiple Choice

Directions: Circle the letter of the choice that BEST completes the statement or answers the question.

1. Tolerances
    A. specify the largest allowable variation for a dimension.
    B. should never be used on drawings of parts that will be manufactured.
    C. both A and B.
    D. neither A nor B.

2. In the limits method of tolerancing, the basic dimension is
    A. followed by a plus/minus symbol and the upper and lower limits of deviation.
    B. not shown.
    C. stated as a percentage of the standard deviation.
    D. both A and C.

3. You can create geometric characteristic symbols and feature control frames by using the
    A. TOLERANCE command.
    B. QLEADER command.
    C. DDIM command.
    D. both A and B.

4. Which of the following can you accomplish from the Symbol dialog box?
    A. place a degree symbol in dimension text
    B. place a true position symbol in a feature control frame
    C. edit the control codes used to place symbols in a drawing
    D. none of the above

5. A surface control is
    A. usually associated with a specific dimension.
    B. the box surrounding a datum reference on a drawing.
    C. information in a feature control frame that refers to a surface specification regardless of feature size.
    D. applicable only when basic dimensioning is being used.

Completion

Directions: In the space at the left, write the word or words that BEST complete the statement or answer the question.

_____ 6. Which tolerancing method should you use in AutoCAD if the upper and lower tolerances for a dimension are equal?

_____ 7. Which tolerancing method should you use in AutoCAD if the upper and lower tolerances for a dimension are not equal?

_____ 8. Symbols that are used to specify form and position tolerances on drawings are called _____ symbols. *(two words)*

_____ 9. Symbols that modify the geometric tolerance in relation to the produced size or location of the feature are _____ symbols. *(two words)*

_____ 10. In addition to positional tolerances, you can specify _____ tolerances to make a tolerance more specific.

Name   Class Period   Time

TEST - Fundamentals Text   *Chapter 29* A Calculating Strategy

Multiple Choice

Directions: Circle the letter of the choice that BEST completes the statement or answers the question.

1. Which of the following commands perform specific inquiries and calculations on objects?
   A. DIST, AXIS, and FILL
   B. AREA, LIST, and ARRAY
   C. CAL, ID, and DIST
   D. LIST, SOLID, and AREA

2. To segment a line into equal parts, use the
   A. DIVIDE command.
   B. MEASURE command.
   C. DIST command.
   D. both A and B.

3. The DDPTYPE command
   A. sets the global linetype for a drawing.
   B. sets the appearance of points in a drawing.
   C. allows you to manage layers in a drawing.
   D. all of the above.

4. The ID command identifies the
   A. distance between two points.
   B. area of a circle or polygon.
   C. coordinates of specific points on the screen.
   D. endpoints of the selected line segment.

5. AutoCAD's online geometry calculator
   A. evaluates vectors.
   B. evaluates real and integer expressions.
   C. can be used within AutoCAD commands to calculate information to be entered at the command prompt.
   D. all of the above.

True-False

Directions: On the line beside each statement, write **True** if the statement is correct or **False** if the statement is incorrect.

_____ 6. The CAL command can be entered transparently.

_____ 7. Object snaps should not be used in conjunction with the CAL command because the results may be unpredictable.

_____ 8. The LIST command displays information about an object, including the object type, layer, space, and area.

_____ 9. You can change the area of a circle using the Properties dialog box.

_____ 10. The DBASE command displays the same information as the LIST command, but in a database format.

Copyright © Glencoe/McGraw-Hill

Name Class Period Time

TEST - Fundamentals Text — *Chapter 30* Groups

Multiple Choice

Directions: Circle the letter of the choice that BEST completes the statement or answers the question.

1. Which of the following can be done using the GROUP command?
   A. create a new group
   B. delete objects from an existing group
   C. change the name of an existing group
   D. all of the above

2. When the Selectable check box is checked in the Object Grouping dialog box,
   A. all members of the group are selected when you pick any member of the group.
   B. each member of the group is selectable independently.
   C. you can select members of the group individually by pressing and holding the CTRL key while picking the objects.
   D. both A and C.

3. The Order Group dialog box
   A. allows you to change the location of group members on the screen.
   B. allows you to change the numerical sequence of objects in a group.
   C. is useful when you are using CNC equipment.
   D. all of the above.

4. The purpose of the Order Group dialog box is to
   A. change the order in which groups are defined in the drawing database.
   B. change the numerical sequence of the objects within a group.
   C. place the objects in the group in alphanumeric order.
   D. none of the above.

True-False

Directions: On the line beside each statement, write **True** if the statement is correct or **False** if the statement is incorrect.

_____ 5. Objects that belong to a group but that exist on locked layers are not affected by commands performed on other members of the group.

_____ 6. Exploding a group causes the objects in the group to become selectable individually, but the group definition is not deleted from the drawing database.

_____ 7. The purpose of the Highlight button in the Object Grouping dialog box is to highlight the members of the group so that they are easily identifiable.

_____ 8. To delete an object from a group, you must delete the group definition and then redefine it.

_____ 9. To rename a group, change the name in the Object Grouping dialog box.

_____ 10. Unchecking the Selectable box in the Object Grouping dialog box deletes the group definition from the drawing database.

Name _____ Class Period _____ Time _____

TEST - Fundamentals Text — *Chapter 31* Building Blocks

Multiple Choice

Directions: Circle the letter of the choice that BEST completes the statement or answers the question.

1. A block is
   A. a rectangular-shaped figure available for insertion into a drawing.
   B. a single element found in a concrete block foundation of a building drawn with AutoCAD.
   C. one or more objects stored as a single object for later retrieval and insertion.
   D. none of the above.

2. Which of the following commands can create, store, and later insert symbols and details in a drawing?
   A. BLOCK and PLACE
   B. BLOCK and RESTORE
   C. SAVE and RESTORE
   D. none of the above

3. The EXPLODE command
   A. breaks a block into its constituent parts.
   B. is used only in conjunction with polylines.
   C. creates two blocks from one.
   D. both A and C.

4. The WBLOCK command
   A. means "Window Block" and allows you to use a window to define a block.
   B. allows you to send a previously defined block to disk, creating a drawing file.
   C. is used in lieu of the INSERT command when the block contains text and dimensions.
   D. none of the above.

5. When you insert a block into a drawing, AutoCAD gives you the option of
   A. rotating the block.
   B. scaling the block.
   C. exploding the block.
   D. all of the above.

6. To change the name of a previously created block, which command should you use?
   A. PURGE
   B. RENAME
   C. BLOCK
   D. INSERT

True-False

Directions: On the line beside each statement, write **True** if the statement is correct or **False** if the statement is incorrect.

_____ 7. The DELETE command allows you to delete unused blocks and other named items.

_____ 8. When you want to use part or all of a drawing in a second drawing, you can insert the entire first drawing into the second using the INSERT command.

_____ 9. The WBLOCK command creates a drawing file from a block.

_____ 10. To transfer a block or set of objects to another drawing on the same computer, you can use the Windows-standard copy and paste feature.

Copyright © Glencoe/McGraw-Hill

Name   Class Period   Time

TEST - Fundamentals Text   *Chapter 32* Symbol Libraries

Multiple Choice

Directions: Circle the letter of the choice that BEST completes the statement or answers the question.

1. The main advantage of using a symbol library is the
   A. elimination of drawing repetition.
   B. speed at which new drawings can be created.
   C. versatility in their creation and use.
   D. all of the above.

2. Previously defined symbols and details can be scaled and rotated
   A. at the time of their insertion.
   B. after they are inserted by using the UPDATE command.
   C. if they are inserted with the * option.
   D. both A and B.

3. To allow a block to inherit the color and linetype of any layer on which it is inserted,
   A. insert the block using the MINSERT command.
   B. create the block on layer 0.
   C. insert the block on layer 0.
   D. create the block using the WBLOCK command.

4. Symbol libraries are
   A. drawing files that contain a collection of blocks for insertion into other drawings.
   B. index files created automatically when you use the BLOCK command.
   C. shape (SHX) files provided by AutoCAD for insertion into drawing files.
   D. none of the above.

5. To insert blocks using AutoCAD DesignCenter,
   A. enter the INSERT command at the keyboard, pick the block in AutoCAD DesignCenter, and follow the prompts at the command line.
   B. enter the DESIGN command, select the block from the resulting dialog box, and pick OK.
   C. pick the block in AutoCAD DesignCenter, and drag and drop it into the drawing.
   D. pick the Insert button on the docked Draw toolbar.

True-False

Directions: On the line beside each statement, write **True** if the statement is correct or **False** if the statement is incorrect.

_____ 6. The main purpose of AutoCAD DesignCenter is to allow you to copy elements of one drawing into another quickly and easily.

_____ 7. The palette in AutoCAD DesignCenter allows you to specify the color of blocks you insert into a drawing.

_____ 8. When you double-click the name of a file in AutoCAD DesignCenter, the blocks in that file insert automatically into the current drawing.

_____ 9. AutoCAD DesignCenter permits you to insert layouts, text styles, layers, and dimension styles, as well as blocks, from other drawings into the current drawing.

_____ 10. To be able to rotate a block while you are inserting it from AutoCAD DesignCenter, you must pick (left-click) the block and drag it into the current drawing while holding down the SHIFT key.

Copyright © Glencoe/McGraw-Hill

Name   Class Period   Time

TEST - Fundamentals Text   *Chapter 33* **Attributes**

Multiple Choice

Directions: Circle the letter of the choice that BEST completes the statement or answers the question.

1. Attributes are the
   A. database information displayed as a result of entering the LIST command.
   B. *x* and *y* coordinate values you enter while inserting a block.
   C. coordinate information of each vertex found in a triangle created with AutoCAD when the triangle is stored as a block.
   D. none of the above.

2. A variable attribute is one that
   A. stores its values only until you end the current session of AutoCAD.
   B. allows you to enter or change values as you insert the block.
   C. changes the block name depending on the values you enter.
   D. both A and B.

3. The Invisible mode
   A. prevents attribute values from displaying when you insert the block.
   B. displays the tags instead of the values when you insert the block.
   C. removes attribute values from the screen temporarily when you enter the REGEN command.
   D. works only when the Constant mode is turned on also.

4. The Edit Attributes dialog box allows you to
   A. delete unwanted attributes.
   B. change the default values of attributes.
   C. change one or more attribute tags.
   D. all of the above.

5. One use of attributes is to
   A. change the properties of objects that have already been created.
   B. list the properties of all the blocks in the current drawing.
   C. provide information that can later be used to create a list or bill of materials.
   D. all of the above.

Completion

Directions: In the space at the left, write the word or words that BEST complete the statement or answer the question.

_____ 6. A(n) _____ attribute is one whose value you define when you first create a block.

_____ 7. To define an attribute, use the _____ command.

_____ 8. The attribute _____ identifies each occurrence of an attribute in a drawing.

_____ 9. The _____ of an attribute is the information contained in a specific instance of a block.

_____ 10. Which command allows you to display the attributes in a drawing?

Copyright © Glencoe/McGraw-Hill

Name Class Period Time

TEST - Fundamentals Text *Chapter 34* Bills of Materials

Multiple Choice

Directions: Circle the letter of the choice that BEST completes the statement or answers the question.

1. AutoCAD attributes can be reported in a simple bill of materials using
   A. the REPORT command.
   B. the File Utilities dialog box.
   C. the extract.lsp file, in conjunction with extract.dcl and attext.txt.
   D. both B and C.

2. Which dialog box allows you to load the program used to create a bill of materials?
   A. the Load/Unload Applications dialog box
   B. the Insert dialog box
   C. the Enter Attributes dialog box
   D. the Attribute Extraction dialog box

3. CDF and SDF are
   A. file formats that allow you to write attributes to an ASCII text file.
   B. variations of AutoCAD's drawing exchange file format.
   C. AutoLISP applications for extracting text files.
   D. none of the above.

4. The ATTEXT command
   A. converts CDF files to a text format that can be read by a word processor.
   B. extracts attributes from a drawing file.
   C. creates applications that can be run from the Load/Unload Applications dialog box.
   D. all of the above.

True-False

Directions: On the line beside each statement, write **True** if the statement is correct or **False** if the statement is incorrect.

_____ 5. Once a CDF file has been created, you cannot view its contents because they are in binary form.

_____ 6. By default, AutoCAD suggests the name of the current drawing as the name of the output file when you extract attributes from a drawing.

_____ 7. Dialog control language (DCL) files define the appearance of dialog boxes.

_____ 8. To print the contents of a dialog box, you can use the ALT and Print Scrn keys to copy the dialog box to the Windows Clipboard and then paste it into a word processing document and print the document.

_____ 9. A template extraction file defines variable attributes for use in a drawing file.

_____ 10. The main purpose of a drawing interchange file is to copy attributes from one drawing file to another.

Copyright © Glencoe/McGraw-Hill

Answer Keys for Fundamentals Text

This section provides answers for the Review Questions and Challenge Your Thinking questions that are found at the end of each chapter in the *Fundamentals* text. In addition, this section provides answers to the chapter tests that are included in this Instructor Resource Guide.

Answers to Chapter Reviews 208

Answers to Chapter Tests 221

Answers to Chapter Reviews for *Fundamentals* Text

The review questions in the textbook are designed to prompt students to practice using AutoCAD software as well as to study the textbook chapter. Many of the questions cannot be answered just by reading the book. For example, a review question may ask the students to describe several AutoCAD command options, but the options may not all be discussed in the textbook. Students need to work with AutoCAD to find the complete answer.

Chapter 1
Review Questions
1. Answers will vary but may include (any 5): map designers, building designers, bridge designers, car parts, stereo equipment, snow skis, and cellular phones.
2. Double-click the AutoCAD 2002 icon or pick the Windows Start button, move the pointing device to Programs, move it to AutoCAD 2002, and pick AutoCAD 2002.
3. Pick the Open Drawings tab in the Today window. Pick the Browse... button. From the Select File dialog box, double-click the folder that contains the drawing files. Single-click any of the drawing files.
4. Shading complex models may make them easier to see and understand.
5. Type EXIT on the command line and press ENTER. Students may also answer that you can select Exit in the File pull-down menu or click the X at the upper right corner of the screen.

Challenge Your Thinking
1. Screen resolution establishes the look of the AutoCAD screen and determines the size of the toolbar buttons and the overall drawing area. To change it, pick the Windows Start button, and pick Settings and Control Panel. Double-click the Display icon and use the Settings tab to access the resolution setting.
2. The buttons permit access to AutoCAD news, product support, catalogs, and other resources. Student examples will vary.

Chapter 2
Review Questions
1. A cascading menu is a menu that displays additional options. The menu is activated by selecting the items in the pull-down menus that have a small arrow to the right.
2. From the View pull-down menu, select Toolbars and pick the box next to the toolbar you wish to display, or move the pointer to any of the toolbars displayed on the screen, right-click, and select the toolbar you wish to display.
3. Click and hold the bar at the top of the toolbar and drag the toolbar to a new location.
4. Pick the X in the upper right corner of the toolbar.
5. A. pull-down menus; B. Object Properties toolbar; C. Standard toolbar; D. Minimize, Maximize, and Close buttons; E. Modify toolbar; F. drawing area; G. Draw toolbar; H. Command window; I. coordinate display; J. Model and Layout tabs; K. status bar, L. scrollbars; M. Solids toolbar; N. crosshairs.

Challenge Your Thinking
1. Answers will vary. It is possible to change the appearance by moving the various windows and toolbars to new locations. To change the colors, select Preferences... from the Tools toolbar, pick the Display tab, and pick the Color... button to display the AutoCAD Window Colors dialog box. The ability to change these characteristics can be valuable for people working in AutoCAD all day under various lighting conditions, for example.
2. The buttons at the top of the screen minimize, maximize, or close the entire AutoCAD program. The lower set is used minimize, maximize, or close the current drawing only.

Chapter 3
Review Questions
1. They allow you to open an AutoCAD drawing file that already exists.
2. The Save Drawing As dialog box.
3. One or more words called *tooltips* appear. The status bar also changes to provide more detailed information about the button.
4. Press the space bar or ENTER.
5. Using abbreviated commands, called *command aliases*; the command aliases for LINE, CIRCLE, and ERASE are L, C, and E, respectively.
6. Type C and press ENTER.
7. While you are creating line segments, Undo backs up one segment at a time and then lets you continue to create line segments.

Challenge Your Thinking
1. Answers will vary. Students may use all the

Answers to Chapter Reviews, *Fundamentals* (Continued)

different methods, depending on which is most convenient in a given situation. However, having multiple input methods increases the time it takes to learn the software. The most efficient method is often the method that you are most comfortable with.

2. You can find the file in a Windows folder and double-click it.

Chapter 4
Review Questions
1. Selecting two points produces a circle passing through the two points. Selecting three points produces a circle passing through the three points. The **TTR** option allows you to create a circle with a specified radius that is tangent to two other objects.
2. The **Draw** toolbar.
3. It allows you to continue producing arcs, each one tangent to the previous arc.
4. It creates thick-walled or solid circles.
5. Inside the imaginary circle.
6. The **LINE** command creates a rectangle with four separate lines that are separate objects. The **RECTANGLE** command requires picking only two points to create a rectangle that is one object. Using the **RECTANGLE** command is generally quicker.
7. **POLYGON** (with four sides) creates a rectangle with all sides equal. Answers will vary, but you might want to use this method to create a square.

Challenge Your Thinking
1. Answers will vary. Entering a negative number for an angle causes the angle to form in the clockwise direction.
2. It is not possible because arcs are circular by definition. Other AutoCAD commands, such as **SPLINE**, can create noncircular curves.

Chapter 5
Review Questions
1. An object is the smallest predefined element you can add to or erase. Examples will vary.
2. Select objects.
3. a. Selects the most recently created object.
   b. Selects the most recently selected objects.
   c. Similar to **Window**, but lets you select objects that cross the window boundary.
   d. If **Remove objects** is active, **Add** changes the prompt back to **Select** objects.
   e. Changes the prompt to **Remove objects**, permitting you to remove objects from the set of objects selected.
   f. If you inadvertently add or erase an item, use **Undo** to remove or restore it.
   g. Similar to basic **Window**, but allows you to create an irregular polygonal window around objects you want to select.
   h. Similar to **Crossing**, but allows you to create an irregular polygonal window that crosses objects to be selected.
   i. Allows you to create a "fence" of connected lines; objects that touch the fence are selected.
   j. Selects all (unfrozen) objects in a drawing.
4. Imagine a box (or window) around the object. Pick one corner of this box; then pick the opposite corner.
5. By picking the **Undo** button located on the **Standard** toolbar or by selecting **Undo** in the **Edit** pull-down menu.
6. By entering the **Remove** option and picking the objects you want to remove.
7. Answers will vary. Possible answers: Enter E for **ERASE** and L for **Last**, or pick the **Erase** button from the **Modify** toolbar.
8. Click and drag.
9. By entering the **Remove Objects** mode and picking the objects you want to remove. If the object you want to remove was the last selected, you can use the **Undo** option.
10. The ability to edit an object without entering a command.
11. Stretch, move, rotate, scale, mirror, and copy.
12. Select the object and pick the center grip, right-click, and pick **Copy**.
13. The noun/verb selection method allows you to select an object before you execute an editing command. The verb/noun selection method requires you to enter a command before you select an object to edit.

Challenge Your Thinking
1. Answers will vary. Although the grips method is quick and convenient, in many cases the commands offer more flexibility by including options not available using grips.
2. The **Remove** option can be useful when you want to select every object in a specific area with the exception of one or two objects. It can be faster to use the **All** option to select

Copyright © Glencoe/McGraw-Hill

Answers to Chapter Reviews, *Fundamentals* (Continued)

all the objects and then use **Remove** to remove a few of the objects than to select all the objects individually.

Chapter 6
Review Questions
1. The AutoCAD world coordinate system is based on the Cartesian coordinate system.
2. Absolute point specification requires entry of *x* and *y* coordinates (*e.g.,* 3,4). Relative point specification requires an *x* and *y* distance relative to an existing point (*e.g.,* @2,3). Polar specification requires a distance and angle from the current point (*e.g.,* @5<90). Polar tracking is similar to polar point specification. Points can be entered by positioning the crosshairs on the desired alignment path and then entering the desired distance from the last point selected and pressing the **ENTER** key.
3. The keyboard allows you to specify accurately any point at any desired location and angle from any other point on the screen.
4. In many instances, it may be faster.
5. The line begins at the last point specified.
6. It forms a line where the direction angle is measured in a clockwise direction.
7. Direct distance entry is similar to polar tracking methods except that direct distance does not use the alignment path to specify an exact angle.

Challenge Your Thinking
1. Because of the addition and subtraction of coordinates required to locate the points.
2. @2.2361<296.5651
   or @2.2361<−63.4349.
3. When creating drawings in which distances between points are known and angles are in the following increments: 90, 45, 30, 22.5, 18, 15, 10, or 5.

Chapter 7
Review Questions
1. Pick the **Open Drawings** tab in the **Today** window. Using **Browse...** choose the file folder you wish to look in. AutoCAD displays thumbnails of each drawing in the folder.
2. The **AutoCAD 2002 Help** dialog box.
3. Enter the **HELP** command and pick the **Contents** tab of the **AutoCAD 2002 Help** dialog box.

4. By picking the **Help** button.
5. Note to instructor: See "Other Sources of Help" in the chapter for the available options.
6. Context-sensitive help allows you to access help in the middle of a command. Pick the **Help** button while the command is active.

Challenge Your Thinking
1. Pick the **Help** button or press the **F1** key and find the topic for which you need help. Select **Print** from the menu.
2. You can search for specific words or phrases, rather than by category. You can control where AutoCAD looks for words, whether the words have to be in a specific order, etc. The **Ask Me** tab enables you to make more sophisticated searches.

Chapter 8
Review Questions
1. The seven items in the upper right area of the **Select File** dialog box, from left to right, allow you to go back, move up one level in the folder hierarchy, search the Web, delete, create a new folder, view file details, and use file organization tools.
2. If you want the copy to be in the same folder as the original, right-click and drag the file to an empty area within the list box. Pick **Copy Here** from the shortcut menu.
3. The size and type of each file and the date on which the files and folders were last modified.
4. Use the **Open a Drawing** button to display the **Select File** dialog box. Select the **Create New Folder** button and assign a name to the folder.
5. As a diagnostic tool, it examines drawing files to check their validity and correct errors.

Challenge Your Thinking
1. It is possible to move and copy files from the **Select File** dialog box to folders on the Windows desktop. It is also possible to copy and move files from the desktop to the **Select File** dialog box. Drawings copied to the desktop can be easily and quickly opened. When they are complete, they can be moved back to a folder.
2. Answers will vary. Example: An AutoCAD user who experiences the same problem more than once may need to record the audit results to help a technical support representative find a solution to the problem.

Answers to Chapter Reviews, *Fundamentals* (Continued)

Chapter 9
Review Questions
1. The object snap modes allow you to snap accurately to specific points in a drawing.
2. You can preset them to run in the background by entering **OSNAP** or selecting **Drafting Settings...** from the **Tools** menu, then selecting the **Object Snap** tab. You can also specify object snaps individually from the keyboard or the **Object Snap** toolbar.
3. Any point on the circle.
4. By specifying running object snap modes for object snaps that you will be using frequently in a given drawing, you avoid having to re-enter each object snap each time you want to use it.
5. You might want to make the target box size smaller if you needed to select specific objects on a complex or crowded drawing.
6. Note to instructor: See Table 9-1 in text.
7. It allows you to create new lines quickly and easily using a combination of object snaps and temporary alignment paths.
8. Object snap tracking acquires the object snap from a point; temporary alignment paths are created from that point based on the settings from polar tracking. Object snap tracking will not work if object snap is turned off.

Challenge Your Thinking
1. Answers will vary. Encourage students to discuss their answers, or use this question as a springboard for a brainstorming session.
2. Answers will vary. One possible use for snapping to an apparent intersection is to position text, leaders, or dimensions on a view that is flat to the screen for plotting purposes. Accept all reasonable responses.

Chapter 10
Review Questions
1. F6.
2. It displays the position of the crosshairs. It also gives the line segment lengths and angles when specifying endpoints of lines.
3. Ortho; F8.
4. In a work or production environment, the **TIME** command tracks specific time spent on each project or job.
5. Note to instructor: See the list under #1, "Tracking Time."
6. F2.
7. Highlight the text to be copied in the **text window**. Then select the **Edit** pull-down menu from the **text window** and select **Copy** to copy the highlighted text to the Windows Clipboard. Open the text editor and use its **Paste** item to paste the text into a document.
8. The **U** command lets you back up one operation at a time. You would have to select **U** five times. The **UNDO** command provides several options, such as backing up five operations by entering **UNDO 5**.
9. Enter **UNDO Mark**. Later in the editing session, enter **UNDO Back** if you want to return to the marked point in the editing session.

Challenge Your Thinking
1. The object snap modes override the ortho mode. For example, when you are creating a line with ortho on, you can snap to an endpoint of an object even if the resulting line is not horizontal or vertical.
2. Answers will vary. Example: If you are having trouble with a particular command or sequence, you can save your entries in AutoCAD to show to a more experienced user. You can copy the pertinent lines from the **command** window and paste them into a text document and then print them.

Chapter 11
Review Questions
1. The grid provides a visual means of referencing distance and reflects the limits. Using **CTRL G**, the **F7** function key, or double-clicking **GRID** in the status bar.
2. The snap feature is useful when you are drawing an object that has no dimensions smaller than a specified snap value. For example, if you want to draw a front view of a cereal box that measures 8 inches by 10 inches, you could set the snap to 1 inch to create the view quickly, without worrying about being a fraction of an inch off. You would toggle off the snap feature to draw objects that do not align wiht the snap grid.
3. By selecting the **Aspect** option of the **SNAP** command. Also by selecting **Drafting Settings...** on the **Tools** menu and selecting the **Snap and Grid** tab. Then set the **X** for horizontal distance and the **Y** for vertical distance.

Copyright © Glencoe/McGraw-Hill

Answers to Chapter Reviews, *Fundamentals* (Continued)

4. Enter the Rotate option of the SNAP command and specify a rotation angle of 45, or select Drafting Settings... on the Tools menu, select the Snap and Grid tab, and set Rotation to 45.
5. XLINE create lines of infinite length through a point, while the RAY command creates lines from a specified point that extend infinitely in one direction. Both can be used to construct objects and layout drawings.
6. Construction lines and rays allow you to insert infinite lines in a drawing. Situations will vary. Example: when you are working on a small portion of a drawing and need a reference line that extends beyond the portion of the drawing currently on the screen.
7. Orthographic projection is the projection of views at right angles to a projection plane, resulting in a 2D view. Orthographic projection is used to create a multiview drawing.
8. One that describes a 3D object completely using two or more 2D views.

Challenge Your Thinking
1. Answers will vary, but students should demonstrate knowledge of the similarities and differences among the snap grid, alignment grid, and object snap features.
2. Answers will vary. Construction lines can be used even when the tracking feature is turned off; however, using AutoTrack results in lines that do not have to be trimmed later.

Chapter 12

Review Questions
1. It allows you to magnify or reduce the apparent size of objects.
2. Answers will vary. Example: if the drawing you are developing is based on a large paper format, you will have to zoom in on portions of the drawing to include detail.
3. a. Shows entire drawing (to drawing limits).
   b. Shows part of drawing.
   c. Shows entire drawing (current extents).
   d. Restores previous view.
   e. Asks for box to be drawn around objects to be enlarged or reduced.
4. The ZOOM command can be used while in another command. For example, it might be useful while drawing a line to locate the endpoints accurately.
5. A process in which AutoCAD recalculates each vector in the drawing individually.

6. The realtime zoom option is often faster than the other zoom options, particularly if you need to move quickly around a large drawing or if you need to see how drawing details affect a drawing overall.
7. It allows you to set the accuracy with which curved lines appear. At lower resolutions, curved lines appear as a series of lines.

Challenge Your Thinking
1. In a vector format, objects are defined as shapes. Each shape is stored with directional information. Most CAD programs, including AutoCAD, use the vector format. In a raster format, everything in the drawing is defined using pixels, or tiny dots on the screen. A line, for example, is stored as a collection of lighted pixels. As such, it cannot be assigned direction or length information. Many "paint" and graphic design programs use the raster format. Drawings can be converted back and forth among these formats. The success of the conversion depends on a number of factors, such as the specific formats involved. Typically, it is much easier to convert from vector to raster than it is to convert from raster to vector.
2. Answers will vary. The ZOOM Center option changes the zoom window by relocating its center point at a position you specify. You can also change the zoom magnification by entering a new zoom factor.

Chapter 13

Review Questions
1. After zooming, PAN provides a means for moving around on a drawing for including detail or for editing.
2. No, you can only pan vertically or horizontally using the scrollbars.
3. It allows you to restore quickly any named view (zoom window) of the drawing for adding detail or for editing.
4. Right-click and use the items on the shortcut menu to alternate between realtime pans and zooms with a single click.
5. Answers will vary. Example: You can keep a sense of perspective about the drawing as you work in a smaller, zoomed area.

Challenge Your Thinking
1. Answers will vary. Different zoom options work best for different applications; with so many options to choose from, many drafters

Answers to Chapter Reviews, *Fundamentals* (Continued)

choose one or two that work best for their applications and tend to ignore the others.
2. The two are similar; in fact, Aerial View incorporates the panning feature. The basic PAN command may be more useful for moving the viewing window once or twice "on the fly" while you are working in a drawing or when you need the viewing window to be as large as possible. Aerial View is more convenient if you need to move around frequently in a drawing or when you need to see where the viewing window is in relation to the entire drawing.

Chapter 14

Review Questions
1. By making the fourth point the same as the third point.
2. FILL controls whether or not objects are solid-filled. FILL is either on or off.
3. The FILL command affects solids, wide polylines, multilines, and hatches.
4. A connected sequence of lines and arcs that is treated by AutoCAD as a single object.
5. Answers will vary. Examples: to define a racetrack, river, or a stream on a map.
6. a. Switches the PLINE command to arc mode.
   b. Causes AutoCAD to draw a line from the current position to the starting point, creating a closed polygon.
   c. Allows you to specify the width from the center of a wide polyline segment to one of its edges, or half the total width.
   d. Allows you to draw a line segment at the same angle as the previous segment, specifying the length of the new segment.
   e. Removes the most recent line or arc segment added to the current polyline.
   f. Allows you to specify the width of the following polyline segment.
7. a. Creates the closing segment of the polyline, connecting the first and last segments.
   b. Finds lines, arcs, or other polylines that meet the polyline at either end and adds them to the polyline.
   c. Lets you specify a new uniform width for the entire polyline.
   d. Allows you to select and perform various editing tasks on one vertex of the polyline.
   e. Computes a smooth curve fitting through all the vertices of the polyline.
   f. Creates a B-spline using the vertices of the selected polyline as the control points.
   g. Removes any extra vertices inserted by the Fit operation and straightens all the segments of the polyline.
   h. Sets the linetype pattern generation around the vertices of a polyline.
   i. Undoes the most recent PEDIT operation.
8. EXPLODE gives you the ability to break a polyline into individual line and arc segments.
9. It enables you to control the type (quadratic and cubic) of B-spline curve to be generated.
10. The curve passes through all the control points.
11. Using grips.
12. The SPLINEDIT, Refine, Add control point sequence allows you to add a vertex to a spline, which changes the shape of the line.

Challenge Your Thinking
1. Answers will vary. The SOLID command is used when a filled object is needed. Examples include electronic symbols, such as a diode, or columns on a floor plan. The FILL command allows you to turn the solid pattern off and allows the screen to regenerate faster.
2. Spline curves are used to describe the complex shape of items such as car bodies and to connect the points in a graph, describing trends.

Chapter 15

Review Questions
1. It produces a chamfered corner at the corner formed by two lines.
2. The smallest element that can be erased using the ERASE command is an object. BREAK allows you to erase parts of objects such as lines, arcs, and circles.
3. Counterclockwise.
4. The Modify toolbar.
5. By selecting the Radius (R) option of the FILLET command and then entering the radius.
6. Two non-parallel, non-intersecting lines can be extended to form an accurate corner.
7. The OFFSET command allows you to produce a line parallel to an existing line at a specified distance from the existing line.
8. Answers will vary. Example: MLINE could be used to create the inner and outer walls of a building on an architectural drawing.
9. Multiline Styles allows you to change the num-

Copyright © Glencoe/McGraw-Hill

Answers to Chapter Reviews, *Fundamentals* (Continued)

ber and spacing of lines drawn when you use the MLINE command, as well as the characteristics of the ends of the lines (caps). These characteristics can be saved as multiline styles that you can later load and use. Multiline Edit Tools allows you to edit existing multilines, including intersections.

Challenge Your Thinking
1. Distance requires two chamfer distances; Angle requires one chamfer distance and the angle for the chamfer. The Distance option is useful when you know both distances. The Angle option is useful when you know only one of the chamfer distances.
2. Students will need to save two multiline styles: one for the 5″ walls and one for the 6″ walls. They should use MLSTYLE to change the offset distance to obtain the correct wall thickness for each. From the Multiline Properties dialog box, they can turn Fill on and select a gray color for the fill, and they should also select start and end caps (lines at 90°).
3. Paragraphs will vary. Students should outline the correct procedure for saving multiline styles as described in this chapter.

Chapter 16
Review Questions
1. The Properties window provides a method of changing an object's properties. The properties listed depend on the object selected.
2. The Modify toolbar.
3. With the MOVE command, you can move an object to a new location. With COPY, the object remains in its original location and a duplicate is produced in a new location.
4. To construct symmetrical objects.
5. Yes, the mirror line can be at any angle to the original object.
6. Rectangular and polar (circular).
7. Answers will vary. The following are typical. Example of rectangular array: arrangement of desks and chairs in a classroom. Example of polar array: number positions on a clock.
8. The objects will not be reproduced in a full circle. For example, you specify 180° to array objects in a semicircle.
9. AutoCAD creates arrays along a baseline defined by the current snap rotation angle. The snap angle can be changed using the SNAP command or through the Drafting

Settings... dialog box located in the Tools menu.

Challenge Your Thinking
1. Answers will vary. Students can often save drawing time and even create more accurate drawings, if they take the time to analyze the object before beginning the drawing. Many objects can be completed by drawing a small part and then copying or mirroring it to create additional parts.
2. Space between rows: 18; space between columns: 16.

Chapter 17
Review Questions
1. STRETCH allows you to move a portion of a drawing, preserving the connections to parts of the drawing that are left in place.
2. 1.5, 3, .5.
3. In reply to Specify scale factor or [Reference]: move the crosshairs to the desired location.
4. Yes. In reply to Specify rotation angle or [Reference]: move the crosshairs to the desired location.
5. The simplest way is to enter −90 in reply to Specify rotation angle or [Reference]:.
6. TRIM erases the portions of selected objects that cross a specified boundary.
7. Answers will vary. One example: it could be used to extend the lines that make up a sidewalk to meet a driveway or vice versa.

Challenge Your Thinking
1. There are several ways to accomplish this. Example: Create a line perpendicular to the house line using the Perpendicular object snap. Then move the line to a point 2′ from the corner of the house using the From and Nearest object snaps. Offset the line by 14′ to create the other side of the driveway. Use EXTEND and TRIM as necessary to complete the driveway.
2. ZOOM changes the size of the viewing window through which you see the drawing, but it does not change the size of the objects in the drawing. SCALE changes the size of the actual objects but does not change the size of the viewing window.

Chapter 18
Review Questions
1. The DTEXT command; DTEXT.
2. Answers will vary. Example: you can spell-

Answers to Chapter Reviews, *Fundamentals* (Continued)

check an entire mtext object in one operation; you can resize the mtext, changing the word wrap, without editing individual lines.
3. Permits you to set a text style previously defined by the STYLE command.
4. Students should list at least six of the standard or TrueType fonts AutoCAD provides.
5. The STYLE command.
6. Enter STYLE. In the resulting dialog box, enter a width factor that is significantly less than the default of 1.00; for example .5.
7. Use MTEXT to get the Multiline Text Editor dialog box, pick the Import Text... button, and select the name of the file to be imported. It may be easier to create long text items using a word processor instead of AutoCAD.
8. Many companies use customized title blocks to provide valuable and necessary information that often includes company name and address, drawing name, designer's name, plot scale, date of any revisions, etc.
9. Answers will vary. Although both DTEXT and MTEXT can create multiple lines of text, the text created with MTEXT is treated as a single object. Multiple lines of text created with DTEXT are individual objects. MTEXT is a good choice when you will need to manipulate text that spans several lines. In many cases, however, DTEXT is simpler and faster to use.

Challenge Your Thinking
1. When you compile a font in AutoCAD, it loads faster; however, some of the font characteristics may no longer be available because it has been saved as an SHX file.
2. PostScript fonts are often (not always) more complex than TrueType fonts, but they are also somewhat more widely accepted, particularly in the publishing industry.

Chapter 19

Review Questions
1. If standard text is selected, the shortcut menu displays the Edit Text... option. If mtext is selected, the shortcut menu displays the Mtext Edit... option.
2. The character map displays all the characters defined for a specific font. If you need to include special or unusual characters in text, the character map can help you find them.
3. In the Multiline Text Editor dialog box, type %%c or select the Symbols button and then choose diameter from the resulting menu.

4. Spell checker may find words that are not in its internal dictionary.
5. One way is to use the Find/Replace tab in the Multiline Text Editor dialog box.

Challenge Your Thinking
1. Answers will vary. Spell checkers cannot replace careful proofreading. Since *test*, *text*, *write*, and *rite* are all words recognized by the dictionary, these errors will not be found by the spell checker.
2. Answers will vary. Building a custom dictionary allows you to define words AutoCAD would otherwise not recognize. This could be very important for someone working in a specialized field such as electronics or aircraft engineering. People who work on more than one type of project at a time may need more than one custom dictionary.

Chapter 20

Review Questions
1. They enhance the appearance and readability of a drawing. Hatch patterns are used to fill in objects or areas with selected patterns that symbolize something, such as a building material or a topographical feature.
2. HATCHEDIT.
3. Note to instructor: See Table 20-1.
4. It determines the length over which movement of the pointer will generate a new line. Thus it establishes the resolution, or accuracy, of the sketch. The smaller the increment, the higher the resolution.
5. Determines whether the SKETCH command generates lines or polylines.

Challenge Your Thinking
1. The Inherit Properties button allows you to give the current hatch the same properties as a hatch that is already present in the drawing.
2. The differences between ANSI and ISO are fundamental. The only real similarity is that they both provide guidelines for people to follow as they create drafted documents. ANSI is used more in the United States, whereas ISO is an international set of standards. Neither is adhered to universally.

Chapter 21

Review Questions
1. A template file is a file that contains settings that can be imported into new drawings files,

Answers to Chapter Reviews, *Fundamentals* (Continued)

which speeds setup time. When a new drawing is established, the contents of the template file are loaded into the new drawing. This is faster than specifying units, limits, layers, etc., individually for each new drawing.

2. Units, limits, layers, dimensions styles, text styles, and linetypes.
3. The smallest fraction displayed will be $1/4''$.
4. Drawing scale and sheet size of the drawing. This can be set using the Use a Wizard button when you create a new drawing or at any time with the LIMITS command.
5. Set Width to 220' and Length to 160'.
6. The display will vary for each drawing. Typical settings displayed include model space limits, display coordinates, base point of drawing, snap spacing, and current settings for grid, layer, color, linetype, lineweight, plot style, elevation and thickness. It also shows disk information such as Free dwg disk space, Free temp disk space, Free physical memory, and Free swap file space.

Challenge Your Thinking
1. Answers will vary. The precision selected must match what is actually being drawn. AutoCAD is very precise, even more precise than the equipment used to manufacture the objects drawn. For example, a large parking lot may be constructed with large tractors and earthmovers. They cannot do work more precise than to the nearest 1". Therefore, the site plan drawing should have its precision set to 0'-0". However, the building can be built to within $1/4''$, and cabinets in that same building may need to be created with precision set to $1/16''$.
2. 1,632" × 1,056". The scale factor for $1/8''=1'$ is 96. The drawing width and length must both be multiplied by 96 (17 × 96 = 1632 and 11 × 96 = 1056).

Chapter 22
Review Questions
1. They allow you to divide objects on a drawing into groups, controlling object properties. They also allow you to control the visibility and editability of the objects on those layers.
2. Select the layer you want to make current and click on the Current button.
3. It allows you to scale linetypes so that they are properly displayed and plotted. It is set using the Linetype Control drop-down box in the Object Properties toolbar.
4. To make the objects on a certain layer invisible and to speed up screen regenerations.
5. (Any five) Dashed, Hidden, Center, Phantom, Dot, Dashdot, Border, Divide, or the ISO linetypes.
6. To keep you from editing objects accidentally.
7. Enter the CHANGE command and select the Properties and Layer options, or use the Match Properties button.
8. Pick the down arrow next to the Layer Control drop-down list and pick the sun in the appropriate row. The sun becomes a snowflake and, when you click outside the drop-down list, the layer freezes.
9. Use the Quick Select dialog box by selecting Quick Select... in the Tools pull-down menu.

Challenge Your Thinking
1. Answers will vary. Example: When layers have already been set up and all you need to do is change layer properties, the drop-down is faster. When you need to create a layer, you must use the Layer Control dialog box.
2. ISO stands for International Standards Organization, a group whose purpose is to approve worldwide standards for various measurements and characteristics in many categories, including drafted documents, quality standards, and many others. ISO standards are used by international companies and by companies that sell their products and services in several different countries.

Chapter 23
Review Questions
1. The Full plot preview shows the drawing as it will appear on the sheet. It allows you to modify the plot settings before you plot, saving paper, ink, and time.
2. It sends the plot output to a file rather than to a printing or plotting device.
3. Limits plots the entire drawing area as defined by the drawing limits. Extents plots the portion of the drawing that contains objects. Display plots the current view. View plots a saved view.
4. One plotted inch represents four scaled inches on the drawing.
5. Select Options... on the Tools pull-down menu. Select the Plotting tab. Then select the Add or Configure Plotters... button. Choose Add-A-Plotter Wizard and follow the instructions.

Copyright © Glencoe/McGraw-Hill

Answers to Chapter Reviews, *Fundamentals* (Continued)

Challenge Your Thinking
1. Answers may vary. Often plot batch files and spooling utilities require the use of PLT files rather than drawing files. Some printers are attached to a plot server (a device that reads PLT files and sends them to the plotter).
2. Paragraphs will vary. A partial preview does not show the actual drawing; instead, it shows the boundaries or extents of the drawing in relation to the drawing sheet.

Chapter 24

Review Questions
1. Most drafting and design work is done in model space. Paper space is used to lay out and plot two or more views of a drawing.
2. Answers will vary. Each viewport can display a unique view, including a different magnification. You can start an operation in one viewport and complete it in another.
3. By picking the desired viewport with the pointing device.
4. Use the Join option of the VPORTS command or select Vports from the View pull-down menu and select Join from the resulting menu.
5. 3 and Below.
6. Change to model space by typing MSPACE or choose the Model tab. Objects in model space cannot be edited while in paper space.
7. Answers will vary. Example: To size the viewports and move them into position in preparation for plotting.
8. You can plot multiple viewports.

Challenge Your Thinking
1. The operating system and display driver place a practical limit on the number of viewports used. The MAXACTVP system variable can also be used to limit the number of active viewports. There is ordinarily no need to use more than four or five viewports. Additional viewports may be necessary for complicated models that require auxiliary views.
2. Answers will vary. Model space and paper space viewports are handled differently by AutoCAD, so it is difficult to convert from one to the other. However, creating viewports in paper space is an easy process; it should not be necessary to convert model space viewports to paper space viewports.

Chapter 25

Review Questions
1. You can use the DDIM command to access the Dimension Style Manager. Pick the Modify button, select the Text tab, and select a new style from the Text Style drop-down list. Students may also use the DIMTXSTY system variable to assign a new dimension text style.
2. When AutoCAD asks for the first extension line origin, press ENTER and pick the line you want to dimension.
3. Aligned Dimension; Angular Dimension.
4. The Radius Dimension button is used for fillets and rounds. The Diameter Dimension button is used for holes and cylinders.
5. Baseline dimensioning is a form of dimensioning in which two or more dimensions share an extension line. It helps eliminate cumulative errors along the length of the piece. Baseline dimensioning is useful for drawings where a common point of reference is needed or desired.
6. Ordinate dimensioning uses a datum, or reference dimension, which is assumed to be correct. Other dimensions are derived from the datum to help prevent cumulative errors in a drawing. Ordinate dimensions show absolute coordinates and are especially useful for mechanical drawings.

Challenge Your Thinking
1. Using grips to change a dimension has no effect on the object that is being dimensioned. However, you can use grips to change the object directly, and then also use grips to change the dimension so that it correctly describes the object. If you use the STRETCH command and include the dimension node (end of extension line closest to the object) in the selection set, the dimension updates with the object's new dimensions.
2. Size dimensions define the part or object in terms of geometric shapes (cylinders, pyramids, etc.) of specific sizes. Location dimensions are used to show the relative position of each piece when a drawing encompasses more than one individual part or object that must fit together. They are generally not needed on single-part drawings.

Copyright © Glencoe/McGraw-Hill

Answers to Chapter Reviews, *Fundamentals* (Continued)

Chapter 26
Review Questions
1. They are used to tailor the appearance of the dimensions to specific style requirements. A company might have specific requirements for how their dimensions should appear on drawings. You can create dimension styles that meet these requirements.
2. Set it at the reciprocal of the plot scale.
3. Center marks are small crosses at the center of an arc or circle. Center lines go completely across the arc or circle and also locate the center. When you use each one will depend on company requirements.
4. The **Continue Dimension** button allows you to continue a previous dimension to create a string of continuous dimensions quickly.
5. The **Dim Text Position, Precision,** and **Dim Style** options allow you to override the settings for the selected dimensions. **Dim Text Position** repositions the dimension text with or without a leader. **Precision** overrides the decimal precision of the dimension. **Dim Style** creates a new style based on the selected dimension(s) or assigns a style to the dimension(s).
6. Spline leaders can be used in "tight" areas of a drawing where other leaders will not fit.
7. Associative dimensions are easier to edit and automatically update when resized with their associated object.
8. Use grips.

Challenge Your Thinking
1. Placing dimensions on a separate layer allows you to freeze them, assign a different color, or plot them at a different width. Freezing a dimension layer while you work on the object makes the drawing less crowded.
2. Change the drawing area to 18′ × 14′. The dimension scale does not need to be changed because the drawing scale remains the same.

Chapter 27
Review Questions
1. AutoCAD allows tremendous flexibility in creating dimension styles to meet the needs of various industries.
2. Alternate units are a second set of dimensions. For example, you could dimension a drawing using inches and use millimeters as an alternate unit.
3. Yes; you may need to rotate dimension text in order to make the dimensioning clearer.
4. The **New** option changes or creates new dimension text for a dimension.
5. You can adjust the angle of a dimension's extension lines using the **Oblique** option of the **DIMEDIT** command (**Dimension Edit** button).
6. None of the dimension editing tools will work on dimensions that are not associative (or have been exploded).
7. Select the dimension, right-click, and select **Properties** to display the **Properties** dialog box.
8. Answers will vary. You may need to suppress a dimension line to fit text in a tight area or to avoid conflicts with other dimensions.

Challenge Your Thinking
1. Change **Dimension Scale** to 25.4.
2. Answers depend on the companies chosen.

Chapter 28
Review Questions
1. Tolerances allow for (and place restrictions on) the normal variation in dimensions that occurs when a part is manufactured.
2. Tolerances are needed for most manufactured components in order to control deviations in dimensions.
3. Examples will vary; students should display the correct format for each dimensioning type.
4. Either deviation or limits.
5. A surface control is a feature control frame not associated with a specific dimension. It establishes the tolerances for the surface of a part. For example, you would use a surface control to establish how flat a surface must be. You create a surface control by picking the **Tolerance** button and specifying the symbol and tolerance values.
6. The **QLEADER** command allows you to use a tolerance box as annotation for the leader.
7. A geometric characteristic symbol specifies the tolerance for the form and position of items on the object being drawn.
8. In the **Geometric Tolerance** dialog box, pick the symbol area to the right of any tolerance or datum value and pick the appropriate material condition symbol.
9. In the **Geometric Tolerance** dialog box, enter the information in the **Tolerance 2** line.

Answers to Chapter Reviews, *Fundamentals* (Continued)

Challenge Your Thinking
1. The easiest way to edit a feature control frame is to use the **DDEDIT** command. The **Geometric Tolerance** dialog box appears.
2. A second feature control frame places more restrictions on the features on the object.
3. Material conditions dictate the allowable tolerances on dimensions.

Chapter 29

Review Questions
1. The **ID** command lists coordinate values.
2. The area and perimeter of an object.
3. The **LIST** command displays all of the information contained in the AutoCAD drawing database for the selected objects.
4. Use the **AREA** command or **LIST** command to calculate the perimeter of a polygon.
5. Use the **AREA** or **LIST** command to calculate the circumference of a circle.
6. By using the **DDPTYPE** command.
7. **MEASURE** allows you to place markers along the object at specified intervals. **DIVIDE** divides the entire object into equal segments. Use **MEASURE** when you know how long the individual segments have to be. Use **DIVIDE** to divide the entire object into equal parts.

Challenge Your Thinking
1. Answers will vary, but student answers should demonstrate that they understand the difference between the two commands.
2. Points created using the **POINT** command are AutoCAD objects; points created by **MEASURE** and **DIVIDE** are not. They are just markers that define lengths.

Chapter 30

Review Questions
1. A group is a collection of individual objects to which a name has been assigned.
2. Groups allow you to move, scale, erase, and perform other editing operations on several objects in one operation.
3. Answers will vary. Students should realize that on a complex drawing, which may have many groups, it can be easy to forget the purpose of an individual group.
4. You can add and delete objects from a group using the **Remove** and **Add** buttons in the **Object Grouping** dialog box.
5. Yes; when the **Selectable** check box is checked, the group is selectable as a single object. When it is not checked, you can edit individual objects within the group and the entire group is not selectable.
6. You might want to reorder the objects in the group when drawing order is critical to an outside process, such as creating tool paths for a CNC machine.

Challenge Your Thinking
1. Answers will vary. Entering a group name in response to the **Select objects** prompt can save time, particularly when the elements of a particular group are scattered around the drawing and interspersed with other objects.
2. Answers will vary. Example: In a group where you want no further changes to take place.

Chapter 31

Review Questions
1. Blocks allow you to combine several objects into one, store them as such, and insert them at any time, thus avoiding repetition.
2. It inserts predefined blocks or drawings, according to coordinates you have given.
3. One way is to pick the **Insert Block** button. This displays a dialog box with the names of all defined blocks.
4. Inserting the block without the **Explode** box checked results in a block that cannot be edited. Selecting the **Explode** check box allows subsequent editing of the newly inserted block.
5. **WBLOCK** allows objects or blocks to be saved as a new drawing file.
6. When you need access to blocks in other drawings, since blocks reside only in the drawing in which they were created.
7. Use the **RENAME** command.
8. Purging unused blocks from a drawing makes the file size smaller and more manageable.
9. Cutting and pasting is a faster method.

Challenge Your Thinking
1. Answers will vary. Examples: using **WBLOCK** to write blocks to files, inserting blocks into a template file, and creating a script file. (Script files are discussed in Chapter 20 of *Applying AutoCAD 2002: Advanced*.)
2. Yes, AutoCAD automatically recognizes the pasted object as a block in the second drawing. Using the "copy and paste" or "cut and paste" methods automatically creates blocks.

Answers to Chapter Reviews, *Fundamentals* (Continued)

Chapter 32
Review Questions
1. To avoid drawing the same item(s) more than once and to standardize.
2. Use layer 0 so that they inherit the properties of the layer on which they are inserted.
3. An organized, hierarchical tree that shows your computer's files, folders, or devices.
4. Drag and drop it from DesignCenter into the current drawing window.
5. (Any three) Dimension styles, layers, layouts, line types, text styles, xrefs.

Challenge Your Thinking
1. Answers will vary. One idea would be to create a symbol library for the desks, chairs, tables, etc. needed for office designs.
2. Answers will vary. Groups are less formal than blocks, and they can only exist inside the drawing in which they were created.
3. Shortcuts are especially useful for inserting often-used symbols. For example, an electrical engineer laying out electrical plans might want to create shortcuts for symbols that represent receptacles, switches, and lights.

Chapter 33
Review Questions
1. Attributes can be used to create reports such as bills of materials.
2. ATTDEF allows you to assign attribute information to drawing components. ATTDISP makes attributes visible or invisible. ATTEDIT lets you edit attributes. BATTMAN lets you edit attribute definitions in blocks, remove attributes, and change the order in which you are prompted for attribute values when inserting blocks.
3. Attribute tags define categories, such as "cost," under which attribute values fall.
4. Attribute values are the specific values (*e.g.*, $200) assigned to and stored in blocks.
5. The Invisible mode does not display the attribute value in the drawing when the block is inserted. The Constant mode gives the attribute a fixed value for all insertions.

Challenge Your Thinking
1. With variable attributes, you can change the attribute values as you insert the block. Fixed attribute values are permanently assigned when the blocks are first created.
2. Answers will vary. Responses may include any items which would benefit from labeling or being associated with other categories of identification.

Chapter 34
Review Questions
1. DDATTEXT displays the Attribute Extraction dialog box, where you can select the format and file from which attributes are extracted.
2. Create a template file to define the format. Then use the DDATTEXT command to select the objects, specify the template file, and specify the output file.
3. It defines the appearance of dialog boxes.
4. Extract.lsp allows you to format and display the contents of comma delimited files (CDF).

Challenge Your Thinking
1. (Answers may vary.) Create a template file that tells AutoCAD how to set up the information. You can display or print them using the appropriate database software.
2. (Answers may vary.) A template extraction file sets up the parameters for displaying text files that include attribute information. Each line of the template extraction file corresponds to one attribute defined in the drawing. The line specifies the name of the attribute tag, character width, and numerical precision for the attribute information.

Answers to Chapter Tests for *Fundamentals* Text

Chapter 1
1. B
2. C
3. A
4. A
5. B
6. toolbars
7. Open
8. EXIT
9. command
10. drawing area

Chapter 2
1. D
2. A
3. C
4. C
5. B
6. crosshairs
7. docked
8. TOOLBAR
9. scrollbars
10. dialog box

Chapter 3
1. A
2. C
3. A
4. D
5. D
6. wizard
7. command alias
8. rubber-band
9. LINE
10. shortcut menu

Chapter 4
1. B
2. B
3. A
4. D
5. regular
6. radial
7. concentric
8. tangent
9. diameter
10. Circles

Chapter 5
1. C
2. C
3. B
4. D
5. A
6. entity
7. noun/verb
8. Grips
9. Fence
10. Remove

Chapter 6
1. C
2. C
3. D
4. A
5. B
6. coordinate pair
7. Cartesian
8. origin
9. vertical
10. @

Chapter 7
1. A
2. D
3. B
4. B
5. C
6. A
7. Thumbnails
8. F1
9. Index
10. Ask Me

Chapter 8
1. B
2. A
3. B
4. C
5. D
6. D
7. attributes
8. AUDIT
9. RECOVER
10. BAK

Chapter 9
1. D
2. C
3. A
4. D
5. A
6. running
7. alignment paths
8. Object Snap
9. aperture box
10. OTRACK

Chapter 10
1. B
2. C
3. B
4. A
5. D
6. ortho
7. F6
8. F2
9. F8
10. elapsed

Chapter 11
1. D
2. A
3. D
4. A
5. A
6. aspect ratio
7. multiview
8. orthographic projection
9. offsetting
10. SNAP

Chapter 12
1. D
2. A
3. B
4. B
5. C
6. transparent
7. regeneration
8. resolution
9. Z
10. .5x

Chapter 13
1. C
2. D
3. A
4. D
5. F
6. T
7. T
8. T
9. T
10. F

Chapter 14
1. A
2. B
3. C
4. B
5. A
6. A
7. B-spline
8. PEDIT
9. Control
10. SPLINEDIT

Chapter 15
1. B
2. C
3. D
4. C
5. C
6. B
7. fillet
8. concentric
9. load
10. MLEDIT

Chapter 16
1. A
2. B
3. D
4. D
5. B
6. A
7. T
8. T
9. F
10. T

Chapter 17
1. A
2. A
3. D
4. A
5. F
6. F
7. T
8. T
9. T
10. F

Chapter 18
1. D
2. A
3. D
4. A
5. C
6. font
7. import
8. romans.shx
9. STANDARD
10. txt.shx

Chapter 19
1. A
2. C
3. C
4. B
5. D
6. F
7. T
8. F
9. F
10. T

Chapter 20
1. D
2. D
3. A
4. D
5. A
6. crosshatch
7. Section
8. associative
9. HATCHEDIT
10. 1

Copyright © Glencoe/McGraw-Hill

Answers to Chapter Tests, *Fundamentals* (Continued)

Chapter 21
1. C
2. D
3. B
4. D
5. D
6. A
7. DWT
8. limits
9. drawing scale
10. 68',44'

Chapter 22
1. D
2. D
3. A
4. C
5. B
6. hidden
7. center
8. freeze
9. lock
10. Filtering

Chapter 23
1. D
2. C
3. B
4. A
5. T
6. F
7. F
8. T
9. T
10. T

Chapter 24
1. C
2. C
3. B
4. B
5. T
6. T
7. T
8. F
9. T
10. T

Chapter 25
1. D
2. B
3. A
4. C
5. D
6. D
7. Baseline
8. datum
9. Ordinate
10. STYLE

Chapter 26
1. D
2. A
3. C
4. D
5. T
6. F
7. F
8. T
9. F
10. T

Chapter 27
1. A
2. A
3. B
4. B
5. A
6. T
7. F
8. T
9. T
10. F

Chapter 28
1. A
2. B
3. D
4. B
5. C
6. symmetrical
7. deviation
8. geometric characteristic
9. material condition
10. projected

Chapter 29
1. C
2. A
3. B
4. C
5. D
6. T
7. F
8. T
9. T
10. F

Chapter 30
1. D
2. A
3. D
4. B
5. T
6. F
7. T
8. F
9. T
10. F

Chapter 31
1. C
2. D
3. A
4. B
5. D
6. B
7. F
8. T
9. T
10. T

Chapter 32
1. D
2. A
3. B
4. A
5. C
6. T
7. F
8. F
9. T
10. F

Chapter 33
1. D
2. B
3. A
4. B
5. C
6. fixed
7. ATTDEF
8. tag
9. value
10. ATTDISP

Chapter 34
1. C
2. D
3. A
4. B
5. F
6. T
7. T
8. T
9. F
10. F

Copyright © Glencoe/McGraw-Hill

APPLYING AutoCAD® 2002 ADVANCED

This section contains materials related specifically to the *Advanced* student textbook. Included are

- A scope and sequence chart, starting on page 224.
- Instructional plans for each of the textbook's 6 parts and 30 chapters. These begin on page 227.
- Transparency masters keyed to the textbook's 6 parts. The transparency masters begin on page 267.
- Chapter tests, starting on page 293.
- Answer keys for the chapter review questions and for the chapter tests, starting on page 325.

Scope and Sequence for *Advanced* Text

Themes and Concepts	Part 1	Part 2
Careers, Productivity, and Employability	Careers Using AutoCAD: Pages 34 and 58	Careers Using AutoCAD: Pages 94 and 120
Communication	Ch. 4: Challenge Your Thinking #2	Ch. 5: Challenge Your Thinking #2 Ch. 7: Challenge Your Thinking #1, #2 Part 2 Project
Mathematics	Ch. 1: Setting Up an Isometric Drawing; Creating an Isometric Drawing Chs. 2 and 4: Entire chapter Ch. 3: X/Y/Z Point Filtering; Snapping to Points in 3D Space; Controlling Visibility of Edges Part 1 Project	Chs. 5, 6, 7: Entire chapter Part 2 Project
Design and Problem Solving	All chapters: Using Problem-Solving Skills Part 1 Project	All chapters: Using Problem-Solving Skills Part 2 Project
Standards, Symbols, and Conventions	Ch.2: Setting Up an Isometric Drawing Ch. 3: Creating a Basic 3D Model	Ch. 9: Attaching Material Finishes; Predefined Landscape Objects
Creating, Editing, Manipulating, and Analyzing Drawings	Chs. 1 through 4: Entire chapter Part 1 Project	Chs. 5 through 9: Entire chapter Part 2 Project
Dimensioning and Tolerancing	Ch. 1: Dimensioning an Isometric Drawing Part 1 Project	
2D, 3D, and Solid Objects	Chs. 1 through 4: Entire chapter Part 1 Project	Chs. 5 through 9: Entire chapter Part 2 Project
Viewing, Printing, and Plotting	Ch. 2: Viewing and Hiding; Viewing Options; 3D Orbit Ch. 4: Generating the Plan View Part 1 Project	Ch. 5: Producing a Revolved Surface Ch. 9: Defining Light Sources; Defining a Scene; Adding a Background Part 2 Project
Computer Equipment and Software	Ch. 1: Setting Up an Isometric Drawing Ch. 2: Creating a Basic 3D Model; Viewing Options; 3D Orbit Ch. 3: Creating 3D Faces Ch. 4: Entire chapter	Ch. 5: Developing a 3D Template File; Controlling the Appearance of Surfaces Chs. 6, 8: Entire chapter Ch. 7: Placing Predefined Primitives Ch. 9: Phong Shading; Editing the Rendered Image

Copyright © Glencoe/McGraw-Hill

Scope and Sequence, *Advanced* (Continued)

Themes and Concepts	Part 3	Part 4
Careers, Productivity, and Employability	Careers Using AutoCAD: Pages 154, 181, 204, and 218	Careers Using AutoCAD: Pages 239 and 250
Communication	Ch. 10: Challenge Your Thinking #2 Ch. 17: Challenge Your Thinking #1, #3 Part 3 Project	Ch. 20: Challenge Your Thinking #2 Part 4 Project
Mathematics	Ch. 10: Creating a Solid Region; Creating a Region from Boundaries; Using Problem-Solving Skills Chs. 11, 12, 13: Entire chapter Ch. 14: Boolean Intersection Ch. 15: Introduction; Defining the Cutting Plane Ch. 17: Slicing the Pulley; Positioning the Solid Model	Ch. 20: Creating a Script
Design and Problem Solving	All chapters: Using Problem-Solving Skills Ch. 12: Applying AutoCAD Skills #1, #3 Ch. 13: Applying AutoCAD Skills #3 Part 3 Project	All chapters: Using Problem-Solving Skills Ch. 19: Entire chapter Ch. 20: Challenge Your Thinking #2; Applying AutoCAD Skills #3 Part 4 Project
Standards, Symbols, and Conventions		
Creating, Editing, Manipulating, and Analyzing Drawings	Chs. 10 through 16: Entire chapter Ch. 17: Slicing the Pulley; Positioning the Solid Model Part 3 Project	Ch. 20: Using Problem-Solving Skills #1 Part 4 Project
Dimensioning and Tolerancing		Part 4 Project
2D, 3D, and Solid Objects	Chs. 10 through 17; Entire chapter Part 3 Project	
Viewing, Printing, and Plotting	Ch. 14: Positioning Adjacent Objects Ch. 15: Creating a Full Section; Creating a Profile Ch. 16: Entire chapter	Ch. 20: Entire chapter Part 4 Project
Computer Equipment and Software	Chs. 10, 11, 15, 17: Entire chapter Ch. 14: Shelling a Solid Object; Testing for Interference	Chs. 18 and 19: Entire chapter Ch. 20: Creating the Slides; Creating a Script; Creating the Library

Copyright © Glencoe/McGraw-Hill

Scope and Sequence, *Advanced* (Continued)

Themes and Concepts	Part 5	Part 6
Careers, Productivity, and Employability	Careers Using AutoCAD: Page 286	Careers Using AutoCAD: Pages 297, 319, and 368
Communication	Ch. 23: Documenting the Routine Part 5 Project	Ch. 27: Challenge Your Thinking #1; Applying AutoCAD Skills #2, #4 Ch. 30: Publishing to the Web; On-line Meetings; Applying AutoCAD Skills #1; Using Problem-Solving Skills #2, #3 Part 6 Project
Mathematics	Ch. 22: AutoLISP Arithmetic; AutoLISP Functions; Applying AutoCAD Skills #1, #4; Using Problem-Solving Skills	Ch. 24: ACIS Files
Design and Problem Solving	All chapters: Using Problem-Solving Skills Part 5 Project	All chapters: Using Problem-Solving Skills Ch. 26: Applying AutoCAD Skills #2 Ch. 27: Applying AutoCAD Skills #2, #4 Part 6 Project
Standards, Symbols, and Conventions		Ch. 24: IGES Files Ch. 26: Preparing the Drawings
Creating, Editing, Manipulating, and Analyzing Drawings	Ch. 23: Parametric Programming; Applying AutoCAD Skills #2, #3	Ch. 25: Mixing Raster and Vector Objects; Editing a Raster Image; Managing Images; all end-of-chapter problems Ch. 26: Preparing the Drawings; Binding an Xref; Binding Parts of an Xref; all end-of-chapter problems Ch. 27: Editing the Server Document; Linking a Document to AutoCAD Ch. 29: Hyperlinks; DWF Files; Using Problem-Solving Skills #1 Ch. 30: Using eTransmit to Package and Send Work; Inserting Content Using i-drop. Part 6 Project
Dimensioning and Tolerancing		Ch. 27: Using Problem-Solving Skills
2D, 3D, and Solid Objects	Ch. 21: Reviewing AutoLISP Examples; Using the Command Line	Ch. 24: 3D Studio Files; ACIS Files; Using Problem-Solving Skills
Viewing, Printing, and Plotting	Ch. 23: Applying AutoCAD Skills #4	Ch. 28: Viewing and Editing Data; Links Ch. 29: Opening a Drawing File Located on an Internet Server; Viewing DWF Files; Using Problem-Solving Skills #2, #3. Ch. 30: Viewing the Files. Part 6 Project
Computer Equipment and Software	Chs. 21, 22, 23: Entire chapter Part 5 Project	Chs. 24, 25, 27 through 30: Entire chapter Ch. 26: Attaching Files As Xrefs; Managing Xrefs. Part 6 Project

Copyright © Glencoe/McGraw-Hill

Instructional Plans for Advanced Text

In the instructional plans, you will find teaching suggestions for each of the text's 30 chapters and 6 parts.

Part 1 3D Drawing and Modeling 229
Chapter 1   Isometric Drawing 230
Chapter 2   The Third Dimension 231
Chapter 3   Point Filters 232
Chapter 4   User Coordinate Systems 233

Part 2 Surface Modeling and Rendering 235
Chapter 5   3D Revolutions..................... 236
Chapter 6   Advanced Surfaces 237
Chapter 7   3D Primitives 238
Chapter 8   Shading and Rendering.............. 239
Chapter 9   Advanced Rendering................. 240

Part 3 Solid Modeling 241
Chapter 10   Solid Regions 242
Chapter 11   Solid Primitives 243
Chapter 12   Basic Solid Modeling 244
Chapter 13   Boolean Operations 245
Chapter 14   Tailoring Solid Models 246
Chapter 15   Downstream Benefits 247
Chapter 16   Documenting Solid Models 248
Chapter 17   Physical Benefits of Solid Modeling...... 249

Part 4 Menus 251
Chapter 18   An Internal Peek at AutoCAD's Menus.... 252
Chapter 19   Custom Menus and Toolbars.......... 253
Chapter 20   Slides and Scripts................. 254

Copyright © Glencoe/McGraw-Hill

Part 5 AutoLISP **255**
Chapter 21   Exploring AutoLISP. 256
Chapter 22   Basic AutoLISP Programming 257
Chapter 23   Advanced AutoLISP Programming. 258

Part 6 Importing and Exporting **259**
Chapter 24   Standard File Formats. 260
Chapter 25   Raster Image Files 261
Chapter 26   External References 262
Chapter 27   Object Linking and Embedding (OLE) . . 263
Chapter 28   Database Connectivity. 264
Chapter 29   Internet Connectivity 265
Chapter 30   Internet Collaboration. 266

Name		Class Period		Time		
Date		M	Tu	W	Th	F

Instructional Plan - Advanced Text *Part 1* **3D Drawing and Modeling**

CHAPTERS AND MAIN TOPICS

Chapter 1: Isometric Drawing—setting up a drawing file for isometric drawing; creating an isometric drawing; dimensioning an isometric drawing

Chapter 2: The Third Dimension—creating a basic 3D model; choosing 3D viewing, such as the VPOINT command, the View pull-down menu, and the View toolbar; using 3D Orbit to manipulate the view of 3D models

Chapter 3: Point Filters—applying X/Y/Z point filters to specify points in 3D space; creating 3D faces; drawing lines in 3D space

Chapter 4: User Coordinate Systems—creating user coordinate systems; changing the current UCS; generating a plan view of a 3D model; deleting unused UCSs

CD-ROM

Use the following from the *Advanced Instructor Productivity CD-ROM* to help you present the textbook's topics and assess student progress.

- Pre-/Post-Test for Part 1, found in the **Exam**View test generator.

- PowerPoint presentation for Part 1. The first slide shows the main topics covered in Part 1 of the textbook. The remaining slides elaborate on the more complex topics. You may want to use the PowerPoint presentations to introduce all the topics in this part before students begin working through the chapters. Later, as they begin each chapter, you could show the related slides for that chapter.

TRANSPARENCY MASTERS

Transparency masters for Part 1 begin on page 269 of this guide.

Title	Use with
TM-1A: 3D Drawing and Modeling	Introduction to Part 1
TM-1B: Isometric Drawing	Chapter 1
TM-1C: 3D Model	Chapter 2
TM-1D: User Coordinate Systems	Chapter 4

HANDOUTS

Saftey (see pages 19-28)

Computer skills (see pages 35-42)

PART 1 PROJECT: 3D Modeling

This project, found at the end of Part 1 in the textbook, provides students the opportunity to apply the AutoCAD commands and procedures they have learned in this part.

- Remind students to read the Hints and Suggestions before they begin drawing.

- Summary Questions/Self-Evaluation may be answered in writing or used as a springboard to class discussion. Students could compare their procedures and exchange ideas about improving efficiency and accuracy.

- Have students keep a log of the methods they used to create their drawings. After they have finished their project, lead a class discussion about the methods that were used and their pros and cons.

- If your students have used the *Fundamentals* text, have them create a 3D model of the cereal box they drew for the project at the end of Part 2.

Copyright © Glencoe/McGraw-Hill

Name		Class Period		Time	
Date	M	Tu	W	Th	F

Instructional Plan - Advanced Text *Chapter 1* Isometric Drawing

FOCUS

- **Gaining Attention.** Pictorial drawings allow an object to appear as if it were shown in three dimensions. They are generally used in conjunction with 2D multiview drawings. Point out that pictorial drawings are helpful to a "nontechnical" person in perceiving the final design or layout of an object.

- **Objectives.** Discuss each of the objectives of the chapter. The objectives are listed at the beginning of each chapter.

- **Orientation.** Types of pictorial drawings include oblique, perspective, and axonometric. Isometric drawings are one kind of axonometric drawing. The other two are dimetric and trimetric. Show examples of each type of pictorial drawing and discuss their similarities and differences.

TEACH

- **Key Terms.** Ask students to write out the meaning of each term in their own words. Discuss the terms with the class until you arrive at a consensus about the meaning of each term.

- **PowerPoint.** Review the PowerPoint presentation for Part 1, provided on the CD-ROM. Slides 2 through 4 apply to this chapter.

- **Drawing Skills.** Assign the step-by-step instructions in the chapter. Skills covered include setting up, creating, and dimensioning an isometric drawing.

- **Isometric Drawings.** Isometric drawings have three axes equally spaced 120° apart. The scales along all three axes are the same. In a regular isometric drawing, the viewpoint is looking down on top of the object. There are other viewpoints, though they are not as commonly used. These are reversed axis isometric (looking up at the bottom of the object) and long axis isometric (looking from the right or the left of the object).

- **Toggling Planes.** While drawing each view, it is important to remain in the proper drawing plane. Use CTRL E to toggle through the planes each time you begin to draw a new view, to verify that you are in the correct plane.

ASSESS

- **Review Questions.** Ask students to complete the Review Questions. Discuss their answers in class. Answers are found in the Answer Keys section of this guide.

- **Applying AutoCAD Skills.** Assign the activities at the end of the chapter.

- **Reteaching.** If students have difficulty making isometric drawings, try giving them an actual object, such as a cube, as a model.

- **Enrichment.** Assign the Challenge Your Thinking questions at the end of the chapter. Assign the Using Problem-Solving Skills activities at the end of the chapter.

- **Mathematics.** Assign Challenge Your Thinking question 2.

- **Communication.** Assign Challenge Your Thinking question 1.

- **Additional Problems.** Assign problems 1, 2, 3, 5, 11, and 27. You may also wish to adapt problem 14 by requiring students to create an isometric view.

- **Test.** Use the Chapter Test printed in this guide, or create a test using the **Exam**View test generator on the CD-ROM. The answers can be found in the Answer Keys section of this guide.

CLOSE

- Have students open an existing multiview drawing file and add an isometric projection, placing it in the upper right-hand corner.

Name		Class Period		Time	
Date	M	Tu	W	Th	F

Instructional Plan - Advanced Text — *Chapter 2* **The Third Dimension**

FOCUS

- **Gaining Attention.** 3D animation is a growing field. This chapter will provide a great opportunity for your students' future success. Have them list several ways in which 3D visuals are used in industry, *e.g.,* TV shows, movies, multimedia presentations, and video games.

- **Objectives.** Discuss the objectives listed at the beginning of the textbook chapter.

- **Orientation.** Briefly review with students material they have previously learned that they will need in order to learn this chapter.

TEACH

- **Key Terms.** Ask students to write out the meaning of each term in their own words. Discuss the terms with the class until you arrive at a consensus about the meaning of each term.

- **PowerPoint.** Review the PowerPoint presentation for Part 1, provided on the CD-ROM. Slides 5 through 12 apply to this chapter.

- **Drawing Skills.** Assign the step-by-step instructions in the chapter. Skills covered include creating a 3D model, viewing and hiding the model, changing the elevation and thickness, using viewing options such as the predefined viewport buttons and the dialog box, and using the 3D Orbit tool.

- **VPOINT Viewing.** This function allows you to fairly accurately rotate a 3D object. Initially it can be rather confusing. A great deal of practice is required to become proficient.

- **3D Orbit.** 3DORBIT gives the ability to shade and rotate 3D images. It is a very "user friendly" feature and helps to make your drawings come to life.

ASSESS

- **Review Questions.** Ask students to complete the Review Questions. Discuss their answers in class. Answers are found in the Answer Keys section of this guide.

- **Applying AutoCAD Skills.** Assign the activities at the end of the chapter.

- **Reteaching.** This is the first step into the next level of drafting. 3D presentations are being used in most multimedia presentations. Allow your students to experiment with the features described in this chapter and encourage them to share their discoveries with one another.

- **Enrichment.** Assign the Challenge Your Thinking questions at the end of the chapter. Assign the Using Problem-Solving Skills activities at the end of the chapter.

- **Mathematics.** Assign Challenge Your Thinking questions 1 and 3.

- **Communication.** Assign Challenge Your Thinking question 2.

- **Test.** Use the Chapter Test printed in this guide, or create a test using the **Exam**View test generator on the CD-ROM. The answers can be found in the Answer Keys section of this guide.

CLOSE

- Have your students create a multilevel object comprising several different shapes, including a cylinder, box, and wedge. Have them add shading and rotate the object in various directions using the 3D Orbit tool. Have them describe what happens as they rotate the object.

Copyright © Glencoe/McGraw-Hill

Name		Class Period		Time	
Date	M	Tu	W	Th	F

Instructional Plan - Advanced Text *Chapter 3* **Point Filters**

FOCUS

- **Gaining Attention.** This chapter continues the 3D modeling instruction that was started in Chapter 2. Show the class an object, such as a cube, and ask students to identify its faces.
- **Objectives.** Discuss the objectives listed at the beginning of the textbook chapter.
- **Orientation.** Briefly review with students material they have previously learned that they will need in order to understand the content of this chapter.

TEACH

- **Key Terms.** Ask students to write out the meaning of each term in their own words. Discuss the terms with the class until you arrive at a consensus about the meaning of each term.
- **PowerPoint.** Review the PowerPoint presentation for Part 1, provided on the CD-ROM. Slides 13 through 15 apply to this chapter.
- **Drawing Skills.** Assign the step-by-step instructions in the chapter. Skills covered include creating 3D faces, X/Y/Z point filtering, mirroring a 3D face, controlling visibility of edges, snapping to points, and creating lines in 3D space.
- **X/Y/Z Point Filter.** The X/Y/Z point filtering feature will be helpful in completing the 3D objects begun in the preceding chapter. This feature has the ability to transcend different elevations with a single command. Students will save time because they don't have to constantly change their point of view to make points accessible.
- **Mirrored 3D Surfaces.** As with 2D drawings, the MIRROR command saves time by allowing the user to make a mirror image of an existing object.

ASSESS

- **Review Questions.** Ask students to complete the Review Questions. Discuss their answers in class. Answers are found in the Answer Keys section of this guide.
- **Applying AutoCAD Skills.** Assign the activities at the end of the chapter.
- **Reteaching.** Show an actual object (such as a foam core model of the "house" in this chapter). Help students identify the different faces and encourage them to compare views of the real object with views on the computer screen.
- **Enrichment.** Assign the Challenge Your Thinking questions at the end of the chapter. Assign the Using Problem-Solving Skills activities at the end of the chapter.
- **Communication.** Assign Challenge Your Thinking questions 1 and 2.
- **Test.** Use the Chapter Test printed in this guide, or create a test using the **Exam**View test generator on the CD-ROM. The answers can be found in the Answer Keys section of this guide.

CLOSE

- Develop a specific multilevel object or use a drawing from the textbook and have students create a 3D surface drawing, attempting to use each of the three methods described in this chapter.

Name		Class Period		Time	
Date	M	Tu	W	Th	F

Instructional Plan - Advanced Text — *Chapter 4* User Coordinate Systems

FOCUS

- **Gaining Attention.** Creating their own user coordinate systems will allow students to alter the plane they are currently drawing on. This feature is similar in function to toggling isometric planes (discussed in Chapter 1), except that it works in 3D drawings. It will permit users to add details to a specific surface while remaining aligned to that plane.

- **Objectives.** Discuss the objectives listed at the beginning of the textbook chapter.

- **Orientation.** Briefly review with students material they have previously learned that they will need in order to learn this chapter. You may wish to review the right-hand rule (see Instructional Plan for Chapter 17, *Fundamentals* text).

TEACH

- **Key Terms.** Ask students to write out the meaning of each term in their own words. Discuss the terms with the class until you arrive at a consensus about the meaning of each term.

- **PowerPoint.** Review the PowerPoint presentation for Part 1, provided on the CD-ROM. Slides 16 through 20 apply to this chapter.

- **Drawing Skills.** Assign the step-by-step instructions in the chapter. Skills covered include creating a UCS, changing the current UCS, generating the plan view, and deleting a UCS.

- **Changing the UCS.** The two methods described attain the same outcome; namely, defining a UCS. The three-point method requires two more steps to define the UCS than the object method. The three-point method is best used to define irregular or complex surfaces. The object method is the preferred method in most other instances.

- **Managing the UCS.** Working with several user coordinate systems on one drawing can prove confusing. It is best to delete each one following the completion of work on a given surface.

ASSESS

- **Review Questions.** Ask students to complete the Review Questions. Discuss their answers in class. Answers are found in the Answer Keys section of this guide.

- **Applying AutoCAD Skills.** Assign the activities at the end of the chapter.

- **Reteaching.** Review the methods of creating and managing UCSs. Allow your students to determine which method is most comfortable for them.

- **Enrichment.** Assign the Challenge Your Thinking questions at the end of the chapter. Assign the Using Problem-Solving Skills activities at the end of the chapter.

- **Communication.** Assign Challenge Your Thinking questions 1 and 2.

- **Test.** Use the Chapter Test printed in this guide, or create a test using the **Exam**View test generator on the CD-ROM. The answers can be found in the Answer Keys section of this guide.

CLOSE

- Have your students add details, such as siding, windows, doors, and skylights to several of the surfaces in drawing prb3-2 from the previous chapter.

Copyright © Glencoe/McGraw-Hill

Name		Class Period		Time		
Date		M	Tu	W	Th	F

Instructional Plan - Advanced Text
Part 2 Surface Modeling and Rendering

CHAPTERS AND MAIN TOPICS

Chapter 5: 3D Revolutions—creating a 3D template; controlling the appearance of surface meshes; creating revolved and ruled surfaces

Chapter 6: Advanced Surfaces—creating tabulated surfaces; producing Coons surface patches; defining surface meshes using coordinate entry; editing basic surface meshes; changing the type and appearance of a surface mesh

Chapter 7: 3D Primitives—placing predefined 3D surface primitives in a drawing; editing the placement and orientation of 3D surface primitives

Chapter 8: Shading and Rendering—shading a 3D model using flat and Gouraud shading; creating a basic rendering of a 3D model; saving and viewing a 3D model in various file formats

Chapter 9: Advanced Rendering—applying Phong shading to a 3D model; producing a photorealistic rendering of a 3D model; adding material finishes, lights, and backgrounds to photorealistic renderings; inserting and editing the appearance of bitmapped landscape objects in a drawing

CD-ROM

Use the following from the *Advanced Instructor Productivity CD-ROM* to help you present the textbook's topics and assess student progress.

- Pre-/Post-Test for Part 2, found in the **Exam**View test generator.
- PowerPoint presentation for Part 2. The first slide shows the main topics covered in Part 2 of the textbook. The remaining slides elaborate on the more complex topics. You may want to use the PowerPoint presentations to introduce all the topics in this part before students begin working through the chapters. Later, as they begin each chapter, you could show the related slides for that chapter.

TRANSPARENCY MASTERS

Transparency masters for Part 2 begin on page 273 of this guide.

Title	Use with
TM-2A: Surface Modeling and Rendering	Introduction to Part 2
TM-2B: 3D Revolutions	Chapter 5
TM-2C: Surfaces	Chapter 6
TM-2D: 3D Primitives	Chapter 7

HANDOUTS

Student and professional organizations (see pages 50-55)

PART 2 PROJECT: Bakery Brochure

This project, found at the end of Part 2 of the textbook, provides students the opportunity to apply the AutoCAD commands and procedures they have learned in this part.

- Remind students to read the Hints and Suggestions before they begin drawing.
- Summary Questions/Self-Evaluation may be answered in writing or used as a springboard to class discussion. Students could compare their procedures and exchange ideas about improving efficiency and accuracy.
- As an alternative project, ask your students to come up with a design for a prototype race car. Have them first create a rough sketch of the concept. Then have them create the AutoCAD 3D drawing of the model. Ask them to combine different mesh surfaces to create the hood, sides, back, and fenders for the model car. Mention that a wise modeler will always create patches in different colors in order to distinguish between the edge lines.

Copyright © Glencoe/McGraw-Hill

Name		Class Period		Time	
Date	M	Tu	W	Th	F

Instructional Plan - Advanced Text — *Chapter 5* 3D Revolutions

FOCUS

- **Gaining Attention.** 3D revolutions can be a lot of fun because they are easy to create and the results can be very pleasing. Ask students if they know how to create a flying saucer, a bowl, apples, or a valve slide for a hydraulic flow control valve. All of these shapes are easy to create if you can produce a profile, create an axis line, and know how many degrees of revolution are required.

- **Objectives.** Discuss the objectives listed at the beginning of the textbook chapter.

- **Orientation.** Briefly review with students material they have previously learned that they will need in order to understand the concepts presented in this chapter. (Students will use the skills they learned in Chapters 2 through 4.)

TEACH

- **Key Terms.** Ask students to write out the meaning of each term in their own words. Discuss the terms with the class until you arrive at a consensus about the meaning of each term.

- **PowerPoint.** Review the PowerPoint presentation for Part 2, provided on the CD-ROM. Slides 2 through 5 apply to this chapter.

- **Drawing Skills.** Assign the step-by-step instructions in the chapter. Skills covered include creating 3D revolutions and creating a 3D ruled surface.

- **Profiles.** Profiles (path curves) used for revolutions can be created using standard lines, circles, splines, polylines, arcs, and ellipses, or any combination of these. The only requirement is that they form a closed loop.

- **Ruled Surfaces.** The purpose of ruled surfaces is to illustrate and cause rendering or surfacing of the area between two other surfaces.

ASSESS

- **Review Questions.** Ask students to complete the Review Questions. Discuss their answers in class. The answers are found in the Answer Keys section of this guide.

- **Applying AutoCAD Skills.** Assign the activities at the end of the chapter.

- **Reteaching.** Students may need a review of underlying concepts. For example, they may need to revisit Chapter 4, "Basic Objects," in the *Fundamentals* text.

- **Enrichment.** Assign the Challenge Your Thinking questions at the end of the chapter. Assign the Using Problem-Solving Skills activities at the end of the chapter.

- **Communication.** Assign Challenge Your Thinking questions 1 and 2.

- **Test.** Use the Chapter Test printed in this guide, or create a test using the **ExamView** test generator on the CD-ROM. The answers can be found in the Answer Keys section of this guide.

CLOSE

- Have students create a bowl and then have them create some apples and oranges to be placed in the bowl. Remind them to use color (red or yellow for the apples, orange for the oranges). Have them save their drawings. In later chapters, you may want to have them shade and render their work.

Name		Class Period			Time	
Date		M	Tu	W	Th	F

Instructional Plan - Advanced Text *Chapter 6* **Advanced Surfaces**

FOCUS

- **Gaining Attention.** Ask your students how they would go about developing a shape like the I-beam illustrated in this chapter. Help them along by using the example of squeezing toothpaste out of a tube. When you squeeze the paste out, you are getting a cylindrical shape that follows along a line (usually along the bristles of the toothbrush). This process is extrusion, something you'll get into in Chapters 13 and 14. However, you can achieve this effect now using TABSURF.

- **Objectives.** Discuss the objectives listed at the beginning of the textbook chapter.

- **Orientation.** Make sure students have their 3dtmp.dwt template file, which they created in Chapter 5.

TEACH

- **Key Terms.** Ask students to write out the meaning of each term in their own words. Discuss the terms with the class until you arrive at a consensus about the meaning of each term.

- **PowerPoint.** Review the PowerPoint presentation for Part 2, provided on the CD-ROM. Slides 6 through 14 apply to this chapter.

- **Drawing Skills.** Assign the step-by-step instructions in the chapter. Skills covered include producing a tabulated surface, creating a Coons surface patch, and using the 3DMESH command.

- **Creating Complex Surfaces.** You can develop a series of complex surfaces using the EDGESURF command. First create 3D boxes to form the boundaries for each complex surface and then form the complex surfaces by using PLINES to shape the ending edge of the surfaces.

- **Editing a Surface Patch Using PEDIT.** When you select a surface mesh for modifications using the PEDIT command, be very careful to position the UCS so that it is perpendicular to the mesh. Also be careful positioning the vertices. Once the object is positioned correctly with its "X marks the spot" location, move the vertices in or out by keying in the new Z axis coordinate. Always smooth your results before leaving the PEDIT command.

ASSESS

- **Review Questions.** Ask students to complete the Review Questions. Discuss their answers in class. The answers are found in the Answer Keys section of this guide.

- **Applying AutoCAD Skills.** Assign the activities at the end of the chapter.

- **Reteaching.** Have students locate examples (pictures or actual objects) of items that would be drawn with tabulated surfaces and with Coons surface patches.

- **Enrichment.** Assign the Challenge Your Thinking questions at the end of the chapter. Assign the Using Problem-Solving Skills activities at the end of the chapter.

- **Communication.** Assign Challenge Your Thinking questions 1 and 2.

- **Test.** Use the Chapter Test printed in this guide, or create a test using the **Exam**View test generator on the CD-ROM. The answers can be found in the Answer Keys section of this guide.

CLOSE

- Ask your students what the differences are between the wire meshes they are using and the meshes that are currently being used by industry, called NURBS geometry.

Copyright © Glencoe/McGraw-Hill

Name		Class Period		Time	
Date	M	Tu	W	Th	F

Instructional Plan - Advanced Text — *Chapter 7* 3D Primitives

FOCUS

- **Gaining Attention.** Tell your students you want them to create an attractive Web page that contains combinations of 3D shapes: spheres, cones, cylinders, boxes, and tori. Ask them if it is possible to combine these primitives to create objects such as a clown's face, Mickey Mouse, a computer monitor, or a keyboard. (It can be done by combining various primitive shapes and using the SHADE command to complete the 3D effects.)
- **Objectives.** Discuss the objectives listed at the beginning of the textbook chapter.
- **Orientation.** Briefly review with students material they have previously learned that they will need in order to learn this chapter.

TEACH

- **Key Terms.** Ask students to write out the meaning of each term in their own words. Discuss the terms with the class until you arrive at a consensus about the meaning of each term.
- **PowerPoint.** Review the PowerPoint presentation for Part 2, provided on the CD-ROM. Slides 15 and 16 apply to this chapter.
- **Drawing Skills.** Assign the step-by-step instructions in the chapter. Skills covered include placing predefined primitives in a drawing and editing primitives.
- **Creating a Cylinder.** Although the cylinder is not specified as one of the predefined 3D primitives, it can be created from the 3D cone primitive. If you specify the same value for both the base radius and the top radius, along with a height value, you have created a cylinder instead of a cone.
- **Creating a Comical Face.** You can create a funny face by using either a sphere or cylinder and editing the mesh of these primitives using PEDIT. It will be painstaking work, but your cartooning results will be worthwhile.

ASSESS

- **Review Questions.** Ask students to complete the Review Questions. Discuss their answers in class. The answers are found in the Answer Keys section of this guide.
- **Applying AutoCAD Skills.** Assign the activities at the end of the chapter.
- **Reteaching.** Make sure students can correctly identify the predefined primitives. Have them identify real-life objects that incorporate these shapes.
- **Enrichment.** Assign the Challenge Your Thinking questions at the end of the chapter. Assign the Using Problem-Solving Skills activities at the end of the chapter.
- **Communication.** Assign Challenge Your Thinking question 1.
- **Mathematics.** Assign Challenge Your Thinking question 2.
- **Test.** Use the Chapter Test printed in this guide, or create a test using the **Exam***View* test generator on the CD-ROM. The answers can be found in the Answer Keys section of this guide.

CLOSE

- One of the fastest-growing industries is 3D model creation for product advertisement, animation, and 3D modeling for VRML (Virtual Reality Markup Language) used on the Internet. Have students check this out through job searches on the Internet.

Name		Class Period		Time	
Date		M	Tu	W	Th	F

Instructional Plan - Advanced Text — *Chapter 8* **Shading and Rendering**

FOCUS

- **Gaining Attention.** Have your students create a sphere, cone, and box. Next, have them use the CHPROP command to change the colors as follows: red for the sphere, green for the cone, and blue for the box. Have them switch to SE Isometric viewpoint. Next, have them open the Shade toolbar, select the Hide button, and note the results. Have them select the Flat Shaded button and note the results. Next, have them select the Gouraud Shaded button and note the results and then select the Flat Shaded, Edges On button and note the results. Finally, have them select the Gouraud Shaded, Edges On button and observe the results. Ask students if they noted any changes to the objects when they switched from one form of shading to another.

- **Objectives.** Discuss the objectives listed at the beginning of the textbook chapter.

- **Orientation.** Briefly review with students material they have previously learned that they will need in order to learn this chapter.

TEACH

- **Key Terms.** Ask students to write out the meaning of each term in their own words. Discuss the terms with the class until you arrive at a consensus about the meaning of each term.

- **PowerPoint.** Review the PowerPoint presentation for Part 2, provided on the CD-ROM. Slides 17 through 20 apply to this chapter.

- **Drawing Skills.** Assign the step-by-step instructions in the chapter. Skills covered are basic shading and creating a rendered drawing.

- **Rendering to Screen vs. Rendering to Image File.** If the video board of your computer is set to 800 × 600 and you have set the colors to 16-bit, the size of your image and the colors will be determined by these settings. This is not significant when viewing your results on the monitor. However, if you proceed to render to an image file, you may have either too large or too small a picture when it is brought over to another program for viewing or editing.

ASSESS

- **Review Questions.** Ask students to complete the Review Questions. Discuss their answers in class. The answers are found in the Answer Keys section of this guide.

- **Applying AutoCAD Skills.** Assign the activities at the end of the chapter.

- **Reteaching.** Discuss the difference between shading and rendering. Ask students to describe situations in which one technique might be preferred over the other.

- **Enrichment.** Assign the Challenge Your Thinking questions at the end of the chapter. Assign the Using Problem-Solving Skills activities at the end of the chapter.

- **Communication.** Assign Challenge Your Thinking questions 1 and 2.

- **Test.** Use the Chapter Test printed in this guide, or create a test using the **Exam***View* test generator on the CD-ROM. The answers can be found in the Answer Keys section of this guide.

CLOSE

- Ask students if they see any association between the shaded or rendered views they are producing and the images they see in animated computer graphics movies they have seen. Ask them if they have ever opened and participated in a VRML Web site. If they haven't, locate some VRML sites through Web searches.

Name		Class Period		Time	
Date	M	Tu	W	Th	F

Instructional Plan - Advanced Text — *Chapter 9* Advanced Rendering

FOCUS

- **Gaining Attention.** Create a 3D model using any of the 3D surfacing methods described in Chapters 5, 6, and 7. Show students the wireframe image as an isometric view and ask them if they can identify the front, back, and side of this object simply by looking at it. Now render the object using all the rendering defaults. Students should be able to identify the views more readily. Next, show students how adding material mapping to the 3D object makes it even easier to distinguish views. Add photorealism to the render properties and re-render. Ask students to note any differences.

- **Objectives.** Discuss the objectives listed at the beginning of the textbook chapter.

- **Orientation.** Briefly review with students material they have previously learned that they will need in order to learn this chapter.

TEACH

- **Key Terms.** Ask students to write out the meaning of each term in their own words. Discuss the terms with the class until you arrive at a consensus about the meaning of each term.

- **PowerPoint.** Review the PowerPoint presentation for Part 2, provided on the CD-ROM. Slides 21 through 23 apply to this chapter.

- **Drawing Skills.** Assign the step-by-step instructions in the chapter. Topics covered include rendering methods, adding backgrounds, adding material mappings, and developing image files of the rendering.

ASSESS

- **Review Questions.** Ask students to complete the Review Questions. Discuss their answers in class. The answers are found in the Answer Keys section of this guide.

- **Applying AutoCAD Skills.** Assign the activities at the end of the chapter.

- **Reteaching.** If students have difficulty with any of the procedures, demonstrate them on the computer. Use projection equipment to display the drawings to the class as you create them.

- **Enrichment.** Assign the Challenge Your Thinking questions at the end of the chapter. Assign the Using Problem-Solving Skills activities at the end of the chapter.

- **Communication.** Assign Challenge Your Thinking questions 1 and 2.

- **Test.** Use the Chapter Test printed in this guide, or create a test using the **Exam**View test generator on the CD-ROM. The answers can be found in the Answer Keys section of this guide.

CLOSE

- Programs like Microsoft® Photo Editor and Adobe® Photoshop® can be used for viewing or editing rendered files. If you have access to these programs, ask students to compare them for viewing or editing. (*Note:* One is primarily used for viewing and the other can also be used for editing.)

Name		Class Period		Time	
Date	M	Tu	W	Th	F

Instructional Plan - Advanced Text — *Part 3* Solid Modeling

CHAPTERS AND MAIN TOPICS

Chapter 10: Solid Regions—creating regions using Boolean operations; performing mass properties calculations on a region; creating a region from boundaries; extruding a solid region to form a 3D model

Chapter 11: Solid Primitives—distinguishing between surface models and solid models; creating solid primitives, including a cylinder, torus, cone, wedge, box, and sphere

Chapter 12: Basic Solid Modeling—revolving a 2D polyline to create a 3D solid model; adjusting the quality, accuracy, and appearance of a solid model; extruding a polyline

Chapter 13: Boolean Operations—using Boolean operations to remove portions of a solid model or to combine composite models

Chapter 14: Tailoring Solid Models—applying bevels and rounded edges to a composite solid; creating a composite solid by intersection; shelling a solid to create a hollow object; checking for interference

Chapter 15: Downstream Benefits—creating a full section from a solid model; creating a profile view from a solid model

Chapter 16: Documenting Solid Models—producing orthographic and section views from a solid model; positioning and plotting orthographic, sectional, and isometric views

Chapter 17: Physical Benefits of Solid Modeling—slicing a solid model; calculating mass properties; creating an STL file

CD-ROM

Use the following from the *Advanced Instructor Productivity CD-ROM* to help you present the textbook's topics and assess student progress.

- Pre-/Post-Test for Part 3, found in the **Exam**View test generator.
- PowerPoint presentation for Part 3. The first slide shows the main topics covered in Part 3 of the textbook. The remaining slides elaborate on the more complex topics. You may want to use the PowerPoint presentations to introduce all the topics in this part before students begin working through the chapters. Later, as they begin each chapter, you could show the related slides for that chapter.

TRANSPARENCY MASTERS

Transparency masters for Part 3 begin on page 277 of this guide.

Title	Use with
TM-3A: Solid Modeling	Introduction to Part 3
TM-3B: Solid Primitives	Chapter 11
TM-3C: Revolved Solid Model	Chapter 12
TM-3D: Solid Extrusion	Chapter 12
TM-3E: Positioning and Plotting Views	Chapter 16

HANDOUTS

Career Handouts: HO-12 through HO-15

PART 3 PROJECT: Designing and Modeling a Desk Set

This project, found at the end of Part 3 of the textbook, provides students the opportunity to apply the AutoCAD commands and procedures they have learned in this part.

- Remind students to read the Hints and Suggestions before they begin drawing.
- Summary Questions/Self-Evaluation may be answered in writing or used as a springboard to class discussion. Students could compare their procedures and exchange ideas about improving efficiency and accuracy.

Copyright © Glencoe/McGraw-Hill

Name			Class Period		Time	
Date	M	Tu	W		Th	F

Instructional Plan - Advanced Text   *Chapter 10* Solid Regions

FOCUS

- **Gaining Attention.** Ask the question: "How are solids used in the everyday world?" Suggest engineering applications, advertisements, graphic analysis to interpret complex functions, or models used for special effects in movies.

- **Objectives.** Discuss the objectives listed at the beginning of the textbook chapter.

- **Orientation.** Briefly review with students material they have previously learned that they will need in order to learn this chapter.

TEACH

- **Key Terms.** Ask students to write out the meaning of each term in their own words. Discuss the terms with the class until you arrive at a consensus about the meaning of each term.

- **PowerPoint.** Review the PowerPoint presentation for Part 3, provided on the CD-ROM. Slides 2 through 5 apply to this chapter.

- **Drawing Skills.** Assign the step-by-step instructions in the chapter. Skills covered include creating solid regions, using Boolean operations, performing mass properties calculations, and making 3D objects from regions.

- **Applying Boolean Functions.** In demonstrating the methods of developing regions from multiple shapes, use the SUBTRACT and UNION commands to show how simple shapes can be transformed into unique and complex shapes.

- **Calculating Mass Properties.** Illustrate how civil engineers can calculate the areas and volumes of concrete shapes used in building skyscrapers, bridges, and highways by applying MASSPROP to a region or extruded solid.

ASSESS

- **Review Questions.** Ask students to complete the Review Questions. Discuss their answers in class. Answers are found in the Answer Keys section of this guide.

- **Applying AutoCAD Skills.** Assign the activities at the end of the chapter.

- **Reteaching.** Let your students know that crossing and closing lines are essential in developing closed shapes for regions. If lines are not touching or are crossing other lines in the shape, the REGION command will not execute.

- **Enrichment.** Assign the Challenge Your Thinking questions at the end of the chapter. Assign the Using Problem-Solving Skills activities at the end of the chapter.

- **Mathematics.** Ask students to determine the cubic foot volume for a 4" × 24' × 40' driveway using the REGION, EXTRUDE, and MASSPROP commands.

- **Communication.** Assign Challenge Your Thinking questions 1 and 2.

- **Test.** Use the Chapter Test printed in this guide, or create a test using the **Exam**View test generator on the CD-ROM. The answers can be found in the Answer Keys section of this guide.

CLOSE

- Ask students to develop plans for a computer using PLINE and then create the shape as a region. Ask them to extrude it into a notebook, tower, or desktop shape. After they complete this activity, have them plot the computer shape in 3D SE Isometric view.

Name		Class Period		Time	
Date	M	Tu	W	Th	F

Instructional Plan - Advanced Text — *Chapter 11* Solid Primitives

FOCUS

- **Gaining Attention.** Find out if any students can associate the primitive models used in AutoCAD with mathematical models used in geometry. Explain that solid primitives can be put together to create complex objects.

- **Objectives.** Discuss the objectives listed at the beginning of the textbook chapter.

- **Orientation.** Briefly review with students material they have previously learned that they will need in order to learn this chapter.

TEACH

- **Key Terms.** Ask students to write out the meaning of each term in their own words. Discuss the terms with the class until you arrive at a consensus about the meaning of each term.

- **PowerPoint.** Review the PowerPoint presentation for Part 3, provided on the CD-ROM. Slides 6 through 16 apply to this chapter.

- **Drawing Skills.** Assign the step-by-step instructions in the chapter. Skills covered include creating a solid cylinder, a torus, a cone, a wedge, a box, and a sphere.

- **Cylinders.** Here's a tip on constructing a cylinder. Remember that after the height is given for the cylinder, you have the ability to taper the side of the cylinder. In tapering, the value of the angle is taken as a doubling effect, so if you enter 2 to mean 2 degrees, you are actually tapering 2 degrees on both sides of the cylinder, resulting in 4 degrees of total taper.

- **Additional Procedures.** Explain the alternate method of creating a box using the Center option, how to make an elliptical cylinder, or how to create a wedge using a negative number for the height.

ASSESS

- **Review Questions.** Ask students to complete the Review Questions. Discuss their answers in class. The answers are found in the Answer Keys section of this guide.

- **Applying AutoCAD Skills.** Assign the activities at the end of the chapter.

- **Reteaching.** Review the basic, underlying concepts that students may not understand clearly. Recall the 3D primitives described in Chapter 7.

- **Enrichment.** Assign the Challenge Your Thinking questions at the end of the chapter. Assign the Using Problem-Solving Skills activities at the end of the chapter.

- **Communication.** Assign Challenge Your Thinking question 1.

- **Mathematics.** Assign Challenge Your Thinking question 2.

- **Test.** Use the Chapter Test printed in this guide, or create a test using the **Exam**View test generator on the CD-ROM. The answers can be found in the Answer Keys section of this guide.

CLOSE

- Ask students how they would draw a drinking glass using only primitives.

- Ask students to draw our solar system using only spheres and tori.

Copyright © Glencoe/McGraw-Hill

Name		Class Period		Time	
Date	M	Tu	W	Th	F

Instructional Plan - Advanced Text *Chapter 12* Basic Solid Modeling

FOCUS

- **Gaining Attention.** Using REVOLVE to create a solid model can result in some very impressive shapes with little effort. You can make a bowl, lamp, pop bottle, gearshift handle, etc. As a demonstration, make a candlestick.
- **Objectives.** Discuss the objectives listed at the beginning of the textbook chapter.
- **Orientation.** Briefly review with students material they have previously learned that they will need in order to learn this chapter.

TEACH

- **Key Terms.** Ask students to write out the meaning of each term in their own words. Discuss the terms with the class until you arrive at a consensus about the meaning of each term.
- **PowerPoint.** Review the PowerPoint presentation for Part 3, provided on the CD-ROM. Slides 17 through 20 apply to this chapter.
- **Drawing Skills.** Assign the step-by-step instructions in the chapter. Skills covered include creating solid models using the REVOLVE command, changing tessellation lines using the ISOLINES command, and developing solid models using the EXTRUDE command.
- **Profile Positioning.** In developing a solid model with the REVOLVE command, it is usual to change the viewpoint to a front view and place the UCS parallel to that view before creating the profile.
- **Tessellation.** Tessellation is sometimes equated with the creation of mesh lines. If you wish to keep the number of tessellation lines low but still wish to have a smooth object shape, export your drawing to 3D Studio MAX and render in this software instead of AutoCAD.

ASSESS

- **Review Questions.** Ask students to complete the Review Questions. Discuss their answers in class. The answers are found in the Answer Keys section of this guide.
- **Applying AutoCAD Skills.** Assign the activities at the end of the chapter.
- **Reteaching.** Review underlying concepts that students may not clearly understand. For example, explain what the differences are between REVOLVE and ROTATE. Explain why it is easier to develop a profile for a solid model using polylines than using lines.
- **Enrichment.** Assign the Challenge Your Thinking questions at the end of the chapter. Assign the Using Problem-Solving Skills activities at the end of the chapter.
- **Communication.** Assign Challenge Your Thinking questions 1 and 2.
- **Additional Problem.** Assign Problem 26.
- **Test.** Use the Chapter Test printed in this guide, or create a test using the **Exam**View test generator on the CD-ROM. The answers can be found in the Answer Keys section of this guide.

CLOSE

- Encourage students to use their imagination. Ask them to create a really unusual profile with the LINE, CIRCLE, and ARC commands. Then have them create a region from these shapes. Next, they should use the REVOLVE command to create a solid model. Awards could be given out for the wildest shape.

Name		Class Period		Time	
Date	M	Tu	W	Th	F

Instructional Plan - Advanced Text   **Chapter 13** Boolean Operations

FOCUS

- **Gaining Attention.** Compare the Boolean operation of SUBTRACT to drilling a hole in a piece of wood. Both are subtractions of material from an object. Likewise, UNION is very similar to gluing two pieces of wood together to form a combined shape. Ask students if they can think of any other associations using SUBTRACT and UNION.

- **Objectives.** Discuss the objectives listed at the beginning of the textbook chapter.

- **Orientation.** Briefly review with students material they have previously learned that they will need in order to learn this chapter.

TEACH

- **Key Terms.** Ask students to write out the meaning of each term in their own words. Discuss the terms with the class until you arrive at a consensus about the meaning of each term.

- **Drawing Skills.** Assign the step-by-step instructions in the chapter. Skills covered include removing portions of a solid model and combining composite models.

- **UCS.** Always observe the positioning of the UCS when combining shapes. Locate the UCS on the face you plan to add to or subtract from. Movements of the UCS are always based from a corner, center position, or object snap position on the object's face.

ASSESS

- **Review Questions.** Ask students to complete the Review Questions. Discuss their answers in class. The answers are found in the Answer Keys section of this guide.

- **Applying AutoCAD Skills.** Assign the activities at the end of the chapter.

- **Reteaching.** Make sure students understand what a composite solid is. Explain the difference between UNION and SUBTRACT when developing a solid object.

- **Enrichment.** Assign the Challenge Your Thinking questions at the end of the chapter. Assign the Using Problem-Solving Skills activities at the end of the chapter.

- **Communication.** Assign Challenge Your Thinking questions 1 and 2.

- **Additional Problems.** Assign problems 24, 25, and 26.

- **Advanced Projects.** Assign one or more of the following Advanced Projects: Bolted Seat Connection (page 414), Bushing Assembly (page 418), or Clothing Rack (page 428).

- **Test.** Use the Chapter Test printed in this guide, or create a test using the **Exam**View test generator on the CD-ROM. The answers can be found in the Answer Keys section of this guide.

CLOSE

- Ask students to create a 3D object with two holes and a slot in it. Then, have them take a bar of soft soap and try to carve the same shape they drew from the bar. (Observe appropriate safety practices.) How closely does the soap's shape resemble the drawing? Award credit for the best carving and also bonus points for the cleanest hands in the class!

Copyright © Glencoe/McGraw-Hill

Name		Class Period		Time	
Date	M	Tu	W	Th	F

Instructional Plan - Advanced Text　　*Chapter 14* Tailoring Solid Models

FOCUS

- **Gaining Attention.** Ask your students where they might apply the INTERFERE command. Consider a case in which a designer models a wheel that partially overlaps a car body. The overlap may be only a few thousandths of an inch, but the result will be that the wheel will not turn. INTERFERE will help avoid that design error by showing the zone where the two objects overlap.

- **Objectives.** Discuss the objectives listed at the beginning of the textbook chapter.

- **Orientation.** Briefly review with students material they have previously learned that they will need in order to learn this chapter. If they need to review chamfers and fillets, refer to Chapter 15 in the *Fundamentals* text.

TEACH

- **Key Terms.** Ask students to write out the meaning of each term in their own words. Discuss the terms with the class until you arrive at a consensus about the meaning of each term.

- **Drawing Skills.** Assign the step-by-step instructions in the chapter. Skills covered include creating fillets, rounds, and chamfers and determining the amount of interference when two or more objects overlap.

- **Chaining Multiple Fillets or Chamfers.** It is easier to connect a grouping of fillets or chamfers than to select one or two edges, perform the fillet/chamfer functions, and then try to select more adjacent edges later.

- **INTERFERE Command.** An easy way to test the operation of the INTERFERE command is to create a box and then create a sphere that is half in and half out of the box. Select the INTERFERE command and select the box and sphere. Press ENTER, and you should see highlighted the half of the sphere that is inside the box.

ASSESS

- **Review Questions.** Ask students to complete the Review Questions. Discuss their answers in class. The answers are found in the Answer Keys section of this guide.

- **Applying AutoCAD Skills.** Assign the activities at the end of the chapter.

- **Reteaching.** If students have difficulty with any of the procedures, demonstrate them on your computer. Use projection equipment to display the drawings as you create them.

- **Enrichment.** Assign the Challenge Your Thinking questions at the end of the chapter. Assign the Using Problem-Solving Skills activities at the end of the chapter.

- **Communication.** Assign Challenge Your Thinking questions 1 and 2.

- **Additional Problems.** Assign problems 10, 15, and 22.

- **Advanced Projects.** Assign one or more of the following projects: Pepper Mill (page 404), Drawing Table (page 408), Mancala Game Board (page 410), or Buffet Tray (page 422).

- **Test.** Use the Chapter Test printed in this guide, or create a test using the **Exam**View test generator on the CD-ROM. The answers can be found in the Answer Keys section of this guide.

CLOSE

- Have students try a variety of fillet and chamfer formats using the primitives cylinder, box, and wedge. Ask them if they could fillet or chamfer all the edges of the box or wedge.

Name		Class Period		Time	
Date	M	Tu	W	Th	F

Instructional Plan - Advanced Text — *Chapter 15* Downstream Benefits

FOCUS

- **Gaining Attention.** Ask your students when it might be necessary or helpful to take a 3D model and develop section and profile views from it. What might be the reasons for doing such a thing? Can one gain a better insight into the shape of the object? Do the procedures result in views that are accepted practice in engineering offices?

- **Objectives.** Discuss the objectives listed at the beginning of the textbook chapter.

- **Orientation.** Briefly review with students material they have previously learned that they will need in order to learn this chapter.

TEACH

- **Key Terms.** Ask students to write out the meaning of each term in their own words. Discuss the terms with the class until you arrive at a consensus about the meaning of each term.

- **Drawing Skills.** Assign the step-by-step instructions in the chapter. Skills covered include creating a full section view from a solid model and developing a profile view from a solid model.

ASSESS

- **Review Questions.** Ask students to complete the Review Questions. Discuss their answers in class. The answers are found in the Answer Keys section of this guide.

- **Applying AutoCAD Skills.** Assign the activities at the end of the chapter.

- **Reteaching.** Review the basic, underlying concepts that students may not clearly understand. For example, explain what section and profile views are. Explain the difference between a full section, half-section, and quarter-section.

- **Enrichment.** Assign the Challenge Your Thinking questions at the end of the chapter. Assign the Using Problem-Solving Skills activities at the end of the chapter.

- **Communication.** Assign Challenge Your Thinking questions 1 and 2.

- **Advanced Project.** Assign the Shackle Assembly project (text page 425).

- **Test.** Use the Chapter Test printed in this guide, or create a test using the **Exam**View test generator on the CD-ROM. The answers can be found in the Answer Keys section of this guide.

CLOSE

- Ask students to create a full section view of a cone with the UCS located at one-half the distance from the center of the cone to the outside edge when the cone is in an elevation viewport. The cut will appear as a parabola.

Copyright © Glencoe/McGraw-Hill

Name		Class Period		Time	
Date	M	Tu	W	Th	F

Instructional Plan - Advanced Text

Chapter 16 Documenting Solid Models

FOCUS

- **Gaining Attention.** Start your class by asking, "Which would be the faster method for drawing orthographic views: (1) drawing a top, front, and right-side view and then an isometric view of the object or (2) drawing a 3D solid model and then taking the top, front, right-side, and isometric views from the solid model?" The answer you should expect is, "drawing the solid model and extracting the views from it."

- **Objectives.** Discuss the objectives listed at the beginning of the textbook chapter.

- **Orientation.** Briefly review with students material they have previously learned that they will need in order to learn this chapter.

TEACH

- **Key Terms.** Ask students to write out the meaning of each term in their own words. Discuss the terms with the class until you arrive at a consensus about the meaning of each term.

- **PowerPoint.** Review the PowerPoint presentation for Part 3, provided on the CD-ROM. Slides 21 through 23 apply to this chapter.

- **Drawing Skills.** Assign the step-by-step instructions in the chapter. Skills covered include creating a solid model, producing orthographic and section views from it, and plotting the views.

- **Setting Up the Orthographic View.** Try the following demonstration. Set up a solid model of the wrench in Problem 6 of the Additional Problems in the textbook. Start by viewing the SE Isometric view of the object in paper space (Layout1). Use a 4-viewport selection. Use SOLVIEW Ortho (select O). From this point on, follow all the information presented in this chapter.

ASSESS

- **Review Questions.** Ask students to complete the Review Questions. Discuss their answers in class. The answers are found in the Answer Keys section of this guide.

- **Applying AutoCAD Skills.** Assign the activities at the end of the chapter.

- **Reteaching.** If students have difficulty with any of the procedures, demonstrate them on your computer. Use projection equipment to display the drawings as you create them.

- **Enrichment.** Assign the Challenge Your Thinking questions at the end of the chapter. Assign the Using Problem-Solving Skills activities at the end of the chapter.

- **Communication.** Assign Challenge Your Thinking questions 1 and 2.

- **Test.** Use the Chapter Test printed in this guide, or create a test using the **Exam**View test generator on the CD-ROM. The answers can be found in the Answer Keys section of this guide.

CLOSE

- Refer to the wrench, Problem 6. Ask students how long they think it would take to develop a three-view orthographic drawing of the wrench. Then ask them how long it would take to create a 3D model of the wrench and acquire the orthographic drawings from it. If the second method takes longer, would it still be worthwhile? Ask them if they can dimension the orthographic drawing created from the 3D model.

Name		Class Period		Time	
Date	M	Tu	W	Th	F

Instructional Plan - Advanced Text
Chapter 17 Physical Benefits of Solid Modeling

FOCUS

- **Gaining Attention.** What do you get when you cut something in half? You get two halves, and two full sections as well! Ask students if they were to cut a watermelon in two, width-wise and again lengthwise, would the cuts width-wise be full sections or half sections? Would the cuts lengthwise be full sections or half sections? Answer: They would all be full sections when considered in terms of the piece they were cut from. When you are cutting a 3D solid, the process really is a lot like cutting that watermelon. The difference is that you still have the whole left, in addition to the section view you've created.

- **Objectives.** Discuss the objectives listed at the beginning of the textbook chapter.

- **Orientation.** Briefly review with students material they have previously learned that they will need in order to learn this chapter.

TEACH

- **Key Terms.** Ask students to write out the meaning of each term in their own words. Discuss the terms with the class until you arrive at a consensus about the meaning of each term.

- **Drawing Skills.** Assign the step-by-step instructions in the chapter. Skills covered include creating 2D section views from a solid, finding the properties of a solid model, and developing an STL output file.

- **Knowing Where the Cutting Plane Is.** It is important to understand the orientation of the cutting plane used with the SLICE command. For example, if you choose the YZ option (as in Chapter 17), the cutting plane is vertical and perpendicular to the screen. To get the section you want, you must orient the object by selecting the appropriate UCS.

ASSESS

- **Review Questions.** Ask students to complete the Review Questions. Discuss their answers in class. The answers are found in the Answer Keys section of this guide.

- **Applying AutoCAD Skills.** Assign the activities at the end of the chapter.

- **Reteaching.** If students have difficulty with any of the procedures, demonstrate them on your computer. Use projection equipment to display the drawings as you create them.

- **Enrichment.** Assign the Challenge Your Thinking questions at the end of the chapter. Assign the Using Problem-Solving Skills activities at the end of the chapter.

- **Communication.** Assign Challenge Your Thinking Questions 1, 2, and 3.

- **Test.** Use the Chapter Test printed in this guide, or create a test using the **Exam**View test generator on the CD-ROM. The answers can be found in the Answer Keys section of this guide.

CLOSE

- Refer to the mass properties report shown in Chapter 17 of the textbook. Have students research the meaning of each term (mass, volume, centroid, etc.) and write a report on their findings.

Copyright © Glencoe/McGraw-Hill

Name		Class Period		Time	
Date	M	Tu	W	Th	F

Instructional Plan - Advanced Text *Part 4* Menus

CHAPTERS AND MAIN TOPICS

Chapter 18: An Internal Peek at AutoCAD's Menus—the contents of AutoCAD's acad.mnu file; AutoCAD's other menu files, including acad.mns, acad.mnc, acad.mnr, and acad.mnl

Chapter 19: Custom Menus and Toolbars—developing a pull-down menu; loading and using a pull-down menu file; loading, using, and removing a partial menu; creating and deleting a custom toolbar

Chapter 20: Slides and Scripts—creating and viewing slide files; developing a slide show as a script; running the script; creating and applying a slide library

CD-ROM

Use the following from the *Advanced Instructor Productivity CD-ROM* to help you present the textbook's topics and assess student progress.

- Pre-/Post-Test for Part 4, found in the **Exam***View* test generator.

- PowerPoint presentation for Part 4. The first slide shows the main topics covered in Part 4 of the textbook. The remaining slides elaborate on the more complex topics. You may want to use the PowerPoint presentations to introduce all the topics in this part before students begin working through the chapters. Later, as they begin each chapter, you could show the related slides for that chapter.

TRANSPARENCY MASTERS

Transparency masters for Part 4 begin on page 282 of this guide.

Title	Use with
TM-4A: Menus	Introduction to Part 4
TM-4B: AutoCAD's Menu Files	Chapter 18
TM-4C: Creating a Custom Toolbar	Chapter 19

HANDOUTS

Career Handouts: HO-16 through HO-18

PART 4 PROJECT: Creating a Trade Show Demo

This project, found at the end of Part 4 of the textbook, provides students the opportunity to apply the AutoCAD commands and procedures they have learned in this part.

- Remind students to read the Hints and Suggestions before they begin drawing.

- Summary Questions/Self-Evaluation may be answered in writing or used as a springboard to class discussion. Students could compare their procedures and exchange ideas about improving efficiency and accuracy.

- As an alternative project, have students create a slide show that demonstrates a particular feature of AutoCAD. The purpose of the slide show would be to educate new users of AutoCAD. For example, the slide show could illustrate the various object snap modes.

Copyright © Glencoe/McGraw-Hill

Name		Class Period			Time	
Date	M	Tu	W	Th	F	

Instructional Plan - Advanced Text — *Chapter 18* An Internal Peek at AutoCAD's Menus

FOCUS

- **Gaining Attention.** Demonstrate how to create a macro (menu item). Ask students to think of ways that macros could make their work more efficient.

- **Objectives.** Discuss the objectives listed at the beginning of the textbook chapter.

- **Orientation.** Briefly review with students material they have previously learned that they will need in order to learn this chapter.

TEACH

- **Key Terms.** Ask students to write out the meaning of each term in their own words. Discuss the terms with the class until you arrive at a consensus about the meaning of each term.

- **PowerPoint.** Review the PowerPoint presentation for Part 4, provided on the CD-ROM. Slides 2 through 4 apply to this chapter.

- **Skills.** Assign the step-by-step instructions in the chapter. Skills covered include interpreting the AutoCAD main menu file, the major sections of the AutoCAD main menu, special character and command functions, and AutoCAD's other menu files.

- **Text Editors.** It is very important to use a low-end text editor when creating or editing AutoCAD menus. Sophisticated word processing software usually adds special control characters to the file, making the file unusable for compiling or operating. Notepad is a wise choice. It is also important to watch the use of the spacebar, because in some cases AutoCAD equates the spacebar with an enter key. Avoid the use of special characters other than those shown in this text.

- **Naming a Menu File.** Caution your students that they should never name their menu files acad.mnu. If they were to use this name, their file would overwrite the original acad.mnu file, and all of AutoCAD's default menus would be lost.

ASSESS

- **Review Questions.** Ask students to complete the Review Questions. Discuss their answers in class. The answers are found in the Answer Keys section of this guide.

- **Applying AutoCAD Skills.** Assign the activities at the end of the chapter.

- **Reteaching.** Review Table 18-1 in the textbook with students. They need to become familiar with these file names and their descriptions in order to create and customize menus in the following chapters.

- **Enrichment.** Assign the Challenge Your Thinking questions at the end of the chapter. Assign the Using Problem-Solving Skills activities at the end of the chapter.

- **Communication.** Assign Challenge Your Thinking questions 1 and 2.

- **Test.** Use the Chapter Test printed in this guide, or create a test using the **Exam**View test generator on the CD-ROM. The answers can be found in the Answer Keys section of this guide.

CLOSE

- Ask students to brainstorm about key commands and functions to include in a menu file. Ask them what command is used to enable their menu file to function in the AutoCAD software.

Copyright © Glencoe/McGraw-Hill

Name		Class Period		Time	
Date	M	Tu	W	Th	F

Instructional Plan - Advanced Text

Chapter 19 Custom Menus and Toolbars

FOCUS

- **Gaining Attention.** Ask your students if they know people who work with CAD software. If they do, have them find out whether the individuals use any special menus that improve standardization of their drawings and reduce drawing time. You could also arrange a field trip or have a drafter or designer come to class to explain the use of custom menus.

- **Objectives.** Discuss the objectives listed at the beginning of the textbook chapter.

- **Orientation.** Briefly review with students material they have previously learned that they will need in order to learn this chapter.

TEACH

- **Key Terms.** Ask students to write out the meaning of each term in their own words. Discuss the terms with the class until you arrive at a consensus about the meaning of each term.

- **Skills.** Assign the step-by-step instructions in the chapter. Skills covered include developing a pull-down menu; loading and using a menu file; converting, loading, and deleting a partial menu; and creating and deleting a custom toolbar.

- **How Many POP Menus?** The number of POP menu areas that are possible depends on the resolution screen setting of your video graphics board. Normally, you will use POP0 through POP12, but if you set your video resolution to 1280 × 1024, you could increase the number of POP menus to 16 without major problems. It is best, however, to stay within a maximum of 12 so that systems with lower resolutions will be able to display all the pull-down menus.

ASSESS

- **Review Questions.** Ask students to complete the Review Questions. Discuss their answers in class. The answers are found in the Answer Keys section of this guide.

- **Applying AutoCAD Skills.** Assign the activities at the end of the chapter.

- **Reteaching.** If students have difficulty with any of the procedures, demonstrate them on your computer. Use projection equipment so that students can see what's happening on your computer screen.

- **Enrichment.** Assign the Challenge Your Thinking questions at the end of the chapter. Assign the Using Problem-Solving Skills activities at the end of the chapter.

- **Communication.** Assign Challenge Your Thinking questions 1 and 2.

- **Test.** Use the Chapter Test printed in this guide, or create a test using the **Exam**View test generator on the CD-ROM. The answers can be found in the Answer Keys section of this guide.

CLOSE

- Refer to the closing activity in the Instructional Plan for Chapter 18. Ask students if they can figure out a way for their menu to bring up a spreadsheet program.

Copyright © Glencoe/McGraw-Hill

Name		Class Period		Time	
Date	M	Tu	W	Th	F

Instructional Plan - Advanced Text — *Chapter 20* Slides and Scripts

FOCUS

- **Gaining Attention.** You should have an especially fun time with this chapter's contents. Make a drawing of a stick figure using the LINE and CIRCLE commands. Show hands and feet. Create running poses by moving the legs and feet into various running positions. Each time you move the legs and feet, use the MSLIDE command to save that pose. Name the slides Runner1, Runner2, etc. When you have made at least 10 to 15 slides, open Notepad. Type in VSLIDE Runner1. On the next line down, enter VSLIDE Runner2 (or whatever sequence you wish to follow), and so on until you have listed all the slides by name. On the last line in Notepad, type RSCRIPT. Save the file with the name runner.scr and now return to AutoCAD. Enter the SCRIPT command, select the runner.scr file, and watch the students' reaction to your animation.

- **Objectives.** Discuss the objectives listed at the beginning of the textbook chapter.

- **Orientation.** Briefly review with students material they have previously learned that they will need in order to learn this chapter.

TEACH

- **Key Terms.** Ask students to write out the meaning of each term in their own words. Discuss the terms with the class until you arrive at a consensus about the meaning of each term.

- **PowerPoint.** Review the PowerPoint presentation for Part 4, provided on the CD-ROM. Slides 5 through 8 apply to this chapter.

- **Skills.** Assign the step-by-step instructions in the chapter. Skills covered include creating slides using MSLIDE, viewing slides using VSLIDE, creating script files, and running the script.

ASSESS

- **Review Questions.** Ask students to complete the Review Questions. Discuss their answers in class. The answers are found in the Answer Keys section of this guide.

- **Applying AutoCAD Skills.** Assign the activities at the end of the chapter.

- **Reteaching.** If students have difficulty with any of the procedures, demonstrate them on your computer. Use projection equipment so that students can see what's happening on your computer screen.

- **Enrichment.** Assign the Challenge Your Thinking questions at the end of the chapter. Assign the Using Problem-Solving Skills activities at the end of the chapter.

- **Communication.** Assign Challenge Your Thinking Questions 1 and 2.

- **Test.** Use the Chapter Test printed in this guide, or create a test using the **Exam**View test generator on the CD-ROM. The answers can be found in the Answer Keys section of this guide.

CLOSE

- Have students apply what they have learned in this chapter to create an animated cartoon character. Give an award to the best cartoon entry. Someone in the class could very well become a special effects animator or programmer in the future.

- Have students research careers in computer animation and report their findings to the class. Their reports should include information about the education needed, the types of companies that hire computer animators, and the salary ranges.

Name		Class Period		Time	
Date	M	Tu	W	Th	F

Instructional Plan - Advanced Text   *Part 5* AutoLISP

CHAPTERS AND MAIN TOPICS

Chapter 21: Exploring AutoLISP—reviewing the contents of an AutoLISP file; loading and invoking an AutoLISP program

Chapter 22: Basic AutoLISP Programming—using AutoLISP's arithmetic expressions; creating an AutoLISP routine by using basic AutoLISP functions; storing AutoLISP routines as files and as menu items

Chapter 23: Advanced AutoLISP Programming—creating a routine to implement a collection of AutoLISP functions; developing an AutoLISP program that creates a drawing border; using a parametric program to create doors and windows for architectural elevation drawings

CD-ROM

Use the following from the *Advanced Instructor Productivity CD-ROM* to help you present the textbook's topics and assess student progress.

- Pre-/Post-Test for Part 5, found in the **Exam***View* test generator.
- PowerPoint presentation for Part 5. The first slide shows the main topics covered in Part 5 of the textbook. The remaining slides elaborate on the more complex topics. You may want to use the PowerPoint presentations to introduce all the topics in this part before students begin working through the chapters. Later, as they begin each chapter, you could show the related slides for that chapter.

TRANSPARENCY MASTERS

Transparency masters for Part 5 begin on page 285 of this guide.

Title	Use with
TM-5A: AutoLISP	Introduction to Part 5
TM-5B: Partial Contents of an AutoLISP File	Chapter 21
TM-5C: Results of Loading an AutoLISP File	Chapter 21
TM-5D: Documenting a Routine	Chapter 23

HANDOUTS

Career Handouts: HO-19 through HO-21

PART 5 PROJECT: Parametric Border Utility

This project, found at the end of Part 5 of the textbook, provides students the opportunity to apply the AutoCAD commands and procedures they have learned in this part.

- Remind students to read the Hints and Suggestions before they begin drawing.
- Summary Questions/Self-Evaluation may be answered in writing or used as a springboard to class discussion. Students could compare their procedures and exchange ideas about improving efficiency and accuracy.
- Have students research careers in programming. What are the educational requirements? The working conditions? The salary ranges and job outlook? What kinds of abilities and personal preferences might help a person become a proficient programmer?

Copyright © Glencoe/McGraw-Hill

Name		Class Period		Time	
Date	M	Tu	W	Th	F

Instructional Plan - Advanced Text — *Chapter 21* Exploring AutoLISP

FOCUS

- **Gaining Attention.** Using PowerPoint slide #3 for Part 5, show the contents of the file mvsetup.lsp. (This file is included in AutoCAD 2002 in the Support folder.) Point out to students that the program lines are written as a string but can be shown as individual lines. Indicate to them that LISP programs can be read in Notepad but, when executed, are compiled for operation within AutoCAD. The mvsetup.lsp file is especially useful because it can correct viewport views of objects so that they are all of the same scale, line up, and enable you to add a title block and paper size.

- **Objectives.** Discuss the objectives listed at the beginning of the textbook chapter.

- **Orientation.** Briefly review with students material they have previously learned that they will need in order to learn this chapter. Ask whether any of them have had programming experience. If so, have them briefly describe to the class what they did.

TEACH

- **Key Terms.** Ask students to write out the meaning of each term in their own words. Discuss the terms with the class until you arrive at a consensus about the meaning of each term.

- **PowerPoint.** Review the PowerPoint presentation for Part 5, provided on the CD-ROM. Slides 2 through 4 apply to this chapter.

- **Skills.** Assign the step-by-step instructions in the chapter. Skills covered include opening an AutoLISP file and loading and invoking an AutoLISP program.

- **Loading and Executing AutoLISP Routines.** Remind students that when they load an AutoLISP program into AutoCAD, a very specific sequence of characters must be keyed in. Begin with a left parenthesis. This is followed by the command name load, which can be entered as upper- or lowercase letters. Next, be sure to add one space. This is followed by a quotation mark, the name of the LISP file, another quotation mark, and a right parenthesis. An example is: (load "mvsetup").

ASSESS

- **Review Questions.** Ask students to complete the Review Questions. Discuss their answers in class. The answers are found in the Answer Keys section of this guide.

- **Applying AutoCAD Skills.** Assign the activities at the end of the chapter.

- **Reteaching.** If students have difficulty with any of the procedures, demonstrate them on your computer. Use projection equipment so that students can see what's happening on your computer screen.

- **Enrichment.** Assign the Challenge Your Thinking questions at the end of the chapter. Assign the Using Problem-Solving Skills activities at the end of the chapter.

- **Communication.** Assign Challenge Your Thinking questions 1 and 2.

- **Test.** Use the Chapter Test printed in this guide, or create a test using the **Exam**View test generator on the CD-ROM. The answers can be found in the Answer Keys section of this guide.

CLOSE

- Ask your students to search the Internet for LISP routines that are given out free by AUGI (AutoCAD Users Group International) or by magazines such as *CADENCE*. Have them try entering a program into Notepad and executing the program in AutoCAD. This is a good opportunity for students to try some excellent LISP programs without knowing how to write code.

Name		Class Period		Time	
Date		M	Tu	W	Th	F

Instructional Plan - Advanced Text
Chapter 22 Basic AutoLISP Programming

FOCUS

- **Gaining Attention.** Demonstrate addition, subtraction, multiplication, and division with AutoLISP arithmetic expressions. Enter the following at the Command prompt: (+ 3 3), then (- 6 3), then (* 3 3), and then (/ 6 3). The results of the operations will show below the typed line after you have depressed the ENTER key.

- **Objectives.** Discuss the objectives listed at the beginning of the textbook chapter.

- **Orientation.** Briefly review with students material they have previously learned that they will need in order to learn this chapter. If they have not already done so, students should complete Chapter 21.

TEACH

- **Key Terms.** Ask students to write out the meaning of each term in their own words. Discuss the terms with the class until you arrive at a consensus about the meaning of each term.

- **PowerPoint.** Review the PowerPoint presentation for Part 5, provided on the CD-ROM. Slides 5 through 8 apply to this chapter.

- **Skills.** Assign the step-by-step instructions in the chapter. Skills covered include using AutoLISP arithmetic expressions, using basic AutoLISP functions to create an AutoLISP routine, and storing AutoLISP routines as files and as menu items.

ASSESS

- **Review Questions.** Ask students to complete the Review Questions. Discuss their answers in class. The answers are found in the Answer Keys section of this guide.

- **Applying AutoCAD Skills.** Assign the activities at the end of the chapter.

- **Reteaching.** If students have difficulty with any of the procedures, demonstrate them on your computer. Use projection equipment so that students can see what's happening on your computer screen.

- **Enrichment.** Assign the Challenge Your Thinking questions at the end of the chapter. Assign the Using Problem-Solving Skills activities at the end of the chapter.

- **Communication.** Assign Challenge Your Thinking questions 1 and 2.

- **Test.** Use the Chapter Test printed in this guide, or create a test using the **Exam***View* test generator on the CD-ROM. The answers can be found in the Answer Keys section of this guide.

CLOSE

- Have your students use AutoLISP to assign values to a point. Then have them enter the LINE command. Instead of numeric values, they should enter the character values for the beginning and ending points of the line.

Copyright © Glencoe/McGraw-Hill

Name		Class Period		Time	
Date	M	Tu	W	Th	F

Instructional Plan - Advanced Text
Chapter 23 Advanced AutoLISP Programming

FOCUS

- **Gaining Attention.** Challenge your students to create a LISP routine that will graphically display their scores in your class. Ask them to use the project scores and test scores as actual values that they would enter in AutoCAD using the AutoLISP functions setq, list, getreal, and getvar and the AutoCAD commands LINE, RECTANG, etc. Ask them to prove their routine really does graphically describe their grade thus far in your class.

- **Objectives.** Discuss the objectives listed at the beginning of the textbook chapter.

- **Orientation.** Briefly review with students material they have previously learned that they will need in order to learn this chapter. For example, in this chapter students will build on the skills they learned in Chapters 21 and 22 to create AutoLISP programs.

TEACH

- **Key Terms.** Ask students to write out the meaning of each term in their own words. Discuss the terms with the class until you arrive at a consensus about the meaning of each term.

- **PowerPoint.** Review the PowerPoint presentation for Part 5, provided on the CD-ROM. Slides 9 and 10 apply to this chapter.

- **Skills.** Assign the step-by-step instructions in the chapter. Skills covered include creating a routine from a collection of AutoLISP functions, developing an AutoLISP program, and using a parametric program.

ASSESS

- **Review Questions.** Ask students to complete the Review Questions. Discuss their answers in class. The answers are found in the Answer Keys section of this guide.

- **Applying AutoCAD Skills.** Assign the activities at the end of the chapter.

- **Reteaching.** If students have difficulty with any of the procedures, demonstrate them on your computer. Use projection equipment so that students can see what's happening on your computer screen.

- **Enrichment.** Assign the Challenge Your Thinking questions at the end of the chapter. Assign the Using Problem-Solving Skills activities at the end of the chapter.

- **Communication.** Assign Challenge Your Thinking questions 1 and 2.

- **Test.** Use the Chapter Test printed in this guide, or create a test using the **Exam**View test generator on the CD-ROM. The answers can be found in the Answer Keys section of this guide.

CLOSE

- Ask your students to develop a simple LISP program that will automatically calculate the combined linear distances of 1 to 5 connected line segments. Tell them they must include information about the operations performed in their program by adding explanatory text inside the program.

Name		Class Period			Time	
Date		M	Tu	W	Th	F

Instructional Plan - Advanced Text — *Part 6* Importing and Exporting

CHAPTERS AND MAIN TOPICS

Chapter 24: Standard File Formats—importing and exporting DXF, EPS, 3DS, and SAT (ACIS) files; differences between ASCII and binary DXF files; the purpose of IGES files

Chapter 25: Raster Image Files—importing, displaying, editing, and managing raster images; mixing raster and vector objects; adjusting the quality of a raster image; exporting a raster image file

Chapter 26: External References—attaching drawing files to a base drawing as external references (xrefs); unloading and reloading xrefs that have been attached to a drawing; binding all or part of an xref permanently to a drawing

Chapter 27: Object Linking and Embedding (OLE)—Using OLE to link AutoCAD to a WordPad document; editing an AutoCAD server document and viewing the changes in the client document; using OLE to link a Word document to AutoCAD

Chapter 28: Database Connectivity—connecting to an external database; configuring a data source connection; viewing and editing records in a database; performing a query to obtain a specific subset of the records in a table; creating a link template in AutoCAD; linking records in a database to objects in a drawing; using links to find objects associated with records or records associated with objects

Chapter 29: Internet Connectivity—inserting a hyperlink into a drawing; opening a drawing file from a Web site; browsing the Internet from within AutoCAD; creating a DWF file; using an Internet browser to view a DWF file

Chapter 30: Internet Collaboration—packaging and sending work over the Internet using eTransmit; inserting AutoCAD content from a Web site using i-drop; creating a custom Web page using Autodesk Point A; preparing a Web page using AutoCAD's Publish to Web wizard; exploring on-line meetings using Meet Now and NetMeeting

CD-ROM

Use the following from the *Advanced Instructor Productivity CD-ROM* to help you present the textbook's topics and assess student progress.

- Pre-/Post-Test for Part 6, found in the **Exam***View* test generator.

- PowerPoint presentation for Part 6. The first slide shows the main topics covered in Part 6 of the textbook. The remaining slides elaborate on the more complex topics. You may want to use the PowerPoint presentations to introduce all the topics in this part before students begin working through the chapters. Later, as they begin each chapter, you could show the related slides for that chapter.

TRANSPARENCY MASTERS

Transparency masters for Part 6 begin on page 289 of this guide.

Title	Use with
TM-6A: Importing and Exporting	Introduction to Part 6
TM-6B: Raster Image Files	Chapter 25
TM-6C: Xrefs	Chapter 26
TM-6D: Xrefs	Chapter 26

HANDOUTS

Career Handouts: HO-22 and HO-23

PART 6 PROJECT: Electronic Art Database

This project is found at the end of Part 6 of the textbook.

- Remind students to read the Hints and Suggestions before they begin drawing.

- Summary Questions/Self-Evaluation may be answered in writing or used as a springboard to class discussion. Students could compare their procedures and exchange ideas about improving efficiency and accuracy.

Copyright © Glencoe/McGraw-Hill

Name		Class Period		Time	
Date	M	Tu	W	Th	F

Instructional Plan - Advanced Text
Chapter 24 Standard File Formats

FOCUS

- **Gaining Attention.** Ask your students where they might use the DXF file format. See if they understand the significance of an exchange file format that allows files to be read and acted upon by other software applications. Mention that the PostScript file format is used to export files to printers. Tell them the reason for exporting AutoCAD 3D solid drawings to 3D Studio MAX. (In many cases, using AutoCAD to develop the drawings is a lot less troublesome than producing the same object using 3D Studio MAX.)

- **Objectives.** Discuss the objectives listed at the beginning of the textbook chapter.

- **Orientation.** Briefly review with students material they have previously learned that they will need in order to learn this chapter.

TEACH

- **Key Terms.** Ask students to write out the meaning of each term in their own words. Discuss the terms with the class until you arrive at a consensus about the meaning of each term.

- **Skills.** Assign the step-by-step instructions in the chapter. Skills covered include creating export files in the DXF, EPS, SAT, and 3DS formats and importing some of these file formats into AutoCAD.

- **DXF Output Files.** It is important to create DXF export files using a different name than the drawing file. AutoCAD will occasionally balk at generating a DXF file simply because it will not interpret the current file with its name. To resolve this problem, simply change the name of the output file so that AutoCAD will proceed with the DXF file generation.

ASSESS

- **Review Questions.** Ask students to complete the Review Questions. Discuss their answers in class. The answers are found in the Answer Keys section of this guide.

- **Applying AutoCAD Skills.** Assign the activities at the end of the chapter.

- **Reteaching.** If students have difficulty with any of the procedures, demonstrate them on your computer. Use projection equipment so that students can see what's happening on your computer screen.

- **Enrichment.** Assign the Challenge Your Thinking questions at the end of the chapter. Assign the Using Problem-Solving Skills activities at the end of the chapter.

- **Communication.** Assign Challenge Your Thinking Questions 1 and 2.

- **Test.** Use the Chapter Test printed in this guide, or create a test using the **Exam**View test generator on the CD-ROM. The answers can be found in the Answer Keys section of this guide.

CLOSE

- Ask your students to search the Internet to find out the names of two software programs that can import DXF files. (No fair using CADKEY as an answer. Students could, however, name GibbsCAM® or Mastercam®.)

Copyright © Glencoe/McGraw-Hill

Name		Class Period		Time	
Date	M	Tu	W	Th	F

Instructional Plan - Advanced Text — *Chapter 25* Raster Image Files

FOCUS

- **Gaining Attention.** Take some 35-mm photos of objects such as a desk (with minimal curves), table, chair, or tool. Take both a top shot (if possible) and a profile shot. Have the photos developed and printed the conventional way but also ask the processing center to make digital files. Be sure to ask what file format your pictures will be in. (They should be BMP, JPG, PNG, TGA, or TIF.) When you receive the files, set up appropriate AutoCAD drawing viewports and insert the digital image of a top view shot into the top viewport. Insert the digital image of the profile into either the front or right side viewport. Show students how you can develop an orthographic or 3D drawing by using a picture and tracing over the edges with lines, arcs, or curves.

- **Objectives.** Discuss the objectives listed at the beginning of the textbook chapter.

- **Orientation.** Briefly review with students material they have previously learned that they will need in order to learn this chapter.

TEACH

- **Key Terms.** Ask students to write out the meaning of each term in their own words. Discuss the terms with the class until you arrive at a consensus about the meaning of each term.

- **PowerPoint.** Review the PowerPoint presentation for Part 6, provided on the CD-ROM. Slides 2 and 3 apply to this chapter.

- **Skills.** Assign the step-by-step instructions in the chapter. Skills covered include importing raster images; using an imported raster image; drawing text, lines, and circles on the raster image; and exporting a raster image.

- **Importing a Raster Image into a Viewport.** When importing a raster image into a viewport, always be certain that the UCS position in that viewport is parallel to the port.

ASSESS

- **Review Questions.** Ask students to complete the Review Questions. Discuss their answers in class. The answers are found in the Answer Keys section of this guide.

- **Applying AutoCAD Skills.** Assign the activities at the end of the chapter.

- **Reteaching.** If students have difficulty with any of the procedures, demonstrate them on your computer. Use projection equipment so that students can see what's happening on your computer screen.

- **Enrichment.** Assign the Challenge Your Thinking questions at the end of the chapter. Assign the Using Problem-Solving Skills activities at the end of the chapter.

- **Communication.** Assign Challenge Your Thinking questions 1 and 2.

- **Test.** Use the Chapter Test printed in this guide, or create a test using the **Exam***View* test generator on the CD-ROM. The answers can be found in the Answer Keys section of this guide.

CLOSE

- Have students create a 3D solid model. After they are finished with it, have them render the drawing to a file using the BMP file format. Now have students develop top, front, and right-side views from the 3D object. In the fourth viewport (assuming they have set up a four-viewport configuration), students should insert the rendered 3D object. Now they can see the practical aspects of their raster image files.

Copyright © Glencoe/McGraw-Hill

Name		Class Period		Time	
Date	M	Tu	W	Th	F

Instructional Plan - Advanced Text — *Chapter 26* External References

FOCUS

- **Gaining Attention.** Describe for students this scenario: You have been creating individual component drawings for parts of a new prototype engine for a race car. You have created all the detail drawings and now you are ready to create the complete assembly drawing. Using the detail drawings and the XREF command, you insert each part drawing and align it correctly. The outcome is the completed assembly drawing. But wait, you discover that one of the parts interferes with another. What do you do? Easy: Just fix the original detail drawings. The assembly drawing will be automatically updated to include the latest drawing revisions!

- **Objectives.** Discuss the objectives listed at the beginning of the textbook chapter.

- **Orientation.** Briefly review with students material they have previously learned that they will need in order to learn this chapter.

TEACH

- **Key Terms.** Ask students to write out the meaning of each term in their own words. Discuss the terms with the class until you arrive at a consensus about the meaning of each term.

- **PowerPoint.** Review the PowerPoint presentation for Part 6, provided on the CD-ROM. Slides 4 through 6 apply to this chapter.

- **Skills.** Assign the step-by-step instructions in the chapter. Skills covered include creating working drawings using xref inserts, unloading and reloading xrefs, and binding xrefs to a drawing.

- **Binding Xrefs.** Remember that until you bind an xref to a drawing, it is not truly a part of the file. When you intend to transport a drawing containing xrefs to another site, either bind the xrefs to the drawing or provide files of the xref drawings along with the base drawing file.

ASSESS

- **Review Questions.** Ask students to complete the Review Questions. Discuss their answers in class. The answers are found in the Answer Keys section of this guide.

- **Applying AutoCAD Skills.** Assign the activities at the end of the chapter.

- **Reteaching.** If students have difficulty with any of the procedures, demonstrate them on your computer. Use projection equipment so that students can see what's happening on your computer screen.

- **Enrichment.** Assign the Challenge Your Thinking questions at the end of the chapter. Assign the Using Problem-Solving Skills activities at the end of the chapter.

- **Communication.** Assign Challenge Your Thinking questions 1 and 2.

- **Advanced Projects.** Assign the Drawing Table project, which begins on page 408 of the text.

- **Test.** Use the Chapter Test printed in this guide, or create a test using the **Exam**View test generator on the CD-ROM. The answers can be found in the Answer Keys section of this guide.

CLOSE

- Have students create two detail drawings consisting of only a front and a top or side view. (All must have the same scale units.) A good example would be a cartwheel axle shaft and retainer. Ask them to create an assembly drawing using xrefs to insert the individual drawings into a new drawing file. Alignment is critical and should be stressed. Then have them change one of the detail drawing's sizes and shape. Have them open the assembly drawing and verify that its shape has changed also.

Name		Class Period			Time	
Date		M	Tu	W	Th	F

Instructional Plan - Advanced Text — *Chapter 27* Object Linking and Embedding (OLE)

FOCUS

- **Gaining Attention.** If you have Microsoft Word® software, start Word and reduce its window size to half the screen. Repeat this process for AutoCAD. Next, create some text in Word. Highlight the text, right-click, and hold. Move the mouse pointer over to the AutoCAD screen and release. From the OLE dialog box, choose to copy or move the text.

- **Objectives.** Discuss the objectives listed at the beginning of the textbook chapter.

- **Orientation.** Briefly review with students material they have previously learned that they will need in order to learn this chapter.

TEACH

- **Key Terms.** Ask students to write out the meaning of each term in their own words. Discuss the terms with the class until you arrive at a consensus about the meaning of each term.

- **Drawing Skills.** Assign the step-by-step instructions in the chapter. Skills covered include creating text in WordPad and transferring this over to AutoCAD and creating a drawing and transferring it to Word or Excel using OLE.

- **The Clipboard.** The application program you are going to use as a server when transferring material (pictures, text, drawing information, spreadsheets) must be able to transfer the material to a Clipboard. An easy way to determine whether the software is capable of this is to look under the *Edit* pull-down menu. If there are selectable items that include *Cut*, *Copy*, and *Paste*, you will probably have very little trouble using object linking and embedding.

ASSESS

- **Review Questions.** Ask students to complete the Review Questions. Discuss their answers in class. The answers are found in the Answer Keys section of this guide.

- **Applying AutoCAD Skills.** Assign the activities at the end of the chapter.

- **Reteaching.** If students have difficulty with any of the procedures, demonstrate them on your computer. Use projection equipment so that students can see what's happening on your computer screen.

- **Enrichment.** Assign the Challenge Your Thinking questions at the end of the chapter. Assign the Using Problem-Solving Skills activities at the end of the chapter.

- **Communication.** Assign Challenge Your Thinking questions 1 and 2.

- **Test.** Use the Chapter Test printed in this guide, or create a test using the **Exam**View test generator on the CD-ROM. The answers can be found in the Answer Keys section of this guide.

CLOSE

- Have students try the examples of object linking and embedding given in this chapter. Then ask them if it would be possible to copy a picture from a Web page and insert it into their AutoCAD graphics screen. (The answer to this is yes, using OLE.)

Copyright © Glencoe/McGraw-Hill

Name		Class Period			Time	
Date	M	Tu	W	Th	F	

Instructional Plan - Advanced Text — *Chapter 28* **Database Connectivity**

FOCUS

- **Gaining Attention.** Talk to your students about GIS (Geographic Information System). Inform them that what they are about to learn in this chapter is a forerunner to GIS. To illustrate the importance of data connectivity as the basis for GIS, ask students if they have ever seen an advertisement from their public utility that said, "Before digging, contact us." If they or their parents were to call the public utility, the probability is that the utility's employee would pull up a map of their sector and in response to their parcel number determine the locations of any gas, electric, water, and telephone lines. Now, how did the employee find this information so fast? The answer is GIS. All the employee had to do was call up the map, click on the area representing the property in question, and up on the monitor appeared the database information pertaining to the utilities, their specific location, depth, and size and type of lines. Now, let's learn what's behind the GIS system and database connectivity.

- **Objectives.** Discuss the objectives listed at the beginning of the textbook chapter.

- **Orientation.** Briefly review with students material they have previously learned that they will need in order to learn this chapter.

TEACH

- **Key Terms.** Ask students to write out the meaning of each term in their own words. Discuss the terms with the class until you arrive at a consensus about the meaning of each term.

- **Skills.** Assign the step-by-step instructions in the chapter. Skills covered include connecting to an external database, configuring a data source connection, viewing data, editing records, sorting data, setting up and formatting columns, querying and reporting data, creating a link template, and linking records in a database to objects in a drawing.

- *Note:* Due to the nature and complexity of database connectivity, you should allow students plenty of time to complete the exercises in this chapter. Keep in mind this is only an introduction to the subject. In-depth coverage is beyond the scope of the textbook.

ASSESS

- **Review Questions.** Ask students to complete the Review Questions. Discuss their answers in class. The answers are found in the Answer Keys section of this guide.

- **Applying AutoCAD Skills.** Assign the activities at the end of the chapter.

- **Reteaching.** If students have difficulty with any of the procedures, demonstrate them on your computer. Use projection equipment so that students can see what's happening on your computer screen.

- **Enrichment.** Assign the Challenge Your Thinking questions at the end of the chapter. Assign the Using Problem-Solving Skills activities at the end of the chapter.

- **Communication.** Assign Challenge Your Thinking questions 1 and 2.

- **Test.** Use the Chapter Test printed in this guide, or create a test using the **Exam**View test generator on the CD-ROM. The answers can be found in the Answer Keys section of this guide.

CLOSE

- Have students search the Internet for information about GIS. Have them write a report about their findings. They should include information about the nature of GIS, who generates the information used in GIS, and how the information is used.

Name		Class Period		Time	
Date	M	Tu	W	Th	F

Instructional Plan - Advanced Text — *Chapter 29* Internet Connectivity

FOCUS

- **Gaining Attention.** Ask students how they think the Internet could help make design and drawing more efficient.

- **Objectives.** Discuss the objectives listed at the beginning of the textbook chapter.

- **Orientation.** Survey the class to determine your students' level of experience with the Internet. For students who are unfamiliar with the Internet, you may wish to copy and distribute the handout on pages 41-42 of this Instructor Resource Guide.

TEACH

- **Key Terms.** Ask students to write out the meaning of each term in their own words. Discuss the terms with the class until you arrive at a consensus about the meaning of each term.

- **Skills.** Assign the step-by-step instructions in the chapter. Skills covered include inserting a hyperlink into a drawing, opening a drawing file from a Web site, browsing the Internet from within AutoCAD, and creating and viewing a DWF file.

- *Note:* To carry out the procedures described in Chapter 29 of the text, students will need computers that have access to the Internet. Observe school policies regarding student use of the Internet. The handouts on pages 39 and 40 of this Instructor Resource Guide include an Internet permission contract and an Internet evaluation sheet.

ASSESS

- **Review Questions.** Ask students to complete the Review Questions. Discuss their answers in class. Answers are found in the Answer Keys section of this guide.

- **Applying AutoCAD Skills.** Assign the activities at the end of the chapter.

- **Reteaching.** If students have difficulty with any of the procedures, demonstrate them on your computer. Use projection equipment so that students can see what's happening on your computer screen.

- **Enrichment.** Assign the Challenge Your Thinking questions at the end of the chapter. Assign the Using Problem-Solving Skills activities at the end of the chapter.

- **Communication.** Assign Challenge Your Thinking questions 1 and 2.

- **Advanced Project.** Assign the Web-Based School Map project, which starts on page 432 of the *Advanced* text.

- **Test.** Use the Chapter Test printed in this guide, or create a test using the **Exam**View test generator on the CD-ROM. The answers can be found in the Answer Keys section of this guide.

CLOSE

- Have students draw a floor plan of the CAD lab, using rectangles to represent the workstations, supply cabinets, etc. Have them insert relevant hyperlinks into the drawing. For example, in a rectangle representing a workstation, they could add a hyperlink to the computer manufacturer's Web site.

Copyright © Glencoe/McGraw-Hill

Name		Class Period			Time	
Date	M	Tu	W	Th	F	

Instructional Plan - Advanced Text — *Chapter 30* **Internet Collaboration**

FOCUS

- **Gaining Attention.** It is common today for the designers and manufacturers of products to be working for different companies and at various locations. Successful collaboration among designers and manufacturers requires good communication tools and skills. Search the Internet for information about collaborative design that you can share with your students. You could start with Autodesk's site, www.autodesk.com.

- **Objectives.** Discuss the objectives listed at the beginning of the textbook chapter.

- **Orientation.** Briefly review with students material they have previously learned that they will need in order to learn this chapter.

TEACH

- **Key Terms.** Ask students to write out the meaning of each term in their own words. Discuss the terms with the class until you arrive at a consensus about the meaning of each term.

- **Skills.** Assign the step-by-step instructions in the chapter. Skills covered include creating a transmittal set of related files, inserting content from a Web site into a drawing file, creating Web pages, using the Autodesk Point A server, and conducting on-line meetings.

- **Note:** Be sure to read this chapter before assigning it to students so that you can determine beforehand which of the exercises you want them to do. The procedures for eTransmit call for the use of e-mail. Using i-drop requires software to be downloaded. To use Autodesk Point A, students will need to register. Using Microsoft's NetMeeting feature requires a setup procedure. Instead of having your students carry out some of these procedures, you may want to demonstrate them for the class yourself.

ASSESS

- **Review Questions.** Ask students to complete the Review Questions. Discuss their answers in class. Answers are found in the Answer Keys section of this guide.

- **Applying AutoCAD Skills.** Assign the activities at the end of the chapter.

- **Reteaching.** If students have difficulty with any of the procedures, demonstrate them on your computer. Use projection equipment so that students can see what's happening on your computer screen.

- **Enrichment.** Assign the Challenge Your Thinking questions at the end of the chapter. Assign the Using Problem-Solving Skills activities at the end of the chapter.

- **Communication.** Assign Challenge Your Thinking questions 1, 2, and 3.

- **Test.** Use the Chapter Test printed in this guide, or create a test using the **Exam***View* test generator on the CD-ROM. The answers can be found in the Answer Keys section of this guide.

CLOSE

- Arrange to work collaboratively with a class at another school. Such a project would be a good opportunity to use several of the features described in this chapter. For example, students could use e-transmit to send drawing files and related information, or one class could publish drawings to a Web page for the other class to download using i-drop.

Transparency Masters for Advanced Text

The transparency masters correlate with the textbook's six parts. The first transparency master for each part lists the topics covered in that part of the textbook. The remaining transparencies illustrate specific topics covered in the part.

You may want to use the transparencies to introduce topics that will be covered in the part before students begin working through the chapters. Later, as students begin each chapter, you could show the related transparencies. See the Part Instructional Plans (such as page 229) for information on which transparencies to use with each chapter.

TM-1A	**Part 1 3D Drawing and Modeling**	**269**
TM-1B	Isometric Drawing	270
TM-1C	3D Model	271
TM-1D	User Coordinate System	272
TM-2A	**Part 2 Surface Modeling and Rendering**	**273**
TM-2B	3D Revolutions	274
TM-2C	Surfaces	275
TM-2D	3D Primitives	276
TM-3A	**Part 3 Solid Modeling**	**277**
TM-3B	Solid Primitives	278
TM-3C	Revolved Solid Model	279
TM-3D	Solid Extrusion	280
TM-3E	Positioning and Plotting Views	281
TM-4A	**Part 4 Menus**	**282**
TM-4B	AutoCAD's Menu Files	283
TM-4C	Creating a Custom Toolbar	284

Copyright © Glencoe/McGraw-Hill

TM-5A	**Part 5 AutoLISP**	**285**
TM-5B	Partial Contents of an AutoLISP File	286
TM-5C	Results of Loading an AutoLISP File	287
TM-5D	Documenting a Routine	288
TM-6A	**Part 6 Importing and Exporting**	**289**
TM-6B	Raster Image Files	290
TM-6C	Xrefs	291
TM-6D	Xrefs	292

Part 1 3D Drawing and Modeling

TM-1A
Advanced

- Ch. 1 Isometric Drawing
- Ch. 2 The Third Dimension
- Ch. 4 User Coordinate Systems
- Ch. 3 Point Filters

TM-1B
Advanced

Isometric Drawing

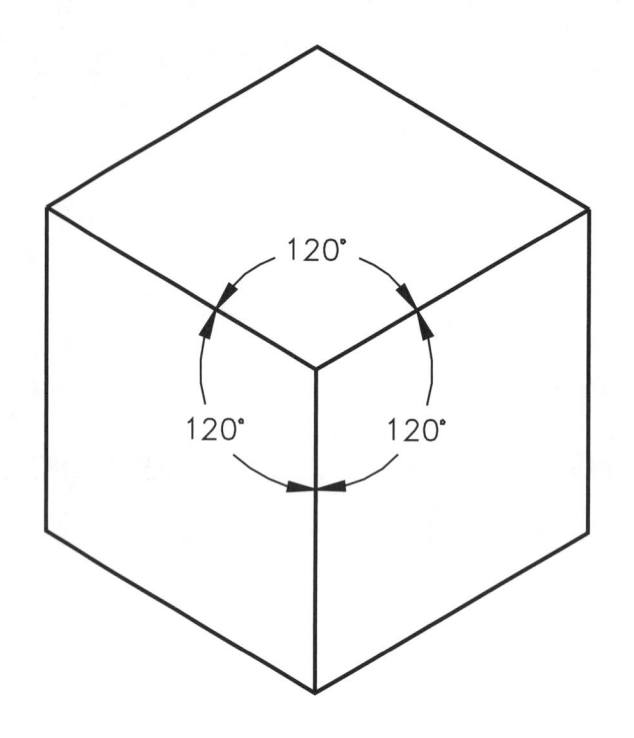

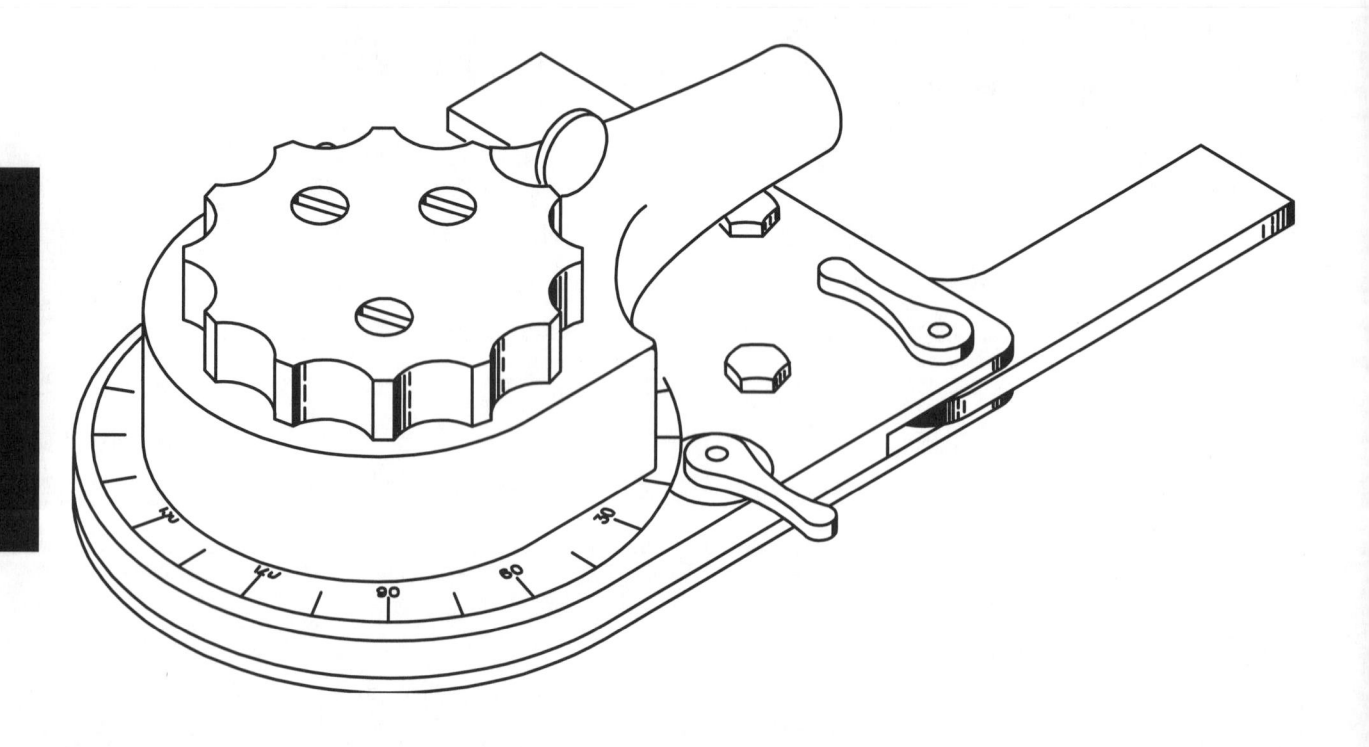

3D Model

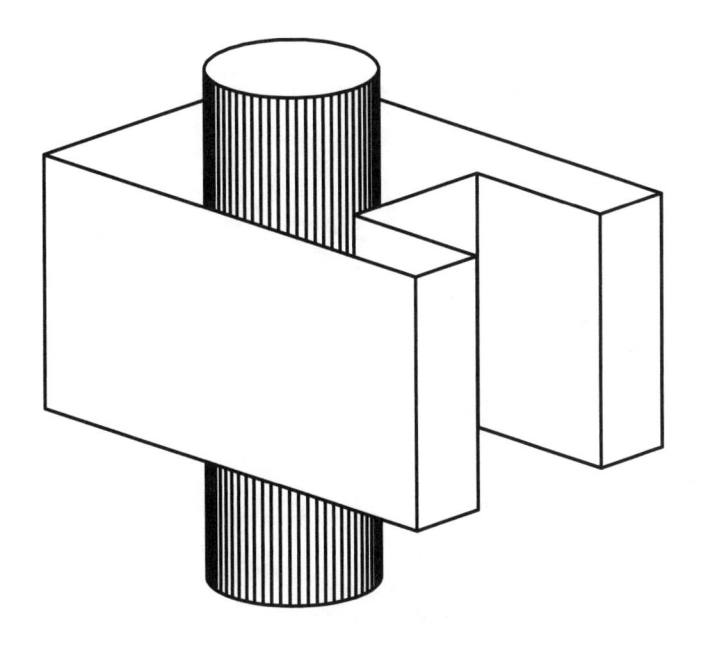

TM-1C
Advanced

3D View

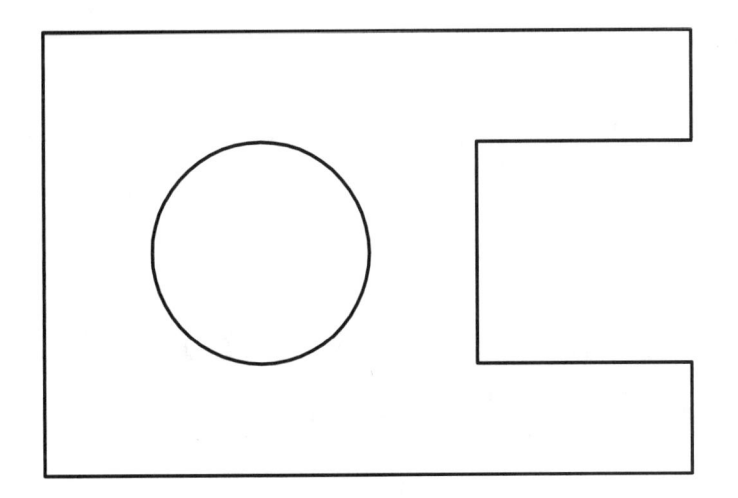

Plan View

TM-1D
Advanced

User Coordinate System

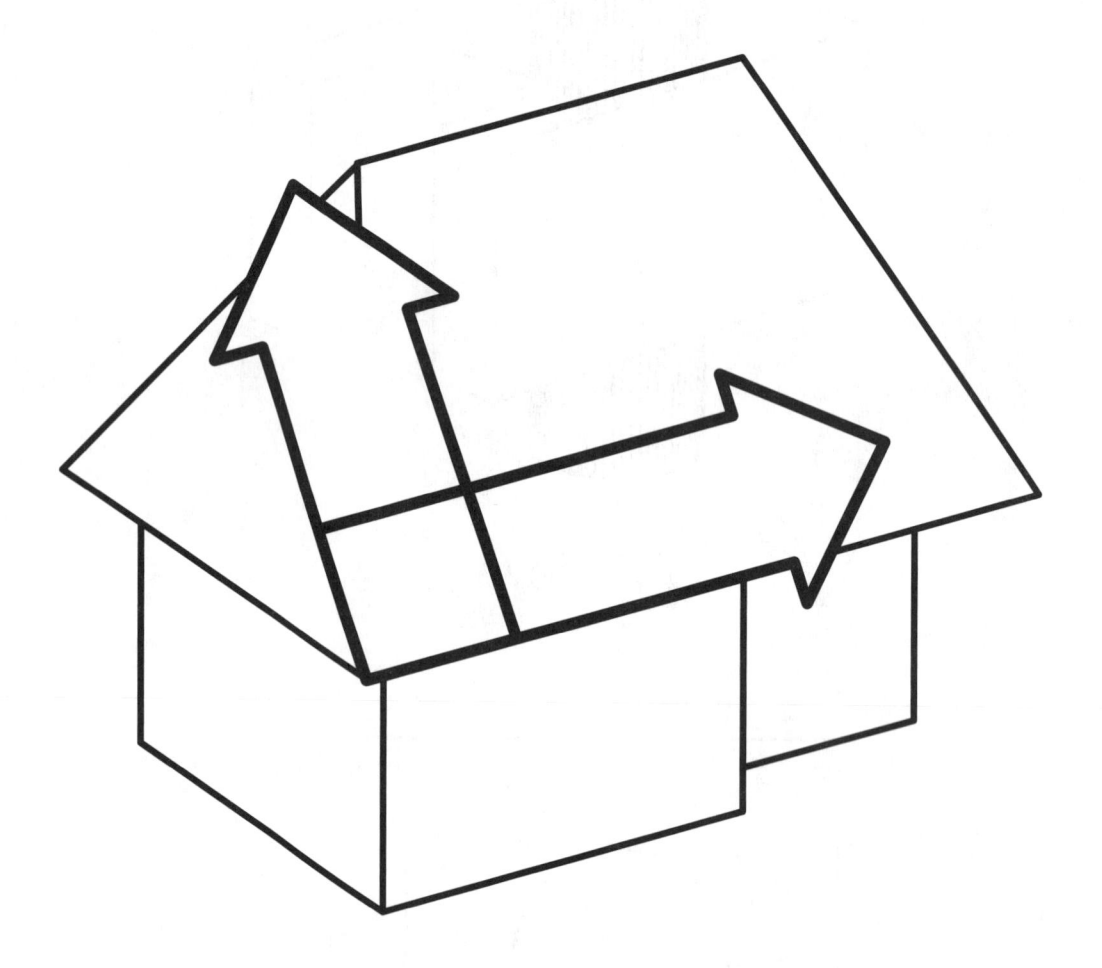

A UCS was defined to match the inclined plane of the roof.

Copyright © Glencoe/McGraw-Hill

Part 2 Surface Modeling and Rendering

Ch. 5 Revolutions

Ch. 9 Advanced Rendering

Ch. 6 Advanced Surfaces

Ch. 8 Shading and Rendering

Ch. 7 3D Primitives

TM-2B
Advanced

3D Revolutions

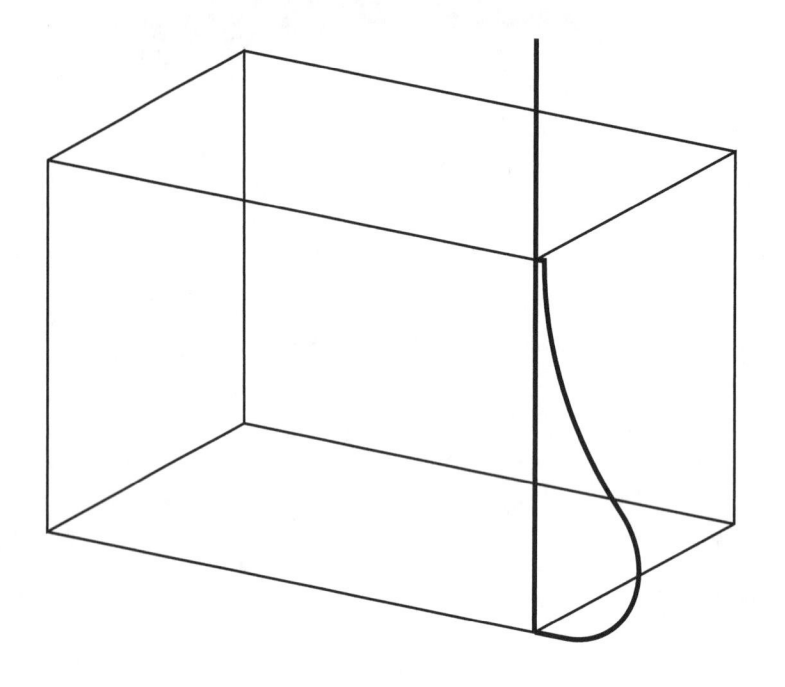

274
Copyright © Glencoe/McGraw-Hill

TM-2C
Advanced

Surfaces

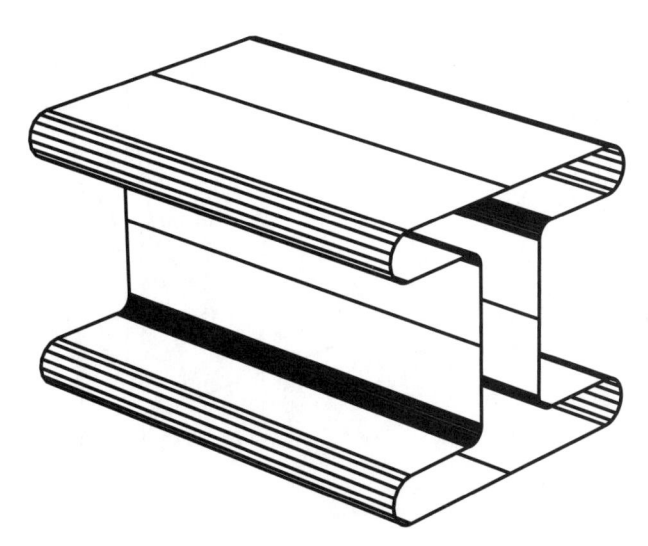

Tabulated Surface

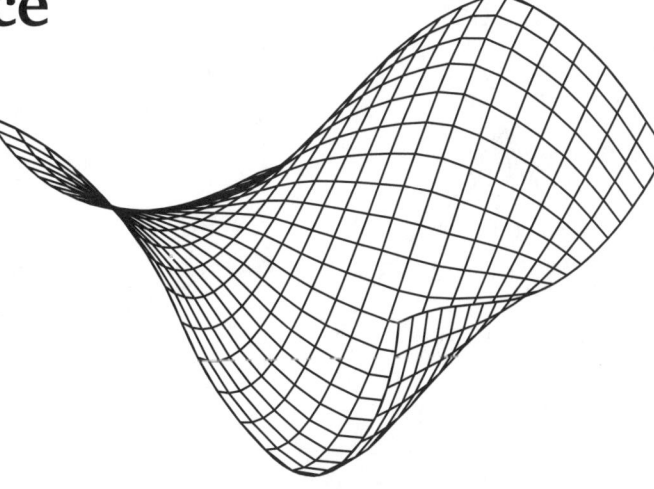

Coons Surface Patch

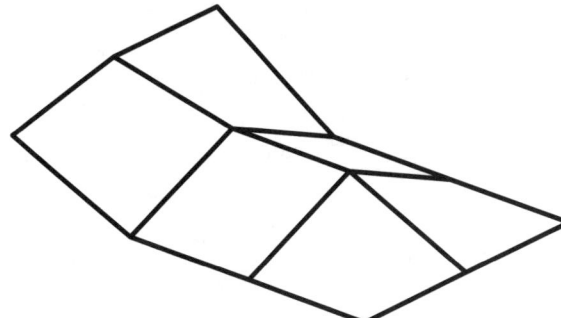

Surface Mesh

3D Primitives

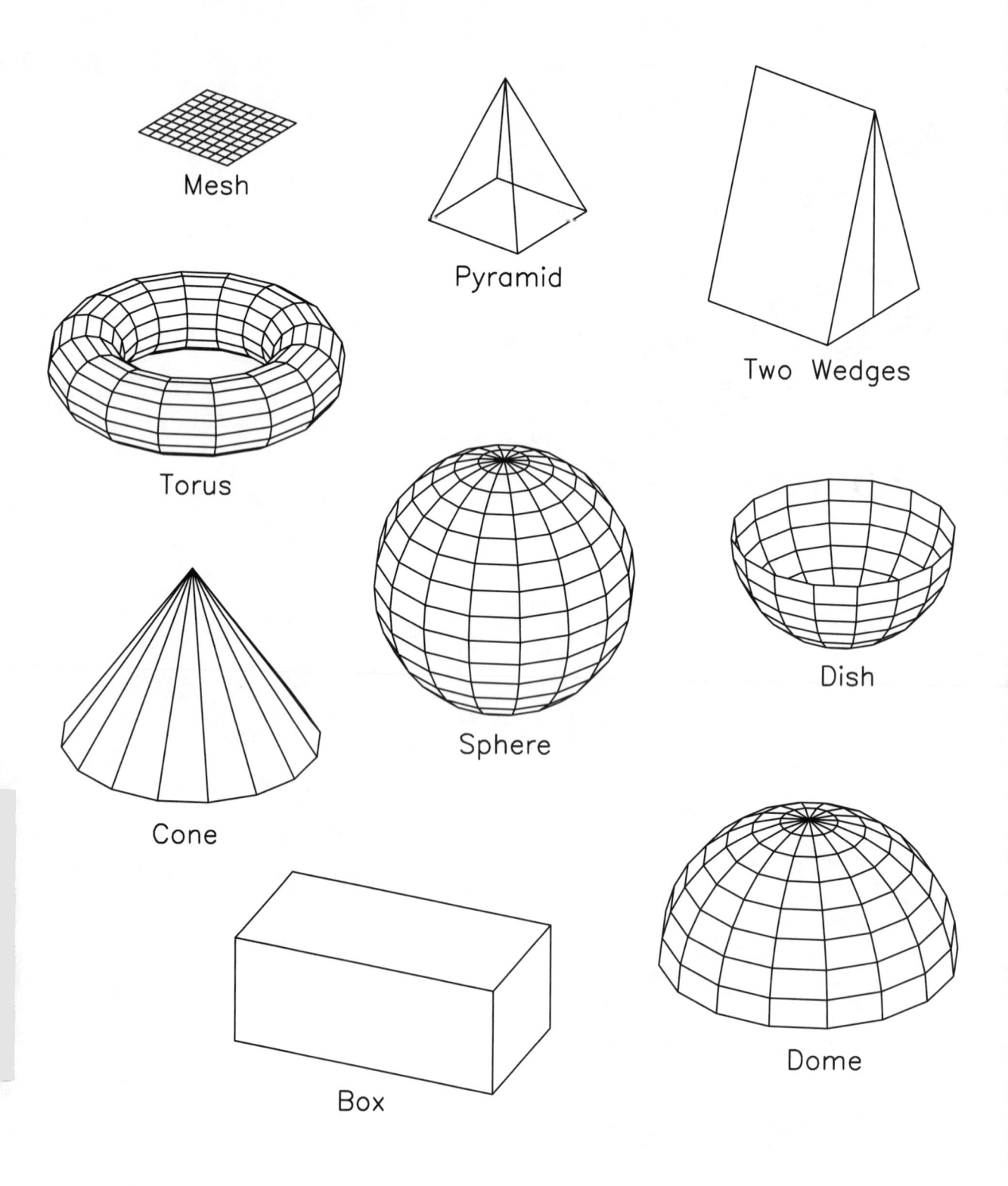

Mesh

Pyramid

Two Wedges

Torus

Sphere

Dish

Cone

Box

Dome

TM-2D
Advanced

Part 3 Solid Modeling

TM-3A
Advanced

- Ch. 10 Solid Regions
- Ch. 17 Physical Benefits of Solid Modeling
- Ch. 11 Solid Primitives
- Ch. 16 Documenting Solid Models
- Ch. 12 Basic Solid Modeling
- Ch. 15 Downstream Benefits
- Ch. 13 Boolean Operations
- Ch. 14 Tailoring Solid Models

Copyright © Glencoe/McGraw-Hill

Solid Primitives

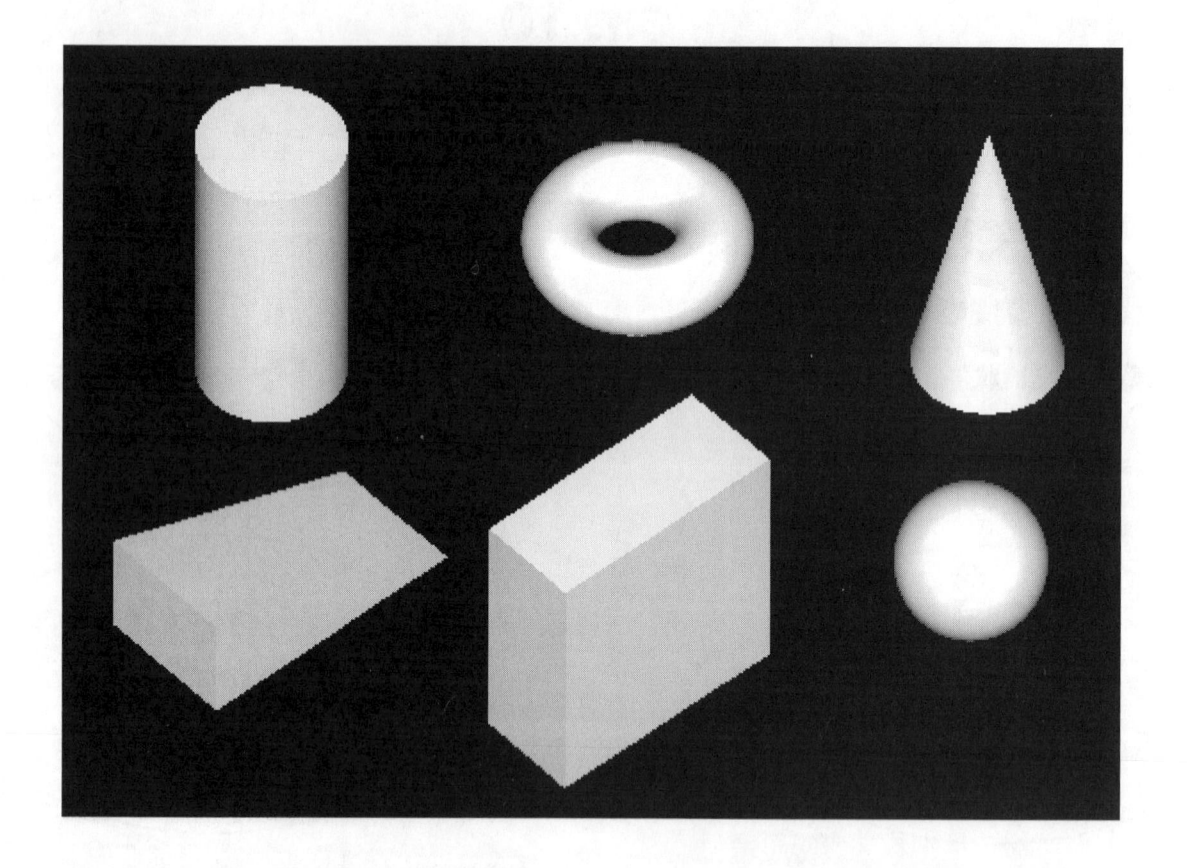

Solid primitives include the cylinder, torus, cone, wedge, box, and sphere.

TM-3C
Advanced

Revolved Solid Model

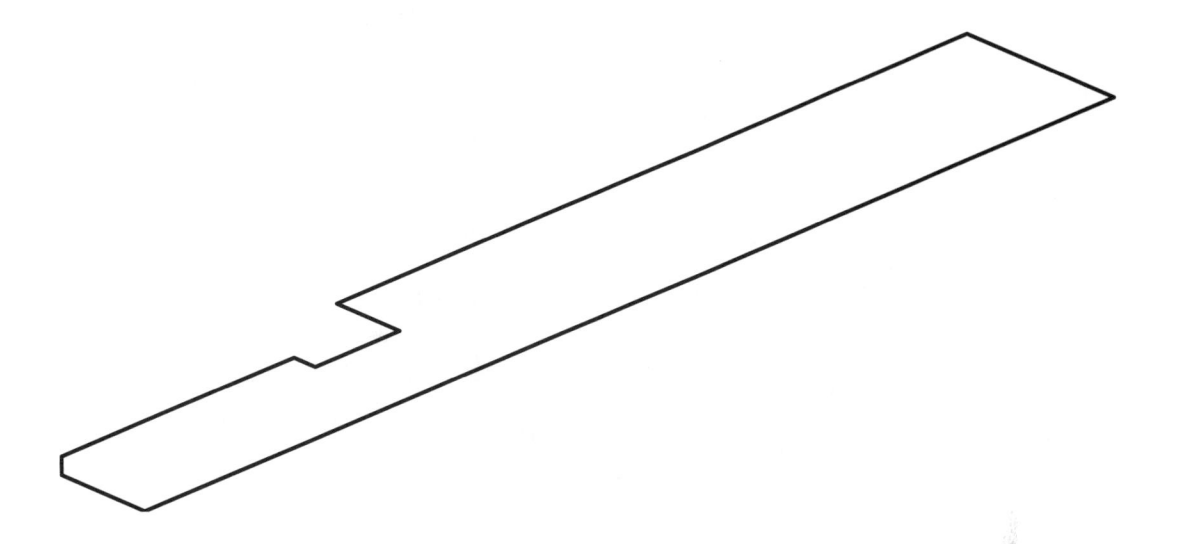

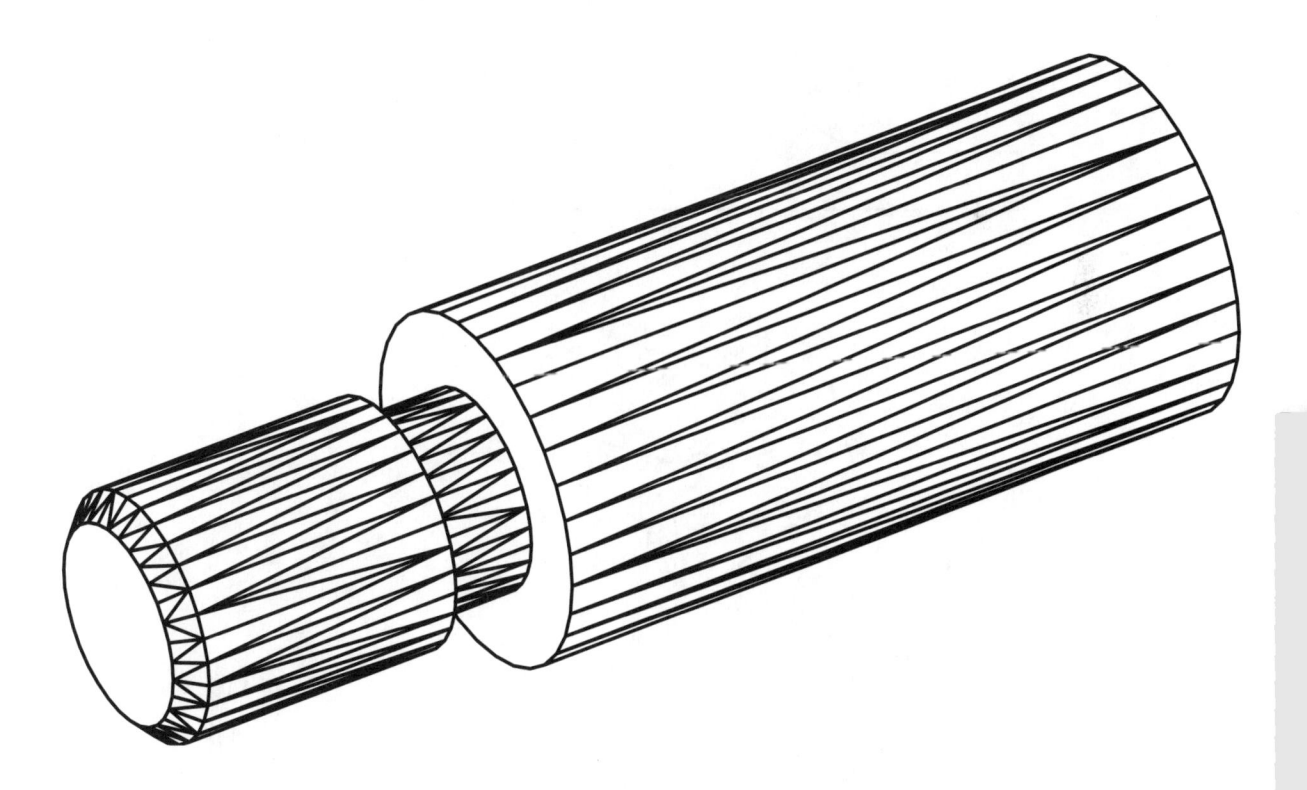

Solid Extrusion

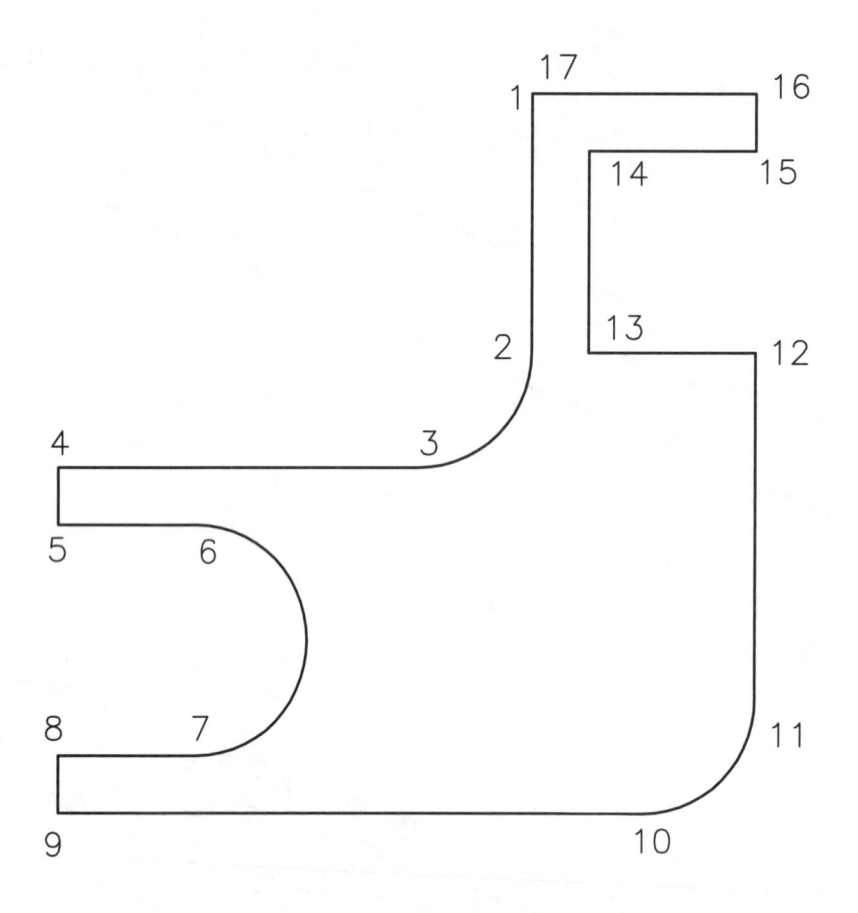

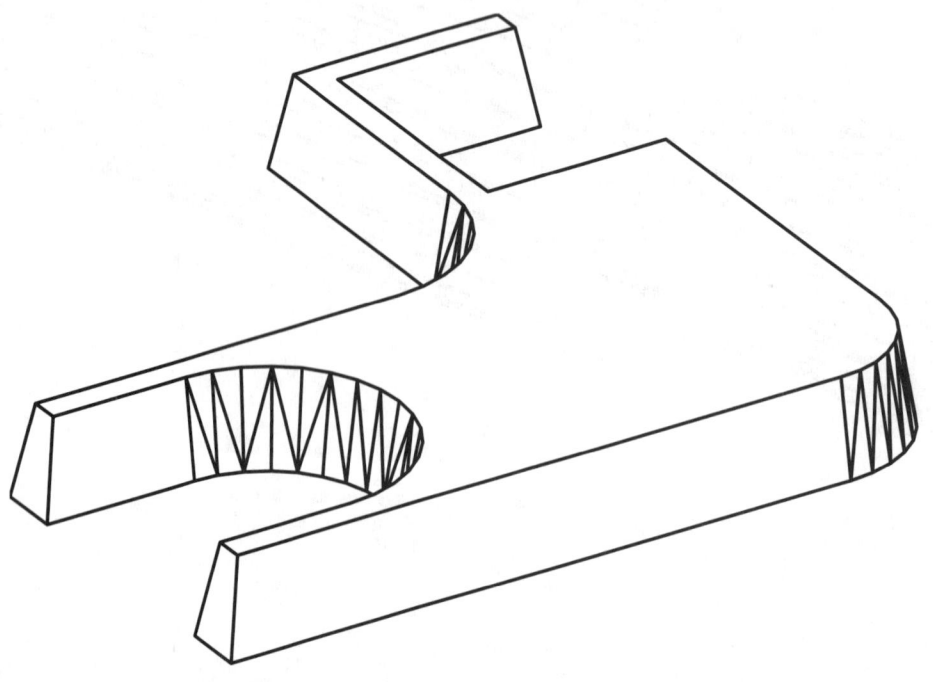

TM-3D
Advanced

Positioning and Plotting Views

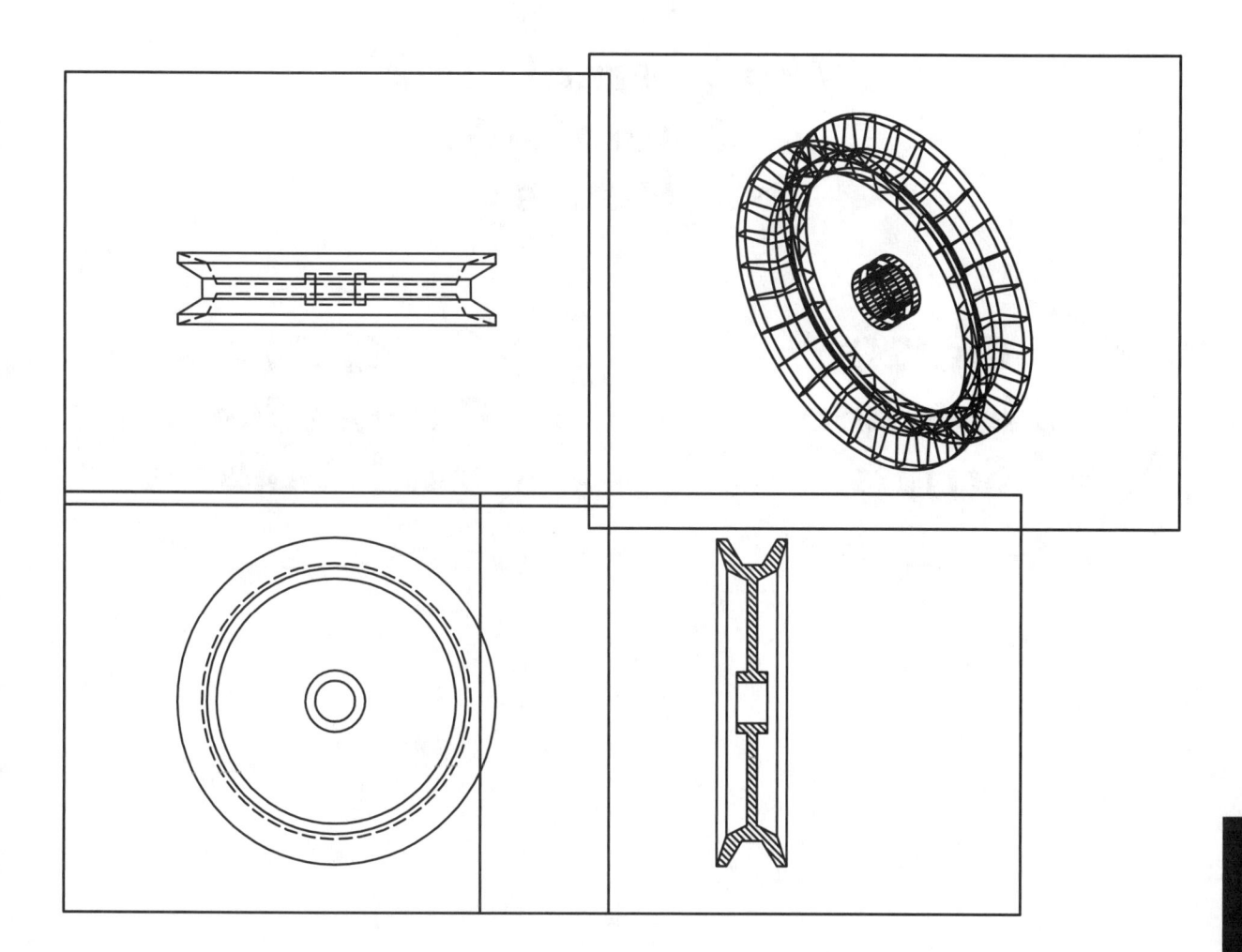

TM-3E
Advanced

TM-4A
Advanced

Part 4 Menus

**Ch. 18
An Internal Peek at AutoCAD's Menus**

**Ch. 20
Slides and Scripts**

**Ch. 19
Custom Menus and Toolbars**

AutoCAD's Menu Files

File Name	Description
acad.mnu	Main menu file
acad.mns	Stores changes to toolbars or menus made from within AutoCAD
acad.mnc	Binary version of acad.mns file
acad.mnr	Contains bitmap images of the buttons
acad.mnl	Menu LISP file

Creating a Custom Toolbar

You can create your own toolbar and copy buttons from other toolbars into it. Be sure to hold down the Ctrl key while you drag and drop the buttons into your toolbar.

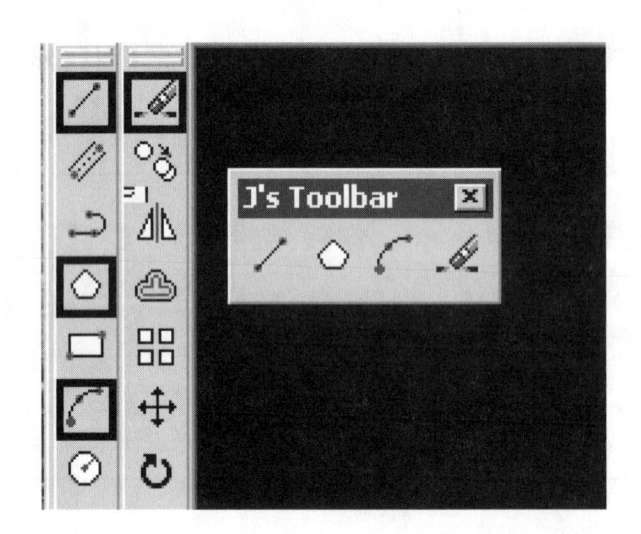

TM-5A
Advanced

Part 5   AutoLISP

Ch. 21 Exploring AutoLISP

Ch. 23 Advanced AutoLISP Programming

Ch. 22 Basic AutoLISP Programming

TM-5B
Advanced

Partial Contents of an AutoLISP File

```
    )
    (if msg
      (alert (strcat " Application error: "
              app
              " \n\n "
              msg
              " \n "
         )
        )
      )
        (exit)
    )

;;; Check to see if AI_UTILS is loaded. If not, try to find it,
;;; and then try to load it.
;;;
;;; If it can't be found or it can't be loaded, then abort the
;;; loading of this file immediately, preserving the (autoload)
;;; stub function.

  (cond
    ( (and ai_dcl (listp ai_dcl)))              ; it's already loaded.

    ( (not (findfile "ai_utils.lsp"))           ; find it
      (ai_abort "3DARRAY"
          (strcat "Can't locate file AI_UTILS.LSP."
              "\ln Check support directory.")))

    ( (eq "failed" (load "ai_utils" "failed"))  ; load it
      (ai_abort "3DARRAY" "Can't load file AI_UTILS.LSP"))
  )

(if (not (ai_acadapp))              ; defined in AI_UTILS.LSP
    (ai_abort "3DARRAY" nil)        ; a Nil <msg> suppresses
)                                    ; ai_abort's alert box dialog.
```

Copyright © Glencoe/McGraw-Hill

TM-5C
Advanced

Results of Loading an AutoLISP File

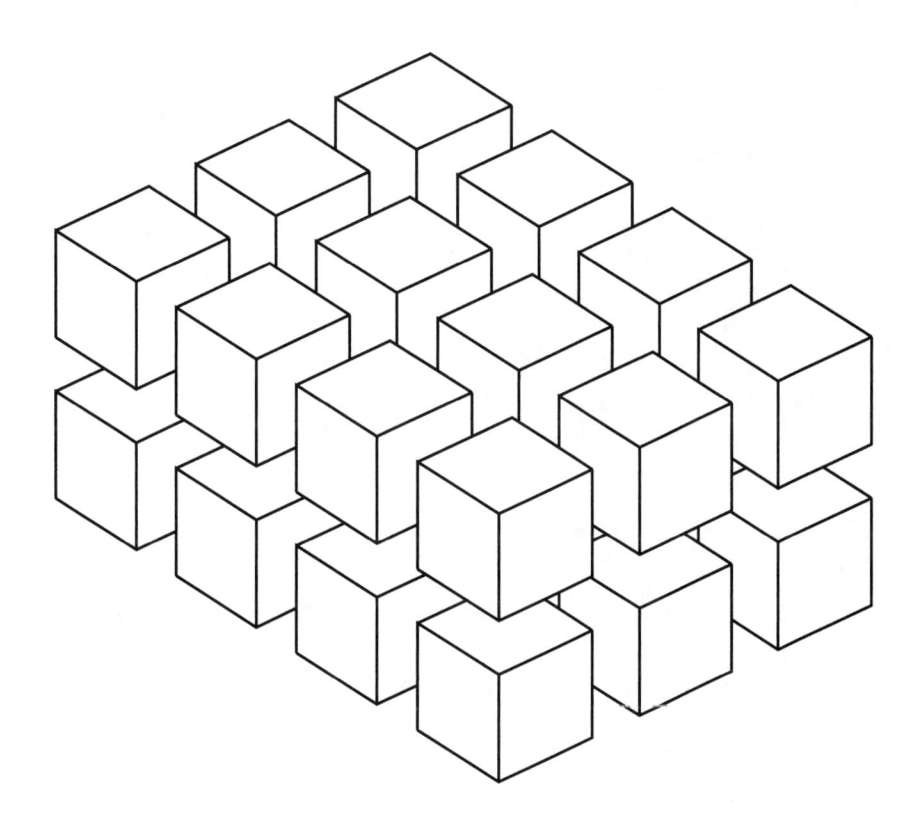

3darray.lsp

Copyright © Glencoe/McGraw-Hill

Documenting a Routine

```
;   This routine establishes a drawing area
;   for a 34" x 22" format (36" x 24" sheet size)
;   and draws a border line.
;

(defun C:34x22 ()
    (setq LL (list 0 0))
    (setq UR (list 34 22))
    (setq LR (list (car UR)(cadr LL)))
    (setq UL (list (car LL)(cadr UR)))

    (command "LIMITS" LL UR) ; sets drawing limits
    (command "ZOOM" "A")     ; zooms all
    (command "GRID" "1");    sets grid
    (command "LINE" LL LR UR UL LL "")
)
```

TM-5D
Advanced

Part 6 Importing and Exporting

TM-6A
Advanced

- **Ch. 24 Standard File Formats**
- **Ch. 28 Database Connectivity**
- **Ch. 25 Raster Image Files**
- **Ch. 27 Object Linking and Embedding**
- **Ch. 26 External References**

TM-6B
Advanced

Raster Image Files

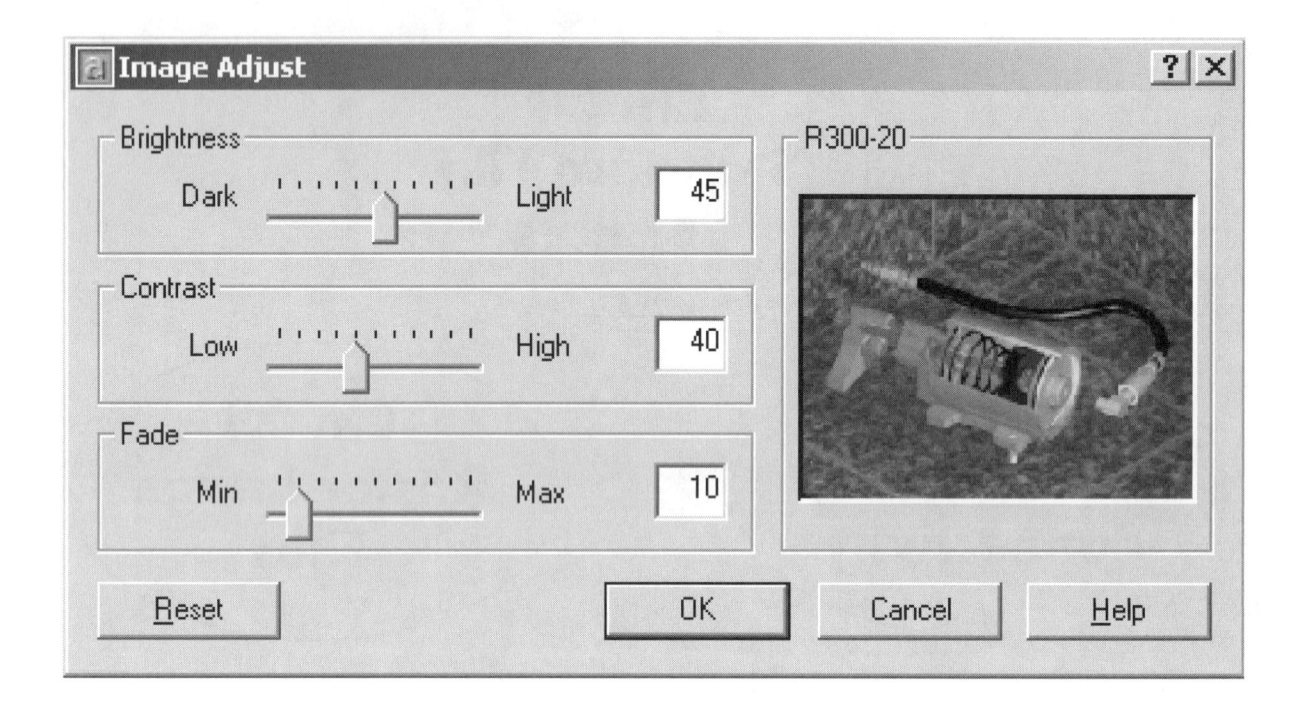

Adjusting Image Quality

Xrefs

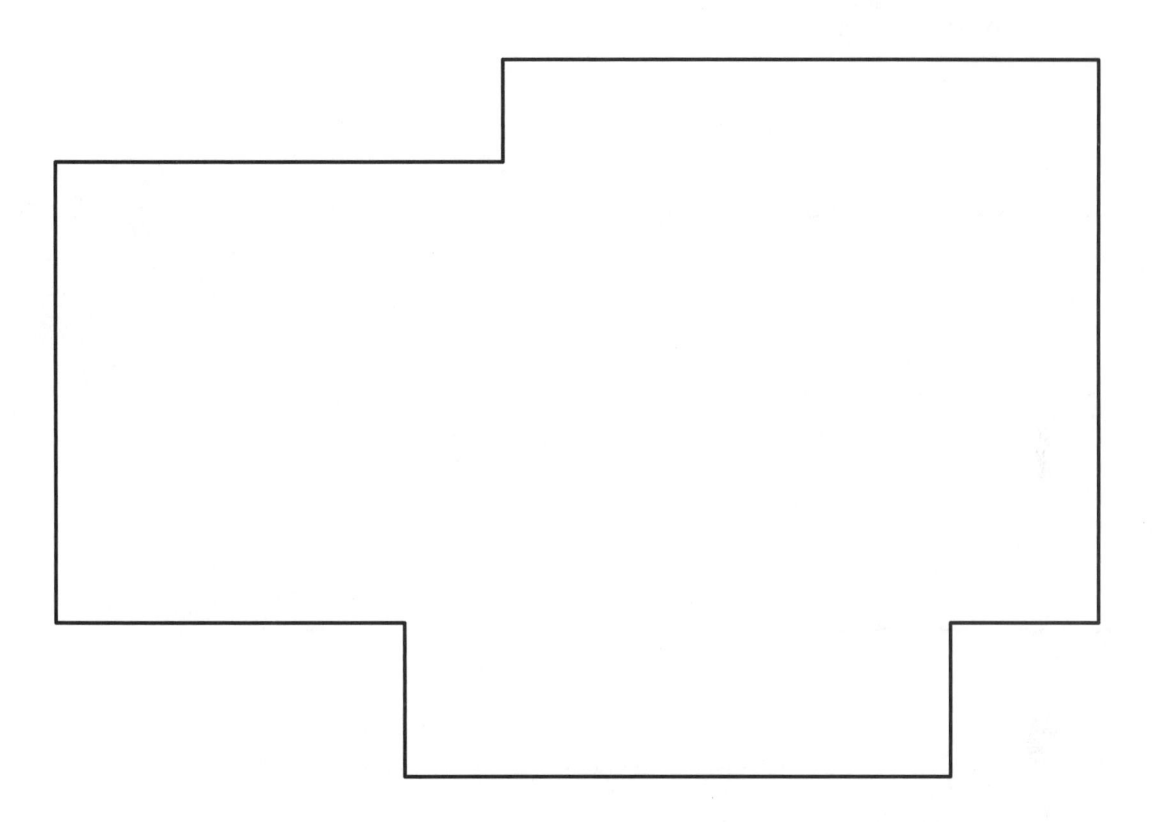

Base Drawing

Xrefs

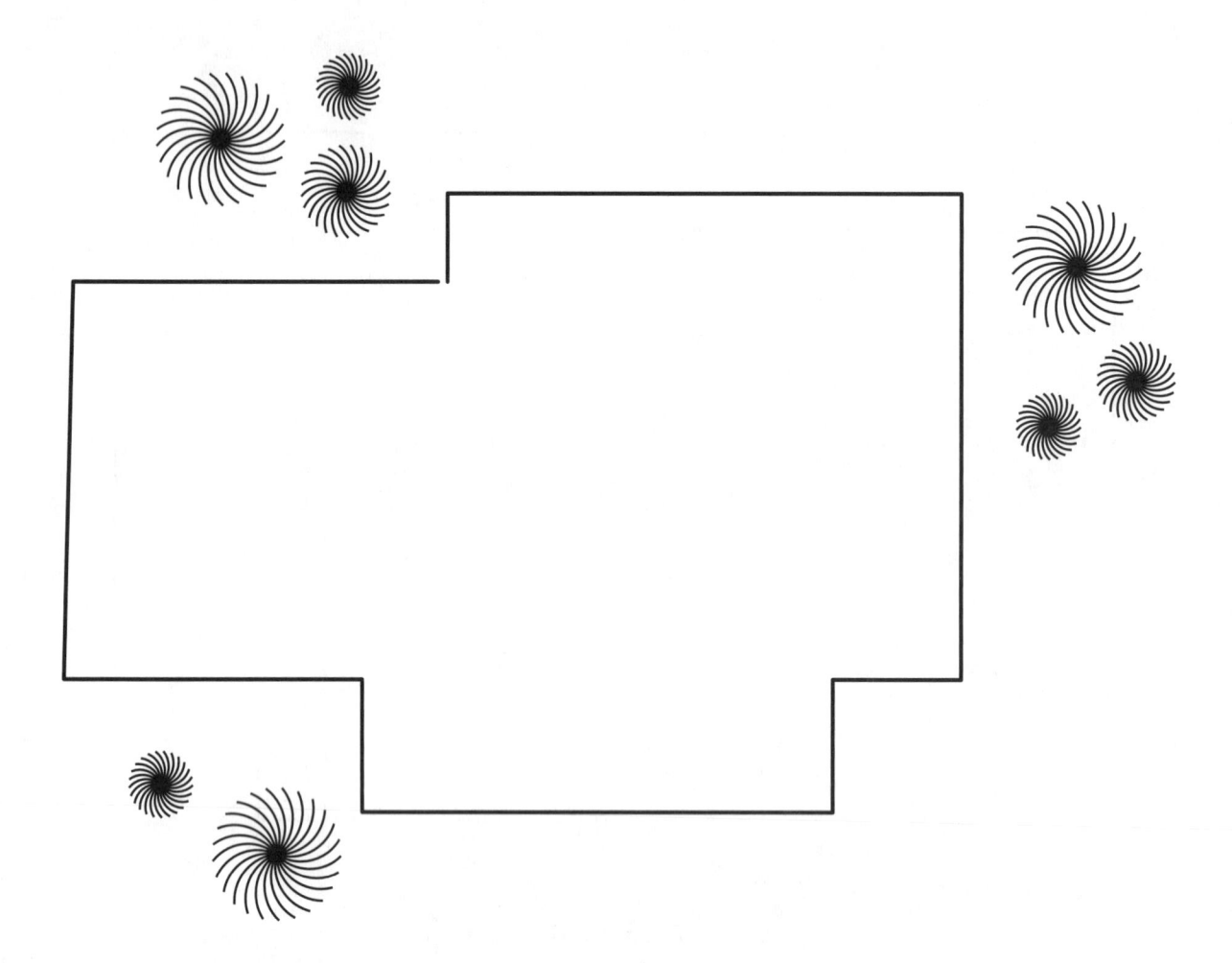

TM-6D
Advanced

Drawing with Xref Attached

Chapter Tests for Advanced Text

This section contains tests for each of the 30 chapters in the *Advanced* text. Answers can be found on pages 335-336.

Part 1 3D Drawing and Modeling
Chapter 1	Isometric Drawing	295
Chapter 2	The Third Dimension	296
Chapter 3	Point Filters	297
Chapter 4	User Coordinate Systems	298

Part 2 Surface Modeling and Rendering
Chapter 5	3D Revolutions	299
Chapter 6	Advanced Surfaces	300
Chapter 7	3D Primitives	301
Chapter 8	Shading and Rendering	302
Chapter 9	Advanced Rendering	303

Part 3 Solid Modeling
Chapter 10	Solid Regions	304
Chapter 11	Solid Primitives	305
Chapter 12	Basic Solid Modeling	306
Chapter 13	Boolean Operations	307
Chapter 14	Tailoring Solid Models	308
Chapter 15	Downstream Benefits	309
Chapter 16	Documenting Solid Models	310
Chapter 17	Physical Benefits of Solid Modeling	311

Part 4 Menus
Chapter 18	An Internal Peek at AutoCAD's Menus	312
Chapter 19	Custom Menus and Toolbars	313
Chapter 20	Slides and Scripts	314

Copyright © Glencoe/McGraw-Hill

Part 5 AutoLISP

Chapter 21	Exploring AutoLISP	315
Chapter 22	Basic AutoLISP Programming	316
Chapter 23	Advanced AutoLISP Programming	317

Part 6 Importing and Exporting

Chapter 24	Standard File Formats	318
Chapter 25	Raster Image Files	319
Chapter 26	External References	320
Chapter 27	Object Linking and Embedding (OLE)	321
Chapter 28	Database Connectivity	322
Chapter 29	Internet Connectivity	323
Chapter 30	Internet Collaboration	324

Name _____ Class Period _____ Time _____

TEST - Advanced Text — *Chapter 1* Isometric Drawing

Multiple Choice

Directions: Circle the letter of the choice that BEST completes the statement or answers the question.

1. To activate the AutoCAD Isometric feature, enter the
   A. CONFIG command.
   B. ISOPLANE command.
   C. SNAP command.
   D. GRID command.

2. To toggle the isometric crosshairs from one plane to another,
   A. press CTRL E.
   B. use the ISOPLANE command.
   C. both A and B.
   D. neither A nor B.

3. To create accurate and properly constructed isometric circles, use the
   A. ELLIPSE command.
   B. ISOPLANE command.
   C. BLOCK and INSERT commands.
   D. none of the above.

4. An isometric drawing is a(n)
   A. three-dimensional model.
   B. two-dimensional drawing that gives a three-dimensional appearance.
   C. highly dimensioned detail of a complex machine part.
   D. none of the above.

Completion

Directions: In the space at the left, write the word or words that BEST complete the statement or answer the question.

_____ 5. The axes in an isometric drawing are _____ degrees apart.

_____ 6. The three drawing planes in an isometric drawing are the left, right, and _____ planes.

_____ 7. To show dimensions in their proper locations on an isometric drawing, you should use the _____ option of the DIMEDIT command.

_____ 8. An isometric drawing produces a(n) _____ representation of an object.

_____ 9. When you work in Isometric drawing mode, the _____ run parallel to the isometric grid.

_____ 10. To place isometric circles correctly on a drawing, you must be sure to toggle the crosshairs to the correct isometric _____.

Copyright © Glencoe/McGraw-Hill

| Name | Class Period | Time |

TEST - Advanced Text   *Chapter 2* The Third Dimension

Multiple Choice

Directions: Circle the letter of the choice that BEST completes the statement or answers the question.

1. To create three-dimensional models and display them with hidden lines removed, which of the following commands should you use?
   A. ELEV, 3D, and VIEW
   B. DISPLAY, VPOINT, and HIDE
   C. VIEW, ELEV, and ROTATE
   D. ELEV, VPOINT, and HIDE

2. You can view a 3D model from
   A. any point in space except from directly above the object.
   B. any point in space except from below the object.
   C. nearly all points in space as long as the drawing contains no cylindrical shapes.
   D. any point in space.

3. Typing VPOINT and pressing ENTER twice
   A. generates the 3D model in perspective projection with hidden lines removed.
   B. displays a "globe representation" that enables you to specify a viewpoint.
   C. creates the top, front, and right-side orthographic projections of the 3D model.
   D. none of the above.

4. You can set the thickness of a three-dimensional object by
   A. entering the ELEV command.
   B. setting the 3DDEPTH system variable.
   C. entering the DEPTH command.
   D. both A and C.

5. The easiest way to view an object from the right side is to
   A. use the Rside option of the VPOINT command.
   B. enter the PLAN command.
   C. pick the Right View button from the View toolbar.
   D. pick the 3D Orbit button from the Standard toolbar.

True-False

Directions: On the line beside each statement, write **True** if the statement is correct or **False** if the statement is incorrect.

_____ 6. When the 3DORBIT command is active, the target of the view moves around a stationary camera.

_____ 7. The target point in 3D orbit is the center of the object(s) you are viewing.

_____ 8. To zoom within the 3D orbit view, right-click and pick Zoom from the shortcut menu.

_____ 9. Perspective projection displays an object with parallel lines that do not converge toward a vanishing point.

_____ 10. The compass in 3D orbit is a 3D sphere within the arcball that is made up of three lines representing the X, Y, and Z axes.

Copyright © Glencoe/McGraw-Hill

Name   Class Period   Time

TEST - Advanced Text   *Chapter 3* Point Filters

Multiple Choice

Directions: Circle the letter of the choice that BEST completes the statement or answers the question.

1. The LINE command
   A. creates objects containing *x* and *y* coordinates only.
   B. creates full 3D lines containing *x*, *y*, and *z* coordinates.
   C. creates 3D faces.
   D. all of the above.

2. Because of their similarities, 3D faces are compared to
   A. shapes produced by the POLYGON command.
   B. blocks.
   C. objects created by the SOLID command.
   D. none of the above.

3. 3D faces
   A. can define visible and invisible edges.
   B. are planar, curved, or cylindrical surfaces in 3D space.
   C. both A and B.
   D. neither A nor B.

4. X/Y/Z point filters
   A. allow you to combine keyboard and pointing methods when specifying a point.
   B. generally are not recommended because they are confusing and seldom useful.
   C. apply only when you are creating large, complex 3D models.
   D. none of the above.

True-False

Directions: On the line beside each statement, write **True** if the statement is correct or **False** if the statement is incorrect.

              5. Point filtering allows you to enter two coordinates of a point in 3D space using the pointing device and add the third coordinate at the keyboard.

              6. 3D faces can be mirrored only within a two-dimensional plane.

              7. *Plan view* is another term for the top view of a 3D object.

              8. The SPLFRAME system variable controls whether 3D face appears solid or in wireframe form.

              9. An advantage of using point filtering is that you can specify points in 3D space without constantly changing your point of view to make the points accessible.

           10. When you are adding lines to an existing object in 3D space, you can use object snap to make point selection easier.

Copyright © Glencoe/McGraw-Hill

Name Class Period Time

TEST - Advanced Text — *Chapter 4* User Coordinate Systems

Multiple Choice

Directions: Circle the letter of the choice that BEST completes the statement or answers the question.

1. Which of the following is *not* true?
   A. A user coordinate system (UCS) is a user-defined construction plane in 3D space.
   B. The UCS command lets you create a new current UCS.
   C. The UCS facility helps you edit objects in 3D space.
   D. The origin of a UCS is fixed.

2. When defining a UCS by selecting 3 points,
   A. the first point you select becomes the origin and the other two define the X and Y axes.
   B. the points you select define the X, Y, and Z axes.
   C. the three points must be on an object that lies entirely within one plane.
   D. you specify the positive direction of the Z axis, and AutoCAD determines the directions of the X and Y axes.

3. The world coordinate system
   A. is AutoCAD's default coordinate system.
   B. has the X axis horizontal on the screen.
   C. has the Y axis vertical on the screen.
   D. all of the above.

4. You can easily generate the plan view of any UCS, including the WCS, by
   A. entering the UCS command and Origin option.
   B. selecting the Restore option of the UCS command.
   C. entering the PLAN comand.
   D. none of the above.

True-False

Directions: On the line beside each statement, write **True** if the statement is correct or **False** if the statement is incorrect.

_____ 5. Changing to a new UCS does not affect the coordinate system icon and grid.

_____ 6. The Z Axis Rotate option lets you specify the rotation angle for the UCS.

_____ 7. You can create a new UCS by moving the origin of the current UCS.

_____ 8. AutoCAD allows you to create a new UCS that is aligned with an existing planar object.

_____ 9. To place a point in the WCS while you are in another UCS, enter an asterisk (*) before the coordinate values.

_____ 10. To delete a UCS from a drawing, enter the DELETE command and select the name of the UCS from the resulting dialog box.

298 Copyright © Glencoe/McGraw-Hill

TEST - Advanced Text
Chapter 5 3D Revolutions

Multiple Choice

Directions: Circle the letter of the choice that BEST completes the statement or answers the question.

1. The REVSURF command enables you to create a surface of revolution by selecting a
   A. line, length, and angle.
   B. path curve and axis of revolution.
   C. polygon mesh and specifying its density and orientation.
   D. none of the above.

2. The RULESURF command
   A. creates a polygon mesh representing the ruled surface between two curves.
   B. asks you to select a defining curve and a straight edge (line).
   C. is nearly identical to the REVSURF command.
   D. all of the above.

3. What controls the density (resolution) of 3D meshes created by 3D commands such as RULESURF and REVSURF?
   A. the SURFTAB1 system variable
   B. the SURFTAB2 system variable
   C. the SURFTAB1 and SURFTAB2 system variables
   D. none of the above

4. AutoCAD uses *M* and *N* vertices to define a
   A. surface mesh.
   B. ruled surface.
   C. surface of revolution.
   D. all of the above.

True-False

Directions: On the line beside each statement, write **True** if the statement is correct or **False** if the statement is incorrect.

_____ 5. As you increase the value of SURFTAB1, the value of SURFTAB2 automatically decreases.

_____ 6. The path curve used by the REVSURF command is often called a *profile*.

_____ 7. One difference between the RULESURF and REVSURF commands is that REVSURF requires a single path curve, but RULESURF requires at least two curves.

_____ 8. An advantage of using more than one viewport as you create a 3D model is that you can see the effects of your work from several different angles simultaneously.

_____ 9. Setting too low a value for SURFTAB2 results in a two-dimensional object.

_____ 10. The process of removing hidden lines becomes faster as you increase the value of SURFTAB2.

Name _____ Class Period _____ Time _____

TEST - Advanced Text *Chapter 6 Advanced Surfaces*

Multiple Choice

Directions: Circle the letter of the choice that BEST completes the statement or answers the question.

1. With the TABSURF command, you create a tabulated surface by
   A. selecting four adjoining edges.
   B. specifying its size (in terms of *M* and *N*) and the location of each vertex in the surface mesh.
   C. revolving a path curve.
   D. none of the above.

2. A Coons surface patch is
   A. created with the EDGESURF command.
   B. a 3D surface mesh interpolated between four adjoining edges.
   C. used to define complex, irregular surfaces such as land formations and manufactured parts such as car bodies.
   D. all of the above.

3. You can edit polygon meshes with the
   A. CHANGE command.
   B. ERASE and BREAK commands.
   C. PEDIT command.
   D. all of the above.

4. The type of mesh created by the 3DMESH command is controlled by the
   A. Surface option of the PEDIT command.
   B. Surface option of the CHANGE command.
   C. SURFTYPE system variable.
   D. TABSURF command.

Completion

Directions: In the space at the left, write the word or words that BEST complete the statement or answer the question.

_____ 5. A 3D line used to provide a direction for a path curve is called a(n) _____. *(two words)*

_____ 6. A(n) _____ is a surface mesh used to create freeform shapes by interpolating between adjoining edges. *(three words)*

_____ 7. Which command should you use to create a path curve or profile so that AutoCAD will treat the profile as a single object?

_____ 8. The _____ command creates basic surface meshes by allowing you to enter the locations of vertices using 3D coordinates.

_____ 9. Which command would you use to create a polyface mesh?

_____ 10. The 3DMESH command can create quadratic B-splines, cubic B-splines, and _____ meshes.

Copyright © Glencoe/McGraw-Hill

Name   Class Period   Time

TEST - Advanced Text   *Chapter 7* 3D Primitives

Multiple Choice

Directions: Circle the letter of the choice that BEST completes the statement or answers the question.

1. Which of the following shapes is *not* available from the 3D Objects dialog box?
    A. plane
    B. sphere
    C. wedge
    D. pyramid

2. The ALIGN command
    A. aligns 3D objects along an imaginary snap grid.
    B. moves objects in 3D space when you specify three sources and three destination points.
    C. aligns two or more 3D objects on a flat, planar surface.
    D. none of the above.

3. Which command(s) can you use to rotate a 3D object?
    A. ROTATE
    B. ROTATE3D
    C. ALIGN
    D. both B and C

4. The MIRROR3D command rotates a 3D object around
    A. an arbitrary plane, which you specify.
    B. a mirror line, which you specify.
    C. the current viewpoint.
    D. none of the above.

5. To create a 3D cube,
    A. pick the Cube button from the Surfaces toolbar.
    B. enter the 3DCUBE command at the keyboard.
    C. pick the Box button from the Surfaces toolbar and select the Cube option.
    D. none of the above.

Completion

Directions: In the space at the left, write the word or words that BEST complete the statement or answer the question.

_____   6. Predefined 3D shapes in AutoCAD are known as _____.

_____   7. When you enter a value higher than zero for the radius of the top of a cone, AutoCAD creates a(n) _____ of the cone.

_____   8. A(n) _____ is a 3D primitive that is shaped like a donut or inner tube.

_____   9. The top point of a pyramid is its _____.

_____   10. When you enter the 3D command at the keyboard, which option allows you to form a polygon of any size and shape by specifying the corner points and *M* and *N* values?

Copyright © Glencoe/McGraw-Hill

Name _____ Class Period _____ Time _____

TEST - Advanced Text — *Chapter 8* Shading and Rendering

Multiple Choice

Directions: Circle the letter of the choice that BEST completes the statement or answers the question.

1. A difference between the SHADE and RENDER commands is that
   A. SHADE produces a higher quality drawing than RENDER.
   B. SHADE is more versatile than RENDER.
   C. SHADE produces a shaded image more quickly than RENDER.
   D. both B and C.

2. To improve the facets in a rendering, you
   A. increase the values of the SURFTAB1 and SURFTAB2 system variables.
   B. decrease the value of the SURFTAB1 system variable.
   C. decrease the value of the SURFTAB2 system variable.
   D. none of the above.

3. The Statistics dialog box contains
   A. the time you have spent on the current drawing.
   B. the coordinates for selected points in the drawing.
   C. information about the most recent rendering.
   D. none of the above.

4. The Save Image dialog box permits you to create which of the following types of files?
   A. TGA
   B. TIFF
   C. BMP
   D. all of the above

5. When you pick the Flat Shaded button on the Shade toolbar, AutoCAD
   A. fills each facet with a single shade of color.
   B. hides the edges of the facets by smoothing their edges.
   C. shows the flat edges of the facets by superimposing the wireframe model on the shaded image.
   D. none of the above.

Completion

Directions: In the space at the left, write the word or words that BEST complete the statement or answer the question.

_____ 6. Another name for smooth shading is _____ shading.

_____ 7. A(n) _____ is a three- or four-sided polygonal element that represents a piece of a 3D surface.

_____ 8. The "stick" representation of a model that AutoCAD shows by default is known as a(n) _____.

_____ 9. Another term for facet shading is _____ shading.

_____ 10. Which command should you use to redisplay an image that you have rendered and saved?

Copyright © Glencoe/McGraw-Hill

Name _____   Class Period _____   Time _____

TEST - Advanced Text   *Chapter 9* Advanced Rendering

Multiple Choice

Directions: Circle the letter of the choice that BEST completes the statement or answers the question.

1. Phong shading is
   A. a method of shading that allows you to assign lights and materials to an object.
   B. shading that takes place within a rendered scene.
   C. similar to Gouraud shading, except that it uses a more advanced method to calculate the lighting effects on the surface of the model.
   D. all of the above.

2. A scene is similar to a view. The only difference is
   A. a scene can contain two or more different material finishes.
   B. a scene can be rendered, whereas a view cannot be rendered.
   C. a scene can contain one or more light sources.
   D. all of the above.

3. When you increase the ambient light setting for a rendered object,
   A. the general light surrounding the object becomes brighter.
   B. the object appears brightly lit against a dark background.
   C. the object appears to be lit from within.
   D. none of the above.

4. When you add a light source, which of the following characteristics does AutoCAD allow you to specify?
   A. color
   B. intensity
   C. position of the light
   D. all of the above

5. The Background dialog box allows you to do all of the following *except*
   A. select a gradient of colors for the background of the rendered object.
   B. use landscape objects to make the background look more realistic.
   C. use a BMP graphic file for the background.
   D. use a customized solid color as a background.

Completion

Directions: In the space at the left, write the word or words that BEST complete the statement or answer the question.

_____ 6. The calculation-intense rendering process in which lines are drawn from the eye to every point on the screen is known as _____.

_____ 7. A(n) _____ is a gradual transition from one color to another.

_____ 8. An object with a bitmapped image mapped onto it, called a(n) _____ object, has a texture, grain, or other quality that helps make it look real.

_____ 9. A model that is _____ resembles a photographic image.

_____ 10. _____ is a method of averaging the edges of a model so that they blend together and provide a smooth appearance.

Copyright © Glencoe/McGraw-Hill   303

Name _____ Class Period _____ Time _____

TEST - Advanced Text   *Chapter 10* Solid Regions

Multiple Choice

Directions: Circle the letter of the choice that BEST completes the statement or answers the question.

1. A region is
   A. produced by combining two or more objects using the REGION command.
   B. made up of 3D elements such as polygon meshes and Coons surface patches.
   C. the result of combining two or more objects using the Boolean union, subtraction, or intersection operation.
   D. both B and C.

2. With what command would you create a composite region by subtracting one object from another?
   A. SOLIDIFY
   B. COMPOSITE
   C. SUBTRACT
   D. none of the above

3. Which of the following commands does *not* calculate the area of a region?
   A. AREA
   B. LIST
   C. MASSPROP
   D. none of the above

4. With which command can you create a region from the intersection of two overlapping 2D objects?
   A. UNION
   B. BOUNDARY
   C. SUBTRACT
   D. none of the above

5. To display the engineering properties of a region, which command should you use?
   A. STATS
   B. MASSPROP
   C. REGION
   D. none of the above

True-False

Directions: On the line beside each statement, write **True** if the statement is correct or **False** if the statement is incorrect.

_____ 6. A region primitive is a basic shape from which more complex regions can be formed.

_____ 7. A composite region is the result of applying Boolean operations to simpler regions.

_____ 8. The outer loop of a region is its outside boundary.

_____ 9. The BOUNDARY command can create both regions and closed polylines.

_____ 10. The EXTRUDE command transforms a closed polyline into a 2D region.

Name _____ Class Period _____ Time _____

TEST - Advanced Text — *Chapter 11* Solid Primitives

Multiple Choice

Directions: Circle the letter of the choice that BEST completes the statement or answers the question.

1. Solid primitives are
   A. the basic building blocks for creating complex solid models.
   B. rarely used to create solid models.
   C. represented ambiguously and are difficult to visualize and apply.
   D. none of the above.

2. Which of the following is a predefined solid primitive in AutoCAD?
   A. mesh
   B. dome
   C. sphere
   D. dish

3. A football-shaped object results when you specify
   A. a radius of 0 for a solid cylinder.
   B. a negative radius for a solid sphere.
   C. a negative radius for a solid cone.
   D. none of the above.

4. To create an elliptical cylinder, you can
   A. enter the Elliptical option of the CYLINDER command.
   B. create an ellipse using the ELLIPSE command and then extrude it.
   C. both A and B.
   D. neither A nor B.

5. One of the reasons that solid models are becoming more widely used than surface models is that solid models
   A. take less time to create.
   B. more accurately reflect a physical prototype.
   C. look better when rendered.
   D. none of the above.

True-False

Directions: On the line beside each statement, write **True** if the statement is correct or **False** if the statement is incorrect.

_____ 6. The DONUT command allows you to create donut-shaped solid primitives.

_____ 7. The most efficient way to create a solid cone is to enter the CYLINDER command and specify a top radius of 0.

_____ 8. To create a solid wedge, you must identify two points diagonally across from each other on the base of the wedge.

_____ 9. The Center option of the BOX command allows you to align the lower left edge of the box with the center of an existing sphere or cylinder.

_____ 10. The 3point option of the SPHERE command allows you to create a sphere that is tangent to three existing solids or surfaces.

Copyright © Glencoe/McGraw-Hill

305

Name Class Period Time

TEST - Advanced Text *Chapter 12* Basic Solid Modeling

Multiple Choice

Directions: Circle the letter of the choice that BEST completes the statement or answers the question.

1. To create cylindrical solid objects, such as a steel shaft, you can use
   A. the CIRCLE and EXTRUDE commands.
   B. the REVSURF command.
   C. the REVOLVE command.
   D. both A and C.

2. The ISOLINES system variable controls the
   A. visibility of solid primitives.
   B. number of tessellation lines used to define curves in solid objects.
   C. shade color when the SHADE command is applied.
   D. both A and B.

3. Which of the following *cannot* be extruded using the EXTRUDE command?
   A. polygons
   B. splines
   C. blocks
   D. regions

4. The function of the REVOLVE command in solid modeling is most similar to which of the following surface modeling commands?
   A. TABSURF
   B. RULESURF
   C. REVSURF
   D. 3DMESH

True-False

Directions: On the line beside each statement, write **True** if the statement is correct or **False** if the statement is incorrect.

_____ 5. A polyline that contains a crossing or self-intersecting segment cannot be extruded.

_____ 6. You can create a hole in an extruded solid without using Boolean subtraction by creating a solid cylinder at the proper location on the part.

_____ 7. Tessellation is the creation of the lines used to describe a curved surface.

_____ 8. By definition, the top surface of an extruded part has exactly the same area as the lower surface.

_____ 9. To improve the quality, accuracy, and appearance of a solid model, you should decrease the number of tessellation lines to a maximum of 4.

_____ 10. Only closed polylines can be extruded.

Copyright © Glencoe/McGraw-Hill

Name _____ Class Period _____ Time _____

TEST - Advanced Text   *Chapter 13* Boolean Operations

Multiple Choice

Directions: Circle the letter of the choice that BEST completes the statement or answers the question.

1. Which of the following is *not* a Boolean operation?
   A. subtraction
   B. composition
   C. union
   D. All of the above are Boolean operations.

2. A composite solid is one that
   A. results when any Boolean operation is applied to two or more solid primitives.
   B. has been converted from another file format.
   C. results when the COMPOSITE command is applied to two or more solid primitives.
   D. does all of the above.

3. Which of the following commands is capable of creating a hole in a solid model?
   A. EXTRUDE
   B. SUBTRACT
   C. BREAK
   D. INTERSECT

4. Which of the following methods would *not* result in a 3D model of a cylinder?
   A. picking the Cylinder button from the Solids toolbar
   B. creating and extruding a circle
   C. applying the UNION command to two circles at different elevations
   D. B and C

True-False

Directions: On the line beside each statement, write **True** if the statement is correct or **False** if the statement is incorrect.

_____ 5. When AutoCAD subtracts one solid from another, it also updates the mass properties of the resulting solid.

_____ 6. The UNION command does not work on composite solids.

_____ 7. To create a hollow pipe with a 2″ outer diameter and a wall thickness of $1/16$″, you could create concentric cylinders with diameters of 2″ and $1\,^{15}/_{16}$″ and then subtract the smaller cylinder from the larger one.

_____ 8. The value of ISOLINES does not have a noticeable effect on composite solids.

_____ 9. To see the effect of Boolean operations on a solid model, the most efficient view to use is generally the plan view.

_____ 10. Composite solids can be broken back into their component parts using the Decurve option of the PEDIT command.

Copyright © Glencoe/McGraw-Hill

Name _____ Class Period _____ Time _____

TEST - Advanced Text   *Chapter 14* Tailoring Solid Models

Multiple Choice

Directions: Circle the letter of the choice that BEST completes the statement or answers the question.

1. The INTERFERE command
   A. detects interfering solid objects and deletes the parts of the objects that interfere with one another.
   B. calculates the mass properties of interfering solid objects.
   C. detects interference (overlap) between two or more solid objects.
   D. none of the above.

2. Which command calculates the solid volume that is common to two or more overlapping solid objects?
   A. INTERFERE
   B. VOLUME
   C. INTERSECT
   D. LIST

3. To create a half-sphere (hemisphere), you can create a sphere and a box and position them so that half of the sphere is inside the box. Then, to finish the hemisphere, you should apply
   A. the SUBTRACT command to subtract the sphere from the box.
   B. the SUBTRACT command to subtract the box from the sphere.
   C. the INTERSECT command.
   D. both B and C.

4. To bevel an edge of a solid model, you should use the
   A. CHAMFER command.
   B. FILLET command.
   C. BEVEL command.
   D. none of the above.

True-False

Directions: On the line beside each statement, write **True** if the statement is correct or **False** if the statement is incorrect.

_____ 5. When you are modifying the edge of a 3D model and AutoCAD selects the wrong surface, you can change the selection by typing N for Next.

_____ 6. The Chain option of the FILLET command allows you to modify several adjoining edges in a single operation.

_____ 7. Shelling a solid model consists of discarding the outer layer so that the inner parts of the model are exposed.

_____ 8. When two solid models occupy the same position in 3D space, the INTERFERENCE command returns the message Interfering Pairs.

_____ 9. The Shell feature works on individual faces of a solid, which you can add to or remove from the selection set before you execute the function.

_____ 10. The only reliable way to position adjacent solids in 3D space is to list their properties and check their coordinates.

Copyright © Glencoe/McGraw-Hill

Name _____ Class Period _____ Time _____

TEST - Advanced Text — *Chapter 15* Downstream Benefits

Multiple Choice

Directions: Circle the letter of the choice that BEST completes the statement or answers the question.

1. Which one of the following is *not* a potential downstream benefit of solid modeling?
   A. fabrication of the physical part
   B. mass properties generation
   C. creation of profile and sectional objects for two-dimensional detail drafting
   D. none of the above

2. You can create a full cross section of a solid model in AutoCAD using the
   A. CUT command.
   B. SECTION command.
   C. PROFILE command.
   D. none of the above.

3. Which command creates 2D profile objects from solid models?
   A. SOLPROF
   B. SECTION
   C. PROFILE
   D. none of the above

True-False

Directions: On the line beside each statement, write **True** if the statement is correct or **False** if the statement is incorrect.

_____ 4. When a curved face meets a flat face, the result is a tangential edge.

_____ 5. Under certain conditions, solid models can be used directly to guide production processes.

_____ 6. A full section of a part shows the interior of the part as it appears at a specified cross section.

_____ 7. AutoCAD automatically hatches sections that you create through solid models.

_____ 8. The SECTION command allows you to define a cutting plane using a 3D polyline or other planar object.

_____ 9. A cutting plane is the plane through an object at which a full section is created.

_____ 10. The SOLPROF command does not work in paper space layouts.

Copyright © Glencoe/McGraw-Hill

TEST - Advanced Text — Chapter 16 Documenting Solid Models

Multiple Choice

Directions: Circle the letter of the choice that BEST completes the statement or answers the question.

1. An orthographic projection
   A. is a view of a solid model that is similar to a two-dimensional isometric drawing.
   B. can be created from a solid model using AutoCAD's SOLVIEW and SOLDRAW commands.
   C. cannot be created from solid models with AutoCAD.
   D. none of the above.

2. Which of the following views *cannot* be calculated by the SOLVIEW command?
   A. auxiliary
   B. sectional
   C. orthographic
   D. isometric

3. When you apply the SOLVIEW command,
   A. AutoCAD automatically creates new layers for each linetype needed in the drawing.
   B. SOLVIEW stores its information on layer 0 so that it is easily accessible.
   C. SOLVIEW saves its information as a block.
   D. none of the above.

4. The SOLDRAW command
   A. uses information calculated by the SOLVIEW command to create a final drawing view.
   B. creates solid models from information calculated by the SOLVIEW command.
   C. both A and B.
   D. neither A nor B.

True-False

Directions: On the line beside each statement, write **True** if the statement is correct or **False** if the statement is incorrect.

_____ 5. SOLVIEW creates viewports and layers to display various linetypes in each view of an orthographic projection.

_____ 6. If you use the SOLDRAW command first, use of the SOLVIEW command is optional.

_____ 7. The Section option of the SOLVIEW command creates a full section, complete with crosshatching.

_____ 8. It is considered bad practice to overlap the borders of viewports because doing so places the top, front, and side views out of alignment.

_____ 9. To reposition viewports, you must be in model space so that you can use the MOVE command.

_____ 10. An auxiliary view is one that is projected onto a plane perpendicular to one of the orthographic views and inclined in the adjacent view.

Copyright © Glencoe/McGraw-Hill

Name _____ Class Period _____ Time _____

TEST - Advanced Text *Chapter 17* Physical Benefits of Solid Modeling

Multiple Choice

Directions: Circle the letter of the choice that BEST completes the statement or answers the question.

1. You can separate a model into two parts using the
   A. STLOUT command.
   B. SECTION command.
   C. PROFILE command.
   D. none of the above.

2. STLOUT enables you to
   A. create a numerical control (NC) tool path.
   B. print a shaded view of a solid model.
   C. create the file type required by most rapid prototyping systems, such as stereolithography.
   D. split a model into two halves.

3. An STL file
   A. describes a 3D model using triangular facets.
   B. can be ASCII or binary.
   C. consists of a list of x, y, and z coordinates that describe connected triangles.
   D. all of the above.

4. It is possible to adjust the size of the triangles in an STL file using
   A. ISOLINES.
   B. FACETRES.
   C. STLSIZE.
   D. none of the above.

5. The SLICE command
   A. cuts through a solid model and retains one or both parts of the solid.
   B. creates a cross section of a solid model along the specified plane.
   C. calculates the mass properties of a solid by determining the properties at a given slice, or cross section, of the model.
   D. none of the above.

Completion

Directions: In the space at the left, write the word or words that BEST complete the statement or answer the question.

_____ 6. ____ is a method of producing physical models quickly using solid model data. *(two words)*

_____ 7. Center of gravity, mass, and surface area are among the ____ AutoCAD can calculate for a solid model. *(two words)*

_____ 8. Fused Deposition Modeling (FDM) and ____ are examples of RP systems that use STL files.

_____ 9. The ____ octant is the area in 3D space where the x, y, and z coordinates are greater than 0.

_____ 10. In general, you should choose to create a(n) ____ STL file, rather than an ASCII file, because it is smaller.

Copyright © Glencoe/McGraw-Hill

Name _____ Class Period _____ Time _____

TEST - Advanced Text *Chapter 18* An Internal Peek at AutoCAD's Menus

Multiple Choice

Directions: Circle the letter of the choice that BEST completes the statement or answers the question.

1. The contents of AutoCAD's pull-down menus
   A. are stored in a file named acad.exe.
   B. are viewed using the DIR command.
   C. can be edited from the acad.mnu file.
   D. all of the above.

2. In an AutoCAD menu file, a semicolon in a menu item tells the computer to
   A. prompt the user for input.
   B. press ENTER.
   C. press the CTRL key.
   D. none of the above.

3. Which of the following is *not* true of the menu element [->&Custom]?
   A. The word Custom appears in the menu.
   B. Custom has a submenu.
   C. The letter C is underlined in the menu.
   D. Custom is the last item in a submenu.

4. Which statement best describes the effect of the following menu item?

   ID_Linetype[Li&netypes...]'ddltype

   A. ID_Linetype is the name tag; Linetypes... appears in the pull-down menu; AutoCAD enters the DDLTYPE command transparently.
   B. ID_Linetype is the name tag; LiNetypes appears in the Linetype pull-down menu; AutoCAD enters the DDLTYPE command transparently.
   C. ID_Linetype appears in the pull-down menu; Linetypes... appears as a submenu; AutoCAD waits for user input and then enters the DDLTYPE command.
   D. ID_Linetype appears in the pull-down menu; AutoCAD enters the LINETYPES command, waits for user input, and then enters the DDLTYPE command.

True-False

Directions: On the line beside each statement, write **True** if the statement is correct or **False** if the statement is incorrect.

_____ 5. Names of menu sections in a menu file are preceded by three asterisks (***).

_____ 6. AutoCAD features such as grid and ortho can be manipulated in menu files by entering control codes such as ^G and ^O.

_____ 7. To ensure that AutoCAD doesn't try to read a comment in a menu file as code, comments must be preceded by two forward slashes (//).

_____ 8. A macro is a collection of elements that create a menu item that performs a specific function in AutoCAD.

_____ 9. The difference between the acad.mnc and acad.mnu files is that the acad.mnu file is a compiled version that cannot be edited.

_____ 10. In a menu file, an apostrophe serves the same purpose that it does at the command line—it enters the following command transparently.

Name _____ Class Period _____ Time _____

TEST - Advanced Text — Chapter 19 Custom Menus and Toolbars

Multiple Choice

Directions: Circle the letter of the choice that BEST completes the statement or answers the question.

1. AutoCAD menu files are stored with what type of file extension?
   A. DWG
   B. DXF
   C. BAS
   D. none of the above

2. The MENU command enables you to
   A. create custom menus.
   B. modify existing menus.
   C. both A and B.
   D. neither A nor B.

3. To convert a menu file named template.mnu into a partial menu,
   A. enter MENULOAD template at the command prompt.
   B. add ***MENUGROUP=TEMPLATE to the top of the template.mnu file, followed by a blank line.
   C. enter ***MENUGROUP=TEMPLATE at the command prompt.
   D. none of the above.

4. To add a button to a new custom toolbar,
   A. pick the Commands tab in the Customize dialog box, make a selection from the Categories list box, and drag the button from the dialog box to the new toolbar.
   B. press the CTRL key and drag the button from another currently displayed toolbar.
   C. drag the button from another currently displayed toolbar and drop it into an open area of the screen.
   D. both A and B.

True-False

Directions: On the line beside each statement, write **True** if the statement is correct or **False** if the statement is incorrect.

_____ 5. A macro can automatically execute several commands or functions in a single operation.

_____ 6. Drawing and editing tasks for 3D objects cannot be executed using a macro when multiple UCSs are needed.

_____ 7. When you load a template menu file, AutoCAD automatically saves the existing MNS file, if one exists, to help avoid accidental overwriting.

_____ 8. The purpose of the MENULOAD command is to load partial menus that can be used with the current base menu.

_____ 9. The Customize dialog box allows you to create, delete, and change the names of toolbars.

_____ 10. The standard acad menu remains loaded in the background even after you load another MNU file; so you retain the functionality of AutoCAD's pull-down menus even while custom menus are active.

TEST - Advanced Text

Chapter 20 Slides and Scripts

Multiple Choice

Directions: Circle the letter of the choice that BEST completes the statement or answers the question.

1. With which of the following commands can you create and view slides?
   A. SLIDE and VIEW
   B. MSLIDE and VSLIDE
   C. SCRIPT and VIEW
   D. both A and C
2. Which of the following commands allow you to view slide shows?
   A. SLIDE, VIEW, and SCRIPT
   B. FILES, SCRIPT, DELAY, and PAN
   C. VSLIDE, DELAY, RESUME, and SCRIPT
   D. VSLIDE, VIEW, and RSCRIPT
3. Which command, when included at the end of a script file, causes a slide show to repeat automatically?
   A. RSCRIPT
   B. RESUME
   C. REPEAT
   D. AutoCAD's script files do not offer this capability.
4. To interrupt a running script,
   A. enter the RSCRIPT command.
   B. press the backspace key.
   C. enter the DELAY command.
   D. none of the above.

True-False

Directions: On the line beside each statement, write **True** if the statement is correct or **False** if the statement is incorrect.

_____ 5. Script files are created using a text editor or word processor and are then compiled into binary SCR files so that they will run more quickly.

_____ 6. A slide show is a collection of slides shown in a continuous sequence that is controlled by a script.

_____ 7. The drawings contained in slides that were created from AutoCAD drawing files cannot be edited.

_____ 8. The REDRAW command removes a slide image from the screen.

_____ 9. The DELAY command delays execution of the next command in a script for a specified number of milliseconds.

_____ 10. To use a slide library, you must store all the slides in the same folder as the slide library file.

Name   Class Period   Time

TEST - Advanced Text   *Chapter 21* Exploring AutoLISP

Multiple Choice

Directions: Circle the letter of the choice that BEST completes the statement or answers the question.

1. AutoLISP is
   A. a simplified version of the C programming language made available to AutoCAD users.
   B. the automatic setting of LISPHEAP.
   C. a user programming language resembling Visual BASIC.
   D. AutoCAD's version of the LISP programming language.

2. To load an AutoLISP program named moon.lsp, enter
   A. (load now).
   B. (load "moon").
   C. the MENU command and then moon.
   D. none of the above.

3. An enhanced version of AutoLISP that includes a compiler and debugger is
   A. ObjectARX.
   B. VBA.
   C. LISt Processing.
   D. Visual LISP.

4. AutoLISP routines can be stored as any of the following *except*
   A. pull-down menus.
   B. DXF files.
   C. AutoLISP files (with the LSP extension).
   D. tablet menu items.

True-False

Directions: On the line beside each statement, write **True** if the statement is correct or **False** if the statement is incorrect.

_____ 5. AutoLISP is embedded in the AutoCAD software.

_____ 6. AutoLISP routines that are stored as files can be loaded and invoked at the command prompt.

_____ 7. The Load/Unload Applications dialog box allows you to load several AutoLISP routines in a single operation.

_____ 8. You can use the Load/Unload Applications dialog box much like the AutoCAD DesignCenter feature to load drawing settings from other files into the current drawing.

_____ 9. You can use the Load/Unload Applications dialog box to free system memory of unneeded AutoLISP files.

_____ 10. In addition to AutoLISP, AutoCAD provides another programming environment known as ObjectARX.

Copyright © Glencoe/McGraw-Hill

Name _____ Class Period _____ Time _____

TEST - Advanced Text *Chapter 22* Basic AutoLISP Programming

Multiple Choice

Directions: Circle the letter of the choice that BEST completes the statement or answers the question.

1. To assign values to variables in AutoLISP, use the
   A. setq function.
   B. cadr function.
   C. command function.
   D. none of the above.

2. What is the value of B if (setq B (–32 6)) is entered at the command prompt?
   A. –26
   B. 26
   C. 1/26
   D. none of the above.

3. The cadr function
   A. obtains the first item in a list, such as the *x* coordinate.
   B. obtains the second item in a list.
   C. assigns a variable to a new list.
   D. none of the above

4. The car function
   A. offers a unique AutoLISP technique for automobile chassis design.
   B. obtains the first item in a list.
   C. gives the second item in a list.
   D. none of the above.

True-False

Directions: On the line beside each statement, write **True** if the statement is correct or **False** if the statement is incorrect.

_____ 5. A computer routine or subroutine that performs a calculation using values that you supply is known as a variable.

_____ 6. If the total number of left parentheses does not equal the number of right parentheses in an AutoLISP expression, AutoCAD displays an error message that tells you how many parentheses are missing and whether the missing ones are right or left parentheses.

_____ 7. The list function can assign only one value to a variable.

_____ 8. To display the current value of a variable, enter a question mark (?) followed by the name of the variable at the command prompt.

_____ 9. The defun function allows you to define a new function or command in AutoCAD.

_____ 10. In AutoLISP arithmetic, the entire operation must be enclosed in parentheses, and the operator (+, –, ×, ÷) must be placed before the numbers to be evaluated.

Name _____ Class Period _____ Time _____

TEST - Advanced Text *Chapter 23* Advanced AutoLISP Programming

Multiple Choice

Directions: Circle the letter of the choice that BEST completes the statement or answers the question.

1. AutoCAD commands are executed from within AutoLISP
   A. using the command function.
   B. by pressing CTRL S and then entering the desired command.
   C. by placing a semicolon before the command.
   D. none of the above.

2. The AutoLISP function that causes AutoCAD to pause for user input of a real number is
   A. getvar.
   B. getnumber.
   C. getdist.
   D. getreal.

3. Parametric programming techniques
   A. involve basic geometry stored in an AutoLISP (LSP) file that can be used repeatedly to create unlimited variations of a part or design.
   B. offer a potential reduction in the number of drawing files created when variations of a part or design are used repeatedly.
   C. both A and B.
   D. neither A nor B.

4. What character must precede any comment or documentation that you include in an AutoLISP file?
   A. /
   B. ;
   C. *
   D. &

True-False

Directions: On the line beside each statement, write **True** if the statement is correct or **False** if the statement is incorrect.

_____ 5. If you respond to an AutoCAD prompt by entering !product, AutoCAD enters the current value of the variable named product.

_____ 6. AutoCAD commands that are included as part of an AutoLISP expression must be enclosed by double quotation marks (" ").

_____ 7. In an AutoLISP expression, entering ^S is the equivalent of pressing the spacebar.

_____ 8. The practice of indenting certain lines of code is discouraged because it makes the code more difficult to read.

_____ 9. The setvar function sets an AutoCAD system variable to a specified value and then returns that value.

_____ 10. Parametric AutoLISP programs are rarely used because they are difficult and time-consuming to develop.

Copyright © Glencoe/McGraw-Hill

Name   **Class Period**   **Time**

TEST - Advanced Text   *Chapter 24* **Standard File Formats**

Multiple Choice

Directions: Circle the letter of the choice that BEST completes the statement or answers the question.

1. Standard file formats for translating drawing files from one CAD system to another are
   A. DWG and COM.
   B. DXF and EXE.
   C. EXE and DWG.
   D. DXF and IGES.

2. Certain CAD characteristics are potential problems when translating file formats. Among these are
   A. layers and dimensions.
   B. blocks.
   C. linetypes, colors, and text.
   D. all of the above.

3. A 25% reduction in file size and a five-fold increase in read/write speed can be achieved by using what file translation format instead of standard ASCII DXF files?
   A. IGES
   B. binary DXF
   C. ASCII DXF is the most efficient format and, presently, there is no substitute.
   D. none of the above

4. A file format that allows you to export complex objects such as NURBS surfaces and solid models to many ACIS-based systems is
   A. SAT.   C. DXF.
   B. EPS.   D. IGES.

5. Which of the following file formats would be the best choice if you needed to export an AutoCAD drawing file to a format in which it could be animated?
   A. SAT
   B. DXF
   C. 3DS
   D. EPS

True-False

Directions: On the line beside each statement, write **True** if the statement is correct or **False** if the statement is incorrect.

_____ 6. To convert AME models to AutoCAD 2002 solid models, you must use the AMECONVERT command.

_____ 7. ASCII DXF files contain all the information of a binary DXF file and are compatible with a wider range of applications.

_____ 8. The information provided by the DXF format is not precise enough to be used with special applications such as generating tool path code for computer numerical control (CNC) machines.

_____ 9. AutoCAD allows you to export and import EPS files.

_____ 10. The accuracy of DXF files cannot be adjusted.

Name _____ Class Period _____ Time _____

TEST - Advanced Text   *Chapter 25* Raster Image Files

Multiple Choice

Directions: Circle the letter of the choice that BEST completes the statement or answers the question.

1. AutoCAD displays raster files in drawing files
   A. if the drawing file contains no vector-based objects.
   B. as unique object types.
   C. as long as you limit the number of raster files to one per drawing.
   D. by importing the contents of the raster file into the drawing database.

2. To resize a raster image in AutoCAD,
   A. pick the border of the image and use the grips that appear.
   B. use the SCALE command.
   C. use the Scale option of the RASTER command.
   D. exit AutoCAD and use other software to resize the image; it cannot be done within AutoCAD.

3. The Image Transparency button allows you to
   A. make the image transparent so that it does not show up on the screen but remains in the drawing database.
   B. control the brightness and contrast of the image.
   C. remove an image permanently from the drawing database.
   D. none of the above.

4. Drawings that contain raster images are typically small (about 30 Kb) because
   A. AutoCAD imports and compresses the raster images into its own DWG format.
   B. raster images are generally smaller than vector images.
   C. AutoCAD attaches raster images as external references, so the raster image size is not reflected in the DWG file.
   D. both B and C.

Completion

Directions: In the space at the left, write the word or words that BEST complete the statement or answer the question.

_____ 5. Another term for raster images is _____ images.

_____ 6. A(n) _____ object is one that is stored as line segments, which are described by the location of their endpoints.

_____ 7. A portion of computer memory that is dedicated to delivering graphic information is known as a(n) _____. *(two words)*

_____ 8. How many shades of gray are displayed by an 8-bit grayscale image?

_____ 9. When you are working on a file that contains a raster image, you can increase computer performance by _____ the raster image; when you do this, the image remains on the screen, but it is no longer retained in working memory.

_____ 10. Which type of image stores objects as a series of dots or pixels without storing any size information about the objects?

Copyright © Glencoe/McGraw-Hill

Name _____ Class Period _____ Time _____

TEST - Advanced Text   *Chapter 26* External References

Multiple Choice

Directions: Circle the letter of the choice that BEST completes the statement or answers the question.

1. External references
    A. remain bound to the drawing until you save it and exit AutoCAD.
    B. become part of the drawing to which they are attached.
    C. load automatically each time you load the drawing file until you detach them.
    D. have to be reattached to a drawing each time you open the drawing.

2. Which of the following is *not* a feature of the XREF command?
    A. The Bind option can make an external reference a permanent part of a drawing.
    B. The Attach option can attach a new xref to a drawing.
    C. The Detach option can remove unneeded external references from a drawing.
    D. All of the above are features of the XREF command.

3. When you attach an xref to a drawing, AutoCAD creates special layers that are
    A. preceded by the file name of the parent xref drawing, separated from the layer name by a vertical bar.
    B. locked so that you cannot change their visibility or color.
    C. frozen; you can change their properties, but only after thawing the layers.
    D. none of the above.

4. The XREF Attach option is similar to what common AutoCAD command?
    A. BLOCK
    B. INSERT
    C. PURGE
    D. FILES

True-False

Directions: On the line beside each statement, write **True** if the statement is correct or **False** if the statement is incorrect.

_____ 5. External references are for visual reference only; you cannot snap to them using object snap.

_____ 6. A drawing into which external references have been inserted is considered the base drawing.

_____ 7. To find out whether an object belongs to an xref, you can select the object and list its properties.

_____ 8. Being linked to related drawings that may change is a disadvantage of using xrefs.

_____ 9. An xref that has been bound to a drawing using the XBIND command can be unbound using the UNBIND command.

_____ 10. Unloaded xrefs remain attached to the drawing file.

Name _____ Class Period _____ Time _____

TEST - Advanced Text *Chapter 27* Object Linking and Embedding (OLE)

Multiple Choice

Directions: Circle the letter of the choice that BEST completes the statement or answers the question.

1. Which of the following statements is *not* true of AutoCAD's OLE capability?
   A. You can link an AutoCAD view to a document in another application, such as a text editor, if the other application supports OLE.
   B. Once another document is linked to AutoCAD, changing either document results in breaking the link.
   C. AutoCAD can be either a client or a server.
   D. The OLE capability saves time and improves accuracy.

2. When a link is set to Manual in the Links dialog box,
   A. you must recreate the link each time you open either of the linked files.
   B. AutoCAD updates the link automatically each time you open the drawing file.
   C. the link updates only when you pick the Update Now button.
   D. the link can be updated only from within the server document.

3. To link an AutoCAD drawing to a document in another application,
   A. pick Copy Link from the Edit pull-down menu.
   B. pick Paste Special... from the Edit pull-down menu.
   C. enter the COPYCLIP command.
   D. display the Links dialog box and pick the Activate button.

4. When you link an AutoCAD view to a document created in the Microsoft WordPad text editor,
   A. WordPad becomes the client.
   B. AutoCAD becomes the client.
   C. both WordPad and AutoCAD are clients; Microsoft Windows is the server.
   D. none of the above.

True-False

Directions: On the line beside each statement, write **True** if the statement is correct or **False** if the statement is incorrect.

_____ 5. A server document is the file to which another file is linked.

_____ 6. The COPYLINK command copies the current view in AutoCAD to the Windows Clipboard so that it can be pasted into another document as an OLE object.

_____ 7. AutoCAD's Paste Special option allows you to link text and objects from other documents to an AutoCAD drawing.

_____ 8. If an AutoCAD drawing has been pasted into a Word document using OLE and both AutoCAD and Word are currently running, changes made to the drawing in AutoCAD are made automatically in the Word file.

_____ 9. Objects that are copied using AutoCAD's COPY command and pasted into an OLE-capable document can be updated at any time by picking Update Now.

_____ 10. AutoCAD's Links dialog box allows you to break existing links between a drawing file and another OLE-capable file.

Copyright © Glencoe/McGraw-Hill

TEST - Advanced Text   Chapter 28 Database Connectivity

Multiple Choice

Directions: Circle the letter of the choice that BEST completes the statement or answers the question.

1. AutoCAD's dbConnect feature allows you to
   A. associate objects in a drawing file with records in an external database.
   B. convert the drawing database for an AutoCAD drawing into a format that can be read by an external database.
   C. import database records into an AutoCAD drawing file.
   D. none of the above.

2. AutoCAD allows you to connect
   A. more than one database to a single AutoCAD drawing file.
   B. more than one drawing file to an external database.
   C. both A and B.
   D. neither A nor B.

3. To move from field to field in a database, which key should you press at the keyboard?
   A. TAB
   B. ENTER
   C. spacebar
   D. ESC

4. Using the column shortcut menu, you can
   A. hide and unhide columns.
   B. freeze and unfreeze columns.
   C. align columns.
   D. all of the above.

Completion

Directions: In the space at the left, write the word or words that BEST complete the statement or answer the question.

_____ 5. Categories of information in a database are known as _____.

_____ 6. A(n) _____ is a group of related fields in a database.

_____ 7. A field or combination of fields that can be used to identify each record in a database individually is known as a(n) _____.

_____ 8. The rearrangement of records based on the contents of one or more fields is referred to as _____.

_____ 9. A new record in a database is identified by an empty row with a(n) _____ in the left margin.

_____ 10. To narrow down the database information that displays on the screen, you can define a(n) _____ that presents only those records that meet specific criteria.

Copyright © Glencoe/McGraw-Hill

Name _____ Class Period _____ Time _____

TEST - Advanced Text — *Chapter 29* Internet Connectivity

Multiple Choice

Directions: Circle the letter of the choice that BEST completes the statement or answers the question.

1. To open a drawing file located on an Internet server, start by
   A. opening your e-mail software.
   B. accessing the Quick Setup wizard.
   C. entering the name of the file.
   D. connecting to the Internet.

2. Drawing files that have been converted to DWF format
   A. can be opened and transmitted faster than AutoCAD drawing files.
   B. must be opened from within AutoCAD.
   C. are in raster-based format.
   D. have lost some of the information contained in the original AutoCAD drawing.

3. A standard method of transferring files over the Internet is
   A. FTP.
   B. URL.
   C. Volo View.
   D. hyperlink.

4. To publish drawing files that others can view on the Web, you can use
   A. hyperlinks.
   B. UCS.
   C. URL.
   D. Drawing Web Format.

5. News and other information related to AutoCAD can be accessed quickly through
   A. Volo View Express.
   B. the Open button on the Standard toolbar.
   C. AutoCAD's Today window.
   D. the FTP button on the Standard toolbar.

Completion

Directions: In the space at the left, write the word or words that BEST complete the statement or answer the question.

_____ 6. A(n) ____ is an electronic connection to another document or to a site on the Web.

_____ 7. You can view Web pages from within AutoCAD by using the Today window or by picking the ____ button.

_____ 8. To create DWF files, pick the ____ button from the Standard toolbar.

_____ 9. To view a DWF file, you need Microsoft Internet Explorer 5.01 or later and the ____ software.

_____ 10. A computer that provides Web sites and files you can access over the Internet is called an Internet ____.

Copyright © Glencoe/McGraw-Hill

323

Name _____ Class Period _____ Time _____

TEST - Advanced Text   *Chapter 30* Internet Collaboration

Multiple Choice

Directions: Circle the letter of the choice that BEST completes the statement or answers the question.

1. With the i-drop feature, you can
   A. send a drawing file and all its related files as an e-mail attachment.
   B. insert hyperlinks into a drawing file.
   C. automatically add your name and e-mail address to the drawing files you create.
   D. insert a drawing file from a Web site into a drawing you are making.

2. To use i-drop, it is necessary to have
   A. a recent version of Microsoft Internet Explorer.
   B. a recent version of Netscape.
   C. Autodesk Point A.
   D. PNG software.

3. Autodesk Point A
   A. is the starting point for creating drawings in AutoCAD.
   B. offers Internet server space at no cost for a period of time.
   C. is a location for storing your drawings in a secure manner; no one else can access them there.
   D. steps you through the process of creating JPEG files.

4. You can create a Web page using the Publish to Web wizard or
   A. Autodesk Point A.
   B. i-drop.
   C. PNG.
   D. Meet Now.

5. The language used to describe and present the contents of Web pages is
   A. JPEG.
   B. DWF.
   C. PNG.
   D. HTML.

Completion

Directions: In the space at the left, write the word or words that BEST complete the statement or answer the question.

_____ 6. The ____ feature allows you to create a set of related files that can be sent over the Internet.

_____ 7. When you create a transmittal set of files, AutoCAD creates a(n) ____ that includes information about the files and also lets you add notes.

_____ 8. A transmittal set of files can be packaged in a compressed self-extracting executable file, a compressed zip file, or a(n) ____.

_____ 9. The Publish to Web wizard allows you to produce Web pages without any knowledge of ____ coding.

_____ 10. AutoCAD's Meet Now feature uses Microsoft's ____ to link people so that they can work collaboratively on-line.

Copyright © Glencoe/McGraw-Hill

Answer Keys for Advanced Text

This section provides answers for the Review Questions and Challenge Your Thinking questions that are found at the end of each chapter in the *Advanced* text. In addition, this section provides answers to the chapter tests that are included in this Instructor Resource Guide.

Answers to Chapter Reviews 326

Answers to Chapter Tests 335

Copyright © Glencoe/McGraw-Hill

Answers to Chapter Reviews for *Advanced* Text

The review questions in the textbook are designed to prompt students to practice using AutoCAD software as well as to study the textbook chapter. Many of the questions cannot be answered just by reading the book. For example, a review question may ask the students to describe several AutoCAD command options, but the options may not all be discussed in the textbook. Students need to work with AutoCAD to find the complete answer.

Chapter 1
Review Questions
1. Enter the SNAP command, select the Style option, and then select the Isometric option, or use the Drafting Settings dialog box.
2. The Ctrl and E keys (or the F5 key) can be used to select the current isometric plane and thus the current pair of axes. You can also use the ISOPLANE command.
3. Use the Isocircle option of the ELLIPSE command.
4. Use the DIMEDIT command to change the oblique angle of the dimension. For greater efficiency, you could create a dimension style for each of the isometric planes with the text and dimension at the proper oblique angles.
5. Right-click on the Snap button in the status bar and select Settings; select Rectangular Snap in the Snap Type and Style box. Or enter the SNAP command and choose Style and Standard.

Challenge Your Thinking
1. Answers will vary. Example: Isometric drawings are often used as pictorials to give clients an idea of what a finished product will look like.
2. Answers will vary. Students will need to use the Oblique option of the DIMEDIT command to position the dimensions correctly for the isometric object. It is important to note both size and location dimensions.

Chapter 2
Review Questions
1. It lets you specify a viewing point in 3D space.
2. Extrusion thickness is an option within the ELEV command. Also, thickness can be specified with the THICKNESS system variable.
3. Use the ELEV command to specify the elevation and extrusion thickness for each object.
4. Directly above it, the same as the plan view.
5. HIDE.
6. Anywhere between the two circles at the twelve o'clock position.
7. 3D Orbit allows you to manipulate 3D models while they are shaded or when hidden lines are removed.
8. Parallel projection shows objects with lines that are parallel to each other. They do not converge toward one or more vanishing points. Perspective projection shows objects as the eye would view them in nature, with depth lines converging toward a vanishing point in the distance.
9. A clipping plane slices through a 3D object, causing the section of the object on one side of the plane to be omitted.

Challenge Your Thinking
1. (1) A (2) D (3) E (4) G (5) C (6) B (7) F
2. Front and back clipping planes are adjustable to allow any "slice" of an object to be selected. Clipping planes may be used to achieve views of 3D objects that are similar to sectional views.
3. A 0,0,0   G 2,2,2
    B 3,0,0   H 2,2,1
    C 3,0,1   I 3,2,1
    D 2,0,2   J 3,2,0
    E 0,0,2   K 2,0,1
    F 0,2,2

Chapter 3
Review Questions
1. It is a 3D planar object defined by *x*, *y*, and *z* coordinates.
2. The SOLID command.
3. Answers will vary. Example: an inclined or oblique surface such as the roof of a house.
4. X/Y/Z point filtering allows two of the 3D points to be entered with a pointing device and the remaining point to be keyed in.
5. They allow you to specify points in 3D space without having to change viewpoints.
6. The LINE command creates lines in 3D space. Therefore, all lines created with AutoCAD are three-dimensional. The thickness is usually 0, but it can be changed with the ELEV command or the THICKNESS system variable.

Challenge Your Thinking
1. Answers will vary. Xlines can be created using the point filters, and they behave similarly to lines except that they extend to infinity in both directions. The point filters can be used with mline only to set the initial point in 3D space. Regardless of further *z* values, mlines remain parallel to the WCS.

Copyright © Glencoe/McGraw-Hill

Answers to Chapter Reviews, *Advanced* (Continued)

2. Answers will vary. Students can use any of the combinations to create points in which only one of the three coordinates is different from an existing point.

Chapter 4
Review Questions
1. They make it easier to construct and edit objects in 3D space that are not aligned with the fixed world coordinate system (WCS).
2. The **3point** option allows a quick alignment of the UCS with an existing object.
3. It indicates the positive direction of the X and Y axes. It is a good visual cue for orientation.
4. This option creates a new UCS perpendicular to the viewing direction; that is, parallel to the screen. This is useful when you want to annotate a 3D model.
5. The **PLAN** command.

Challenge Your Thinking
1. A view is the point of view from which you see a 3D object. A UCS represents the current drawing plane, which may or may not be parallel to the view. Together, views and UCSs allow you to create complex surfaces and to create detail on 3D objects.
2. The **UCSFOLLOW** system variable generates a plan view whenever you change to a different coordinate system. This is useful when working with multiple UCSs because it provides a consistent visual reference.

Chapter 5
Review Questions
1. It allows you to create a revolved surface by rotating a path curve (profile) around a selected axis.
2. It lets you create a polygon mesh representing the ruled surface between two curves. To use it, you select two defining curves. The polygon mesh appears after you pick the second curve.
3. UCSs help you place objects when using these two commands. For instance, you may choose to create the path curve required by the **REVSURF** command by placing a polyline on a UCS named **FRONT**.
4. They control the density (resolution) of 3D meshes created by 3D commands such as **REVSURF** and **RULESURF**.
5. The appearance of 3D models improves, but they require more time to regenerate.

6. Models regenerate quickly on the screen, but they may not represent your design adequately, appearing rough-faceted.
7. A three dimensional grid defined in terms of $M \times N$ vertices.

Challenge Your Thinking
1. Answers will vary. It is not impossible to create a 3D object without creating and using UCSs. Using the UCS makes such jobs easier and faster. In this case, the path curve for the lamp had to be viewed perpendicular to its vertical axis, a task easily accomplished through the UCS.
2. Paragraphs will vary, but students should note that the options are the same except that 2D lines have **Join** and **Width** options. Also, the **PEDIT** command allows independent editing of 3D mesh vertices when a mesh is selected.

Chapter 6
Review Questions
1. Select the path curve (the profile from which the tabulated surface is created) and direction vector. The tabulated surface generates on the screen.
2. This is a vector (line) on the screen that, when picked, specifies the direction and length of the tabulated surface.
3. It is used to construct a Coons surface patch (a 3D surface mesh interpolated between four adjoining edges).
4. UCSs help you place the four objects required by the **EDGESURF** command.
5. Coordinate entry is tedious, time-consuming, and error-prone unless it can be automated using a program.

Challenge Your Thinking
1. Answers will vary. The simplest method is to use **PEDIT** to join the four parts of the I-beam before using **TABSURF**.
2. Answers will vary. The biggest difference among quadratic, cubic, and Bezier curves is the manner in which they are calculated, although the mathematics become complicated.

Chapter 7
Review Questions
1. (Any five) 3D box, pyramid, wedge, dome, sphere, cone, torus, dish, mesh.
2. The torus radius is the distance from the center of the torus to the center of the tube.

Copyright © Glencoe/McGraw-Hill

Answers to Chapter Reviews, *Advanced* (Continued)

The tube radius determines the radius of the torus "tube" itself.
3. You must pick four points to form a polygon and enter *M* and *N* values.
4. Enter the ALIGN command and select the 3D object to be moved. Pick a source and a destination point.
5. It allows you to rotate an object around an arbitrary 3D axis.
6. It allows you to mirror 3D objects around an arbitrary plane.
7. Answers will vary. Using primitives saves time whenever an object to be drawn incorporates the available primitive shapes.
8. Answers will vary. You might want to have students form small groups to evaluate their ideas and determine the most efficient way to create each of their designs.

Challenge Your Thinking
1. MIRROR3D requires a plane defined by three points to determine the "mirror line." MIRROR requires only a line. ROTATE3D requires a 2D vector to define the rotation axis. ROTATE requires only a single rotation point.
2. Answers will vary, but students should realize that the two have similar underlying concepts. *M* and *N* values create a grid that resembles the Cartesian coordinate system.

Chapter 8
Review Questions
1. On large, complex models, it may be faster to shade the image using the Shade toolbar.
2. A facet is a three- or four-sided polygon that represents a piece of a 3D surface.
3. Flat shading simply shades the facets of the objects. Gouraud smooths the edges and provides a more realistic, rounded appearance on curved surfaces.
4. The Statistics dialog box displays details about the last rendering, such as rendering time and original and projected extents. The values can be saved to a file.
5. BMP, TGA, and TIFF.
6. It displays TGA, TIFF, and BMP files.

Challenge Your Thinking
1. The system variables that control the appearance of shaded objects are SHADEDIF and SHADEDGE. SHADEDIF sets the ratio of diffuse reflective light to ambient light. SHADEDGE controls the shading of edges of the object. Answers for situations will vary. Situations calling for a specific visual emphasis might require changing options.
2. Answers will vary. Make students aware of suitable graphic and illustration programs available to them at your school or company.

Chapter 9
Review Questions
1. Smooth shading requires a blending of the facets through a mathematical process called *interpolation*, which requires many calculations, consuming more computer time.
2. Predefined materials may be attached to an object by selecting from those available in the materials library (Render toolbar).
3. Light sources.
4. Select them through the Render toolbar.
5. Using the basic Render option, you can render a model without applying a material, adding any lights, or setting up a scene. The Photo Real rendering type can display bitmapped and transparent materials and generate shadows; it can look more realistic.
6. An object with a bitmap image mapped onto it, allowing you to add realistic landscapes to a drawing.

Challenge Your Thinking
1. Answers will vary. The colors behave similarly to the way they would behave in the real world. For example, if you shine a blue light onto a yellow sphere, the sphere appears to be green when you render it. This property is useful for mimicking the effect of colored lights on objects, as in a special museum display or in theater lighting.
2. Answers will vary. Under most circumstances, Gouraud shading is probably sufficient. Because Phong shading uses a more complex algorithm, it takes a slightly longer time to shade.

Chapter 10
Review Questions
1. The outer loop is the outside boundary of a region. Inner loops are "islands" within the outer loop that do not belong to the region.
2. A composite region is the result of applying Boolean operations to two or more regions.
3. SUBTRACT.
4. (Any) AREA, LIST, or MASSPROP.
5. It calculates engineering properties of regions.
6. The UNION command creates a composite region by combining the area of two or more 2D objects or regions.

Copyright © Glencoe/McGraw-Hill

Answers to Chapter Reviews, *Advanced* (Continued)

7. Region or polyline.
8. Use the EXTRUDE command.

Challenge Your Thinking
1. Answers may vary. Students should list occupations in which engineering properties are needed for design tests and manufacturing.
2. Answers will vary. Regions can have mass properties, which makes them more useful in some situations. However, polylines may be better when the drawing needs frequent editing because polylines are easier to edit.

Chapter 11
Review Questions
1. CYLINDER creates a solid cylinder. TORUS creates a solid donut-shaped object. CONE, WEDGE, BOX, and SPHERE create solid cones, wedges, boxes, and spheres, respectively.
2. TORUS.
3. BOX.
4. They allow you to create elliptical cylinders and cones using prompts similar to those used in the ELLIPSE command.

Challenge Your Thinking
1. The shapes used earlier are surface models; those in this chapter are solids. You can only get engineering properties from a solid model.
2. It is not possible using just the solid primitive commands to create a cylinder or cone at any angle other than 90° from its base. To achieve other angles, you would need to use Boolean operations to add or subtract portions of the primitives.

Chapter 12
Review Questions
1. REVOLVE creates a solid volume by turning a polyline around an axis. EXTRUDE creates a closed volume from a planar 3D face, closed polyline, polygon, circle, ellipse, closed spline, donut, or region.
2. REVOLVE.
3. The ISOLINES system variable controls the number of tessellation lines used in a solid object, which in turn controls the quality and accuracy of curved areas in the object.

Challenge Your Thinking
1. Answers will vary. Although higher settings result in more accurate solid models, they require more processing time.
2. It is possible to extrude a wide polyline; however, AutoCAD discards the width information and extrudes from the center of the polyline's path.

Chapter 13
Review Questions
1. Create a solid model with a cylinder. Using the SUBTRACT command, subtract the cylinder from the solid to create the hole.
2. Composite solids are composed of two or more solid primitives. A union, subtraction, or intersection creates a composite solid.
3. SUBTRACT performs a Boolean operation that creates a composite solid by subtracting one solid from another. UNION joins two solid objects to form a new composite solid.

Challenge Your Thinking
1. Answers will vary. Example: Set up the computer so that you're working in the front viewpoint; create a polyline for the top part of the bracket and extrude it; create a cylinder for the hole and subtract it from the extruded solid; change to the top viewpoint and repeat the process for the bottom part of the bracket. Changing the viewpoint and UCS as necessary, position the two pieces as shown and use UNION to join them.
2. Answers will vary. Example: Using viewports for the front and top views, create a cylinder for one of the large ends of the object with an appropriate height. Create the smaller cylinder and give it a longer height. Copy the first large cylinder to the other end of the small cylinder to create the dumbbell. Use UNION to join the cylinders.

Chapter 14
Review Questions
1. They create a beveled (CHAMFER) or rounded (FILLET) edge on the outside corners.
2. By overlapping two or more solid objects and entering INTERSECT. AutoCAD calculates the solid volume common (intersecting) to each of the objects.
3. It allows you to create a shell or hollow object from a solid.
4. INTERFERE allows you to check for interference (overlap) between two solids.
5. Answers will vary. The fit of various parts of an assembly is very important. The INTERFERE command helps them make sure the parts of the assembly fit together correctly.

Copyright © Glencoe/McGraw-Hill

Answers to Chapter Reviews, *Advanced* (Continued)

Challenge Your Thinking
1. Answers will vary. The CHAMFER and FILLET commands create inside bevels and fillets in a manner similar to creating outside bevels and rounds; the appearance varies, depending on the surfaces you select.
2. Answers will vary. Creating a solid using interference solids requires careful preplanning.

Chapter 15
Review Questions
1. (Any two) Mass properties generation, detail drafting, finite element analysis, and fabrication of the physical part.
2. It creates a cross section from a solid model.
3. Define a cutting plane using an object such as a closed polyline. AutoCAD creates a cross section where the plane intersects the object.
4. Two-dimensional profile objects.
5. They contain the profile lines.

Challenge Your Thinking
1. Answers will vary. To display the section, students must thaw layer 0. To orient the section and the profile in relation to each other and print them, they should create and use paper-space viewports.
2. Answers will vary. Students may find that a company's use for solid models varies not only with tooling and available equipment, but also with owner/stockholder preferences.

Chapter 16
Review Questions
1. It sets up new layers and calculates orthographic, auxiliary, and sectional views in paper space for use by SOLDRAW.
2. Ucs creates a profile view relative to a specified user coordinate system. Ortho creates an orthographic view from an existing view. Auxiliary creates an auxiliary view from an existing view. Section creates a sectional view, complete with crosshatching.
3. Layers for visible lines, hidden lines, dimensions, and hatch patterns.
4. SOLDRAW uses the information gathered by SOLVIEW to create the final drawing views.
5. No, because SOLDRAW needs the information calculated by SOLVIEW to create the various drawing views.

Challenge Your Thinking
1. Answers will vary. Many objects with surfaces that are not parallel to any of the standard orthographic planes of projection require an auxiliary view.
2. Answers will vary. With complex models, the Ucs option makes it easier to produce a profile view relative to a user coordinate system. If no viewports exist in the drawing, the Ucs option is a good method of creating an initial viewport.

Chapter 17
Review Questions
1. The SLICE command permits you to cut a solid model into two or more parts.
2. Answers will vary. Example: you could cut a symmetrical solid model into halves and save one half. Use it to fabricate a pattern to create identical halves of a mold.
3. Enter the MASSPROP command and generate a report; enter Yes in reply to Write analysis to a file? An MPR file contains the list of mass properties in standard ASCII format.
4. (Any three) Mass, volume, bounding box, centroid, moments of inertia, products of inertia, radii of gyration, and principle moments.
5. It creates an STL file.
6. STL is the file format required by rapid prototyping systems such as stereolithography. These systems enable you to fabricate a physical part from the STL file without tooling, milling, or fixturing.
7. FACETRES.
8. A binary STL file is smaller. You can view the contents of an ASCII STL file.

Challenge Your Thinking
1. Paragraphs will vary. The SLICE command cuts a solid along a plane and allows you to retain one or both parts of the original solid. The SECTION command isolates a cross section of a solid without changing the solid.
2. Answers will vary. For example, you might need to use the 3points option if you need to align a cut through a solid with the edges of other, neighboring solids in an assembly.
3. Essays will vary. Students should mention at least some of the major technologies.

Chapter 18
Review Questions
1. Displays Properties in the menu (the underlined P indicates the mnemonic key); issues cancel twice; enters the PROPERTIES command. (Students will need to do some

Answers to Chapter Reviews, *Advanced* (Continued)

research within AutoCAD. Have them select Ask Me in AutoCAD's Help feature and key in the phrase custom menus. The section on Menu Item Syntax contains the information students will need in order to arrive at the answers.)

2. Displays Dimstyle in the menu and enters the DIMSTYLE command.
3. Displays Zoom in the menu and indicates that Zoom has a submenu. (The underlined Z indicates the mnemonic key.)
4. Specifies the Line submenu.
5. Displays New in the menu, issues cancel twice, and enters the NEW command.
6. Displays Window in the menu and enters the Window option.
7. Displays Text Style... in the menu (the underlined S indicates that it is the mnemonic key); the apostrophe allows for transparent command entry; enters the STYLE command.
8. Displays Start, Center, End in the menu (the underlined S indicates the mnemonic key); issues cancel twice; enters the ARC command; pauses for user input; enters the Center option.

Challenge Your Thinking
1. Answers will vary depending on the menu items students choose.
2. Answers will vary. Encourage students to explore further if the item is different from what they thought it would be.

Chapter 19

Review Questions
1. A menu item that automatically executes a series of AutoCAD inputs.
2. Because they speed the selection of certain AutoCAD functions and commands.
3. A base menu is loaded when you first start AutoCAD or when you use the MENU command. You can add partial menus to the base menu using the MENULOAD command.
4. The MENU command.
5. MNC and MNR files.
6. Add a new first line to the menu file: ***MENUGROUP=[NAME] where [NAME] is the name of the menu file. Add a blank line after the new first line.
7. Enter TOOLBAR at the keyboard or select Toolbars... from the View pull-down menu. Create the new toolbar, turn it on, pick the Commands tab, and drag the Polyline button from the Draw toolbar to the Custom toolbar.

8. Acad.mns, acad.mnc, and acad.mnr.

Challenge Your Thinking
1. A drawing or symbol could be selected and inserted by picking this menu item
2. No. The entire flyout is selected.

Chapter 20

Review Questions
1. MSLIDE makes a slide from the current display. VSLIDE displays a slide file. SCRIPT executes a command script. RSCRIPT restarts a script from the beginning. DELAY delays execution of the next command for a specified time. RESUME resumes an interrupted script.
2. It allows commands to be read from a text file and executes a predetermined sequence of commands. You can invoke these commands when you start AutoCAD, or you can start a script from the Command prompt.
3. SCR.
4. The length of the delay in milliseconds.
5. Slide (SLD) files.

Challenge Your Thinking
1. It is more practical to store a drawing setup in a drawing template file, and it is easier to access and modify settings. A template file may be quicker to use because a script takes time to start and run.
2. Answers will vary. To develop a plan, students should follow a method similar to the one used in this chapter.

Chapter 21

Review Questions
1. AutoLISP is AutoCAD's version of the LISP programming language. AutoLISP enables you to write and execute custom routines in the AutoCAD environment.
2. Answers will vary. Example: It could draw the border and title block and prompt you for title block information.
3. LSP.
4. Creates 3D rectangular arrays by specifying rows, columns, and levels; also creates polar arrays around a specified axis.
5. At the command prompt, enter (load "project"). If the project.lsp file is in another drive or folder, you would enter (load "drive:\folder name\project"). Substitute the correct name of the drive or folder.
6. Select Load Application from the Tools pull-down menu. Using the down arrow in the field Files of type, select *.lsp. Select the

Answers to Chapter Reviews, *Advanced* (Continued)

drive and folder level you will be working in. Select project.lsp and pick the Load button.

Challenge Your Thinking
1. Answers will vary. AutoCAD's usefulness for various applications can be enhanced by creating additional commands or menu items or to automate a task that would otherwise require many tedious steps.
2. Answers will vary. For large amounts of customization, AutoLISP might be better because it takes up less RAM. It would also depend upon the type of customization being done. Visual LISP might be used more for graphic user interfaces and customizing buttons. AutoLISP can be used effectively for short customization routines.

Chapter 22
Review Questions
1. 20.
2. It is used to assign values to a variable.
3. 129.5.
4. The car function obtains the first item in a list, such as the *x* coordinate. The cadr function gives the second item of a list, such as the *y* coordinate.
5. The list function displays the value assigned to a variable or variables.
6. Enter (load "RED") or use the Load AutoLISP, ADS, and ARX Files dialog box to load the file; then enter RED.
7. Saving as a file allows you to load it by typing the file name at the Command prompt. Saving as a menu item allows you to pick the item from the menu.

Challenge Your Thinking
1. To load AutoLISP functions automatically each time you start AutoCAD, place the load function calls into a file called acad.lsp. For example, to load the AutoLISP functions red, green, and blue, enter the following into acad.lsp. (If acad.lsp doesn't exist, create it.)
(load "red")
(load "green")
(load "blue")
2. Add the code directly to acad.mnu and save it. (Save acad.mnu with a different name before you make any changes to it.)

Chapter 23
Review Questions
1. Because you only need to load AutoLISP, rather than all of the individual functions.
2. The command function executes AutoCAD commands from within AutoLISP.
3. To add documentation to the program.
4. Getvar retrieves the value of an Auto-CAD system variable. Getpoint pauses for user input of a point. Getdist pauses for user input of a distance.
5. Parametric programming enables you to create and insert unlimited variations of a part or design. The basic geometry that makes up the object is described with AutoLISP. This technique reduces the number of drawing files as well as the disk space they require.

Challenge Your Thinking
1. Any application in which a fairly standard sequence of commands is used to create a variety of items is a good choice for parametric programming. Examples will vary.
2. Answers will vary. Students should first decide what questions need to be asked at the prompt line to make all the drawing size possibilities available, then determine all the possible answers to the questions. Only then should they begin writing the program.

Chapter 24
Review Questions
1. DXF is a standard format for conveying drawing files from one CAD system to another.
2. In addition to DWG files, AutoCAD 2002 can export files in these formats: DXF, WMF, BMP, PostScript (EPS), ACIS, 3DS, SLA, DWF, and XML. (Students can find this information by selecting Ask Me in AutoCAD's Help feature and keying in the phrase export drawings to other file formats.)
3. Binary DXF files are approximately 25% to 40% smaller, and they can be written and read by AutoCAD faster than ASCII DXF files.
4. EPS format is used in many graphics programs for desktop publishing and presentation applications.
5. Yes. No.
6. SAT.
7. It converts Advanced Modeling Extension (AME) rel. 2 or 2.1 solid models to AutoCAD 2002 ACIS-based solids or regions.
8. IGES stands for Initial Graphics Exchange Specification. Its purpose is similar to DXF.
9. Layers, blocks, linetypes, colors, dimensions, and text.

Answers to Chapter Reviews, *Advanced* (Continued)

Challenge Your Thinking
1. The **DXF** file overwrites the existing file, so the original objects are lost.
2. Answers will vary. The **3DS** model generates according to the export and import options students specify, with varying results. The current view in the AutoCAD drawing is not retained; the initial view is the plan view.

Chapter 25
Review Questions
1. Any six of the following: BMP, RLE, DIB, RST, GP4, MIL, CAL, CG4, FLC, FLI, BIL, GIF, IG4, IGS, JFIF (JPG), PCX, PICT, PNG, RLC, TGA, TIF.
2. You can resize a raster image in AutoCAD by picking the grips and dragging to a new size.
3. **Unload** removes the image from working memory but does not erase it from the drawing database. **Reload** loads the image.
4. Instead of importing all the contents of the images, AutoCAD attaches the images to the drawing as external references.
5. BMP, WMF, EPS.
6. Answers will vary. Examples: geographical surveys and annotated photographs taken for reference in various circumstances.

Challenge Your Thinking
1. It allows you to adjust the display to **High** or **Draft** resolution. Setting the image quality to **Draft** speeds up the display time. The setting has no effect on the printed image.
2. Choose the **Detach** button when you are sure you no longer need the image in the drawing process; **Detach** permanently removes the image from the drawing database.

Chapter 26
Review Questions
1. They can be shared by several users and appear in several drawings. As the xref is modified, all drawings it appears in update automatically to show the modifications.
2. **Attach** allows you to attach a new xref to the drawing. **Detach** detaches one or more xrefs from the drawing; detaching an xref erases all instances of a specified xref. **Reload** reads and displays the latest version of the xref drawing. **Unload** suppresses the display and regeneration of the an xref definition to improve performance while the reference is not needed. Unloading an xref does not remove the xref permanently from the drawing database. **Bind** converts an external reference into a permanent part of the drawing.
3. **INSERT**.
4. **LIST**.
5. It permanently binds a subset of an xref's dependent symbols, such as blocks and layers, to the drawing.

Challenge Your Thinking
1. Answers will vary. The **Overlay** option is similar to the **Attach** option, but if you create an external reference to a drawing that also contains xrefs, the referenced drawing's xrefs do not appear in the current drawing. Overlaid drawings cannot be nested.
2. Answers will vary. One advantage of using xrefs is that they can be updated easily, so if several different people are working on different parts of a single drawing, everyone can work with the latest version. When a project has been finished, the xrefs can be bound to the drawing to become part of the permanent record.

Chapter 27
Review Questions
1. To link or embed objects from one application into another application.
2. AutoCAD is the server.
3. In WordPad, pick **Links...** from the **Edit** menu.
4. The spreadsheet document is the server because it is the document from which the object (the spreadsheet) is being linked.

Challenge Your Thinking
1. Answers will vary. Linking maintains a link between the documents that can be updated. Embedding takes a "snapshot" of the object and embeds it in the document.
2. Answers will vary. Students don't have enough information to say which is the better option. Xrefs are probably a better idea if AutoCAD will be available for the actual presentation and all the companies have access to a network that allows the files to be updated. Embedding is the only choice if AutoCAD is not available for the presentation.

Chapter 28
Review Questions
1. To associate objects in a drawing file with records in the external database.

Answers to Chapter Reviews, *Advanced* (Continued)

2. The process of making it available to you through AutoCAD's **dbConnect** feature.
3. Connect to the data source (and configure it, if this is the first time you have connected to it). Then use the **View Table** or **Edit Table** option to view or edit the records.
4. A group of related fields, where the fields have unique names that you can reference.
5. A database composed of fields and records.
6. A key field is a unique identifier used to identify one or more fields that in turn identify the record.
7. Structured Query Language.
8. By refining a query to perform a unique search of data.
9. It provides information that AutoCAD needs to link objects in drawings to unique records in a database table.

Challenge Your Thinking
1. Possible answers: Because the database file was deleted, stored in a different folder, or the drawing file has to be located in some other location out of reach of the database; a key field was removed, so the AutoCAD drawing file cannot correctly link to it.
2. Answers will vary. The **Query Builder** provides an interface that is easier to use. Users do not need to understand SQL to use **Query Builder**. For complex queries, using SQL directly provides more flexibility and more power for the SQL programmer.

Chapter 29
Review Questions
1. The hyperlink makes it easy to visit a Web site related to the AutoCAD object.
2. Connect to the Internet. Within AutoCAD, pick the **Open** button from the **Standard** toolbar and key in the URL of the desired file.
3. You can save the file to an Internet server only if you have permission to write to that server's disk drive.
4. Answers will vary. Students may say that the file could have information that's needed for their work or that they want to show the file to a coworker. Also, it is possible to save the file to your computer's hard disk.
5. Connect to the Internet. Within AutoCAD, pick the **Open** button from the **Standard** toolbar and then pick the **Search the Web** button.
6. AutoCAD's Drawing Web Format is a compressed vector file used to publish AutoCAD drawings. Compressed **DWF** files open and transmit faster than AutoCAD drawing files, and the vector-based format ensures that precision is maintained.
7. **FTP** is a standard method of transferring files over the Internet.

Challenge Your Thinking
1. Both methods require the user to connect to the Internet. To view **DWG** files, users need AutoCAD. The **DWF** files can be viewed without AutoCAD, but users need Volo View or Volo View Express. Since **DWF** is a compressed file format, opening and transmitting a **DWF** file will be faster than opening and transmitting a **DWG** file.
2. Answers will vary but should point out that files in the **DWF** format will be faster to open and transmit.

Chapter 30
Review Questions
1. Answers can vary. Two types that students may list are fonts and xrefs.
2. The recipient may need the related files in order to use the drawing file.
3. The i-drop capability is a fast way of inserting a drawing file from a Web site into a drawing.
4. Autodesk Point A allows users to create a custom Web page. It also allows access to disk space on an Internet server. Students may list other benefits as well.
5. It supports **DWF**, **JPG**, and **PNG** images.
6. Answers will vary.
7. These enable people to meet and work collaboratively on-line.

Challenge Your Thinking
1. The transmittal set includes all the files related to the AutoCAD drawing. It's easier to send this one package with your e-mail message than to attach several files individually.
2. You can edit the contents and format of the page by clicking **Edit Profile and Content**.
3. Answers will vary, but students should note that different formats produce different sizes of files.

Answers to Chapter Tests for *Advanced* Text

Chapter 1
1. C
2. C
3. A
4. B
5. 120
6. top
7. Oblique
8. pictorial
9. crosshairs
10. plane

Chapter 2
1. D
2. D
3. B
4. A
5. C
6. F
7. F
8. T
9. F
10. T

Chapter 3
1. B
2. C
3. A
4. A
5. T
6. F
7. T
8. F
9. T
10. T

Chapter 4
1. D
2. A
3. D
4. C
5. F
6. T
7. T
8. T
9. T
10. F

Chapter 5
1. B
2. A
3. C
4. D
5. F
6. T
7. T
8. T
9. F
10. F

Chapter 6
1. D
2. D
3. C
4. C
5. direction vector
6. Coons surface patch
7. PLINE
8. 3DMESH
9. PFACE
10. Bezier

Chapter 7
1. A
2. B
3. D
4. A
5. C
6. primitives
7. frustum
8. torus
9. apex
10. Mesh

Chapter 8
1. C
2. A
3. C
4. D
5. A
6. Gouraud
7. facet
8. wireframe
9. flat
10. REPLAY

Chapter 9
1. C
2. C
3. A
4. D
5. B
6. raytracing
7. gradient
8. landscape
9. photorealistic
10. Interpolation

Chapter 10
1. C
2. C
3. D
4. B
5. B
6. T
7. T
8. T
9. T
10. F

Chapter 11
1. A
2. C
3. D
4. C
5. B
6. F
7. F
8. T
9. F
10. F

Chapter 12
1. D
2. B
3. C
4. C
5. T
6. F
7. T
8. F
9. F
10. T

Chapter 13
1. B
2. A
3. B
4. C
5. T
6. F
7. T
8. F
9. F
10. F

Chapter 14
1. C
2. C
3. D
4. A
5. T
6. T
7. F
8. F
9. T
10. F

Chapter 15
1. D
2. B
3. A
4. T
5. T
6. T
7. F
8. T
9. T
10. F

Chapter 16
1. B
2. D
3. A
4. A
5. T
6. F
7. T
8. F
9. F
10. T

Chapter 17
1. D
2. C
3. D
4. B
5. A
6. Rapid prototyping
7. mass properties
8. stereolithography
9. XYZ
10. binary

Chapter 18
1. C
2. B
3. D
4. A
5. T
6. T
7. T
8. T
9. F
10. T

Chapter 19
1. D
2. D
3. B
4. D
5. T

Copyright © Glencoe/McGraw-Hill

Answers to Chapter Tests, *Advanced* (Continued)

6. F
7. F
8. T
9. T
10. F

Chapter 20
1. B
2. C
3. A
4. B
5. F
6. T
7. T
8. T
9. T
10. F

Chapter 21
1. D
2. B
3. D
4. B
5. T
6. T
7. T
8. F
9. T
10. T

Chapter 22
1. A
2. B
3. B
4. B
5. F

6. T
7. F
8. F
9. T
10. T

Chapter 23
1. A
2. C
3. C
4. B
5. T
6. T
7. F
8. F
9. T
10. F

Chapter 24
1. D
2. D
3. B
4. A
5. C
6. T
7. T
8. F
9. F
10. F

Chapter 25
1. B
2. A
3. D
4. C
5. bitmapped

6. vector-based
7. bit plane
8. 256
9. unloading
10. raster

Chapter 26
1. C
2. D
3. A
4. B
5. F
6. T
7. T
8. F
9. F
10. T

Chapter 27
1. B
2. C
3. A
4. A
5. T
6. T
7. T
8. T
9. F
10. T

Chapter 28
1. A
2. C
3. B
4. D
5. fields

6. record
7. key
8. sorting
9. asterisk (*)
10. query

Chapter 29
1. D
2. A
3. A
4. D
5. C
6. hyperlink
7. Search the Web
8. Plot
9. Volo View (or Volo View Express)
10. server

Chapter 30
1. D
2. A
3. B
4. A
5. D
6. eTransmit
7. report
8. folder
9. HTML
10. NetMeeting

Copyright © Glencoe/McGraw-Hill